"Taking his readers on a global journey, Keener marshals evidence from biblical accounts of miraculous life restorations, responds to skeptics who reject miracles, and presents many Christian and non-Christian accounts of miracles as divine decisive acts that changed their lives. It is one thing to read about how miracles happen and change other peoples' lives; it's another to actually hear Keener describe how his life and thought as a New Testament expert was shaped and moved by a miracle. *Miracles Today* is a unique, intriguing, incisive, and invaluable book that makes Keener's research accessible to a wide readership. I have read, learned from, and used many of Keener's books in my courses for years and will do the same with *Miracles Today*."

—**Aliou Cissé Niang**, associate professor of New Testament,
Union Theological Seminary

"Once again, Keener treats readers to an exciting overview of recent miracle accounts, this time arranged by category. Cases involving brain death? Those who were blind? Cerebral palsy? Video accounts? Testing and other evidence from the physicians themselves? Skeptical objections? This volume is an absolutely fascinating read—a veritable one-stop study that is sure to relate to a very wide audience and needs to be on your shelf. Very highly recommended!"

—**Gary R. Habermas**, Distinguished Research Professor of Apologetics
and Philosophy, Liberty University

"*Miracles Today* is an in-depth examination of God's supernatural intervention in human life. Dr. Keener's superlative scholarship is evident. As a physician, I found Keener's descriptions of physical healing credible and compelling. I was particularly fascinated by some of the medical facts and physician comments. Keener also discusses the theology of miracles and artfully disarms philosophical arguments against the miraculous. His own personal testimony of conversion and healing is powerful. This is a must-read for those longing to know more about modern-day miracles."

—**Joseph Bergeron**, MD, author of *The Crucifixion of Jesus: A Medical Doctor
Examines the Death and Resurrection of Christ*

"Keener is among a handful of today's top Christian intellectuals. But he is also a tenderhearted, humble Jesus-lover who is fully immersed in supernatural Christianity. His new book reads like a warm and very personal conversation between Keener and the reader. It is brimming with new, authentic, credible, shocking accounts of the triune God's activity all over the world. My own faith was deeply strengthened by reading it. *Miracles Today* is suited for believers and unbelievers and could be the spark that lights a fire of more supernatural activity in a world that needs to see and experience it. This book is nothing short of stunning!"

—**J. P. Moreland**, Distinguished Professor of Philosophy, Talbot School of Theology,
Biola University; author of *A Simple Guide to Experience Miracles*

"Keener has done it again. In the midst of a global pandemic, in a time in which many people, including me, have suffered so much loss and so many deaths of loved ones, he encourages us to continue to trust God for miracles today and to believe that God is at work in our world. Keener documents miracles and tackles hard questions, such as what happens when healings don't happen and when healing is temporary. This book is timely and calls the reader to see 'healings as kingdom samples' and 'foretastes of the future.'"

—**Lisa Bowens**, associate professor of New Testament,
Princeton Theological Seminary

"*Miracles Today* defends the claim that God still acts in miraculous ways in the contemporary world, offering dozens of credible testimonies for many different types of special actions of God. Keener sees miracles as signs that are fragmentary foretastes of God's final victorious kingdom; he honestly faces the fact that until that kingdom arrives, all of us face death as mortal beings. Even in this ambiguous world, these miraculous signs offer inspiration and hope, pointing to a world where suffering and death will be no more."

—**C. Stephen Evans**, University Professor of Philosophy and Humanities,
Baylor University

MIRACLES TODAY

the supernatural work of God in the modern world

CRAIG S. KEENER

B

Baker Academic

a division of Baker Publishing Group

Grand Rapids, Michigan

© 2021 by Craig S. Keener

Published by Baker Academic
a division of Baker Publishing Group
PO Box 6287, Grand Rapids, MI 49516-6287
www.bakeracademic.com

Printed in the United States of America

Library of Congress Cataloging-in-Publication Data
Names: Keener, Craig S., 1960– author.
Title: Miracles today : the supernatural work of God in the modern world / Craig S. Keener.
Description: Grand Rapids, Michigan : Baker Academic, a division of Baker Publishing Group,
    [2021] | Includes bibliographical references and index.
Identifiers: LCCN 2021009285 | ISBN 9781540963833 (paperback) | ISBN 9781540964298
    (casebound) | ISBN 9781493431380 (ebook)
Subjects: LCSH: Miracles.
Classification: LCC BT97.3 .K44 2021 | DDC 231.7/3—dc23
LC record available at https://lccn.loc.gov/2021009285

The author's profits from this book will be divided among SIM medical missions, Compassion International, and Iris Mozambique (Gen. 14:22–24).

22   23   24   25   26   27   7   6   5   4   3   2

Dedicated to medical professionals, counseling professionals, and all who pray for divine healing—for all who seek to relieve the suffering in our broken world

Contents

Acknowledgments

I am very grateful to the Carl F. H. Henry Center for Theological Understanding for the study leave grant for spring 2020, during which I wrote this book (most of it on the campus of Trinity International University, until COVID-19 sent me home); also to Asbury Theological Seminary and my doctoral students, who were willing to spare me during that leave. The COVID pandemic canceled some other research travel for interviews and collection of documents, but this book can provide at most a sample account in any case.

I cannot name all the individuals who encouraged me to write this book, or all the venues that influenced me to do so, but they include Jane Campbell of Chosen Books; Jim Kinney of Baker Academic; an editor for IVP Academic; and a meeting of the Society of Vineyard Scholars several years ago, particularly because of the topic I was assigned to speak about there. I am also grateful to my copyeditor, Corrie Schwab, proofreaders Ryan Davis and Kristie Berglund, and my project editor, Tim West. While editors do get paid for editing, it is commitment rather than paychecks that make them do a good job.

I am also very grateful to those who provided information or referred me to their own sources for interviews, including Jack Deere, Ken Fish, Micael Grenholm, Dean Merrill, Lee Schnabel, and Elijah Stephens.

I am immensely grateful to the physicians who evaluated or gave feedback on some of the healing case studies for me, some extensively and in great detail. These physicians include Joe Bergeron (physical medicine and rehabilitation), Thomas Coburn (family medicine), Scott Kolbaba (internal medicine), Ruth Farrales Lindberg (family medicine), David McCants (internal medicine), Todd Stokes (family medicine), and Matthew Suh (surgery). Nicole Matthews provided advice on some of the cases I have carried over from the first book. I mention these doctors here at the front of the book but could have cited their specific counsel in many of my endnotes. Several other physicians also provided case studies and are mentioned at appropriate points in the book.

I also thank Global Medical Research Institute, which follows stringent scientific standards that often require a significant degree of medical uniqueness. (These standards exceed those even possibly applicable in historiography, the standards I must follow in my normal line of work, in New Testament studies.) GMRI was thus able to point me to several of the most scientifically secure, well-documented, already published cases.

Responsibility for any errors or misinterpretations, of course, remains with me. (To respect the medical reviewers' time, I have tried to check what I could on my own and saved the harder calls for them.)

Although in this book I deliberately focus on accounts that I did not use before, some come from my larger, more academic book *Miracles: The Credibility of the New Testament Accounts*[1] or from my article "The Dead Are Raised," published in *Bulletin for Biblical Research*.[2] I am grateful for permission to use this material. At this point my initial manuscript also acknowledged those who allowed me to not only cite but also reproduce their published medical documentation in an appendix. After I had collected much of it, however, my publisher, while allowing me to cite it in my endnotes as needed, decided that I could not actually reproduce it visually in the book for logistical and legal reasons, the latter apparently becoming increasingly complex these days. Happily, it does appear in some of the sources I cite and in more journal articles available today than in 2011.

Besides the divine Miracle Worker, I express the greatest gratitude to those who shared their stories, both those that I have included and those that I lacked room to include. I do not take for granted the price at which your testimony came—namely, the suffering you experienced before experiencing healing. You are the ones who lived through these stories, and you graciously shared with me the privilege of telling them.

Preface

Get Up and Walk

When I was an atheist, I didn't believe in miracles. After I was converted through a dramatic encounter with the Holy Spirit, I understood that God did spiritual things, but I still didn't expect him to do anything *visible*. That is, as a Christian, I now believed in miracles *in principle*, but I did not really expect to see one. That was when I met the first of the two women I will introduce in this preface, both of whom are coincidentally (but really) named Barbara.

Barbara in a Nursing Home

After my first summer of college I was helping at a Bible study at Rose Lane Nursing Home in Massillon, Ohio. There, every week, Barbara—an older woman bound to her wheelchair—lamented, "I wish I could walk! I wish I could walk!"[1]

We were normally careful to avoid anything so controversial as actually praying for someone present to be healed. But one week Don, the middle-aged Bible study leader and a student at Fuller Theological Seminary, had had enough. He jumped from his seat and strode toward Barbara. "I'm sick of this," he announced, then grabbed her hand. "In the name of Jesus Christ, I command you to rise up and walk!"

If faith is a bias, I was entirely innocent of it that evening. Frozen with panic, I expected Barbara to fall on the floor, possibly injured, and the nursing home to ban us from holding further Bible studies there. Moreover, the expression on Barbara's face conveyed what I felt: utter horror. When I recount the story today, I observe that if somebody's confidence healed a merely psychosomatic disorder, the confidence certainly wasn't hers. Still less was it mine.

Yet Don then walked Barbara around the room with his hand in one of hers. She stepped cautiously at first, utterly astonished at what was taking place. After Don had brought her around the room, she asked him to let her sit down, so he walked her back to her wheelchair. She sat down, still confused and trying to make sense of what had happened. Yet her newfound ability proved to be no mere momentary burst of emotion. From that day forward, Barbara came to the Bible studies each week, the first time holding on to a walker for security, but soon proudly abandoning it as she saw that now she really could walk completely by herself. Now Barbara would always declare, "I love this Bible study! I love this Bible study!"

A Barbara Sent Home to Die

Let me tell you now about a different Barbara, Barbara Cummiskey.[2] When she was a teenager, doctors diagnosed Barbara with multiple sclerosis (MS). Although MS can come in milder forms, Barbara's condition deteriorated quickly. One day, she looked out the hospital window. With all her heart, she wished that she could just be a regular person, able to drive and live a normal life. Yet, no matter what, Barbara had decided that she was totally in love with the Lord. He was her reason to live.

From the age of fifteen to the age of thirty-one, Barbara spent three-quarters of her life in the hospital; the rest of the time she was being cared for at home. She had chronic pulmonary disease, with frequent infections and pneumonia. A surgeon, Dr. Harold Adolph, describes her condition toward the end of her suffering:

> Barbara was one of the most hopelessly ill patients I ever saw. She was diagnosed at the Mayo Clinic as having multiple sclerosis. She had been admitted to the local hospital seven times in the year that I was first asked to see her. Each time she was expected to die. One diaphragm was completely paralyzed so that the lung was nonfunctional, and the other worked less than 50 percent. She had a tracheotomy tube in her neck for breathing, always required extra oxygen, and could speak only in short sentences because she easily became breathless. Her abdomen was swollen grotesquely because the muscles of her intestine did not work. Nor would her bladder function. She had not been able to walk for seven years. Her hand and arm movements were poorly coordinated. And she was blind except for two small areas in each eye.[3]

She was hooked up to various machines. Because her bowel was paralyzed, Dr. Adolph disconnected it and doctors provided her instead with an outside hookup. Another machine helped her breathe. Because she could not swallow, she had a feeding tube in her stomach.

Barbara needed so much care that, when she was home, a nurse or nurse's aide remained with her most of the time. In her words, she was wrapped up like a pretzel. Her feet pointed down, unable to rest flat against the floor—even had someone tried to stand her up. Her arms remained tight against her chest; normally when anyone tried to pull one of her arms away from her body, it would automatically clamp back up against her chest. Her hands curled up against the inside of her wrists, leaving them full of dead skin except when, periodically, someone would pry them open to clean them out.

Dr. Thomas Marshall had assumed her palliative care in what appeared to be the final weeks of her life. He recalls that her body was "contracted in a permanent fetal position." "Her hands were so permanently flexed that her fingers nearly touched her wrists."[4] He sadly explained to the family that the next infection would likely kill her, and everyone agreed not to prolong her suffering with any further hospitalization or by attempting resuscitation with CPR.

Unable to free herself from her pretzel position or even to breathe normally, Barbara felt trapped inside her own body. Now, after sixteen years of physical deterioration, doctors had sent her home from the hospital one last time. They had regretfully warned her parents, "It's unlikely that she'll survive long enough for us to see her here again."

The Voice

For more than four years, Barbara had not been able even to visit her Wesleyan church in Wheaton, Illinois. Nevertheless, her faithful pastor had visited her every day during that time. Now it was Pentecost Sunday, June 7, 1981, and two friends from her church visited her after the morning worship service. This time they showed up laden with cards and letters. Someone had called in a prayer request about her to the local Christian radio station, WMBI. Now 450 letters came to her in care of her church.

As her friends began reading the new letters to her, she suddenly heard a booming, authoritative voice over her left shoulder. "My child: *Get up and walk.*"

Because of the breathing tube, she could speak only when someone plugged the hole in her neck. They would do this whenever she looked agitated, and her friends, seeing her current agitation, plugged the hole. "God just told me to get up and walk," she gasped. Her friends grew quiet, but Barbara insisted. "Go get my family!" she ordered urgently. Feeling her excitement, they dashed out of the room to find her family.

The sense of urgency in Barbara's heart suddenly became too intense for her to wait for their return. Normally, it would take two people about two minutes to get her out of bed. They would slide her onto a lapboard and then into a chair. But now she did not have time to ponder what should have been impossible for her.

Abruptly, she jumped out of bed toward the direction of the voice. Equally abruptly, she found herself standing. Her feet had been too deformed even to wear slippers, but now she found them flat on the ground. Then she noticed that her hands were both open at her sides, like anyone else's. What struck her next was that she could *see* her hands and feet—she was no longer blind! Freeing herself from the connected apparatus, she disconnected her tracheostomy tube from the oxygen tank and fastened the catheter bags to her clothes with safety pins.

At this point her friends returned to the room. As they caught each other's eyes, her friends started screaming and jumping. Her mother came running behind them, assuming from her friends' urgent summons that something terrible had happened to Barbara. As Barbara's mother burst into the room, however, she froze, transfixed with amazement. Not only was Barbara healed from her condition; beyond possible natural explanation, her muscles were not even atrophied as they normally would have been from years of nonuse. (Instant reversal of muscle atrophy is not usual even in miracle accounts.)

"Barbara—you have calves again!" her mother exclaimed. Barbara examined her own legs with astonishment.

"Dad!" Barbara now shouted.

"Just a minute," he called. He had not heard the cause of all the commotion. Since Barbara had become unable to speak normally, her father assumed that it was her sister calling him. But Barbara realized that she no longer had to wait for him to come to her.

At about this time, Angela, a friend who often came to see Barbara, arrived for a visit. Angela was an occupational therapist who knew that Barbara had reached a point of no return for MS. As she witnessed Barbara bolting out of the room, Angela was horrified. Nobly, she rushed to try to get Barbara's pulse. "Wait!" she shouted fearfully. "You can't be in bed that many years . . . and then just get up . . . and have a normal heartbeat!"

But Barbara could not wait for Angela. She raced down the wheelchair ramp. Angela desperately grabbed the oxygen tank, wheeling it down the ramp after her. "But you can't . . . you can't . . ." she kept protesting, while those who had followed Barbara out of her room just kept laughing.

Finally Barbara's dad spotted her. Overcome with joy, he waltzed Barbara around the room, her catheter bags still attached to her clothes. Soon, she recounts, she "ran outside and hit the blacktop on that 93-degree sunny day with feet that could now feel and [with new] sight! And what a dance I did as I inhaled the fragrant summer air and saw sights I had so missed!"[5] Jesus was already Barbara's reason to live, but by this healing he had enabled her to live a normal life.

Word Spreads

The next day Barbara visited her doctor's office. Dr. Marshall recounts his feelings when, in the hallway of his medical office, he first saw Barbara walking toward him. "I thought I was seeing an apparition! Here was my patient, who was not expected to live another week, totally cured."

Over the next three and a half hours, she saw virtually every doctor in the office. Dr. Marshall reports that none of his colleagues "had ever seen anything like this before." X-rays showed that even her collapsed lung was no longer collapsed.[6] He removed all the tubes that could be removed without surgery. Barbara reports his verdict that day: "I'll be the first to tell you: You're completely healed. I can also tell you that this is medically impossible." Dr. Adolph remarks that "her breathing was normal. The diaphragms were functioning normally."[7] He soon reconnected her bowel, which was now functional; her only health problem involved some complications from this new operation.

That week, WMBI broadcast her testimony. Eventually, the *Chicago Tribune*, some television stations, and many magazines and books carried her story. Dr. Marshall told Barbara, "You are now free to go out and live your life." And Barbara has—now for roughly four decades with no recurrence of MS.[8] Dr. Marshall deems it his "rare privilege to observe the Hand of God performing a true miracle."[9] Dr. Adolph notes that Barbara eventually studied surgical technology at the hospital "and even assisted me on several simpler operations. Both Barbara and I knew who had healed her."[10]

One day the man who normally delivered oxygen to Barbara's house arrived to bring more oxygen, and Barbara herself answered the door with a big smile. He was shocked: she would not be needing any more oxygen deliveries![11]

Just the Beginning

In December 2015, I first interviewed Barbara Cummiskey Snyder. Even though it was now many years after her healing, Barbara still brimmed with excitement as she shared her story. Dr. Adolph also confirmed his report for me personally, providing additional details.[12] Another doctor who had worked with her, Dr. Scott Kolbaba, further confirmed her story for me.[13] He also sent me his recent book, *Physicians' Untold Stories*. It collects accounts from twenty-six medical colleagues of what they believe have been various kinds of supernatural experiences, including Dr. Marshall's account of Barbara's healing. But I already have way too many accounts to include in this book! Indeed, in some months I receive multiple accounts of significant healings from sources that I trust (as well as some that I cannot adjudicate with confidence).

The interpretation of some accounts in this book may be somewhat ambiguous; the events may not be completely unique, but their coinciding with prayer will impress at least those more open to faith. The story of the first Barbara might be such a case: a nonbeliever might dismiss such an account as an interesting anomaly that just "happened" to occur during prayer. Barbara just "happened" to be able to walk but didn't know it, and Don just got lucky when he commanded her to rise in Jesus's name. To me, that seems a considerable stretch, but some prefer to take the leap of faith required by such an explanation rather than to trust a God who sometimes acts unexpectedly. The story of the second Barbara, physically incapable of walking but completely restored when she heard a divine voice, seems harder to dismiss in such terms.

I will spend most of this book sharing some of the healing reports from around the world that eyewitnesses have shared with me. Toward the end of the book, I will explore what such reports may mean for us today.

Whether you start from much faith, little faith, or no faith at all, I invite you to explore this book's interesting "anomalies"—and see whether some challenge you to believe more. Before I turn to such accounts, though, I need to explain why I'm writing this book at this time.

Introduction

Miracles Books, Old and New

Many scholars assume that biblical accounts of miracles could not ultimately reflect information from the reports of eyewitnesses. This assumption, however, does not match known reality since millions of eyewitnesses today claim such experiences. To challenge many fellow scholars' skepticism that such experiences occur, I wrote my 1,100-page *Miracles: The Credibility of the New Testament Accounts*.[1] In it I provide modern analogies for most of the sorts of miracle accounts we have in the New Testament.

Miracles the Last Time Around

The book won several awards, including one in *Christianity Today*, but what took me particularly by surprise was how widely the book was received. There remains enough prejudice against miracles in many academic circles that I had feared I was committing academic suicide. Nevertheless, I was convinced that the reality the book described was genuine and needed to be heard. Although I felt that I was sticking my neck out, the guillotine's blade—for whatever reasons—proved less lethal than expected.

Some vocal atheists on the internet predictably panned the book, but they demurred mainly regarding the book's secondary thesis: that many purported miracles are genuine acts of God. They did not (and could not) object so much to the book's primary thesis: that eyewitnesses experience what they consider to be miracles today, and that there is no reason to suppose that matters were different in the first century. Meanwhile, Christians from a wide range of traditions embraced the book, as did, for different reasons, some members of other faith traditions.

One problem with such a massive volume was that many people were more likely to talk about it than to actually read it. Both detractors and supporters on the internet sometimes claimed more for the book than it actually argued. In fact, detractors often criticized examples from the section of the book illustrating the range of contemporary testimonies without noticing that it differs from the part of the book where I engage potential explanations and highlight some cases as particularly compelling.

Given the time needed for research and being a full-time professor, I usually cannot respond to internet critics with too much time on their hands, especially when they have not actually bothered to *read* the book. Often critics present a skewed critique, caricaturing the work to produce impressions of it quite different from those someone actually reading the work would get.[2] Moreover, some protest against healing by using logically irrelevant arguments, such as the argument that healing often does not happen. No one, however, claims that healing always *does* happen. By way of analogy, even the best medical technology does not *always* bring healing, but we do not for that reason dismiss its value when it does. (More thoughts on this later.)

Miracles This Time Around

In fairness to those who did not read the entire book, reading 1,100 pages can take a rather long time. Although some PhD programs use *Miracles* as a textbook, it does not seem suitable as a supplemental undergraduate or seminary textbook. Nor is it the sort of book I can hand to a new acquaintance on a plane (at least, not without injury to my aged arm), in contrast to my frequently given little book, *Impossible Love*, cowritten with my wife.[3] For a number of years, then, I have realized the need for a more concise, less detailed work about miracles.

In December 2016, Lee Strobel interviewed me extensively for his book *The Case for Miracles*.[4] As I have told Lee, his excellent book meets the need for a solid but more readable book on the subject (not unlike some other fairly popular-level books).[5] Thus I wavered about whether I needed to write this second, shorter book on miracles.

But while these other books communicate to their audiences on a better level than I could, I gradually realized that I still had something valuable to contribute to my own usual readership. I simply needed some time to get it written. When the Henry Center at Trinity International University provided the opportunity for a study leave specifically on this topic, it appeared that the time had come.

I have tried to keep the chapters short enough to be readable, although some subjects required somewhat longer-than-average chapters and others allowed shorter ones.

Although I have reused some stories from the larger book on miracles, especially some testimonies I could verify from within my own circle and some medical accounts, I have focused more here on newer accounts. I have thus omitted hundreds of older accounts and included some accounts of varying evidential weight, especially in the earlier chapters, simply because they are new and thus supplement the samples in the earlier volume.

What Not to Expect

Nevertheless, what I include here remains merely *samples*, and I have also omitted many newer accounts. Indeed, so many testimonies have come my way since the publication of *Miracles* that I probably could have written another massive volume. I have omitted some well-documented miracles because some sources, on reflection, preferred to keep their stories private. Other times I have omitted stories simply because I lacked further room. I apologize to the vast number of sources, including academic colleagues and students, whose stories I did not include here.

With just a few exceptions, I also omitted a majority of accounts associated with figures well known for ministries of healing. Some, like Daniel Kolenda, whose ministry I appreciate and trust, have witnessed far more healings than a book such as this one could begin to describe.[6] (One can, for example, watch what everyone present understood as the healing of the Muslim king of Tamale, Ghana, in the film *Finger of God 2*, when Kolenda prays in Jesus's name.) Though I pause to acknowledge it here, Kolenda's ministry merits books of its own, as do some other ministries. For the sake of welcoming the broadest range of Western readers, however, I have chosen to focus in this book more often on individual stories from less widely known settings.

I should warn readers at the outset that the samples included in this book are not meant as models for everyone to follow. Whatever patterns might emerge in how I recount the stories, the differences among them preclude us from taking any one expression of faith as the right expression and others as wrong ones. As in the Bible, God chooses to work today with different people in different ways. Moreover, because of its subject, this book recounts more dramatic healings than non-healings, but God works through people with different abilities and disabilities, and those who are healed in one area do not always experience healing in all areas. Despite limited reflections in later chapters (especially in part 7), this book is more about the reality of miracles than about the theology of why or how miracles sometimes happen or do not happen. This does not mean that those questions do not matter; they are, however, sometimes harder to answer.

Except for brief treatment in appendix B, I chose to limit this book to reports of Christian miracles rather than opening up another can of worms. (Still, in the earlier book I did survey a large range of sources regarding non-Christian miracle claims—contrary, again, to comments from some reviewers who did not actually read that book.)[7] I have also chosen, however, not to restrict it further. Some Christian groups mistrust other Christian groups, and so perhaps they will recommend this book with a warning label: "Ignore testimonies from [fill in the blank: Catholics? charismatics? evangelicals? mainline Protestants?]." Likewise, some critics complain about examples of particular ministries or witnesses they mistrust, using them to excuse overlooking other witnesses. This commits a logical fallacy akin to supposing that if one appears to discredit one witness in court, the entire slate of witnesses must thereby collapse. As a New Testament scholar, I probably have disagreements with everybody on something; what would we scholars have to write about if we never held some different views? But as important as theological distinctives may be to those who affirm them, they are not the subject of this book. If there seems reason to me to believe that God has acted on behalf of someone he loves, regardless of this person's theological orientation, I am more than happy to celebrate God's choice. Meanwhile, I still have plenty to learn myself, including from friends whose views differ from mine on various matters. When the Lord heals anybody, the credit goes to him as healer, not to those of us who are healed or who petition him.

Anyone who fears that the present book lacks sufficient documentation regarding complex philosophic and other issues should feel free to consult *Miracles: The Credibility of the New Testament Accounts*, which cites some four thousand sources. The present book is designed to be more useful to general readers, as a supplemental classroom text, and for those who liked the earlier book very much without ever getting around to actually reading it.

Readers who want something even more reader-friendly than my opening discussion are free to skip ahead to the miracle stories. (Though the graphic nature of some of the medical ailments described there is less reader-friendly than the healings, it serves to explain why they are healings.) But those who want to learn more about why some people argue against miracles and why I argue for them should start from the beginning.

PART 1

Perspectives on Miracles

Beliefs are not only a matter of evidence but also a matter of the interpretive grids through which we read the evidence. If a preacher gets struck by lightning, does this mean that God is judging a hypocrite? That the devil hates preachers? Or maybe just that preachers, like other people, shouldn't run around too much outside during thunderstorms?

The same issue arises with miracle claims. Everyone acknowledges the occurrence of some anomalies—experiences that do not easily fit current understandings of nature. But do we think of it differently if a striking anomaly happens just when some people pray for it to happen? Or if it happens on multiple occasions, just when some people pray for it to happen? Or if a particularly improbable anomaly happens after someone predicts it?

Because of different assumptions, different people require different standards of evidence. Someone particularly gullible may accept as a miracle anything that anyone claims to be such. Someone particularly skeptical may reject an event as a miracle regardless of the attestation and natural improbability. Someone who believes in a God active in the universe allows for the potential of miracles occurring; someone adamantly opposed to God's existence cannot allow for that possibility. As we shall see, skepticism is no less a historically conditioned assumption than the reverse.

But speaking of miracles occurring, what *is* a miracle? Good question.

Chapter 1

What *Is* a Miracle, Anyway?

One problem for anyone writing a book about miracles is that there is no universally agreed-upon definition.[1] In popular usage, miracles might include the New York Mets winning the World Series in 1969 or the Anaheim Angels winning it in 2002. While it might indeed take a miracle at least for a team including any Craig Keeners to win a baseball game, this book is using the term in a more precise way. Still, not *too* precise.

Extraordinary Divine Action

Probably the most common definition of a miracle throughout history, from Augustine to Aquinas, has been a divine action that transcends the ordinary course of nature and so generates awe. By "transcending the ordinary course of nature," these thinkers don't just mean an unusually awesome sunset. They mean something you would never expect to happen on its own.

Now, that is a somewhat subjective definition, because some things are more unexpected than others. Likewise, not everybody responds to even the most dramatic "miracles" with awe. In the Bible, when God parted the sea so his people could escape their pursuers, his people were impressed. Their pursuers, by contrast, had a different theology. They didn't doubt that the God of their former slaves had *some* power (he was, after all, a god), but they were sure that their own gods (including their king) were stronger, so they continued their pursuit.

David Hume, whom you'll meet more officially in chapter 3, defined a miracle as a violation of natural law. One problem with this definition is that barely any of the biblical miracles, which Hume has at least partly in view, ever claimed to violate natural law. Even the particularly dramatic miracle of God's parting of the sea did not work against natural law: the Bible says that God used a strong east wind to part the sea (Exod. 14:21). A strong-enough wind can move water; what meteorologists call "wind setdown" sometimes does. But moving water in such a way as to part the sea, letting all the Israelites cross precisely when their lives depended on it, does not look very much like an accident. The odds of such a coincidence are so low that ordinarily, for practical purposes, we would not seriously consider them. Even in dramatic acts of God in the Bible, God typically uses what he has already created rather than starting over by creating something new.

There are other problems with Hume's definition of *miracle* (not least his definitions of *violation* and *natural law*), but suffice it to note for now that his definition is unhelpful for the present subject. Apart from creation, the virgin birth, and the new creation introduced with Jesus's bodily resurrection, the Bible itself does not claim many miracles in the law-violating sense. A book giving examples of such miracles today might prove rather concise.

Theologians today thus often echo the more traditional historic approach to miracles, referring to them as "special divine action."[2] This label is meant to differentiate miracles from divine action more generally, since Christians affirm that God works in all sorts of ways around us all the time. But what is the cutoff where "general" divine action becomes "special" divine action? How do we classify, for example, an extraordinarily fast recovery from surgery?

The boundaries are fuzzy, but we can at least provide paradigmatic examples of each. By analogy, the boundary between "long hair" and "short hair" may be unclear, but most of us would at least recognize Samson's proverbial hair as long and the hair on a mostly bald head (mine, for example) as short. In the same way, those of us who believe in God regard life as God's gift to everyone who is alive, but if someone comes back to life who has been clinically dead for an hour, and suffers no brain damage, most of us regard that as a miracle. Between examples that would convince nearly everyone and those that would convince scarcely anyone exists a broad middle range that will probably include some inauthentic cases and exclude some genuine ones; but enough genuine and convincing ones should remain to make the point. Miracles don't always happen—but sometimes they do.

Burden of Proof

Many passages in the Bible speak of miracles as "signs," experiences that get people's attention. The Bible does speak of some less extraordinary events, such as circumcision or a rainbow, as signs that signify or communicate something. But often the Bible speaks of more extraordinary signs as special acts of God that get attention and communicate something about him. These include events such as the exodus plagues (e.g., Exod. 10:1–2; Ps. 78:43), kingdom healings (e.g., Acts 2:22, 43; 4:16, 22, 30), and nature miracles (e.g., John 2:11; 6:14). Again, not everyone responds positively to such signs. In one town where the apostle Paul and his colleague Barnabas preached, signs got people's attention, but not all the attention was positive. Some, to be sure, responded to the signs by accepting their message; others, who refused the message, just became more hostile (Acts 14:3–4).

We all evaluate miracle reports through our own assumptions. If a person who has not walked for ten years can suddenly walk after prayer, albeit with some support, I would normally see that as divine enablement. Barring an additional miracle, the person will need some support because her muscles will still be atrophied for a time; achieving suddenly what might take physical therapy weeks or months remains extraordinary. Some reject such a healing as incomplete, demanding that divine intervention restore every organ to perfection. We do not, however, live in a currently perfect world; unless you are Superman or the Hulk, even what we accept as normal functionality has limits. Likewise, if after prayer eyesight immediately improves from legal blindness to functional sight, vision need not be 20/20 for us to infer special divine action. If God has improved your sight beyond available human means but you still need glasses, don't complain. Lots of the rest of us have to wear glasses too. If Jesus resuscitates a twelve-year-old young woman, he may still request that her parents feed her rather than supernaturally filling her empty stomach (Mark 5:43). But again, some people work with different assumptions about how a God must display himself, and they therefore dismiss evidence that does not match their assumptions.

How extraordinary must an event be to get someone's attention? Further, how much evidence does it take to convince someone? That depends on who the person is and what the person's starting assumptions are. If I am adamant that miracles are impossible, in principle I might reject any amount of evidence. If I already trust God, I will thank God for even the smallest details of my life.

Most people, even if they do not trust God in details, are open to evidence. Yet standards for evidence vary. It is possible to be too gullible and be convinced by simple magic tricks. Conversely, some people are so opposed to miracles that they keep raising the bar of evidence to evade them. They may say, "There is no medical documentation for miracles." If I show them medical documentation, they may say, "Just because that was unusual doesn't mean it couldn't happen on its own. Show me someone who was raised from the dead." If I give examples of people raised from the dead, they may say, "Well, *I* didn't see that happen."

Twice I have asked skeptical academic friends, "Would you believe it was a miracle if you did see someone raised from the dead?" and they have replied, "No." I think what they meant was, "Miracles can't happen, so I would just say it was unexplained." But if someone uses this approach, what sort of evidence *would* they accept? If they say "none," then it's clear that they value their starting premise more than any amount of evidence, making it disingenuous for them to ask for any. They had better not accuse all *Christians* of being closed-minded!

Fortunately, most people are not *that* skeptical. It is thus helpful to provide solid evidence where we can. And fortunately, there is a lot of evidence for those who are willing to believe.

I should conclude this section with a caution, however: miracles do not "prove" God. If you are inflexibly committed to finding another explanation, you always will. Even if you see the sea part at just the right time, you could choose to dismiss it as a one-chance-in-a-billion coincidence. (In the Bible itself, Pharaoh, at least, did not seem sufficiently impressed to halt his pursuit.) But if you are open to the reality of God, what you recognize as miracles will get your attention and invite your faith in him. And if you already believe in God, they will give you additional reasons for gratitude.

"Ordinary" Blessings

There are greater miracles than the ones this book addresses, but people regularly ignore or even reject them. Because they are part of the "normal" course of nature, available to everybody, most people take them for granted. Hidden in plain sight, they're not "extraordinary," hence not what we usually call miracles.

Although this book is about "special" divine action, Christians (and most other theists) believe that general divine action is all around us. The psalmist already marvels at God's glory in nature (Ps. 19:1). Ancient, non-Christian Stoic philosophers recognized divine design in nature.[3] The apostle Paul says that God's power is evident in his creation, especially in our own selves. He explains that our proper response should be gratitude (Rom. 1:19–21).

One need not believe that God micromanages every detail to affirm that something about our universe seems to exceed random chance. Both the Bible (Gen. 1:24) and our knowledge of the cosmos suggest that God likes to create things that not only exist but develop and replicate on their own. But is their existence an accident? What are the odds of a universe accidentally arising with just the right, extraordinarily precise conditions to support life? Exact calculations vary, but the parameters are so exquisitely fine-tuned that their generation by chance seems utterly implausible—often calculated as far less than even one in a trillion trillion trillion trillion trillion.[4] In daily life, none of us would stake our lives on such minuscule odds. From a Christian perspective, it seems a testament to some thinkers' faith commitment in anything-but-God that they would desperately cling to such minute possibilities. This may be one reason why a far greater number of academic works about theism in philosophy of religion today defend rather than contest the existence of God.[5]

Some respond that we just blissfully happen to live in the one life-permitting universe that exists out of a seemingly infinite number of (unattested) universes. In terms of economy of logic, however, it seems much simpler to posit a single designer beyond the universe than to posit trillions of trillions of universes.[6] And even if one does opt for this multiverse hypothesis (the idea of many unconnected universes), one merely pushes the design question back one level: so far, all the models for generating many universes require immense precision in the settings.[7]

At a 2012 Harvard Veritas Forum that may be viewed online, John Lennox, now emeritus professor of mathematics at Oxford University, recounted a discussion he once had over dinner with a reductionist colleague.[8] The colleague insisted that nothing exists beyond physics and chemistry. Lennox then pointed out two words on their menu. "Explain to me those marks based only on the paper and the ink," he demanded. After a moment of silence, his colleague, a leading biochemist, admitted, "One cannot explain meaning apart from intelligence." Random marks communicate little, but specifically arranged marks designed to represent meaning communicate information.

Lennox goes on to point to a much more complex language, one we must use computer information technology to describe. Human DNA uses an alphabet of four letters, arranged in base pairs in a mostly specific sequence to compose a word some three billion letters long. Did chance and necessity organize these from scratch? Their design suggests both intelligence and benevolence: God purposed and desired our existence.[9]

What are the odds that we humans, the most intelligent form of physical being we know of in the universe, would, merely by random chance, have the abstract reasoning capable of figuring these things out? Christians differ among ourselves about how we got here. Some say God created us directly, whereas others say that God used evolution as a process with some predesignated outcomes. Either way, our existence does not make sense apart from an ultimate designer. Throughout most of history, natural selection by itself has lacked much incentive to produce abstract mathematical reasoning.

Some people view such a design as wasteful. Why would some God create billions of trillions of stars in the universe if life on our planet is supposed to be so special? Why would he allow the development of matter for more than thirteen billion years before forming humanity? Why would he allow suffering in the world before someday creating a world without suffering? But we can speak of "waste" as a problem only if there is a limited supply.[10] Some thinkers also suggest that there had to be enough matter in the universe for the universe to expand at the right rate for galaxies, stars, and thus planets to form.[11] Humans make up very little of the matter in the universe, but in terms of information content, we are, so far as we know empirically, its most complex entities. We are the pinnacle of God's creation, his special delight. The Bible suggests that someday we will be able to look back over history and see God accomplishing his purposes for those who will be his forever, despite what looks to us now like a lot of waste as other things run their own course.

Everyone has starting assumptions. Biblical faith provides glasses that enable our eyes to see God's work all around us. Yet when people look around with nonbelieving sunglasses, they do not recognize God's activity around them. In that sense, they take for granted sunlight, air to breathe, and often life itself.

Special divine action reinvites most people's attention. If it weren't special—that is, if miracles happened all the time when we wanted them—we might take them for granted the same way we do the more "regular" patterns God authored in nature. God arranged for our bodies to be able to heal themselves of many infections, for example. But if healing *always* took place, spiritual sunglasses-wearers might well dismiss that gift as simply the ordinary course of nature as well.[12]

New Life in Christ

Most of this book is about special events. But I would be remiss to leave the impression that only what appears to others as extraordinary is divine action. Whether we label it a "miracle" or not, it is divine action that makes possible a relationship with God. The creator who made humans special, intelligent, and relational desires a relationship with us. We humans cut off that relationship from our side by neglecting him and mistreating others who are no less special to him. Yet this God who desired us enough to create us for himself sacrificed his own heart to restore us to him. He thus sent his own Son united with our humanity and mortality so he could bring us back into relationship with himself.

My own faith is God's merciful gift to me; I surely didn't deserve it. I started out as an unchurched atheist who knew a lot more about ancient Greek myths than about Christianity, while for years some devout Methodist relatives prayed faithfully for my family. As an atheist, I allowed Christianity only about a 2 percent chance of being true. (Technically, by that point I was somewhat agnostic since I was no longer 100 percent certain about atheism. But I didn't tell anyone that, since I enjoyed looking down on most theists.)

It looked to me as though most people who claimed to be Christians (back then it was maybe 80 percent of Americans) did not live as if they took their faith seriously. With a few exceptions that I treated as anomalous outliers, Christians didn't seem to live like people who owed their entire existence and purpose to a creator. Either these people who claimed to be Christians were quite stupid, or they didn't believe what they claimed. "If I ever believed there was a God," I reasoned, "I would owe God everything. I would give God everything." But if Christians didn't take their faith seriously, why should I?

Once I started thinking about it, however, I didn't want to stake my eternal destiny on even a 2 percent possibility of being wrong. I wasn't familiar with Pascal's wager, but that concept would have made sense to me: the stakes involved in trusting or denying God are rather high. I had been convinced enough of my atheism to make fun of Christians, but I was scared to make fun of God. I was not so sure of myself that I wouldn't consider evidence if somebody presented some. Indeed, on occasion I secretly asked any superior being that might be listening, if there was one, to show me the truth. For a seeker, asking God to show himself to you is not a bad place to begin. He shows himself more often where he is more welcome—though he does not usually show himself on our terms. I was hoping for empirical or historical evidence, of which, I now know, there is a lot.[13] A book like this one could also have gotten my attention. In my case, though, the Lord chose a more humbling route.

What convinced me initially was not historical evidence, scientific evidence, witnessing a miracle, or anything of the sort. One day, some Bible-wielding, conservative Baptist street preachers in black suits—students at a local, church-run Bible college—confronted me with what their Bible said about Jesus: God's Son, Jesus Christ, died and rose to save me. I argued with them for forty-five minutes and finally demanded, "If there's a God, where did the dinosaur bones come from?" The question is logically fallacious—why should the existence of God conflict with the existence of dinosaurs?—but neither I nor (apparently) they yet understood that point. On the spot and having to come up with a quick answer, one retorted, "The devil put them there." Disgusted, I walked away. (Their off-the-cuff response to my question about dinosaurs still draws my hearers' laughs; they were certainly not paleontologists. But they *did* know what their Bible said about being made right with God.)

Yet I experienced a sort of evidence that was less public but more compelling on the personal level. Over the next hour or two, I was overwhelmed with God's own presence until my knees buckled under me and I gave in. I didn't understand how God made me right with him by Jesus's death and resurrection, but since that was what he was saying, I accepted it. I'd studied various religions and philosophies, but I experienced something that day that I had never experienced before. The presence, which I have often experienced since then, was more real and direct than that of another person physically talking to me in the same room. I actually felt God come inside me.

The next few years were a journey of finding out the answers to the kinds of questions those Baptist Bible college students understandably hadn't been able to answer. Nevertheless, biblically speaking, God himself had entered my life and begun to make me new. No physical healing I have experienced or witnessed has been as clear a divine action in my life as the adventure of becoming new and thus experiencing a foretaste of the future new creation. So while that experience is too personal, and hence "subjective," to count as "evidence" for most people who haven't experienced it, to me personally it is no less persuasive than any "public" miracle I recount in this book.

All this is to say that, even though this book is about what people call miracles, more narrowly defined, those of us who are believers would never limit God's action to what gets everybody else's attention.

Chapter 2

Why Do Some People Assume That Miracles Don't Happen? Worldviews

M any people simply take for granted that miracles don't happen. Sometimes this is because of bad experiences with miracle claims or hopes. There are, for example, charlatans, unfulfilled promises, and disappointments. I can certainly understand such sentiments; besides having some health problems over the years, my wife and I suffered a series of miscarriages, which are even more devastating in her culture of origin than in the West. But counterfeit money is no reason to abandon the real thing, and receiving one plate empty is no reason to turn down food on the next one. Though the subject of this book is miracles, I'll talk more in some later chapters (esp. 37–39) about times when miracles don't happen.

But besides personal, emotional reasons for doubting miracles, there are also ideological ones.

Perspectives Make a Difference

Assumptions shape how we approach evidence. A person who already believes in miracles may find her faith confirmed even if she simply experiences a better-than-usual recovery. By contrast, someone else might not believe even if he sees his name and a call to faith spelled out in the sky. "My wife must've paid somebody to do that," he might insist.

Although some skeptics are open-minded, others place the bar of evidence so high that they will never have to believe. I have friends and relatives who are open-minded, "agnostic" skeptics, or at least tolerant ones.[1] But there are also dogmatic skeptics and hostile skeptics. When I was an atheist, I was not quite 100 percent dogmatic, but I was hostile; I used to make fun of Christians. Being converted, therefore, was a humbling experience for me in more than one way: I had to eat crow.

Hardline skeptics argue that coincidences and anomalies (unexplained occurrences) happen often enough that we should *never* accept claims for miracles, no matter how unusual. Although they may understandably bristle when a Christian appeals to anything currently unexplainable as divine action, they may prove less critical of their own position. When they cannot currently explain an apparent miracle, they may dismiss it as an anomaly that will *someday* be explained.[2]

They would rather accept an explanation that they admit is in a given case highly improbable (or as yet unknowable) than wrestle with the possibility of a God who does not fit their worldview (that is, what they believe about reality). As one scrupulously honest atheist medical historian points out, this approach "also arises from a kind of faith—the absolute belief in the nontranscendence of earthly events."[3] In essence, inflexible supporters of this approach would allow nothing to persuade them; their minds are made up.[4] When the most reasonable faith is the ability to perceive divine truth, critics who speak of blind faith can be blind to their own blindness of antifaith.

Many people in the West today have embraced a worldview of unbelief (usually with a more respectable title).[5] Because of this, they may prefer any possible naturalistic explanation—even no explanation at all—to admitting the possibility that God has acted. No amount of evidence, therefore, will convince them. Ironically, I have spoken with some advocates of this approach who insist that all believers are closed-minded.

Such a posture should not surprise us. In the Bible itself, think again of Pharaoh, when he was confronted with the plagues announced by Moses. Pharaoh's own magicians duplicated the first couple of plagues, though on a much smaller scale. Yet it soon became clear—to almost everyone except Pharaoh—that Israel's God was bringing plagues that Pharaoh's gods could not stop (see Exod. 12:12; Num. 33:4). Pharaoh was too committed to a different worldview to recognize what became obvious to others. From Pharaoh's perspective, while Israel's God might have some power, the single god of a powerless, enslaved people must be far less powerful than the many gods who had built Egypt into a mighty empire. Indeed, Egyptians believed that Pharaoh was a god himself; acknowledging the greater power of Israel's God would have undercut Pharaoh's entire belief system, including his lifelong sense of his own identity.[6]

Likewise, when Jesus raised Lazarus (John 11:43–44), reactions were mixed. Most apparent resuscitations in the Bible, like most apparent resuscitations today, occur within a few hours of death. The raising of Lazarus was different. Not only were all his brain cells certainly dead, but he was beginning to decompose; he had been dead for four days (11:17, 39). You would think that, even without modern medical knowledge, everyone who witnessed this public miracle would have become a believer. The Fourth Gospel reports that many people were so impressed that they believed in Jesus (11:45). Others, however, reported Jesus to hostile authorities (11:46), who wanted to kill him before he led any more people astray with his unusual acts (11:46–50). Jesus's hometown did not welcome his miracles (Mark 6:5), and Jesus himself denounces towns whose response to his miracles was too bland (Matt. 11:20–24//Luke 10:13–15).

In the Bible, divine signs get the attention of those who are open, but bring to the surface the hostility of those who are not (note again Acts 14:3–4). The biblical standard for a sign's "success" is not that it convinces everyone. It is that it gets their attention—and often in the process it exposes the attitude of their heart (see John 3:19–21; 15:22–24).

Some today classify all belief in supernatural activity as superstitious because they lump all supernatural claims together as part of a "primitive" worldview.[7] This approach, aside from being ethnocentric, fails to recognize that its own framework constitutes a worldview. This skeptical worldview is in fact far more idiosyncratic historically and culturally than are worldviews that allow for supernatural activity. Yet it assumes an elite position of superiority in evaluating other worldviews, while denying others the same opportunity.

What we believe does affect how we understand what we see. One time as a very new Christian I wanted to command a storm to stop but felt that the Lord did not want it to stop, and I had better run for cover. Usually I simply carry a small umbrella in my bag just in case it rains. I have only twice in my life commanded storms to stop; the first time the rain immediately stopped, but I don't have much else to say about it. It is the other time I will mention here.

One day I was working hard at my computer during a long thunderstorm. My son, then quite young, burst into the room. I was happy for his company, but he came to warn me that it was dangerous for me to work on the computer during a thunderstorm. Despite my good surge protector, he was technically correct. Nevertheless, the odds of a direct strike were low, I had a tight deadline, and all but that afternoon's work was already backed up. Finally, and without thinking about what I was doing, I shouted, "Thunder, stop! In Jesus's name!" The lightning and thunder stopped immediately.

"Did you see that?" I asked.

"You just didn't want to take a break from your computer!" he charged. He didn't notice the end of the lightning and thunder, which did not resume for the rest of my working day. Both of our observations were correct, but our different interests and frames of reference shaped what we chose to notice. I cite this not as proof of a "miracle" but as proof that our lenses affect what we perceive.

Does Science Disprove Miracles?

In terms of *ideological* reasons for rejecting miracles, many people start with the assumption that modern science has disproved miracles. The relationship between science and miracles, however, is not strictly a matter of scientific data but one of the philosophy of science—that is, of what science is designed to explain. Science rightly shows what normally occurs; it does not address what God might cause for a special purpose in a special situation. "By definition," apologist Amy K. Hall notes, "a miracle does not happen as a result of a naturally repeating cause."[8]

As we shall see in the next chapter, it was not science but a particular philosopher (David Hume) who persuaded many academics that miracles cannot occur. Many leading scientists before Hume were also theologians, who affirmed both the normally predictable course of nature and that in special circumstances God could act differently with nature. As I and many others have argued elsewhere, Hume's redefinition of miracles simply takes for granted that these affirmations are incompatible. Indeed, Hume's argument, though influential, offers little good reason to force a reductionistic choice between these affirmations.

Different disciplines require different approaches. Physical science is superb and necessary within its sphere and also has valuable contributions to make to the study of miracles. When most narrowly defined, science is about measurements and about what happens all the time under certain circumstances; it is not, however, about divine purpose or human meaning.[9] Just as one does not weigh an object by its color or measure love by its height, the tools of science are designed only to explore particular sorts of questions. Science can tell you how much cyanide will kill your friend or whether a nuclear weapon should work, but science *as science* does not tell you whether it's right to kill your friend or fire your nuclear weapon.

Science does offer the best means to verify that someone was sick and is now well. So long as we exclude talk about God, however, we cannot talk about a miracle. What if we expand our definition of science to hypothesize about intelligent causes? Surely any real God should be able to act as a cause no less than any human person does. In this case, science might even help quantify probabilities that a particular event is a divine act. But the variables for such equations would be legion, and most scientists understandably define their discipline more narrowly. Rather than dismissing the possibility of miracles, science when defined most narrowly simply excludes them from its sphere of discussion.

Although some scientists have accepted the false historical narrative that religion and science are opposed, others see them as simply addressing different subjects or even as different avenues to truth.[10] At a 2014 conference at Oxford University where I and other participants presented papers regarding special divine action, I learned from and spoke with Sir John Polkinghorne, a former professor of mathematical physics at Cambridge and president of Queen's College, Cambridge. But Polkinghorne's voice at the conference was by no means his first word on the subject; he addressed the question of special divine action in earlier books. He notes that while God usually works in consistent ways, God is not bound to act in those ways.[11] Oxford mathematician John Lennox, Oxford religion and science scholar Alister McGrath (who holds PhDs in both molecular biophysics and theology), MIT scientist Ian Hutchinson, and a host of other prominent thinkers reject the idea that science forces one to dismiss miracles.

I am not suggesting that all scientists believe in miracles or that science as such compels belief in miracles. My point is simply that believing in miracles does not make one opposed to science. Science is about measurements, but the interpretation of those measurements overlaps with philosophy. Science makes predictions on the basis of what is repeatable; but distinctive, detailed events in history—such as miracles would be—are not repeatable.[12] (For example, we do not kill someone again to check how the person died; we infer it on the basis of the evidence available.) Those who refuse to believe in miracles unless God acts predictably in a scientific experiment are looking for God in the wrong place, ignoring signs that God more normally provides. The god they are seeking is not the one revealed in the Bible.

Nevertheless, scientific evidence remains very helpful when studying miracles because in some cases it can help us decide whether an event happened. For example, X-rays, when available, can reveal extraordinary changes even though they cannot prove that God performed the changes. Much of part 3 and some cases in parts 4 and 5 of this book provide examples of this sort. Medical data can also give us an idea about how irregular or extraordinary an experience may be.

Did Miracles Stop Happening a Long Time Ago?

Although the focus of this book is responding to skepticism that miracles have ever happened, some people believe that miracles used to happen but do not do so any longer. Since that is a theological position I have addressed elsewhere,[13] I will respond to it here only briefly.

I believe that biblical spiritual gifts are for today, but some of my esteemed colleagues among Christian scholars believe that particular spiritual gifts have ceased. This position is called "cessationism." There are some senses in which virtually everybody, including those who affirm that gifts continue, is cessationist. That is, nobody believes that God regularly parts the sea to let Israelites flee their pursuers. Nobody believes that Jesus has to keep dying and rising from the dead; the Bible says that he did that once for all, accomplishing the foretaste of believers' future resurrection. Nobody believes that the first apostles who knew Jesus in the flesh are still alive; while some of us affirm that "apostolic" ministries continue in some sense (in the form of special strategists, missionary church planters, bishops, or the like), nobody affirms the continuation of the original Twelve. And to my knowledge, no Christians believe that anybody is writing Scripture today that we should add to our Bibles.

Likewise, few people who believe that particular spiritual gifts have ceased reject them all; normally they consider teaching, for example, as continuing today. I view this selectivity as inconsistent, but for the purposes of this book, it doesn't really matter. Very few cessationists deny that God still does miracles. They acknowledge that God is sovereign and can do whatever he wants to do. If Jesus is Lord of the universe, enthroned at the Father's right hand, why *wouldn't* he sometimes open blind eyes and raise the dead where his message is breaking new ground?

A much smaller minority of Christians, however, deny that God even performs miracles today. Historically, their views go back partly to some of the Protestant Reformers, who were reacting against Catholic miracle claims. (Some of them were also originally against missions since they viewed missions as something that Catholics did!) Even these Reformers did not deny that God might still do miracles at times, but many of their successors came to embrace more radical views, especially as they sought rapprochement with later Enlightenment critics of miracles.

In the Gospels, however, miracles are often signs of the coming kingdom (Matt. 12:28//Luke 11:20)—the fullness of which, in the usual Christian view, is still coming. Moreover, the New Testament emphasizes that Christians live in the era of the Spirit: the "last days," in which God pours out the Spirit on all believers (Acts 2:17). Biblically, this outpouring is characterized by experiences such as prophecy, visions, and dreams (2:17–18); it is a promise to all Christ's followers throughout the world and throughout history (2:38–39). The Western denial of all miracles in this age therefore must reject signs of the kingdom and truncate an essential promise of the gospel.

Those who deny all miracles today rightly point out some false teachings, practices, and miracle claims that pervade some extreme miracle-claiming circles. Nevertheless, is it possible that denial of miracles may itself be a false teaching? Certainly it lacks explicit biblical support. It is not the possibility of miracles but the denial of that possibility that conflicts with Scripture. Biblically, we are in the era of the foretaste of the kingdom, the time between Jesus's first and second coming—the era of Pentecost.

Western Christianity has much to teach Christians elsewhere, but many Christians outside the West have rightly rejected the common erroneous teaching in the Western church that undercuts current access to the gift of the Spirit. This may be one reason why many churches outside the West are growing: they embrace the power of the Spirit for ministry. Some Western Christians recognize the Spirit only when God works within accepted structures. Thus they readily welcome some gifts that fit within those structures (especially teaching) while explaining away, and hence rarely experiencing, others.

Still, a foretaste differs from the consummation. Miracles foreshadow the world made new, but they do not eliminate the problem of suffering. Although I address suffering briefly in chapters 37–39, that subject calls for a different book.

At this point, however, we need to look more closely at why some people assume that miracles don't happen—and never did.

Chapter 3

Why Do Some People Assume That Miracles Don't Happen? David Hume

W hy do many people embrace a worldview that won't even consider evidence for miracles? Sometimes they assume that science opposes miracles, but that assumption goes back not to scientific inquiry itself but to an eighteenth-century philosopher. Knowingly or unknowingly, many people have followed the thesis of Scottish skeptic David Hume (1711–1776).

Hume was probably the most prominent philosopher of his generation, and surely the most influential from his time on subsequent generations. He wrote on a wide variety of topics, sometimes very insightfully but sometimes (as with his ethnocentric approach to history) in ways that would not be accepted today. Hume's intellectual stature, earned from other works, eventually lent credibility to his (originally) 1748 essay on miracles.[1] In this essay, Hume dismisses the credibility of miracle claims, appealing to "natural law" and uniform human experience. Although an appeal to natural law might sound scientific, Hume was not a scientist; in fact, some of his views on causation would make scientific inquiry impossible. Hume's essay on miracles also contradicts his own approach to discovering knowledge.[2]

Moreover, Hume's essay has generated serious intellectual counterarguments since the time it was first published.[3] One of these counterarguments was history's first public use of Bayes' theorem, today an essential staple in statistics. Mathematician and Presbyterian minister Thomas Bayes originated the theorem but died before publishing it. His close friend Richard Price, also a mathematician and minister, therefore published it and then used Bayes' theorem to refute a probability claim Hume had made in his essay about miracle witnesses.[4] Hume himself acknowledged the force of that argument, though he did not adequately revise his essay in light of it.[5] Mathematician Charles Babbage, designer of the first mechanical computer, also issued a refutation of Hume's probability argument against miracles.[6]

Most early English scientists believed in biblical miracles. Such scientists included Isaac Newton and early Newtonians. Modern science originally developed in contexts that affirmed that a superintelligent God created the universe and that it therefore should make sense.[7] Newton popularized the idea of natural law—and saw it as a design argument *for* God's existence. Likewise, Robert Boyle, the father of chemistry, used his discoveries about nature to argue for an intelligent designer. Boyle, Newton, and Newtonians believed in biblical miracles: they affirmed that the God who set up the universe to normally work in an orderly way was not subject to that order.[8] Some modern scientific thinkers concur, such as Sir John Polkinghorne, as noted earlier.[9]

Most early modern scientists worked from a Christian worldview. Examples include Blaise Pascal, the mathematician who developed the precursor of the modern computer; Andreas Vesalius, the founder of the modern study of human anatomy; Antonie van Leeuwenhoek, the founder of microbiology; William Harvey, who described the circulatory system; Gregor Mendel, a monk and early leader in genetics; Francis Bacon; Nicolaus Copernicus; Galileo Galilei (despite conflicts arising from contemporary academic and ecclesiastical politics); Johannes Kepler; and, more recently, Michael Faraday, James Clerk Maxwell, and George Washington Carver—the list could go on.[10] The myth of a historic war between science and religion stems especially from two late nineteenth-century books that historians have subsequently debunked as antireligious propaganda.[11]

It was not, then, scientists who came up with the idea that miracles violate natural law. It was other thinkers such as Hume. Hume liked Newton's mechanistic universe; he used it, however, in a way quite different from Newton. Hume adopted much of his argument from a movement of his day called deism.[12] Deists believed that God designed the universe, but they often denied that he acted in the world much after that.[13] Hume developed much of his argument precisely to oppose the sort of evidentialist apologists who had led England's scientific revolution.[14]

Hume's argument was twofold: First, miracles are violations of natural law. Second, uniform human experience warns against trusting miracle reports.

God versus Nature?

Although some earlier writers had viewed miracles as beyond laws of nature, Hume treated them as "violations" of laws of nature. Once he adopted this definition, he insisted that miracles are miracles only if they violate natural law. Then he argued that natural law cannot be violated, so therefore miracles do not happen. Although this clever play with words does not fit Hume's own normal way of arguing, he conveniently defines miracles this way in hopes of defining them out of existence.[15] This approach spares him the trouble of having to argue against them one by one.

As Hume's critics have always pointed out, this language loads the deck of the argument. No one who believes in a God who created laws of nature believes that God is subject to such laws—as if God illegally "violates" them by doing a miracle. Hume's god that cannot violate natural law is not the God of Judaism, Christianity, or Islam. Nor do "violations" of nature correspond with most of the biblical miracles that Hume wished to undermine. Hume was thus refuting a straw man—a caricature of what people actually believed.

In the Bible, God often acts through other agents. When Judges 20:35 says that God struck the tribe of Benjamin, the context makes it clear that God executed this judgment through human warriors. Likewise, when God gave the Israelites Canaan, the Bible claims that he accomplished this gift through their military victories (Deut. 3:18; 4:1). When God sent swarms of locusts into Egypt by a strong east wind (Exod. 10:13), he was not breaking any natural law. This was not the only time locusts struck Egypt; it was simply the most severe and timely— the one that came right after Moses predicted it. And we already discussed the parting of the sea.

Human beings regularly act within nature; they do not, for example, "violate" the law of gravity by catching a falling pencil or lifting an eraser. Nor does a surgeon violate natural law when she restores someone's sight. Why should a putative creator be any less able to act within nature than those he created?[16] One must essentially assume deism or atheism from the start for Hume's argument to work at all.

Another problem with Hume's argument today is how he viewed natural laws. Today philosophers of science tend to define laws of nature in primarily descriptive ways.[17] That is, these "laws" describe what happens rather than causing it. If scientists find some things that do not fit the pattern, they may rethink the law, but they do not ordinarily say that something violated the law. Moreover, laws of nature describe nature at particular levels and under particular conditions; they function differently in settings such as superconductivity or black holes.[18] Why should special divine action not create a different set of conditions than those to which we are accustomed?

Are There Credible Eyewitnesses?

The second half of Hume's essay offers his second and more important major argument, which essentially says that we lack credible eyewitness evidence for miracles. When Hume argues that miracles violate natural law, his understanding of natural law depends on known human experience, which is known partly on the basis of human testimony. Most known human experience of extraordinary "miracle" events, like knowledge of most events in history and today, also depends on human testimony. Thus Hume must show that eyewitness claims for miracles are untrustworthy.

We cannot trust testimony for miracles, Hume argues, because uniform human experience leads us to not expect miracles. But, as noted above, if we have eyewitness experiences of miracles, human experience against miracles is hardly uniform.[19] Eyewitness experiences of miracles existed already in Hume's day, but he denied their credibility. He insisted that this testimony always came from unreliable sources.

Hume even gives examples of such unreliable sources. One of his examples is the healing of Blaise Pascal's niece Marguerite Perrier, treated later in this book (chap. 6). Hume points out that this miracle was public, organic, and medically documented, far better attested than any miracle reported in the Bible. So how does Hume respond to Perrier's healing? He does not really offer an argument. Rather, he basically says, "We know that this miracle could not have happened, so why would we be tempted to believe any other accounts?"[20]

How could Hume get away with simply dismissing this documented miracle? Divisions among Christians themselves pried open the door for Hume. This healing occurred among Jansenists, who were Catholic, and Hume was writing in a setting where Protestants readily dismissed Catholic testimonies.[21] If you are going to dismiss this testimony, Hume says (implying "and you should"), then why not be consistent and dismiss them all? Rather than such an all-or-nothing approach to witnesses, which would undermine all legal reasoning and historiography, a sounder way of handling the evidence would have been to acknowledge that the evidence does in fact support Perrier's healing. We can come up with a nonsupernatural way to explain it if we wish, but merely dismissing inconvenient evidence is not a fair way to argue.

Hume's argument depends largely on his dismissal of sufficiently credible eyewitnesses. As we shall see, however, this argument does not work today; there are simply too many credible eyewitnesses now.

Hume claims that uniform human experience leads us to not expect miracles. But what happens when eyewitnesses report experiences of miracles? How then can human experience be "uniformly" against miracles? Many things happen that are not *typical* experience; we do not for that reason deny that they *ever* happen. Hume might protest that miracles are a *kind* of experience that has never been shown to happen, but that argument simply assumes without evaluation that miracles have never been shown to happen.

Not surprisingly, a majority of philosophers writing on the subject today recognize that Hume's traditional argument against miracles does not work. These include Oxford philosopher Richard Swinburne as well as the authors of works published by major university presses such as Cambridge, Cornell, and Oxford.[22] This is because Hume's argument is circular: it assumes what it pretends to prove.[23]

That way it can rule out miracles from the beginning rather than having to examine any evidence.

Do "Modern" People Believe in Miracles?

One British tabloid, complaining about government waste, notes that a pastor's wife healed at a Christian conference had trouble getting the government to stop her benefits. She had spent six years in a wheelchair, but after prayer she "was able to fold away her wheelchair and stop taking painkillers." Unfortunately, the government computer "wasn't programmed to allow the payments to end until her death." There was no "button to push that says miracle."[24]

For several centuries, some have dismissed those who believe in miracles by supposing that miracles differ from what everybody in the modern world takes for granted. Never mind that most people in the modern United States or the world globally never stopped believing in miracles![25] If you can dismiss the intelligence of those who disagree, though, it saves you the courtesy of having to offer an argument.

One scholar influenced by Hume's argument was the nineteenth-century New Testament scholar David Friedrich Strauss. Strauss allowed for some psychosomatic recoveries but denied that eyewitnesses could have attested the sorts of miracles sometimes reported in the New Testament. Instead, he argued, they were legends that grew over the course of generations.

Strauss, however, should have known better. He had a friend by the name of Eduard Mörike. Because of a diagnosed spinal problem, Mörike could walk only with great difficulty. Then he visited with German Lutheran pastor Johann Christoph Blumhardt, who was known for a ministry of healing. Soon Strauss heard from Mörike that the latter was hiking in the mountains. Strauss dismissed the previous condition as psychosomatic, but he did not, and could not, attribute it to a legend that arose over the course of generations.[26]

In the heyday of skepticism, Ethan Allen (1738–1789), a Revolutionary War hero who was a deist, published a pamphlet called *Reason the Only Oracle of Man*. Despite Allen's fame, the work sold perhaps two hundred copies.[27] In the work, Allen insists that "in those parts of the world where learning and science have prevailed, miracles have ceased; but in those parts of it as are barbarous and ignorant, miracles are still in vogue."[28] In other words, genuine modern learning banishes the superstitious idea of miracles. Ironically, one of Ethan Allen's most prominent subsequent namesakes (perhaps his grandson, if we give credence to the unfortunately debatable claim of his hometown paper), Ethan O. Allen (1813–1902), was known for his effective ministry of divine healing.[29]

One famous twentieth-century New Testament scholar, Rudolf Bultmann, dismissed the reality of miracles by claiming that nobody in the modern world who uses electric lights and telegraph machines accepts New Testament ideas about miracles and spirits.[30] Bultmann, who lived later than Strauss, also dismissed stories about Blumhardt's nineteenth-century healing ministry as legends.[31] But now we have access to the diaries, letters, and so forth attesting the reports about Blumhardt from the very times that the events were occurring![32]

Ironically, Bultmann's antimiraculous "modern world" excludes most of humanity today. Most people in the world believe in miracles or something like them. This includes orthodox Jews, Christians, and Muslims along with spiritists and traditional tribal religionists—in short, the majority of the world's population.

Certainly most of global Christianity affirms the reality of miracles. Cuban Lutheran bishop Ismael Laborde, who shared with me his experience of miraculous healing from liver cancer, notes that it is hard to find Latin American Christians who do not believe in miracles.[33] Citing Latino churches, renowned scholar Justo González notes that "what Bultmann declares to be impossible is not just possible, but even frequent."[34] Retired Methodist bishop Hwa Yung, a Malaysian scholar, notes that Bultmann's approach to the supernatural is irrelevant in Asia,[35] and he suggests that antisupernatural Western Christianity is "the real aberration."[36] Philip Jenkins's works on global Christianity for Oxford University Press emphasize belief in the supernatural outside the West.[37] The Presbyterian and Methodist churches of Ghana, for example, host formal healing ministries, sometimes citing instant and visible public healings.[38]

David Hume denied the existence of credible eyewitnesses for miracles. So we should ask, How often do dramatic healings happen? More often than many of us think. In the next chapter, we will look at evidence that suggests that millions of people experience extraordinary recoveries.

———— PART 2 ————

Witnesses of Miracles

espite some critics' dismissal of the value of eyewitness testimony, eyewitness testimony is accepted as a form of evidence in law, journalism, sociology, anthropology, and (to cite my own line of work) historiography. None of these disciplines could exist apart from testimony, so those who a priori dismiss the value of testimony are actually dismissing entire spheres of knowledge and investigation. Indeed, were I to reject all testimony, I could not accept anyone else's claims about what they experienced. For example, I could not reasonably ask my wife, after she has been outside, whether I need a jacket today.

No one lives by such a constrictive epistemology; instead, we critically *evaluate* testimony. I turn to medical documentation later, but in this part of the book I explore some eyewitness accounts. (Eyewitness accounts also appear in later chapters where they are relevant to particular issues, such as healings from blindness, raisings from the dead, nature miracles, and so forth. Some accounts here and later also include medical documentation, just as medical test reports often require a narrative from the patient—a witness—to give them context.) For miracle reports from before modern medicine, as for example in the Gospels and reports from many parts of the world where medical technology is not yet widely available, such accounts are nearly our only window into what people have experienced.

Chapter 4

Are There Many Witnesses of Miracles?

Minister Ken Fish shared with me that he prayed for a woman dying from acute liver failure in the ICU. Her heart monitor was beeping very slowly; she was gray and looked as if she were already dead. He says that when he put his hand on her, he suddenly felt a surge of power. The heart monitor came alive as she began shaking, and it beeped wildly for some ninety seconds. She was healed and discharged that night and remains well today. Fish recounts that this fits a pattern of many healings when he prays.[1]

Dramatic healings such as those of Barbara Cummiskey (now Snyder), which I recounted in the book's preface, are not an everyday occurrence in most of our individual lives. Nevertheless, when we take into account the span of the entire globe, they are occurring regularly.

The Stats: Hundreds of Millions of Witnesses

A 2006 Pew Forum survey of just ten countries on four continents suggests that about two hundred million Pentecostal and Protestant charismatics in those countries alone claim to have witnessed divine healing. Perhaps more surprisingly, some 39 percent of Christians in those countries who are *not* Pentecostals or Protestant charismatics *also* claim to have witnessed divine healing.[2] Hundreds of millions of people around the world claim to have witnessed such experiences.

Such figures are at best merely estimates; nevertheless, it seems clear that we are talking about a *lot* of people. No one would claim that all these reports involve genuine miracles—but neither is it reasonable for anyone to simply ignore all of them while claiming there are no credible witnesses for miracles. Indeed, it is surely intellectually dishonest to dismiss them all from the start on the basis of "uniform" human experience, or to simply go cherry-picking among the least plausible examples to justify neglecting more plausible ones.

These experiences seem more common in some places and times than others. One Western researcher, for example, was astonished to discover that 83 percent of the people he interviewed at a church in the Philippines had experienced significant healings.[3] Nevertheless, even societies less prone to express such experiences may include members who have experienced them. Another survey shows that more than a third of Americans claim to have *witnessed or experienced* what they believe to be divine healing.[4] Still another survey reports that more than a quarter of Americans (27 percent) "experienced a physical healing that could only be explained as a miraculous healing and not solely as a result of normal process, medical procedure or the body healing itself."[5] While many may be too intimidated to discuss these experiences publicly, some 38 percent—close to one hundred million Americans—expressed belief that they had experienced some sort of divine miracle.[6]

Doctors as Witnesses

Indeed, another survey suggests that nearly three-quarters of doctors in the United States believe in miracles. More important, over half of the physicians surveyed noted that they had *witnessed* what they considered to be miracles.[7]

Three factors make this figure appear even more compelling. First, the context of the survey question mentions biblical miracles, which most people think of as fairly *dramatic* events. Second, doctors' scientific training appropriately leads them to look for ordinary causes first, so many may not have counted as miraculous cases in which God could possibly have used ordinary causes in nature to achieve a miraculous outcome. (Remember our paradigmatic case of the east wind parting the sea.) Third, any respondents inflexibly opposed to belief in miracles would not have interpreted an event as a miracle, no matter how extraordinary it was.

Other studies show us that most of those who pray for and believe they have experienced miracles do not even inform their physician that they prayed.[8] Physicians are thus not always even aware of a spiritual context for many of the recoveries they witness.

Researching Eyewitnesses Claims

Some people complain that there are plenty of stories about miracles, but they're like rumors: the information is always second- or thirdhand. That's why I like to trace stories back to witnesses. I recount hundreds of such cases in *Miracles: The Credibility of the New Testament Accounts*.

In addition to collecting more generic stats, I wanted to know the sorts of experiences people have in mind when they say they have experienced "divine healing." Some of the stories shared with me were less dramatic, such as warts vanishing overnight or someone recovering from an illness that often goes away on its own. (I could even recount a number of experiences of my own, for example, in which severe sickness disappeared during a simple prayer; see chap. 34.) But many of those who shared their experiences recounted more dramatic incidents.

As noted earlier, different disciplines require different approaches. Although we always need to evaluate witnesses' reliability, eyewitness testimony is accepted as a form of evidence in law, journalism, sociology, anthropology, and (in my line of work) historiography.[9] When eyewitnesses are otherwise credible people with something to lose, we normally value their testimony over the skepticism of nonwitnesses.

For example, imagine that, as an officer is interviewing witnesses to an accident, a passerby interrupts: "That's not what happened!" The officer may invite the passerby to give an account of what he witnessed. What would you think of this passerby's approach if he responded, "I didn't witness anything happen. I wasn't there. That's why I know it didn't happen!" We probably wouldn't be inclined to take his opinion very seriously. Nor would we take it more seriously if even a hundred nonwitnesses offered the argument that, because they were not present, an event did not happen.

Why should it be any different in the case of miracles? One does not even have to start with the premise that God exists to accept evidence for miracles; one simply has to be open-minded about the possibility. And if evidence supports the authenticity of some miracles, then there is reason to be open to the possibility of other ones. Those who dismiss all claims for miracles have often never even looked at evidence for any of them.

Someone will object, "Miracles are different from accidents, because we have witnesses all over the world to accidents, but we don't have any for miracles." Yet this objection simply assumes what it claims to prove. As we have noted, hundreds of millions of people report miracles, many of them very significant. David Hume's argument against miracles rests on the lack of credible eyewitnesses. Yet I believe that if Hume had had access to the range of testimony we have today, he would not have ventured this argument. At the least he would have had to adjust it, because his argument in its original form simply does not work today.

Discounting Witnesses

Some people today counter, "You can't trust all eyewitness claims. Think how many people claim to have seen space aliens!"[10] The analogy is not very evenhanded, however. In the United States, the best estimates of the number of people who claim to have witnessed space aliens run to many thousands,[11] but in the same country some 34 percent of the population—more than one hundred million people—claim to have witnessed divine healing (according to a 2008 Pew Forum survey).[12] That is, witnesses of divine healing easily outnumber witnesses of space aliens more than a thousand to one. Much of the evidence cited for alien abductions comes from memories recovered through hypnosis, which is also noted for planting false memories.[13] The majority of people who believe in divine healing do not believe in space aliens, and simply lumping them together because one disagrees with both is an ethically questionable substitute for an argument.[14]

One might explain some miracle accounts as the misinterpretation of coincidence, others as the result of misdiagnosis, and yet others as the curing of psychosomatic illnesses. Initial misdiagnosis is not uncommon,[15] and correct diagnoses are not always correctly interpreted. Some apparent healings are adrenaline-driven excitement without long-term benefit. Some suggest that as many as half of ailments treated on a regular basis by doctors lack detected organic causes.[16] Even if this figure is high, mental and emotional components to health are certainly significant.[17] God can work psychologically as well as physically, but skeptics are naturally less impressed by nonphysical claims. Further, God designed our bodies to be able to recover naturally in many circumstances; God often works through natural means, as we have seen (remember again the parting of the sea in Exod. 14:21). Moreover, some healing claims are simply attempts to deny reality. Some are even fraudulent attempts to gain publicity or financial support for ailing ministries.[18]

Nevertheless, these explanations do not easily account for all kinds of claims. Sometimes we have multiple independent witnesses. Sometimes we have clear medical evidence that precludes misdiagnosis. In some of these instances, a skeptical response is, "The mere fact that we cannot explain it, and that it seemed coordinated with prayer, does not mean that God did it. Maybe there's some natural explanation that we simply don't know." It is true enough that there are many things that we do not know. But if one is prepared to dismiss any *possible* evidence for miracles in this way, it seems disingenuous to demand evidence to begin with. Open-mindedness ought to invite openness to evidence.

Moreover, we can observe a *pattern* of miracles in some times and places that suggests that God sometimes works in special ways. For example, nearly all of those in my or my wife's immediate circle who reported nonmedical resuscitations in the context of prayer were people of prayer working to honor Jesus.

When miracle accounts cannot be explained by natural means, some, like Hume, are ready to dismiss all witnesses as psychotics or liars.[19] In the past, for example, skeptical researchers often crudely dismissed women's miracle claims as the result of feminine hysteria.[20] But those who choose to explain away all miracle accounts in these terms should be clear about what they are doing. They are so committed to believing that miracles cannot occur that they are willing to dismiss as liars millions of people, not because these people have already been shown to be untrustworthy, but simply because their reported experience conflicts with the skeptics' prior assumptions. Again, those who explain away all miracle claims without considering them should not pretend to be neutral.

As we will see in chapter 5, millions of non-Christians have been convinced and converted as a result of their extraordinary experiences. Sometimes the experience of miracles has changed even Western scholars' views. Walter Wink, a founding member of the generally skeptical Jesus Seminar, notes that at one time he disbelieved in miracles. Then, he says, he encountered some, such as a large uterine tumor disappearing apparently immediately after prayer. He points out that those who disbelieve others' testimonies because of their own lack of experience are at a disadvantage in understanding the world.[21]

Hume and his critics used an imaginary case to argue back and forth about whether it is rational to consider testimony for miracles. In this imaginary story, Dutch visitors told a South Asian ruler that in their own country people could ride horses on rivers frozen as hard as stone. The ruler concluded that these visitors must be liars, since their report contradicted reality. Hume argued that the ruler was correct to disbelieve them, given his local reality. Hume's critics argued that the ruler was wrong because he limited reality to his own experience and so denied the eyewitness experience of others.[22] We cannot always extrapolate from the settings with which we are most familiar to all settings universally.

Are All Witnesses Uneducated?

Hume dismissed some healing reports by stereotyping the reporters as ignorant and uneducated.[23] Aside from the fact that it does not take any specialized education to notice that one is no longer blind or deaf or that water now looks, smells, and tastes like wine, the prejudice is unfair. While education can make us less gullible, some kinds of education can also make us more skeptical than we need to be about particular topics.

Moreover, there are, in fact, plenty of educated eyewitnesses of miracles. This is why I have sometimes mentioned witnesses' doctoral degrees in the book. Degrees do not by themselves make witnesses more reliable, but they do challenge the prejudice that educated persons do not witness events they experience as divine.

Here I focus on one circle in which a number of highly educated people attest witnessing miracles: Iris Ministries in Mozambique, founded by Rolland and Heidi Baker. Accounts in this book represent various denominations and theological perspectives, not all of which appreciate each other. Rolland and I have had numerous discussions of theology, however, and, for what it's worth, our theological perspectives seem pretty close. (One of Rolland's theological mentors was the respected New Testament scholar Gordon Fee, who has also been a mentor to me.) I have met some people who have criticized these friends by highlighting clips of off-the-cuff, out-of-context, or now-out-of-date[24] statements on the internet, but I know them well enough to affirm this couple's integrity and intelligence.

Heidi, who speaks seven languages, holds a PhD in theology from King's College London; Rolland holds a doctor of ministry degree from United Theological Seminary in Ohio. Their ministry supports some ten thousand orphans in Mozambique. As for integrity, they have suffered extensively and laid their lives on the line for the people they serve. Yet they also offer eyewitness reports of instant healings of deafness and blindness and of raisings from the dead.[25] Most often, these experiences occur in non-Christian villages where no one expects them. The healings generally culminate in many of the people in these villages, people who knew firsthand the previously deaf or blind people, following Christ.

Highly educated outsiders have also witnessed these miracles. My friends Wendy J. Deichmann and Andrew Sung Park are both Methodist professors at United Theological Seminary. Andrew did his PhD at Graduate Theological Union in Berkeley and Wendy did her PhD at Drew University, and they visited Mozambique along with a number of their students. Wendy reports that she witnessed various healings, including that of a blind man. Afterward, she further witnessed the entire village, "previously violently hostile to Christianity," choosing to follow Christ.[26]

Brandon Walker, who did his PhD at the University of Nottingham, spent several years with Iris Ministries in Mozambique. Although he did not witness dramatic healings daily, he shared with me some of what he did see. This included nonbelievers healed of blindness and thereupon converted, a girl who was healed of both deafness and inability to speak, and a couple of cases of men unable to walk being instantly healed and walking away. At one conference, a disabled man was carried in by friends. The man explained that he had not been able to work since he became disabled, and that his family therefore beat him and mocked him. It was difficult for him to forgive his family, but Brandon prayed for him that God would help him to let go of the anger. For ten minutes the man lay shaking while Brandon and his friends prayed. Afterward, others helped him up and then he walked away on his own.[27]

Don Kantel, who wrote a doctoral dissertation that focused on Iris Ministries, told me about witnessing miracles, and recounts some of these incidents elsewhere in print: "I've watched the indescribable excitement in young village children when one of their friends who had been totally deaf from birth could suddenly hear and repeat sounds and words. I've held a boy's badly broken forearm and watched the arm straighten and be completely healed as I prayed."[28] He also reports that food was unexpectedly but clearly supernaturally multiplied on some occasions.[29]

Chapter 5

Do Only Christians Report Christian Healings?

Someone might protest that Christians have a bias that leads them to report experiences as miracles. While that is probably true in some cases, that explanation does not stretch far enough to address all claims. It also fails to take into account the cases where those with a bias against miracles dismiss them by reaching for any other remotely possible explanation, no matter how much simpler the miracle explanation is.

In fact, reports of Christian healing are not even limited to Christians. Millions of non-Christians around the world have changed centuries of many of their ancestral beliefs, often despite considerable social pressure, and become committed followers of Jesus as a result of extraordinary healings. If all these healings were simply ordinary, run-of-the-mill recoveries of the sort that they witnessed in their pre-Christian experience (religious or otherwise), why would they risk social ostracism and leave familiar traditions for a faith completely new to them?

God may act anywhere, and some of the experiences reported in this book, like that of Barbara Cummiskey Snyder (narrated in the preface), happen in mainstream US settings. Nevertheless, we learn about these experiences most *often* on the cutting edge of evangelism, where Jesus's message is breaking fresh ground. That is the way it was in the biblical Gospels and book of Acts too. Biola University's J. P. Moreland points out that up to 70 percent of the rapid evangelical growth in the past few decades has been due to "signs"—the sorts of divine acts that get people's attention for the message about Christ.[1]

A Friend's Eyewitness Account

Suriname is a multicultural nation in South America whose national language is Dutch. Although many people in Suriname have long been Christians, one population group in Nickerie, Suriname, had another dominant faith and had resisted the Christian message for centuries. For generations, only a few hundred Christians lived there, and churches competed with each other for the same members. When I met with Dr. Douglass Norwood in 2006, he shared with me his eyewitness experience from twelve years before, also recounted in his dissertation.[2] He was a Moravian pastor, and Moravians had been among the pioneers of churches there. In November 1994, after he preached, the churches there repented of their divisions and cried out to God for an outpouring of the Holy Spirit.

Believers went out and began to share their faith with surprised neighbors, who had never known the Christians to act this way before. That night, many non-Christians gathered at the church—a few of them hostile. One hostile visitor, perhaps in his seventies, had been paralyzed on his right side virtually all his life. Because he could not walk, his friends had brought him on a blanket or rug and plopped him down on the ground in front of Norwood.

This man was not happy. "Your religion is garbage!" he shouted. "My religion is garbage too! I've prayed to Shiva, and to Vishnu, and to my other gods, and nothing happens. Now you want me to pray to *Jesus*?"

As he uttered the name Jesus, his paralyzed arm suddenly shot up into the air. He stared at his own arm, shocked. No one had prayed for him, but when he mentioned Jesus, God healed his paralysis. Norwood reports, "At that instant, he jumped up, grabbed my mike, and began screaming, 'Look what Jesus did for me!' as he danced around, waving his now-healed arm in the air." The other visitors were converted almost as quickly as he was.

This was the beginning of a movement that, over the next few years, brought tens of thousands of people to faith in Christ, most of whom had previously had little exposure to him. The massive growth of the Christian movement in Nickerie in recent decades is well known.

Conversions through Healings in Asia

China was not included in the Pew Forum survey that I noted earlier; statistics are notoriously difficult to obtain there, and the figures I provide in this section are simply some observers' estimates. Nevertheless, behind these figures are undoubtedly a significant number of people convinced by healing experiences.

For example, one source from within the state-authorized church suggests that half of all Christian conversions over a period of two decades in the late twentieth century were due to "faith healing experiences."[3] One rural house church estimate puts this figure closer to 90 percent.[4] Whatever the exact percentage, we may be talking about *millions* of people converting because of healings.[5]

Likewise, Dr. Bal Krishna Sharma, principal of Nepal Theological College, shared with me that 80 percent of Christian conversions in Nepal are due to healings or deliverance from spirits. Keep in mind that in 1950 outside observers knew of no Christians in Nepal; now there are more than half a million. In a country of fewer than thirty million people, we are therefore speaking about a lot of conversions. Sharma himself has some good reason to believe in miracles, since his wife was healed in 1997 of inoperable tuberculosis of the brain, with no lasting effects. The Hindu doctor remarked, "Your Jesus has healed you."[6]

The mass conversion of the Nishi tribal people in northeast India is well documented. One dissertation explains how the movement began.[7] A government official's son died. Neither medicine nor sacrifices had helped the boy, but a pharmacist had suggested prayer to Jesus, the Christian God, who had once raised Lazarus. The official laid his hand on his boy's head and promised to worship this Christian God if God would heal his son. The child's eyes opened and he recovered, sparking hundreds of conversions in the region.

Moreover, because of other beliefs or social pressure, some non-Christians remain non-Christians even after being healed, further weakening charges of Christian bias in reporting.[8] According to one 1981 survey, 10 percent of *non*-Christians surveyed in Chennai, India, reported that they had been healed when someone prayed for them in Jesus's name.[9]

When I taught at a Baptist seminary, Pastor Israel—a Baptist doctor of ministry student I knew well—told me about his healing experiences in India.[10] The conversation came about because he prayed for my splitting headache—and nothing happened. (Of course, it did go away eventually!) "It's because I don't have any faith," I complained.

"No, it doesn't work here," he observed sadly. "Everybody I pray for in India gets healed." Pastor Israel explained that healing was so common there because God was reaching out in a special way to these precious and desperate people who had never before known about Christ's love for them.

Pastor Israel told me that his church grew from maybe half a dozen people to six hundred, nearly all from non-Christian backgrounds, as God answered prayer to heal the sick in his community who came for prayer. Because of ancestral and cultural ties, however, many others who were healed did not become Christians, though they remained appreciative of Jesus.

Sai Ankem, a doctor of ministry student at Trinity Evangelical Divinity School, shared with me the story of how his family in India came to follow Jesus.[11] When Sai was seven or eight years old, his father, who had regularly ridiculed Christians, was injured in an accident. His mother visited the temples of many deities, promising offerings if they would save her husband. After the father had spent a month in a coma, the doctors declared that he did not have much longer to live.

A relative who had become a Christian suggested that the mother try Jesus, who would "definitely save your husband." Sai's mother knew Jesus only as the god of people of lower caste, but she now had nothing to lose. Without knowing how to pray to this god, she cried, "Oh, Jesus, you were not our God, yet I come to you pleading for the life of my husband. If you would save his life, we will serve you all of our lives!" Sai's father in the ICU then experienced Jesus touching him and speaking to him, and by morning he was completely restored. Despite great social opposition, the family became followers of Jesus. Sai himself later experienced an audible voice calling him to ministry.

Rita Jeet prayed to Hindu deities and was a popular radio personality in Fiji.[12] At a point of deep brokenness in her life, she prayed for Jesus to show himself to her if he was real, whereupon she saw a bright man coming from the sky. She became a follower of Jesus, and she began experiencing various miracles. One that she shared involved the twofold healing of a relative. He had abused her when she was younger, but he later became paralyzed from the waist down. Jeet, now a Christian and finding grace to forgive him, felt divine compassion and prayed for him. He was immediately healed, and that family also became followers of Jesus. Other miracles have followed.

Nor is the pattern limited to Asia. In Ethiopia, for example, 83 percent of believers surveyed in a Lutheran (Mekane Yesus) church several decades ago attributed their conversions to healings or exorcisms.[13] In the US, too, healings may lead to conversions.[14]

But are such healings merely a recent fashion? Or have they happened at other times in history?

Chapter 6

Is Healing Just a New Thing?

I n the introduction to her Oxford University Press book *Healing in the History of Christianity*, Amanda Porterfield admits that she did not expect "the extent to which I would come to see Christianity as a religion of healing."[1] In this chapter I trace only a very small sample of historic healing claims.

Reports of miracles are not a new discovery or a post-postmodern fad. They appear in the Old Testament, especially, though not exclusively, in the times of Moses, Joshua, Elijah, and Elisha. They fill the pages of the New Testament—roughly one-fifth of the book of Acts and nearly one-third of the Gospel of Mark address miracles. Although Paul's letters to established churches focus more on those churches' current issues, Paul mentions that miracles accompanied his ministry wherever he established new churches (Rom. 15:19). He also appeals to his audience's direct experience with his miracles (2 Cor. 12:12) and their awareness that such gifts continue among them (1 Cor. 12:8–10; Gal. 3:5). James expects healing to continue in answer to the believing prayers of church leaders (James 5:14–15). But healing and miracles did not stop at the close of the first century.

Even second- and third-century critics of Christianity, both Jewish and pagan,[2] acknowledged that healing occurred through this movement that they disliked. Although later rabbis disagreed with Jesus's movement theologically and often attributed the works of Jesus and his followers to evil magic, they recognized that unusual things happened when Christians prayed.[3]

In the early third century, the Egyptian church leader Origen testified that he had witnessed healings and exorcisms.[4] The third-century North African bishop Cyprian noted that Christians were sometimes healed during baptism.[5] In the 300s, the African bishop Athanasius, known as his era's leading defender of the Trinity, praised the miraculous feats of the desert monk Anthony. Athanasius invited skeptics to come witness the efficacy of exorcism for themselves.[6] Ordinary letters from this period also report healings.[7] Although many medieval reports of miracles stem from subsequent hagiography, some are contemporaneous accounts dependent on witnesses,[8] including some reports of resuscitations from conspicuous death.[9]

Augustine

The famous theologian and North African bishop Augustine (354–430) once believed that miracles had mostly died out. Then he and people close to him experienced some miracles, and he changed his mind. One of the key experiences involved Augustine's good friend Innocent. Innocent had severe anal fistulas, and an operation had not resolved all of them.

No anesthesia was available back then, and people sometimes bled to death during surgery. Yet Innocent's doctors all agreed that another operation was necessary. Augustine and other friends prayed with Innocent the night before his second surgery, but Augustine found himself distracted from prayer by Innocent's plaintive wailing. "If you cannot be moved by a prayer like Innocent's," Augustine asked God, "what can possibly move you?" The next morning, Augustine accompanied Innocent to the surgery. The doctors removed the recent bandage—and found that Innocent was completely healed.

Once Augustine recognized the continuing reality of miracles, he became very serious about documenting them. Over a period of just two years, Augustine's diocese collected documentation from firsthand witnesses for some seventy significant healings, including healings of blindness and of long-term inability to walk, as well as raisings from the dead. He testifies that other centers of healings, which had been collecting reports longer, had even larger dossiers.[10]

Converted through Healings

I mentioned earlier that in recent decades many people around the world have become Christians after witnessing healings. Conversion in response to healing has much ancient precedent. Many early church fathers reported that many polytheists were converting to Christianity because they witnessed healings. In the late second century, for example, Irenaeus, a bishop in what is now France, described the same sorts of miracles occurring in his day as appear in the Gospels and Acts, leading to many conversions.[11] One North African theologian, Tertullian, even offered to name prominent pagans who were grateful to Christians for bringing them deliverance from evil spiritual powers.[12] Ramsay MacMullen, a leading Yale historian, has reluctantly concluded that the leading cause of conversion to Christianity in the 300s was healing and deliverance.[13]

Miracles are associated with the earliest missionaries who evangelized England, Scotland, Ireland, Germany, Persia, and elsewhere.[14] In some more recent periods as well, healing has been associated with Jesus's message coming to new peoples—for example, during the predominantly Presbyterian revival in Korea in the early twentieth century.[15] By 1981, a thesis that surveyed more than 350 other theses reported more accounts of miracles in new mission contexts than the author had room to use.[16] Healing remains a major feature in Majority World evangelism.[17]

Protestants versus Catholics

Although healing has continued in various ways throughout history (including several examples noted later in this book), leading Protestant Reformers initially reacted against medieval Catholic miracles because of Catholic polemic and popular gullibility about relics of the saints. A relic was something that had belonged to a particularly holy person, now deceased, and it was supposed to retain some of that person's spiritual power. On the basis of several biblical incidents[18] and some subsequent experiences, relics associated with holy people became a focal point for healing in the early centuries of the church.[19] Despite opposition to relics, the Reformers were not against prayer for recovery; Luther, for example, prayed for Melanchthon's recovery and accepted the possibility of miracles in missionary situations and extraordinary times. Toward the end of his life, Luther also taught about praying for the sick.[20]

But Luther hated the abuse of relics, fakes of which were circulating for profit everywhere by this time. (Charlatans' exploitation of people's illnesses in the name of healing is not a new practice.) Various sites laid claim to one of Jesus's baby teeth, his newborn umbilical cord, and—last but not least—claimed by eight sites, the holy foreskin remaining from his circumcision.[21] Luther complained, sarcastically, that eighteen of the original twelve apostles were buried in Germany.[22]

But God does not always play by our rules, even when we have good reason for them. Blaise Pascal was one of history's most brilliant mathematicians, as well as the inventor of an adding machine that was a forerunner of computers. Pascal was also a committed Christian who had a powerful experience with the Holy Spirit. He had sympathies with the Jansenists, members of an Augustinian sect within the Catholic Church. His niece Marguerite Perrier had a severe, long-term fistula in her eye, which produced a foul odor. At a Jansenist monastery, however, she was touched with an alleged thorn from Jesus's crown of thorns on March 24, 1656.

Was this thorn *really* from Jesus's crown? Most of us today would consider that suggestion highly unlikely. Nevertheless, the relic provided a contact point for Perrier's faith, and she was instantly and publicly cured. The cure generated so much attention that the queen mother of France sent her own physician to investigate, and he verified the cure.[23]

Before the influence of the radical Enlightenment, many Protestants, including Scots Reformers, Friends, and Baptists, did continue to affirm and experience miraculous healings.[24] Subsequent Protestants, however, often developed further the Reformers' overreaction against miracles among Catholics, an overreaction that served and was further amplified by the anti-miracle polemic of deists and David Hume.

Yet God continued to sometimes tweak these theologians' scripts. When healings like those in the Bible occurred, Protestants who did not believe in miracles sometimes called them "special providences." This helped them avoid the language of miracles, since they were careful not to use language that made them sound like Catholics! But special providences were essentially what many theologians today call special divine action; the line between such providences and miracles was sometimes quite thin.[25]

For example, Mary Maillard's left leg had been weak from birth, but in 1693, as she heard the account of the healing of a disabled man in Mark 2:1–12 being read, "she thought she heard a Voice saying, '*Thou art healed*,'" whereupon she found herself cured. Because she was a French Huguenot refugee in England rather than a Catholic, British Protestants accepted the healing, and Cotton Mather, recounting Huguenot miracles, in 1696 even speculated that miracles, once restrained because of Roman Catholic "Apostasy," might now be being renewed in a new "age of miracles."[26]

In another notable case, Mercy Wheeler had been bedridden since 1726. That year, she also lost much of her vision, and she drooled, unable to eat solid food, though she reported that by 1733 God had blessed her with the ability to speak again. Finally, on May 25, 1743, as others prayed with her, she trembled, shook, and spoke something like gibberish as she felt God's presence. The shaking began with her hands but finally racked her whole body, until when it passed she felt the first strength she had experienced in many years. Feeling then a compulsion to act, she got up and walked sixteen feet, crying out, "Bless the Lord Jesus, who has healed me!" to the amazement of all present. The preacher attempted to calm her, but she walked around the room a few more times, and over the next five months she kept walking farther and farther.[27]

Some theologians were not sure what to make of this event.[28] Following James 5:14–15, contemporary Protestants regularly prayed for people's healing, but they expected recovery "through providential means," not an instant miracle.[29] This is by no means the most dramatic account of healing we have encountered, but it was certainly enough to disturb some eighteenth-century conservative Protestants!

Christian Healing Is . . . Widely Christian

These accounts are not limited to any particular denomination, movement, or for that matter social or political perspective. For example, the most prominent healing ministry in Germany in the nineteenth century was that of Lutheran pastor Johann Christoph Blumhardt, mentioned in chapter 3.[30] Other leading figures were Swiss Protestants Dorothea Trudel and Otto Stockmayer.[31] Early nineteenth-century Methodist circuit riders in the United States reported healings and other supernatural experiences.[32] Leading North American advocates of divine healing in the late nineteenth century included Baptist A. J. Gordon (for whom Gordon College and Gordon-Conwell Theological Seminary are named) and Presbyterian A. B. Simpson, founder of the Christian and Missionary Alliance. Reformed minister Andrew Murray was a leading advocate in South Africa.[33] Both Simpson and Murray reported experiencing major healings themselves.[34]

Some of the most spectacular and consistent reports of healings come from Anglican bishops around the world in the 1920s. These bishops offered eyewitness attestation of dramatic healings, including of deafness, blindness, shriveled legs, and so forth, through the ministry of Anglican layman James Moore Hickson.[35] Also in the early twentieth century, many dramatic miracles were happening in China through the ministry of John Sung, who remained independent of Western denominations.[36]

Partly because of early Protestant criticism, Catholics have often been particularly careful about seeking documentation for miracles.[37] Alfred Bessette, who became Brother André, was from near Montreal and had a gift of healing in the late nineteenth and early twentieth centuries. An associate for fifteen years remarked that he witnessed miracles virtually every week: "Often a paralytic would be cured, or one blind, or someone who had to be brought here on a stretcher." The medical bureau established there considered many cases exaggerated or psychosomatic, but for others the officials lacked naturalistic explanations.[38]

A number of mid-twentieth-century healings associated with the ministry of Italian Capuchin friar Padre Pio include medical attestation.[39] Padre Pio himself sometimes noted, as have many others associated with healing, "I didn't do the miracle. I only prayed for you. The Lord healed you."[40]

My students over the years (because of the seminaries where I have taught) have been most frequently Baptists, Methodists, and Pentecostals, and they have shared with me numerous experiences. A conservative Presbyterian scholar friend recounted to me two extraordinary healings he has witnessed in answer to prayer, including "the sudden, total disappearance of a cluster of tumors," immediately after prayer.[41] The activity of God's Spirit is not limited to a single denomination or circle (though on average miracles probably occur more often among groups that pray for them more often).

God acts in history not because all his people have identical, precise theology. God acts, as in Jesus's ministry in the Gospels, to show compassion on many of the needy and to provide foretastes of Christ's kingdom.

Chapter 7

Baby Pics

Chapter 6 surveyed healing in some younger eras of the church. Here I sample briefly some accounts about younger individual lives.

Just about everyone likes baby pictures. Pictures of the babies in the following stories would be worth a thousand words, but reproducing photographs would raise the cost of the book. I will, however, provide some verbal pictures of the events surrounding their births. Even those who doubt divine activity can celebrate with the parents in the following stories. While one might view some of the cases simply as rare anomalies (in contrast to some accounts in later chapters), some of the following stories appear more difficult to explain purely naturalistically. At the very least, no one should be tempted to dismiss the cures of newborns as psychosomatic.[1]

"It's Because They're Christians!"

In Malia Wiederhold's third trimester, a routine prenatal ultrasound revealed a tumor on her baby's heart.[2] After a second ultrasound confirmed the presence of a tumor in the heart, the doctor warned that the child would probably be mentally challenged and experience multiple seizures throughout the day, and would not be able to do much in his life. Malia's husband, Jeff, assured her that everything would be all right. The doctor responded, "I don't think you understand. Everything will *not* be all right. You need to be prepared for this." Jeff, who is also a health professional, remained insistent, and so did the doctor.

As the couple got back in their car, Jeff took Malia's hand and reminded her of something that the Lord had shown her earlier, restoring her own confidence.

Jeff encouraged Malia, but given other recent tragedies, she still felt emotionally shaken by the diagnosis. Malia's close friend Valerie (who had been one of her bridesmaids) recalls Malia calling her in tears after the appointment, informing her about the tumor.[3] Valerie agreed to pray and soon shared that she felt that God was holding the baby.

Denial is a frequent response to grief, and in the ensuing weeks the medical professionals assumed that the couple's insistence that God would heal their child was just that. Nevertheless, Malia and Jeff felt a confidence that in this case God was going to act. Malia even felt a specific date on which her child, whom they named Jeremiah, would be born: the 28th. Although Malia went into labor on the 26th, Jeremiah was indeed born on the 28th. During the difficult childbirth, Malia felt God saying that he was removing the tumor, but she was kept in suspense even once she delivered. Expecting serious medical difficulties, the medical team rapidly whisked the baby away for more detailed evaluations.

For several tense minutes, Malia and Jeff waited for a report, yet the sense of God's peace continued. Finally, the pediatric cardiologist returned and announced, dumbfounded, "The tumor is gone."

The midwife, who had seen two ultrasounds a couple of weeks apart, protested. "What? I saw it with my own eyes!"

"Well, where did it go, then?" the cardiologist demanded.

The midwife shook her head. "It's because they're Christians!" she blurted out. Of course, this is not the experience of all Christians, but the midwife knew of this couple's insistence that God had spoken to them.

God's activity didn't stop at Jeremiah's birth. Malia's friend Valerie recounts an experience she witnessed when she was babysitting Jeremiah when he was eighteen months old. When he heard an Elevation Worship song, he "stopped what he was doing. He was on his knees with his head looking up to heaven and his arms lifted to the sky. He was worshiping God!"[4]

The medical documents provided to me in this case are clear.[5] I also have the review of internal medicine doctor David McCants, who, having heard Malia's story, went over her medical records independently. He was able to verify the disappearance of the cardiac tumor, as described in her story:

Malia's son was diagnosed with a cardiac rhabdomyoma. Cardiac rhabdomyomas are benign tumors that can be identified pre-natally on ultrasound or early in the newborn period or infancy. They can sometimes cause severe cardiac arrhythmias or obstruction of cardiac function by blocking normal flow. They can rarely even cause fatal complications. Cardiac rhabdomyomas are often, but not always, associated with a separate medical condition called tuberous sclerosis, in which seizures and cognitive problems are common occurrences. This is one reason the physician who saw Malia prior to her delivery warned, "Everything will *not* be all right." The described time frame for spontaneous regression of rhabdomyomas, if it occurs, is over months to years. This is why its disappearance over the span of

2 weeks was completely unexpected by her physicians, and I could find no similar cases described in the medical literature, in my review on the subject. Malia's story is compelling, and I believe, like her, that it is a story of God's intervention on behalf of her son.[6]

"Siara, Come Forth!"

Manuel and Maria Hernandez were looking forward to the birth of their next child. Since Maria's diagnosis of diabetes in 2002, the prospect of more children had seemed unlikely. Eventually, however, they discovered, through a miscarriage in November 2005, that Maria could still become pregnant.

On November 27, 2006, after fourteen hours of labor, Siara began to be born at Hemet Valley Medical Center in Hemet, California. Suddenly, it became clear that she was stuck in the birth canal, with only her head emerging. Manuel noticed the medical staff starting to act frantic and saw that his daughter's face was blue. Siara's compressed umbilical cord was wrapped around her neck, and she lacked a heartbeat or respiration. When the delivery was complete, Siara's Apgar score was zero. (The Apgar score is used by doctors to assess a baby's life signs immediately after birth.) Staff called out a Code Blue, and more medical personnel streamed into the delivery room. Even Annette Greenwood, executive director of nursing, joined the group.

Dr. Renato Judalena, the ob-gyn, and Becki Gomez, an RN working in the labor and delivery unit, initially kept working with Maria, who did not yet know what was happening. Soon they joined the other physician and the rest of the medical team, who labored valiantly over Siara for twenty-one minutes. Everyone did their best, but they observed no signs of life—cardiac or respiratory—during these twenty-one minutes. Believers among the staff prayed quietly as they worked, but Manuel, Maria, and their daughter Cherissa were praying more vocally.

"Zero," rang a nurse's voice a few times, reading the monitor. Finally, she queried the doctor. "Are you going to call it?"

After sighing dejectedly, he pronounced Siara dead at 2:59 p.m. The baby had been without oxygen for close to half an hour. The staff was distraught; Gomez, the main delivery nurse, was in tears. Most of the staff who had filled the small room began filing out, as equipment was removed from the still form of the hoped-for child.

Siara's father, however, suddenly felt an overwhelming sense of certainty. He could not give up. God had done so much for them already by bringing them to the point of birth, and he had spoken so clearly. They could not lose this child!

Word had gone out for prayer, and Starla, their pastor's wife, was now praying in her home. Suddenly she felt led to cry out, "She will live and not die!" Meanwhile, Maria overheard staff saying the child was declared dead; in the midst of her shock, however, she felt the Lord's comfort and envisioned Starla crying out precisely those words: "She will live and not die!" She did not learn until later that Starla was in fact crying out those exact words.

Manuel now prayed fervently over the body, the remaining staff patiently permitting him to express his faith and grief. Alluding to Lazarus, he cried, "God, so that everyone here will know you are alive and love your children, I say, 'Siara, come forth!'" Other Christians present felt God's presence, and Manuel began praying in tongues. But the body remained lifeless.

Perhaps sensing the discomfort of an ensuing silence, a nurse carried the baby's still form over to her mother's bed. It had been perhaps five minutes since the doctor had pronounced Siara dead. "Come on, Mija, wake up!"[7] Maria pleaded—and suddenly noticed Siara's chest moving.

"I'm sorry, sweetie," the respiratory therapist tried to explain. "That's just the oxygen we pumped into her coming out now."

But as Dr. Judalena drew close to add his own voice of comfort, he also felt something: the child's heart had started beating! "Unbelievable!" he exclaimed. "Call Code Blue again!"

Given how long Siara had lacked a heartbeat, however, most of the medical staff were certain that if she survived at all, she would have severe brain damage. They initially debated whether to try to revive the child further. But when Annette Greenwood, director of nursing, saw the pink spreading across the baby's chest, she knew that the child was recovering.

Greenwood recounts, "In all my twenty years of experience, I have never seen a baby come back from that length of time. I would say she was resurrected. It was God's divine intervention."

Nurse Gomez concurs: "She was pronounced dead. She was dead. So definitely—she was resurrected."

"I'm a Catholic," Dr. Judalena adds. "She was resurrected. It was a miracle. It's beyond medical explanation."

Not only did Siara survive, but MRIs, EEGs and so on all showed her to be normal. Finally, eleven days after her birth, the hospital sent her home with her parents. Nothing at all was wrong with her. As the story circulated, many churches invited Manuel and Maria to come share their testimony, and they brought their miracle baby with them.

Their pastor, Peter Edwards of New Life Open Bible Church in San Jacinto, California, was with the family during their crisis. "Today," he recounted a few years ago, "she is a normal, active ten-year-old in our church."[8]

By the time I interviewed Siara's father, Manuel, she was going on fourteen, and her father spoke proudly of her intelligence.[9] Through interviews conducted by Peter Edwards, I also watched testimonies about the miracle from Dr. Judalena, Becki Gomez, and Annette Greenwood, all long-serving medical staff at Hemet Valley Medical Center.[10] (For additional accounts of unexpected resuscitations from death in religious contexts, see part 5 of this book.)

Lone Survivor

When I interviewed Anthony Wainaina Njuguna, he and his wife, Edwina, were PhD students at Trinity International University near Chicago.[11] They told me about the birth of their son Adiel in Kenya. About an hour after his birth, Adiel began to experience difficulty breathing. When the baby's breathing did not stabilize, the doctor grew concerned and advised Anthony and Edwina to seek out a larger medical facility.

Because the hospital lacked a neonatal intensive care unit, and because Anthony and Edwina could not afford the more elite hospitals, they transferred the child to Kenyatta National Hospital. The neonatal nursing staff there were professional and caring, but most infants who ended up there were in severe condition. On the morning after his transfer to this hospital, Adiel stopped breathing for a full ten minutes. A doctor was able to revive him but warned that the brain damage from oxygen deprivation would be irreparable. Adiel would never be able to walk or talk; at best, he would stare blankly into space. Over the next twenty days the couple witnessed the tragic death of thirty-three infants—all the infants in the unit except for Adiel.

At first the doctors shook their heads sadly at Wainaina (Anthony), who would read psalms and pray for his unconscious child, but as Adiel continued to live, they welcomed his father's continued prayers. But then doctors detected a serious heart problem that, if Adiel lived, would require open-heart surgery in six months.

A couple of days later, they checked Adiel's brain. The doctor looked confused, rechecked his file, and then called over colleagues to examine both the scan and the chart. Then they called over the nurse and insisted that this was either the wrong baby or the wrong file. There was nothing wrong with Adiel's brain. Trying to figure out what had happened, staff prodded and poked Adiel so much that for days afterward he continued to recoil when touched. The discharge document admitted that the doctors did not know what had happened.

At his one-month review, a similar scene unfolded as doctors checked and rechecked his heart. His heart, too, was cured, and he was completely healthy. Nine years later, Anthony and Edwina introduced me to Adiel, who smiled as his father shared his story.

"We're Calling This One a Miracle"

Born at just twenty-five weeks and one day and weighing a pound and a half, Gavriel Nesch had a lengthy stay in the neonatal intensive care unit.[12] (Average birth weight tends to be about seven and a half pounds [three and a half kilograms], with normal birth weight roughly two pounds in either direction.) Gavriel thus received significant medical attention. Nevertheless, one expected aspect of attention proved unnecessary. We have all the relevant medical records in his case, and they clearly show that at nine months Gavriel had an inguinal hernia.

This is a condition in which a loop of intestine can descend into the groin area and is at risk of becoming trapped there. The condition occasionally leads to dangerous complications, and, as Gavriel's doctor rightly pointed out, it can be corrected only by surgery. The only known exceptions are extremely rare, and in these particular cases the patients were prematurely born girls.

Nevertheless, the family continued to pray that God would help their child without this operation. Some forty-five minutes after the operation was scheduled to begin, the doctor reappeared and showed them pictures. "You can see the scar tissue here where the hernia was before. But . . . he must have healed himself. It's as if somebody had performed the surgery already."

"The Lord healed him," Gavriel's father, Elliott, suggested. The doctor, who had earlier explained that an inguinal hernia cannot go away without surgery, conceded the point. Gavriel's mother, Harmony, asked a nurse if this happened often. The nurse replied, "We're calling this one a miracle."

Tumor Treatment

Accounts abound of God enabling mothers to bear children after years of unsuccessful attempts—for example, of a pregnancy immediately following prayer after fifteen years without giving birth.[13] Another example is that of Sandra Rivera. In 1997, her doctors discovered a pituitary tumor that they believed would preclude pregnancy. Because of the tumor's location within the brain, the doctors ruled out surgery. Soon after this, Rivera committed her life to Christ and also received a prophecy that she would bear a child. Testing a year and a half after the initial diagnosis showed that the tumor was growing. Nevertheless, Rivera refused in faith to let go of what she believed God had said, and on Valentine's Day 1997, her doctor appeared confused as he examined her new test results. The medical report attests that a small cavity remained where the tumor had been, but the tumor itself was gone. Since then, Rivera has had two children.[14]

A Special-Needs Adoption

In his younger days, Jeff Durbin, a world champion martial artist, portrayed Johnny Cage in *Mortal Kombat: Live Tour* (1996) and Michelangelo and Donatello of the Teenage Mutant Ninja Turtles. Today, after his conversion, Jeff is one of the pastors of Apologia Church in Arizona. Pastor Jeff and his wife, Candi, decided to adopt a baby whose prenatal testing identified special needs. I contacted Jeff after a mutual friend drew my attention to his public testimony.[15]

While in the womb, the boy they hoped to adopt was officially diagnosed with spina bifida;[16] the birth mother had to see the doctor more than once a week for the rest of her pregnancy. Multiple ultrasounds made the condition clear: the baby was on the better side of the fourth, and worst, type of spina bifida. Once

he was born, doctors would need to close the opening in his spine; they therefore expected that he would need to remain in the hospital for two to six weeks.
Doctors warned that the Durbins would not be able to hold him directly after
his birth because of the hole in his spine. "They had also planned for a possible
brain shunt," Jeff shared with me, "due to complications they observed in the
ultrasounds."[17]

Christians around the world were praying for this baby's wholeness, but the
answer to their prayers exceeded their expectations. Baby Augustine was supposed to be in the newborn ICU, but when Jeff and Candi arrived at the hospital
to meet him, they found someone holding him, which was not supposed to be
allowed. Smiling, the nurse opened the bundle and turned Augustine over: his
back was already whole. Jeff and Candi alternated between stunned silence and
praising God. What were they to make of this? Like everyone else, they had seen
the ultrasounds. "I don't know any explanation for this," a nurse volunteered.

She noted that the team had been ready for the surgery once he was born, but
when he arrived, they kept flipping him over, saying, "I can't explain this." They
kept running tests, but Augustine had no open spine. Turning the child over again,
a surgeon with more than thirty years of experience seemed mystified. "This is a
normal baby," he observed to the birth mother. "Do you have another baby inside
you?" A colleague asked, "Have you ever seen anything like this?" He shook his
head. "This is my first time in over thirty years ever having seen anything like this."

Visible Growth

Kathleen and Michael Bratun were referred to a high-risk doctor because ultrasounds showed abnormal growth in their preborn infant, Brielle.[18] Brielle's
arms were so short that doctors suspected achondroplasia, a form of dwarfism
that can have potentially severe complications. Around twenty weeks, the doctor
suggested abortion, but Kathleen and Michael maintained that all human life is
valuable. They began fetal monitoring three times a week, the third time with a
full ultrasound, and kept praying for a miracle. At thirty-six weeks, a month early,
the doctor decided to induce labor right away because of a dangerous reverse
flow of the placenta.

Contrary to expectations, Brielle was born healthy and able to breathe on
her own. Her upper arms, however, remained short, as both pictures and medical reports attest. By the time Brielle was six months old, her pediatrician was
demanding more testing: because of potential complications, mere observation
was no longer sufficient.

Sunday morning during worship, Kathleen, who had seen others healed when
she prayed, prayed for Brielle with fresh faith. "Arms, grow, in the name of Jesus!"
she commanded. Suddenly Kathleen saw the arm she was looking at get longer:
the tip of her elbow was now peeking out of her jacket. So Kathleen urged, "Lord,

do it again." And it grew a second time, until Brielle's entire elbow was sticking out. When Kathleen took Brielle to the pediatrician several days later, the doctor declared, surprised, "Wow, her arms are longer! She doesn't need testing after all."

Liver Disease

Cameron and Caden Sturtz of Clinton, Iowa, born several years apart, suffered from glycogen storage disease IXa—a rare, incurable genetic liver disease. Their cases also had distinctive features. Their mother, Korene, reports that though Cameron and Caden received regular special feedings, their doctor was concerned: their livers were becoming incapable of storing iron, and their arteries were hardening. Cameron's muscles grew so weak that sometimes he could not walk; his liver increased to five times the normal size, and his spleen doubled in size. His liver damage nearly approximated cirrhosis. His younger brother, Caden, whose heart enzymes became three times higher than normal, had even worse episodes. Caden was malnourished because he could not keep food down; he needed trips to the emergency room weekly.

Their father, Darin, challenged their mother, Korene, to be willing to accept however God healed them: in this life, or by taking them home to heaven. Korene resisted the latter idea angrily. But at a revival service in Rochelle, Illinois, she finally told God that she surrendered everything. She would praise him whether he healed them or took them. Then she felt God say, "Now that you have released control to me, go get your boys, because I will heal them tonight." In the same service, Darin and Korene's older child, Madison, began to pray for the afflicted, witnessing bones visibly shifting as she prayed. Madison laid hands on her younger brothers, and each of the boys felt that God had just healed them. One week later, medical tests on their blood confirmed that their blood values were normal, and their livers and spleens were now of normal size. Cameron's healing was instant and complete; Caden's began at the same time, but some features of his recovery were more progressive.

In less serious forms of the disease, symptoms sometimes disappear gradually before adulthood, but one would not expect this to begin (and, in one case, become complete) for both brothers simultaneously. Nor in their case had survival to adulthood been guaranteed, especially in Caden's case. Pediatrician Dr. Neeru Aggarwal, who had followed the boys from birth, testifies on a video now online, "It's a miracle."[19]

Jesus Heals a Flow of Blood

In Mark 5:25–34, Jesus heals a woman with a long-term flow of blood. When I was visiting a seminary in India, seminarian Syam Jeevan Babu shared with me his mother's experience. Each of her three babies died, and then she suffered a flow of blood for many years. Despite petitions to other gods, she was not healed. Finally she prayed to Jesus, and he healed her and promised her a son for ministry. Syam is that son.[20]

///////////

These are merely samples of some reports about the healing of infants or young children. Some reports appear to be even more dramatic than these, such as reported healings from AIDS[21] or raisings within the womb.[22] If some readers do not consider these reports concrete enough to allow for the possibility of cases of special divine action, perhaps some accounts in part 3 of this book will invite further consideration.

Videos and Doctors' Reports

Physicians are particularly well qualified to certify cures today. Whether cures are divinely caused is a theological question, but whether they are genuine is a medical one. Admittedly, some physicians are more prepared to certify cures than others, and some are more willing to call them miracles than are others. Records can, however, show whether a person who once had a condition has it no longer. Subsequent parts of the book will also note some doctors' reports, but I cite more here than in earlier chapters. (I have tried to compromise between grouping events by kind, such as healings of infants or brain recoveries, and a section focused on videos and medical reports. Naturally, there is some overlap, and I could have placed some accounts elsewhere.)

Before proceeding, I should respond to one objection some critics raise against even some medical documentation. Some skeptics want to dismiss medical reports by doctors who believe in miracles, calling them biased. Such an approach, however, itself stacks the deck in a biased way: it accepts evidence of miracles only from those who disbelieve in miracles, who will naturally be reluctant to define a recovery as a miracle. We do not ordinarily follow this kind of logic. Nations that allow freedom of conscience, for example, do not ordinarily require witnesses to deny their belief systems before providing legal evidence, whether those belief systems are theistic, atheistic, or something else. In most cases of medical documentation, we actually lack knowledge of the physicians' personal beliefs—though in some settings, such as the Catholic shrine at Lourdes, investigators deliberately seek some verdicts from experts of other faiths or no faith. The issue in medical documentation is not a physician's theological opinion but the medical certification of before-and-after conditions. In this section, we consider what some deem "harder" evidence: videos and medical reports. So: what would the doctor say?

Chapter 8

Do Healings Ever Get Captured on Video?

Some years ago, when I presented a public lecture at Wheaton College on the subject of miracles, a science professor there reasonably asked why healings were never caught on video. The short answer is that sometimes they are. Since that time, I have found many videos of healings. Unfortunately, many videos posted online are of uncertain authenticity, because with sufficient funds or expertise, unscrupulous marketers can fake videos, just as charlatans can fake cures in person. Some experiences, however, cannot reasonably be faked, and video can sometimes help substantiate these cures. In this chapter I focus on a particular case in greater detail.

Feeling in Her Legs

Injured by a drunk driver in a terrible car accident, Delia Knox was confined to a wheelchair for more than twenty-two years because of nerve damage.[1] Because she was a widely noted singer, her paralysis was public knowledge throughout this period, attested in many newspaper articles and videos that are still widely available online. For years Knox prayed for healing, but after ten years she began to lose hope. She came to dread healing services, where at times well-intentioned but apparently rash ministers tried to pull her from her chair, expecting her to walk.

One night during a crowded conference service, however, evangelist Nathan Morris prayed over Knox. (Others have also experienced healing when Morris prayed.)[2] Suddenly she began to feel something in her legs, though she had not felt anything there for twenty-two years. With her husband and other ministers

helping to support her, she began to walk. Video captured these first steps. Internet critics scoffed that Knox needed support to walk, ignoring the fact that she
was the one controlling legs that she had never moved for twenty-two years. Her
muscles were still atrophied, so she had to relearn how to walk.[3]

Another video shows Knox marching into a church service three weeks later,
stable and ready to pray for others' healing. How did critics respond now? Some
scoffed that after one's muscles had atrophied for twenty-two years, one would
not be able to walk so quickly. Not only is this the exact opposite of the earlier
complaint, it misses the point. Hardline skeptics do not want to call anything
that could possibly happen naturally a miracle, but when God does something
that cannot happen naturally, they deny that any such thing is possible.

How can one explain the disappearance of paralysis after twenty-two years?
Since Knox was now obviously able to walk, some internet critics insisted that
she had simply faked paralysis for twenty-two years so she could claim healing
now. They were actually suggesting that someone would endure more than two
decades of not walking in public just to claim a miracle later! This sort of skeptical speculation convinced me of only one thing: that some hard skeptics will
go to any lengths to avoid believing. Some who demand evidence are really not
open-minded enough to accept any. Before my own conversion, I was an atheist,
but I valued truth enough to want to follow where the evidence led. Fake miracles
exist, but this one cannot qualify as such.

Delia Knox's Friends

Delia Knox's previous disability was well-documented public knowledge. But even
had I lacked access to such documentation, I soon encountered people who knew
her. I heard Knox's story originally because one of her old friends shared news of
it with a friend of mine. When I was lecturing for a conference at Northeastern
Seminary in Rochester, New York, I learned further details. When I recounted
what I knew by then of Knox's story, Bob Tice, a pastor from Buffalo, New York
(Knox's hometown), offered his direct insight and some details I hadn't known.[4]
Before planting a new church in inner-city Buffalo, Tice had been one of the pastors at the Tabernacle, Knox's original home church in Buffalo. Because she was
disabled, he had often helped lift her up onto the platform when she would sing.
He witnessed how valiantly she labored against her physical struggles.

Tice connected me with Bishop Tommy Reid, Knox's then eighty-four-year-old
former pastor at the Tabernacle in Buffalo.[5] In recent decades Reid has helped
spearhead the urban renewal of that city. Because I was traveling for the next
couple of weeks, I delayed calling him. On the afternoon of Friday, July 8, 2016,
however, I felt an urgency to call right away. To my amazement, Reid noted that
Knox and her husband were sitting across from him at that very moment; they
happened to be visiting Buffalo. So I was able to talk with her directly.

Bishop Reid noted that he had known Delia Knox well for many years. She was like a second daughter to him, and his daughter always calls Knox her little sister. Knox had often traveled with Reid's ministry team, singing from her wheelchair. In his younger days Reid had been healed from polio and he had witnessed many extraordinary miracles, but he now considered Knox's healing the most extraordinary miracle he knew firsthand, because she had not walked for more than twenty years. "Before the miracle, she couldn't have felt her legs even if someone had driven a nail through them," he explained. She was singing from her wheelchair for Reid's church when she met her husband, Bishop Levy Knox. Bishop Reid even officiated at their wedding.

Because of Delia Knox's wheelchair, however, he had never been able to look at her eye to eye without getting down on his knees. He tried to describe for me his emotion on the day when he first saw her eye to eye, when she returned to Buffalo after the miracle. "I'll never forget the first time when I could look directly in her face. She walked off the plane pushing the wheelchair with her luggage in it."

The conference at which I spoke in Rochester had been in June. The next time I recounted Knox's story was in July, at a Methodist renewal conference. When I told what I knew of the story, a minister there named Gregory Helinsky informed me that he had attended Tommy Reid's church in Buffalo for ten years.[6]

Helinsky was involved in the music ministry at the church and knew of Knox's disability, though he thought of her especially "as a Spirit filled Woman of God with an extraordinary singing voice." She often sang at church, but her ministry went far beyond her singing. As she spoke about God's love, "she was exuberant and joyful as if she would love to dance as well as sing . . . if she were able!"

Every time Helinsky saw her, Knox was confined to her wheelchair. With much effort, some people would push or lift her onto the platform in her wheelchair. There was no sign that she could use her legs. "Her chair, as far as my perception was concerned, was part of who she was."

Years later, after moving to Ohio, Helinsky saw a Facebook video of a woman leaving her wheelchair and being able to walk. It was clear that this was Delia Knox, and it was so amazing to him that he called his mother- and father-in-law, who still attended the church in Buffalo and had been ushers there for some twenty years. "Yes!" they confirmed. "Delia is now able to walk by the miraculous hand of God!"

Still later, when I gave a guest lecture at Houghton College in New York State, someone else in that room also had known Knox and testified directly to her healing.[7] By that point, though, further interviews seemed superfluous!

Spiritual Backstory

Long before Delia Knox's healing, various ministers who passed through her church had prophesied that one day she would be healed. This was not something they prophesied to everyone who was disabled; there was simply a consistent sense from the Spirit regarding Knox. Bishop Reid often reminded her of this; indeed, most of her friends had confidence that she would be healed. Over time, though, the prophecies faded. Her sister Enid notes, "I knew she would be healed in heaven." About a month before Knox's healing, however, someone called Enid and unexpectedly prophesied again that Knox would be healed, and this time Enid felt differently about it. Knox might well be healed in this life.[8]

On the night that Delia Knox was healed, she was deeply moved with compassion for an ill baby. She was not praying for her own healing, but when she prayed for the baby, feeling began to return to her own legs. She and her husband believe that compassion helped unlock the miracle. When feeling returned to her legs, she needed both faith to try to move them as best she could and humility to not care what people thought if she fell.

The test of her faith did not end with the twenty-two years of disability or her act of faith during the service. Her nerves now worked, but, in contrast to Barbara Cummiskey Snyder's healing (described in the preface), Knox's muscles remained atrophied from years of disuse. When she got home after the service, she again could not walk. Nor could she walk in the Sunday church service. In faith, she had to keep exercising the new gift of mobility, trying until she built up enough muscle strength to walk normally. Even once she could walk, her feet, unaccustomed to being flat on the ground, remained painful at first. But soon she was walking again.

Some weeks after Knox's healing, she returned to visit her home church. When Bishop Reid escorted her to see her mother, he suggested to her mother, "You must be thrilled to see her walking!" This was the first time Knox's mother had seen her walk in over twenty years. She responded, "I knew she'd be healed. I knew this all the time." Now, in Knox's home church, a thousand people who had known her for years in her wheelchair gathered to celebrate her healing.

There are many other examples of healings captured on video,[9] some of which are noted in my previous book on miracles.[10] But Delia Knox's decades of public presence in a wheelchair make her case particularly conspicuous. As noted earlier, an inflexible skeptic actually posted online that Knox must have faked her disability for two decades so she could later claim healing. When that is the best public argument that a hard skeptic can muster, skepticism is walking on thin ice.

Chapter 9

Medically Attested Catholic Cures

Partly because of often-justifiable Protestant complaints about late medieval Christian gullibility and fake relics, the Roman Catholic Church began to put strict protocols in place for testing healing claims. Sometimes these protocols have been so strict as to exclude from consideration even most events that we would probably regard as miracles, but this approach means that the miracle reports that do pass muster in these conditions have a very high degree of certainty. (Other cures in Roman Catholic contexts appear elsewhere in the book; I separate this chapter from others in part 3 partly to keep each chapter concise.)

Already in chapter 6, I noted the medically verified healing of Pascal's niece in 1656. Over the past four centuries, the Roman Catholic Church has reported more than 1,400 miracles, often with considerable testimony and medical documentation, associated with saints and other figures.[1] As a Protestant myself, I do not share all the theology connected with these healings[2] (or, for that matter, all the theology connected with many of the other healings recounted in this book). But I do believe in a God who hears the desperate cries of his children, whether these cries are directly or implicitly addressed to him. (I pause to address this objection only because some voiced it in response to the previous book.)

Indeed, despite the still somewhat polemical character of the age, even a number of prominent nineteenth-century evangelicals, such as A. B. Simpson, affirmed the genuineness and divine character of such Roman Catholic miracles while disagreeing with some Catholic theology.[3] (If God answered only prayers that were theologically precise, probably few people of any theological persuasion would be healed.) Protestants, too, have reported healings at the Catholic shrine at

Lourdes,[4] and one of the major twentieth-century publications regarding Lourdes comes from a sympathetic Protestant author.[5]

Nor are such observations limited to Christians. A friendly atheist medical historian authored one of the best and most thorough studies of Catholic medical documentation available. After examining medical evidence from past cases of healings attributed to saints, she acknowledges that many of these were miracles, which she defines as cures of conditions that were in those eras incurable.[6]

Various Catholic Reports

In over one hundred cases in the Vatican dossiers, doctors acknowledged their astonishment at patients' inexplicable recoveries.[7] I include here only a small sample of reports. For example, in 1824, Ann Mattingly had suffered for seven years "from an 'ulcerated back' and had a 'tumor' the size of a pigeon's egg." She was considered beyond medical help at the time, but in Washington, DC, on March 10, 1824, she recovered within hours after receiving the sacrament. Thirty-five affidavits affirmed the genuineness of her sickness and recovery.[8]

When two-year-old Teresa Benedicta McCarthy swallowed sixteen times the lethal dose of Tylenol on March 20, 1987, the Massachusetts General Hospital warned that she would die unless she received a liver transplant. After a few days of requests for the intercession of the saint for whom she had been named, her liver and kidneys recovered fully without a transplant. Her main physician, Dr. Ronald Kleinman, associate professor of pediatrics at Harvard Medical School, was Jewish. He considered her cure "miraculous," reporting the cure both to the Vatican and in a 1997 interview with *CBS Evening News*.[9]

Benedict Heron, prior of the Benedictine Monastery of Christ the King in Cockfosters, North London, recounts many cures, providing comments from physicians. For example, one doctor was bedridden from malignant tumors of the spine, and other physicians had relinquished hope for him. He was then healed after being anointed with oil by women from a British Catholic charismatic prayer group. We lack reports of this condition naturally disappearing after it has reached such an advanced stage.[10] In another case, the medical editors of Heron's book note that "severe heart failure with fluid in the lungs following several heart attacks almost invariably leads to near incapacity and ultimately death." Yet they report a case of complete healing.[11]

Victor Agbeibor is a medical doctor, as is his wife, Catrell, whom I have known since our time at Duke University some thirty years ago. They attend a non-denominational church, but when Victor was extremely sick in Ghana many years ago, a Catholic charismatic priest who had once been schoolmates with his mother prayed for him. Victor's malaria had become so severe that he developed hemolytic anemia; his urine was turning red from his red blood cells breaking down. This condition required medical treatment such as blood transfusions, so he was about to make his way to Accra, Ghana's capital. The priest said that this trip wouldn't be necessary. He instructed Victor to kneel, explaining that he would lay hands on him and pray. After praying, the priest declared, "Your faith has made you well." "Immediately," Victor recounts, "my fever went away. When I went to urinate the next time, it was all clear. I never needed any medication."[12]

Some Dramatic Cures at Lourdes

Most pilgrims to Lourdes are not ill, and most who are do not experience dramatic cures. Nevertheless, the latter do receive spiritual and emotional as well as medical care there, which is especially meaningful to those facing the end of their earthly lives. "For those whom I met in terminal stages of illness," one physician explains, "biomedicine can only provide a pain-free and comfortable death. It cannot help them accept their situation and prepare themselves to meet God."[13]

But dramatic cures do occur at Lourdes. Whatever one makes of some of the roughly seven thousand claims, some (for which medical documentation remains available) seem impressive. In 1878, a "gangrenous ulcer" on Joachime Dehant's right leg was twelve inches by six inches and had "penetrated to the bone." Her companions on the train, nauseated by the odor, vomited. Nevertheless, the second time she bathed in the pool at Lourdes, she was healed within two or three hours—only a scar remained. Investigators gathered testimony not only from physicians at Lourdes and her own physicians who had treated her for over a decade but also from her traveling companions, family, and others who knew her in her hometown.[14]

Tuberculosis, while treatable today, was not medically curable in the era in which such cures appear in the Medical Bureau's records.[15] Tuberculosis sometimes goes into remission spontaneously, but some cases do not appear to fit the profile of such natural remissions. For example, Mademoiselle Brosse had large abscesses and was dying, yet within hours was so fully healed that the wounds had closed and she could walk under her own power.[16]

Even were we to explain such cures purely naturally, other cases surely elude such explanations. Consider, for instance, the case of Francis Pascal, cured of "blindness" and "paralysis of the lower limbs" at the age of three years and ten months, on August 28, 1938.[17] While the keenness of his vision remained less than the average person's,[18] this child—who had been completely blind before the cure—was soon an active reader and writer.[19] Other blind persons were also cured of documented, organic optic atrophy, able thereafter to see.[20] One might also consider Marie Bigot, cured of blindness, deafness, and hemiplegia on October 10, 1954.[21]

Unable to work and deemed an invalid owing to verified physical causes, the nearly blind Serge Perrin visited Lourdes and, on May 1, 1970, was anointed. Within hours his vision unexpectedly returned fully, and he was able to walk unaided.[22] Doctors verified that no trace of his previous medical problems remained; six years later, in view of his continued health, the cure was recognized by the church as miraculous.[23]

The medically documented instantaneous healing of a swollen and paralyzed arm drew public attention and television coverage in France in 1954 and 1960.[24]

As already suggested, standards at Lourdes are so strict that they undoubtedly screen out many genuine cures.[25] The Medical Bureau at Lourdes officially endorses only a minute percentage of cures, those that both medical examiners and theologians consider airtight. Of some seven thousand claims of unexplained cures, the bureau has endorsed only seventy—that is, 1 percent. For example, in one case not endorsed, a Methodist visitor was immediately healed at Lourdes of much of her naturally incurable blindness (due to macular degeneration), though she still cannot see perfectly.[26]

The Lord at Lourdes?

In one half-year period noted by a journalist (April to October 1965), some sixteen hundred physicians from thirty-two nations and a diverse range of religious or nonreligious perspectives visited the Medical Bureau at Lourdes, where they were able to examine the evidence for themselves.[27] The fact that infants and unbelievers have been healed precludes purely psychosomatic explanations in those cases.[28] Other observers, reticent to endorse a supernatural explanation and emphasizing the possibility of prayer stimulating psycho-neuroimmunological and biochemical healing, still recognize that many of the cures exceed present medical explanation.[29]

In 1902, Alexis Carrel, who did not believe in miracles himself but had learned that patients of his had been cured at Lourdes, decided to investigate. On the train he cared for a dying girl, Marie Bailly, who was also traveling there. Her abdomen was swollen, she had peritonitis and was deathly pale and skeletal, and he believed that she was in danger of dying at any moment.[30] At Lourdes, she was removed from the train by a stretcher, with almost no pulse. To the "stupefaction" of the physicians, she was cured, the "tumors" vanishing in front of them; one astonished medical observer added that such a serious affliction "has never been cured [naturally] in a few hours like the case on record here."[31] Because Carrel was now interested in miracles, the University of Lyon medical faculty rejected him in 1905; he joined the Rockefeller Institute instead and in 1912 received the Nobel Prize in Physiology or Medicine. His memoir of the healing was published only later.[32] Although he prescinded from supernatural explanations, Carrel believed that science should study factors at Lourdes that could be used in medical healing.[33]

One scholar who articulates a more skeptical approach grants that "some utterly extraordinary cures" have occurred at Lourdes. He notes that enemies of the Catholic Church and leading medical scientists such as Alexis Carrel have been persuaded by the data,[34] and reports that scientists "unanimously" concur that these healings take place there.[35] Among clearly nonpsychosomatic cures he includes "the instant healing of a terribly disfigured face, and the instantaneous healing of a club foot on a two and one half year old child," shown by non-Catholics to be permanent. Further, he cites a news article about a three-year-old with terminal cancer whose bones were being eaten away; after the healing, even "the bones in her skull grew back. Her doctor, a Protestant, said that 'miracle' would not be too strong a word to use."[36]

Nevertheless, this scholar concludes that a natural explanation would be possible if only sufficient evidence were available, even if such cases have happened only one in a million times.[37] What makes the scholar so sure that a natural explanation must be possible? It seems that such certainty reflects an inflexible commitment to an exclusively natural explanation *always* being the most plausible one. By this approach, one cannot accept *any* evidence for miracles because one will always be required to dismiss such evidence; one's assumptions predetermine one's conclusion.

Granted, anomalies occur, and the fact that a recovery is medically inexplicable today does not mean that it will always be inexplicable. Biblical theology itself does not deny that God works through natural causes—in the Bible, God usually *does* work this way.[38] Moreover, a biblical perspective recognizes divine providence even in easily *explicable* recoveries. But, as I noted in part 1, evaluation of miracles also depends on the assumptions one brings to the discussion. If someone demands medical evidence for miracles, such evidence is available. If a person rejects such evidence by saying, "I will not accept that God did it even if I lack a better explanation than one chance in a million," this says more about that person's assumptions than it does about evidence. How much more is that the case when they appeal to this explanation for many such cases?

Chapter 10

A Few Vignettes
of Brain Recovery

This is one of the book's shortest chapters, since more detailed accounts of brain recovery follow later in the book. Testimonies abound of recovery from near-death experiences—and they are not by any means confined to believers, especially given current technology. Some of these cases are more significant for our subject than others. When the person's heart has not pumped blood to the brain for four or more minutes, we have reason to expect permanent brain damage; when the person ends up with little or no brain damage, we see that as extraordinary, even if not unparalleled. Believers thank God for what we see as divine activity in overcoming brain damage and near-death experiences, and believers usually define such experiences as miraculous.

Such events seem providential and medically rare but are not naturally impossible when effective CPR or a fairly limited time frame has allowed oxygen to reach the brain. Some readers might thus debate some of the examples in this chapter, depending on their starting assumptions. If you are tempted to disregard accounts in this chapter, you may find further insight in chapter 11, which recounts a recovery from virtual brain death. Beyond that, part 5 of this book (chaps. 24–31) contains accounts of raisings from death, in the majority of which death had lasted longer than in the accounts related here.

Nevertheless, the following accounts remain intriguing, and most differ from usual expectations. Certainly, believers *experience* such cases as miraculous. For example, on June 9, 2018, nine-year-old Annie Powell drowned in warm water. She was without oxygen for roughly ten minutes: most of her upper body was blue, and her eyes had rolled back in her head. Medical staff worked hard and Annie's Assemblies of God church prayed hard. Less than a week after the accident, Annie walked out of the hospital without brain damage.[1] This does not appear as dramatic as recovery after an hour without oxygen, but neither is it a typical outcome.

Overdose

On May 29, 2014, at the age of twenty-four, Dina Cafiso overdosed on heroin. Her mother, Maria, found her facedown, and her brother called 911.[2] The emergency medical team reports that her heart stopped for ten minutes, but they and hospital personnel continued to labor over her. The CT scan and her curled hands suggested the possibility of significant brain damage.

Maria was already a person of prayer, but now she began pouring her heart out desperately to God to give Dina another chance. She continued to express her trust in God despite subsequent hard news about Dina's fever and pneumonia.

After a week, Dina awoke from her medically induced coma without brain damage but with nerve damage in her left arm, on which she had been lying when her mother found her. For Dina, however, the experience was a wake-up call. She devoted her life to God and entered rehabilitation through Brooklyn Teen Challenge. Through prayer and therapy, she recovered full use of her left arm and now helps lead worship on her electric guitar. When I corresponded with Maria and Dina, both continued to overflow in their gratitude to God.

Traffic Accidents

On April 10, 2003, a pickup truck smashed into Natalie Elders's car near Asheville, North Carolina. An MRI showed that the impact had almost completely severed her brain stem; doctors concluded that she would be a lifetime quadriplegic if she ever woke up. Her husband, Dewayne, solicited widespread prayer, but on Good Friday, April 18, the doctor warned that she would never wake up without divine intervention. On Monday, they would need to make a decision about whether to take her off life support. Before that time arrived, she woke up—on Easter Sunday morning. Within two weeks she was sent to a rehabilitation center. While doctors did not expect her release until after Christmas, more than eight months away, she walked out in May. Dr. Edgardo Diez notes her relatively quick recovery, considering that she arrived needing total care.[3]

Valerie Paters was injured and near death after a traumatic accident; at least one source in the hospital suggested that life support was sustaining her so that her surviving organs could help someone else in need. While her sister Cheryl travailed in prayer, Valerie experienced Jesus's presence in heaven; Valerie and Cheryl shared some spiritual experiences independently during this time. Although a painful convalescence followed Valerie's unexpected return to physical consciousness, her near-death experience brought her an extraordinary, fresh revelation of Jesus's love for her.[4]

Giving Up

Some years ago PAX TV's program *It's a Miracle* researched and reported the case of Isaias Sevilla. After successful medical intervention for his otherwise terminal cancer, Isaias's lungs suddenly collapsed and filled with blood—his entire body was shutting down. His wife, Silvia, kept praying, but eventually the doctors suggested that she disconnect life support. That evening, Silvia visited her husband one last time, praying. When the technicians shut off life support, however, there was suddenly a commotion behind the curtain. Isaias sat up alive, as if nothing had ever happened. The doctor testified that he had never seen anyone in this condition recover so fully. Isaias returned home well twenty-one days later.

Running Back

In contrast to stories reported by *It's a Miracle* or other national outlets, sometimes extraordinary recoveries invite only local media coverage. For example, one January morning in southern Ohio, two-year-old Malachi Reissig was running around while his mother, Kelly Reissig, was chatting with her sister on the phone and making breakfast.[5] Realizing she had not heard her son for a few minutes, Kelly stepped into the living room and, horrified, dashed the phone to the floor. Malachi had accidentally hanged himself from a treadmill cord and was already stiff, his eyes fixed.

Malachi's father, Jim, reached the local hospital just before Malachi was to be airlifted to the children's hospital in Columbus, Ohio. The physician explained that it appeared that Malachi's oxygen had been cut off for nearly ten minutes. If he survived at all, he would probably be a vegetable. Glancing at his unmoving child, Jim Reissig broke down, fell to his knees, and began crying out to God. To the astonishment of everyone in the room, color began to return to Malachi's body and the swelling visibly diminished.

So how did things turn out for Malachi in the long run? My account comes (in this case, exclusively) from the September 19, 2013, sports section of the *Chillicothe Gazette*. The newspaper reported Malachi's baby story because he was now, at age fifteen, a running back for the local football team.[6]

Chapter 11

Back from Virtual Brain Death

C hapter 10 included some vignettes of brain recoveries experienced as miracles by those who prayed. These accounts usually include medical intervention fairly soon after cardiac arrest. Sometimes, however, so much of the brain is dead that reviving it is, even with today's best medical resources, technically impossible. This chapter recounts the story of a young man in that condition.

Impact

Years ago one of the testimonies featured on *It's a Miracle* was that of sixteen-year-old Dallas Pullum, nearly killed in a terrible accident. Regional news outlets covered the story; in 2002, Larry King interviewed the family on CNN;[1] and *It's a Miracle* publicly displayed the medical documentation. Eighteen years later, I caught up with the Pullums as they recounted the fateful day of the accident and the intense weeks that followed.[2] I learned several morals from the story; one of them is the importance of keeping your promises.

A couple of weeks before the accident, Dallas and his mother, Regina, both began to have night anxieties about Dallas's safety, and Regina began praying for his safety. Two nights before the accident, Regina dreamed that Dallas had experienced a wreck but was standing beside his vehicle, without a scratch on him or the vehicle. He held out both hands and said, "It's okay, Mama. I'm going home." Regina would soon have reason to believe that this meant "going home to be with Jesus."

On April 7, 2000, as Dallas was heading out, Regina and her husband, Stevie, each told him, "I love you! Be careful," as they regularly did. But as Dallas and a friend were racing on their four-wheelers, the vehicle occupied by Dallas and his girlfriend, Christina, collided with another vehicle. Christina's arm was broken, but Dallas—who was not wearing a helmet—was hurled into a windshield, lacerating his head and throat.

Dallas's brother Wayne confesses that the accident was "the scariest day of my life." By the time Wayne reached Decatur General Hospital, Dallas was bleeding from his ears, eyes, mouth, and throat, yet was still conscious and in agony. "Am I going to be okay?" Dallas pleaded. "Yeah, buddy, you're going to be all right," Wayne assured him. "Do you promise me?" Dallas pressed. "Yeah, Dallas, I promise you, buddy," Wayne responded.

But Dallas no longer looked as though he was going to be all right, and the hospital was preparing to transfer him to one of Alabama's leading trauma centers, in Huntsville. As Wayne spoke with his mother outside, he confessed, "Mama, I just did something I said I'd never do. I'd never told Dallas a lie. But I may have just lied to him."

On the way to Huntsville, Dallas began to decline quickly. His father was in the transport vehicle and his heart sank—he feared they had lost him. Trauma surgeon Deepak Katyal notes that roughly an hour after Dallas reached Huntsville, he experienced a seizure that revealed that his apparently minor head injury was not actually minor. By the time the family got to Huntsville, Dallas's brain was swelling and he was placed in a medically induced coma. Doctors warned that even far less intracranial pressure than Dallas was experiencing usually causes brain damage. Insufficient blood was reaching his brain, and over the next few days CT scans showed his brain cells irrecoverably dying.

Losing Dallas

Regina could not yet bear to see her son in this condition, but Stevie and Wayne spent time with him. "His hand was cold," Wayne notes. "He looked dead." As Wayne shared with me his memory of that occasion, he was racked with sobs and struggled to regain his composure. "I just couldn't handle the last thing I said to him being a lie." Wayne says that he could not sleep for days, until exhaustion finally overtook him involuntarily. In the hospital chapel, "I prayed harder than I'd ever prayed in my life." One day, as he was crying out to God, he heard a voice in his heart as clear as if it came from outside: Dallas would be okay. After that, "I told Mama and Daddy that he's gonna be okay."

But his parents, struggling with their own grief, urged Wayne to face reality. Doctors had already shown them the scans of his brain. "Anything you see black in the brain is dead," the doctor had explained. The scan of a normal brain looked mostly white; the scan of a brain with partial function had more black. The latter is common in severe brain injuries, and the condition is irreversible. The scan of Dallas's brain was completely black except for three small white spots, the only places that had not been starved of oxygen. He lacked brain stem function and was for all practical purposes brain-dead.[3] If Dallas woke up at all, he would be a vegetable, so one doctor was pressing them to donate his organs. Dallas was virtually dead already; life support was merely preserving his organs.

One day some doctors called family members into the meeting room. "You might as well accept the fact that your brother's dead," a physician admonished sadly.

"Do you believe in miracles?" Wayne demanded.

"Yes, I do," the doctor replied, "but I don't see one happening here. With the kind of damage we see here, it's medically impossible."

Wayne felt his temper rising. "But do you believe in miracles?" he repeated.

"Yes," the doctor explained patiently, "but this isn't going to be one." The doctor was speaking on the basis of considerable experience. Other families prayed for loved ones too, but at this stage recovery was virtually impossible, like raising the dead.

Wayne's parents kept trying to help Wayne accept his brother's death. "These doctors know what they're talking about," they explained.

"No, not in this case," Wayne objected. "Normally it's right to believe the doctors. But the one who's telling me something different outweighs their opinion. Just have a little faith."

Mustard Seed

Wayne confesses, "I didn't read my Bible the way I should, but I know that I'd heard that the faith of something as small as a mustard seed can move something as big as a mountain. God told me he was going to heal my brother, and the good Lord's not gonna lie. Anybody can have just that little bit of faith like a mustard seed."

On the basis of the doctors' extensive trauma experience, however, Regina and Stevie made the difficult decision to take Dallas off life support. When Wayne learned of this, he sat down by his cousin Ronald, who was like a brother to him. "It's not his time to die!" Wayne insisted. Ronald agreed. Ronald had lost his own brother, Billy, and said that he kept dreaming that Billy was telling him that Dallas would be okay. "You need to try to talk your mama out of this or you'll never be able to let go of this."

Wayne took Regina outside to the parking deck, insisting, "I need to talk to you away from everybody."

"Dallas ain't ready to die," he pleaded. "Don't let them take him off life support." Regina was crying and repeating what the doctors had said. "I know what they're saying," he agreed, "but I can't live without my brother."

Finally, Regina relented, feeling that Wayne was simply emotionally exhausted and needed a little more time to let Dallas go. "I'll give you one more day if you promise to come home and get some rest. But after that, you need to accept what the doctors said." He consented.

They returned to the room and told the nursing staff, "Wayne isn't ready to let go of his brother yet. Maybe tomorrow." The nurse called the doctor, who was already on the way up to detach life support.

As they left the building, Wayne hesitated. "I can't leave him."

"You promised," she reminded him. She needed him home with her, Stevie, and their daughter, to try to remember and cherish the good times they had had with Dallas. And Wayne needed to get some rest.

"I know I promised, and Dallas wouldn't want me to break a promise, but I just feel like I need to be with him." They lived in rural Alabama, about an hour from the hospital. Wayne knew that his mother would not bring him back to the hospital that night, and Wayne, who was legally blind, could not drive there himself.

Ronald broke the mounting impasse. Although he lived an hour further away from the hospital, he said to Wayne, "Go on home with your mother. If you feel you need to come back later, I'll give you a ride." Wayne made him promise, and then went home with Regina. When they reached home, Regina picked out Dallas's clothes to bury him in, including the shirt he had worn to school the previous Friday. Brokenhearted, Stevie made arrangements at the funeral home, picking out the casket.

Wayne spent time with the family, but that night he called Ronald, who had just gotten home. "I really feel like I need to get back to the hospital."

"Are you serious?" his dismayed cousin asked. But Wayne reminded Ronald of his promise. "Okay," Ronald acquiesced. "I'll see you in an hour."

As Ronald's car pulled up, Regina asked, "Who'd be here at this time of night?" Someone wanting to console them surely wouldn't come this late. She started to cry as Wayne explained that he was going back to the hospital. "You promised!"

"I kept my promise," he answered. "I came home and got rest. But I need to go back."

New Beginnings

A surprise awaited Wayne at the hospital: Dallas had just emerged from six days in a coma. "You couldn't tell he was any different from looking at him, but the heart monitor and all the stats were better." Wayne took Dallas's right hand and said, "If you can hear me, squeeze my hand." Dallas's fingers closed around Wayne's hand.

Wayne called the nurse. "It's just an involuntary spasm," she explained calmly.

"Dallas, you've got to show us right now that you're not ready to go!" Wayne begged desperately.

Suddenly, Dallas squeezed his hand again—multiple times. "Oh my God!" the nurse exclaimed. "Let me get the doctor." The doctors didn't know what to make of this new situation. "We have pictures. This boy has no brain stem function!" But Dallas was responding fully. Something had happened to his brain.

Wayne wasn't allowed to call his parents immediately for fear that the news would shock them too much, but a surprise greeted them when they returned to the hospital. Dallas tightly squeezed his mother's hand, and when his father announced his presence, Dallas released his mother's hand and squeezed his father's. "We were in utter disbelief at this point," Dr. Katyal notes for the televised *It's a Miracle* interview. "I have no other way of describing this except that it was a miracle."

But Dallas's recovery was only beginning. Although he could use his right hand, the left side of his body remained paralyzed. Doctors warned that he would probably not regain much movement on his left side, but Wayne insisted, "The good Lord don't start something and then not finish it." Attached to a ventilator, Dallas could not speak, but his gestures soon let Wayne know that he wanted to communicate.

Wayne asked the nurse for a pencil and paper. "He can't write," she explained, but Wayne insisted, so she shrugged and brought him one. Dallas immediately wrote, "Who did I hit? Are they okay?" He had no memory of the accident himself. "They're fine," Wayne assured him. Dallas kept writing notes, to the appreciative amazement of the staff.

While at the hospital, Wayne ran into the trauma doctor who had said that a miracle would not happen in this case. "I eat my words," the doctor offered humbly. "From now on I'll be careful what I tell families about their faith."

Still, Dallas was not out of the woods yet. One day his fever reached 107 degrees; Regina went to the chapel and prayed. When she returned, it had dropped to 102 degrees. After that, whenever his fever spiked, the nurses informed his mother so that she could pray.

Altogether, Dallas was in the hospital for thirty-one days. Although he has no memory of the accident or of his time in the coma, he remembers clearly the arduous time of convalescence. "They said I'd be a vegetable, and I did have to learn how to walk and talk again." His left side recovered, but he returned home using a wheelchair, not least because of his broken femur. The accident had cut Dallas's throat and paralyzed his vocal cords; although his speech was recovering, others found it difficult to understand him at first. This frustrated Dallas.

"I went to this therapy," he noted, "and I hated it." But Dallas was determined. After three months of therapy he could stand without trouble. In six more months he was walking, and within about a year he had fully recovered all his previous physical ability.

Meanwhile, although he had missed the conclusion of tenth grade, he was able to start eleventh grade alongside his peers. The following year this young man who had lacked brain stem function graduated high school with honors.

Looking Back

A priest who visited Dallas in the trauma center had sadly warned his family that Dallas was dead. Learning of Dallas's recovery shortly before Easter, the priest made Dallas's testimony the centerpiece of his Easter sermon. As of the writing of this book, Dallas is thirty-six, has a family of his own, and works hard in his lawn service.

"I think my brother was with Jesus for a little while," Wayne shared with me, becoming emotional again. He believes that Dallas really was not in his body for a time. "There's no way you can tell me that there's not a God. Jesus didn't raise the dead just back then. I watched him do it in our time."

Wayne knows that God does not always heal people. Two years ago Wayne lost one of his other best friends—Ronald, who had driven him to the hospital. "I don't know why God does it sometimes and not for others. God has a time for everybody. But I think sometimes he changes outcomes when people pray." Baptists and Methodists were praying for Dallas's recovery; a Pentecostal cousin touched him and prayed in tongues over him. "Can I say which prayer helped him? Was it one prayer? I don't know. A part of me wants to be selfish and say God gave him back to me, but I think God really gave him back to make believers of a lot of people."

What about Dallas's own thoughts? "Miracles happen every day, but when something that dramatic happens, it touches not just me and my family, but the whole community, my school, and others. I think the good Lord meant it as a testimony for everybody."

Chapter 12

More Medically Attested Twentieth-Century Cures

A re there medically attested cures in the context of faith? I know of no central repository of such evidence, but I have been able to find plenty of samples. Indeed, that is why this chapter addresses other "twentieth-century" cures; dividing material by centuries is somewhat arbitrary, but it allows me to keep the samples in this chapter from growing too long.

For example, a woman with a confirmed diagnosis of tuberculosis of the cervical spine, unable to stand, was healed after prayer; her doctor, who had been trying to secure her a place in a sanatorium, "was bewildered to find there was no evidence of disease in her body." Her illness was certain, her cure permanent, and the witness virtually incontrovertible. The witness, John White, could attest to this incident and its permanence because not only was he the person who prayed for her, and an MD himself, but he later married this woman and spent the rest of his life with her.[1]

Healings in Sweden

Besides perhaps Antarctica,[2] no continent has as low a proportion of reported believers in divine healing as Europe. Nevertheless, healings are reported there as well. Chapter 7 of editor Micael Grenholm's *Dokumenterade Mirakler* presents some medical records from Sweden.[3]

For example, in midsummer 1985, neurologist Lars Olof Ronnevi diagnosed Pär-Ola Malm, then surnamed Karlsson, with ALS (amyotrophic lateral sclerosis)—Lou Gehrig's disease.[4] ALS progressively destroys nerve cells in the muscles; it is incurable and ultimately fatal. The typical life expectancy after diagnosis is three years, though roughly one-fifth of sufferers live five years, and some have survived for ten years.

By September, Pär-Ola needed a wheelchair. In October, he asked two fellow Pentecostals to pray for him. They anointed him with oil and laid hands on him in prayer. The next night, October 31, 1985, he felt that Jesus told him, "Pär-Ola, I have seen your tears. I carried the cross in your place." He then saw Jesus carrying a cross and walking away, and he felt a warm current passing through his body. In the morning, he began to walk, and over the following few weeks his atrophied muscles began to regain strength.

When Pär-Ola next visited his neurologist, Dr. Ronnevi was astonished. After new tests, he certified Pär-Ola's health. In the certificate, dated April 3, 1986,[5] he reports, "For reasons unclear to us, and completely contrary to the almost invariable prognosis of the said disease, we have seen a gradual and now practically total symptom regression. The case is assumed to be very strange." The Swedish Pentecostal movement's newspaper interviewed Dr. Sebastian Conradi, another physician at Karolinska Hospital who had cared for Pär-Ola and had researched ALS. Dr. Conradi noted "that there is a lot that you can't explain medically," including in the present "exciting and fascinating" case. Pär-Ola remains alive and well, and Grenholm interviewed him in 2019.[6]

In 2003, Sofi Berggren and Ingela Ronquist (later Aminoff) wrote their graduate medical project work about a man who had recovered from extensive skin problems.[7] By late August 1998, this man felt as if his skin, which was red and crusted, was starting to burn; he needed to change his sheets daily because they "were soaked in blood." In December 1998, after medical tests, his doctor concluded that he had lymph node cancer that had spread to his skin. The man's friends then undertook extensive prayer for him, including two days of twenty-four-hour prayer. A week before Christmas, the man awoke thinking about Jesus, and then was astonished to discover that all his rashes had vanished.

His doctor acknowledged this transformation "without my intervention or treatment." Nevertheless, on the basis of the tests that had been conducted, the doctor insists that his original diagnosis was correct. Subsequent checkups in March and June 1999 revealed that no skin disorders had returned. While recognizing that believers might call this a miracle, the doctor is satisfied to conclude medically that the overnight recovery "cannot be explained scientifically."

British Healing Miracles

In his book *Healing Miracles*, British physician Rex Gardner[8] records numerous verified healings, such as that of a woman supposed to need traction for many weeks who rose immediately after prayer,[9] and the healing of a person disabled from a heart condition.[10]

More dramatically, in January 1975 a young medical trainee in North Wales was dying in the hospital of meningitis and meningococcal septicemia, but those praying for her felt that she would recover, against medical opinion. X-ray films of her chest initially revealed "extensive left-sided pneumonia with collapse of the middle lobe." Two days later, however, new X-rays showed "a normal chest." Because of scarring on her eye, the ophthalmologist assured her that she would have "permanent blindness in that eye," despite her confidence that she would be healed.

Although sometimes patients' insistence may be a result of psychological denial, the trainee proved correct. Her eye recovered completely, for which the ophthalmologist could offer no explanation. "The four consultants who saw her on admission to hospital remain confident of their initial diagnosis. She is shown at post-graduate medical meetings as 'The one that got away.'"[11]

In one of Dr. Gardner's other examples, a doctor examined a Baptist woman's ulcer that was daily exuding pus and concluded that even if it healed, skin grafting would be necessary. The morning after prayer, nearly the entire ulcer disappeared; a week later, during another prayer, the skin was completely healed. Gardner notes that he was one of the examining physicians and had also inquired of the witnesses.[12] I will reserve his documented account of the healing of a girl's deafness for my chapter on healings from deafness (chap. 23).

After reporting various other case studies, Gardner openly challenges anti-supernaturalist presuppositions: "That God does heal in the late twentieth century should be accepted on the evidence of all these Case Records." He invites those who reject such evidence to "ask yourself what evidence you would be prepared to accept. If the answer proves to be 'None,' then you had better face the fact that you have abandoned logical enquiry."[13]

The Healing Evangelist

Many cases from the United States appear elsewhere in this book, but here I cite a particular conglomeration of reports. Richard Casdorph, MD, PhD, provides in his book more substantial medical documentation, including X-rays and the like, for the following cases of extraordinary healings after prayer, though some of these are more "medically inexplicable" than others:

- Lisa Larios, healed of reticulum cell sarcoma of the right pelvic bone (see more fully chap. 14)[14]
- Elfrieda Stauffer, healed of chronic rheumatoid arthritis with severe disability[15]
- Marie Rosenberger, healed of a malignant brain tumor of the left temporal lobe[16]
- Marion Burgio, healed of multiple sclerosis[17]

- Marvin Bird, healed of arteriosclerotic heart disease[18]
- B. Ray Jackson, healed of carcinoma of the kidney (hypernephroma) with diffuse bony metastases[19]
- Pearl Bryant, PhD, healed of mixed rheumatoid arthritis and osteoarthritis[20]
- Anne Soults, healed of a probable brain tumor[21]
- Paul Trousdale, instantly healed of massive gastrointestinal hemorrhage with shock[22]
- Delores Winder, healed of osteoporosis of the entire spine with intractable pain requiring bilateral cordotomies[23]

Dr. Casdorph consulted at least nine other named doctors and medical researchers to verify the diagnoses noted in his book.[24]

The spiritual context of the healings is significant. Here I take as examples just the last two cases mentioned. In December 1973, the stool of well-known businessman Paul Trousdale[25] was jet black and his blood count very low despite multiple transfusions. But John Hinkle, pastor of the church Trousdale had recently begun attending, came to the hospital and prayed for him with great confidence. Trousdale says that he suddenly saw Jesus on his other side, who took his other hand. Equally suddenly, he felt better and asked to be sent home. The hospital naturally ran tests on him. They not only discovered that he was no longer bleeding but that they could not locate any source for the previous hemorrhage. Trousdale committed himself more fully to Christ.

What makes several of Casdorph's other cases surprising, including the book's final case, is their connection with Kathryn Kuhlman. In the introduction, I warned that this book would not discuss many healing evangelists. Because of prior publications medically documenting healings surrounding Kuhlman, however, she constitutes one of the few exceptions. Although I did not begin my original study of miracles skeptical about miracles per se, I did begin skeptical of Kuhlman. Yet, while many seekers who attended her meetings were not healed, as Kuhlman herself recognized, significant cures did occur in the context of her ministry.

Casdorph's final chapter deals with Delores Winder. Winder's osteoporosis and consequent disabling pain led to five spinal surgeries and pain treatment often reserved for terminal cancer patients, which failed to control all her pain. For some fourteen years, she wore either a brace or a full-body cast; she was told that she was dying. Casdorph notes that his medical records on Winder are "an inch thick."[26] At a friend's urging, she attended a Methodist conference about the Holy Spirit on August 30, 1975. She was stunned to feel something like fire in her legs when Kathryn Kuhlman began praying from the front of the auditorium; Winder had been unable to feel her legs since her cordotomies. (Cordotomies seek to destroy the tracts of the spinal cord that conduct feelings of pain to the brain.)

But Winder did not believe in instant healing, and as Kuhlman began ministering, Winder turned to leave. As she did, a man approached who seemed to discern that something unusual was happening to her, and she found that she was able to remove the cast. The man was Dr. Richard Owellen of the Johns Hopkins medical school, one of Kuhlman's medical advisers.[27] Not only was Winder healed, to her astonishment, but even her nerves that had been medically interrupted to control pain now functioned normally. She was able to continue her life without braces, medication, or numbness.

Perhaps more dramatic are some accounts in secular investigative reporter Allen Spraggett's *Kathryn Kuhlman*. Spraggett is no apologist for orthodox Christianity; he tries to explain the healings that took place in terms of parapsychology, and he has denounced most other healing evangelists. Yet he and others (including Kuhlman's biographer, Jamie Buckingham) cite doctors' eyewitness reports of instant and public healings in Kuhlman's meetings.

Although these accounts do not reproduce their medical documentation, as does Casdorph's book, they do report the testimony of doctors who were firsthand witnesses of healings:

- Dr. Cecil Titus, on staff at a Cleveland hospital, claimed that he witnessed, at close range, a ten-year-old's clubfoot instantly straighten during prayer.[28]
- Dr. James Blackann witnessed spastic conditions and large cysts vanish in front of him and people crippled with arthritis set free.[29]
- Dr. Kitman Au, a radiologist in Burbank, California, is quoted by a newspaper as witnessing in Kuhlman's meetings "healings . . . that . . . go beyond human power."[30]
- Spinal specialist Dr. Martin Biery witnessed frozen spines suddenly achieve full mobility.[31]
- Dr. Richard Owellen of Johns Hopkins University observed in amazement as the dislocated hip of his own baby, cradled in his arms, shifted until it was fully healed during a healing service.[32]
- Dr. Viola Frymann witnessed children being healed of paralysis and blindness.[33]
- Dr. E. B. Henry was healed of a false joint and hearing difficulties.[34]
- Dr. Robert Hoyt in 1969 witnessed the sudden and miraculous healing of an eye.[35]
- More recently, Dr. Raquel Burgos testified about her own medically documented healing as a child. Her short leg grew two inches to match her other leg days after she attended one of Kuhlman's meetings; because she had been seeing an orthopedist, she says, she has medical records verifying her claim.[36]

These are simply samples of healings evaluated by doctors; some other samples appear in subsequent chapters. As noted at the beginning of this chapter, healings did not end in the twentieth century.

Chapter 13

Some Medically Attested Twenty-First-Century Cures

Healings continue to occur, as the cases in this chapter suggest. The examples in this chapter include a healing of an incurable stomach condition (severe gastroparesis), a cardiologist's multiple experiences witnessing extraordinary healings, and summaries of many other reports of healing. Some other medically attested twenty-first-century cures appear in the appropriate topical chapters regarding healings of blindness, deafness, and so forth.

Gastroparesis

This case study of gastroparesis was unusual enough that it made it into a medical journal.[1] At the age of two weeks, Chris Gunderson was vomiting profusely. Medical tests at the hospital confirmed a diagnosis of gastroparesis, which required the installation of feeding tubes. Gastroparesis hinders the stomach from emptying properly. While medical technology can treat the symptoms of idiopathic gastroparesis, the condition is lifelong and cannot be cured.[2] When Chris was eleven months old, surgeons inserted a Roux-en-Y limb—something like an artificial tube to reroute stomach emptying. For the next sixteen years, Chris was entirely dependent on feeding through the attached jejunostomy tube.

He recounts, "Growing up being an active child, it was difficult to get the hydration and nutrition necessary with a drip feeding process."[3] Divine healing was not an option the family considered, since they and their church believed that miracles had ceased. On November 6, 2011, however, they visited a Pentecostal church in Oregon. The person speaking, Bruce Van Natta, had himself been miraculously healed of a life-threatening abdominal condition, in a story I will recount in chapter 22. As Van Natta spoke, Chris experienced an unusual feeling in his abdomen and realized that God was getting him ready for something. In his heart, Chris promised that if God healed him, he would let everyone know about it.

After the service, Chris spoke with Van Natta, and the two bonded over their common experiences of multiple surgeries. Van Natta invited the entire family to join them, and they gathered around. Van Natta explained that he had no authority of his own to heal, but that he was calling on the authority of Jesus's name. He laid his hands on Chris's shoulders.

Chris shared with me what happened next.[4] Two or three minutes into the prayer, he felt something like electricity from his right shoulder shooting into his abdomen, as if God was jump-starting his stomach with the shock. He bent over, so Van Natta checked to see whether he was okay. Chris was, so Van Natta said they would continue praying for the moment, since they were not finished yet. As the prayer continued, Chris kept feeling a "pulsing" or "contraction sensation" in his abdomen. After a total of five to seven minutes of prayer, they finished.

That night, Chris ate his first meal orally without complications. He continued to eat orally in the months that followed. His primary care physician, who was also his gastroenterologist, could think of no medical explanation for this resolution of symptoms, but noted that if the situation continued for several months, Chris's tubes could be permanently removed. Finally, four months after the healing, the tubes were surgically removed. As already mentioned, his healing has been written up as a case study in a medical journal.[5]

"Since I have been healed of my illness, I have had more energy than ever before, and have thoroughly enjoyed the new adventure of trying all different types of foods," Chris testifies. More than six years later, Chris remains well. At the time we talked, he had been working as a nurse in an ICU for two and a half years. Because of everything he has been through, he wanted to work in health care, "to give back for all the great care I have received, and also to give people hope."[6]

Healing Gifts, Natural and Supernatural

Though I do cite other such published cases in various chapters (such as an article attesting healing after twelve years of blindness in chap. 17, and another attesting healings of blindness and deafness in chap. 23), busy doctors write up only a minority of unusual cases for medical journals. Nevertheless, cases attested by medical evidence and by doctors' eyewitness testimony abound.

Florida cardiologist Chauncey Crandall acknowledges that most people are not immediately healed, yet once he added prayer to his medical expertise, he began to witness cures far exceeding his expectations based on his past medical experience alone. He prayed with fairly little faith for a man whose lung cancer had metastasized to his brain; all the man's tumors vanished after minimal treatment.[7] A forehead tumor for which Dr. Crandall prayed vanished within a day.[8] He offers eyewitness accounts of a disabled woman, man, and child each instantly cured during prayer; of a child's deafness instantly cured during prayer;[9] and of the full recovery of a dying woman whose organs had been shutting down.[10] Another woman's large, inoperable tumor disappeared spontaneously after prayer, and CT-scan results attested the quick healing of a man's inoperably large lung tumor after prayer.[11]

Dr. Crandall has seen the deaf healed (though especially outside the West) and those unable to walk suddenly gain that ability.[12] One Thursday, a man whom Crandall had known for many years came to his office.[13] Crandall had not seen this man in six months, and during that time the patient had developed a grapefruit-sized, flesh-eating ulcer on his leg. The wound had reached the bone, eating through the calf muscles. Treatments had failed, and he was scheduled to have his leg amputated the next week. The family had come to Dr. Crandall for a second opinion. He concurred with the other doctors: the wound was incurable. Nevertheless, he would pray. After unwrapping the leg, he placed his hand inside the wound and prayed for the wound to be healed. He then wrapped the leg up and confessed, "I've done what *I* can do; the rest is up to God." Four days later the man's wife called, noting that the ulcer was melting away and new skin was forming. Should they amputate the leg anyway? she wondered. Because a miracle was clearly taking place, he advised against that. By the following week, the man's leg was completely whole.

"Can that happen on its own?" I probed in an interview.

"It can't happen on its own," Dr. Crandall replied, sounding astonished at my medical naivete. "Impossible."

Not everyone is healed, but Crandall has seen so many miracles since he began praying for patients that he cannot doubt their reality.[14] During the year before our interview, he had been keeping notes on the cases.[15]

Broken Ankle

Carl Cocherell belongs to a Baptist church pastored by my friend and former academic colleague Dr. John Piippo. In March 2006, after a spiritual retreat in Branson, Missouri, Cocherell was checking the oil in his car when he stepped down and felt a sharp crack. Although he is a Vietnam veteran, he says that he had never felt such pain, and he fainted. X-rays at the emergency room in the Branson hospital revealed such a serious break of the ankle that after setting the break the orthopedist ordered him to stay overnight. During that night, though, Cocherell recounts that he experienced a voice from the Lord assuring him that his foot was not broken. The doctor put his foot in a cast and warned him that he would need months of therapy, referring him to his family physician.

Cocherell's wife drove them back to Michigan, and the next day his family doctor sent him to the hospital for more X-rays. After receiving the X-rays, his doctor called him into the office and explained that there were no breaks, or even tissue indicating where the break had been. "You never had a broken ankle," the doctor insisted. Cocherell pointed out the X-rays from Missouri. "*That* is a broken ankle," the doctor admitted. But now there was no sign that Cocherell had even had one, so the doctor removed the cast right away. The ankle was blue for a couple of days, but Cocherell had no further problems with it. At church that Sunday, where he used no crutches or other support, he testified about how God had healed him. Cocherell provided me with the radiology reports from before and after the healing, supporting his claim.[16]

Sampling Many More Reports

Who can adequately "declare all the LORD's acts of power?" (Ps. 106:2). The author of the Fourth Gospel notes that he included only samples of Jesus's miracles sufficient to invite faith (John 20:30–31), hyperbolically adding that the world itself could not contain accounts of all of Jesus's acts (21:25).[17] The same could be said of Jesus's works today.

Various other doctors have shared their reports of healings in theistic contexts:[18]

- Dr. Debra Gussman had removed both of a patient's fallopian tubes because of successive ectopic pregnancies. Tests confirmed this, and yet two years later the patient experienced a normal pregnancy and a healthy baby. The patient regarded this as miraculous, and Dr. Gussman testifies that "I couldn't disagree."[19]
- Dr. Jeannie Lindquist notes that a patient was healed of kidney failure through prayer.[20]
- Dr. Raquel Burgos testifies of her own medically documented healing as a child.[21]
- Dr. Alex Abraham, a neurologist, reports cures of severe epilepsy, tumors, heart failure, and other serious conditions.[22]
- Dr. Mirtha Venero Boza provides an eyewitness report of a severe burn that healed during prayer.[23]
- Dr. Tonye Briggs attests as an eyewitness to the dramatic closing of a massive wound overnight after prayer (see chap. 22).[24]
- Dr. David Zaritzky documents the cure of a middle-aged patient who had suffered for several years with Sjogren's syndrome, a currently incurable autoimmune disorder. The woman neither produced saliva nor was expected

to ever be able to produce it. After prayer, and without medication, her mouth began producing saliva.[25]

- Dr. William Wilson, professor emeritus in psychiatry and behavioral sciences at Duke University, notes the healing, after three hours of prayer, of a Methodist pastor friend of his, who had previously had "75% occlusion of his major arteries."[26]
- Wilson also reports that a nurse was healed of her depression and the asthma she had suffered from for thirty years when he prayed. He also reports a healing of severe ankylosing spondylitis, among other accounts.[27]
- Dr. William Standish Reed reports cures of metastasized cancers.[28]
- Dr. Christopher Woodard testified to a number of inexplicable healings after prayer, which he believed to be divine healings.[29]
- Dr. Ronda Wells reports that a critically ill baby experienced an extraordinary recovery within five minutes after prayer.[30]
- Feeling consistently urged by the Spirit, Dr. Dave Walker prayed for Tessa, a comatose toddler who had swallowed insecticide. Although he felt awkward in his prayer, within ten minutes "Tessa opened her eyes, sat up and said she was thirsty," "completely healed in an instant" and with "no after-effects whatsoever."[31]
- Dr. David Kimberlin celebrated the inexplicable (though progressive) recovery of a patient named Casey and especially her family's deep faith. Scans showed that fungus had "burrowed over seven inches into [Casey's] brain," so that "she should have died or at the very least been severely brain-damaged." Yet not only did the fungus simply vanish, but her leukemia went into remission. She never showed signs of brain damage.[32]
- At age forty, Australian radiologist Ginney MacPherson had never been able to conceive. At that time, Ken Fish prayed with her, and, with no medical intervention, she soon became pregnant. After that child was born, she again was unable to conceive for two years, so she invited Fish to pray again, after which she had twins.[33]

Sometimes some factors add more to the miraculous verdict than others. Dr. Kathleen Farrell reports the case of an "entirely nonresponsive" two-year-old whose lungs were "completely filled by fluid"; the child had fallen into the deep end of a pool and inhaled the water. Yet the next day this child was playing as normal, and a new X-ray showed "no traces of fluid," a rapid recovery that Dr. Farrell would normally deem "impossible."

Yet she reports another factor that, for most of us, confirms this restoration as miraculous. It was the toddler's five-year-old cousin, who herself did not know how to swim, who rescued her. She brought the victim from the bottom of the deep end of the pool to the surface of the shallow end. When asked why she did this, the five-year-old responded immediately, "The man all dressed in white told me to." Afterward one of the doctors suggested wryly that the medical staff should get the family swimming lessons so they wouldn't have to depend on angels the next time someone fell into the pool![34]

Nor is it the case that doctors who report these experiences necessarily reflect a faith bias, though naturally people of faith are often more ready to recognize such occurrences as miraculous. Dr. Richard Westcott, an atheist, recounted an event in the *British Medical Journal* and reflected further on it a decade later in an article for a book on medical miracles. His patient Jim was a nonreligious man with metastasized mesothelioma, a lung cancer related to asbestos exposure, which had spread throughout much of Jim's abdomen. To the surprise of both doctor and patient, after the unexpected ministry of a nun and a priest in a Greek Orthodox monastery that Jim visited as a tourist, Jim's strength immediately began returning, and tests revealed that the tumor had completely (and permanently) vanished.[35] Dr. Westcott concludes, "A couple without religious faith . . . and their atheist doctor [that is, Westcott himself] had to face the question: If not this, what *is* a miracle?"[36]

Doctors differ among themselves as to what, if anything, they would call a miracle. The question for you as a reader is what *you* would consider a miracle. I hope that by this point in the book you have recognized quite a few. Chapters recounting cures of blindness (chaps. 16–17), deafness (chap. 23), and death (chaps. 24–31), for example, should provide some more.

Chapter 14

Cancer Cures

I deal in this book only briefly with cancer cures, because cancers sometimes do go into remission, and because nearly all cases that have medical documentation have it because the patient underwent medical treatment. (This is as it should be. It would be unethical to have patients under medical observation while withholding available treatment that might prove beneficial.)

At the same time, spontaneous cures of most kinds of cancer are quite rare if the cancer has metastasized—that is, if it has spread to other organs.[1] Some of the following cases (such as that of Lisa Larios, those of the Lourdes records, the pancreatic cases, and, in the following chapter, that of Ruth Lindberg) are stronger than some others, for which fewer records are available (such as that of William Burton). All are, however, merely samples of the many reports of cancer healing today.[2] Healing testimonies are frequent enough that even an older friend of mine from the church small group that meets in my home celebrated one recently, although the healing happened during an early stage of cancer.[3]

Cancer in Earlier Times

The Gospels' reports of healings that witnesses see and hear (Matt. 11:4–5//Luke 7:22) do not specify cancer healings, for natural reasons. First, most internal cancers are not visible. Second, ancient Galileans probably thought more in terms of symptoms (such as skin growths or inability to walk) than in terms of the diseases that we label "cancer" today. Although a Greek medical term related to cancer existed,[4] it was not likely known to ordinary Galileans. Third, osteoarchaeologists have surveyed ancient bones and argued that cancer was much less common before the sixteenth century. Today it is the leading cause of death next to heart disease; many medical historians believe that it was much rarer in antiquity.[5]

Although cancer might not have been identified as such in antiquity, it was certainly widespread and greatly feared in much of the twentieth century. Examples of reported cures could be multiplied, but one will suffice here. Historian David Emmett shared with me information about British missionary William Burton, some of whose reports about other miracles appeared in my previous miracles book. Enough correspondence from Burton's circle survives to inspire confidence that he was expected to die, barring a miracle. Burton, who was serving in Congo, doubled over with abdominal pains in February 1944. Burton noted that barium X-rays showed his colon to be seriously obstructed, with waste backing up. Further X-rays in a Johannesburg hospital revealed the rapid development of growths in his colon, and in May doctors performed a cecostomy to drain waste products. They informed Burton's wife that cancer had spread throughout his colon and gave him a maximum of six months to live. Burton reports the verdict of the hospital register: "Mr. Burton was discharged from the hospital at his own request in a dying condition."

Enough correspondence survives to underline the seriousness of these expectations. In various letters to friends, Burton noted the doctors' assessment that he had less than a year to live. Nevertheless, he expressed hope that God would hear the prayers of Congolese believers and enable his ministry to continue.[6] He "continued to wear a cup and rubber bag . . . to receive the waste products" from his body. Six months after his operation, in January 1945 he returned to his ministry in Congo. A public prayer request soon after noted that he was expected to die in June.[7] His fellow missionaries grew increasingly concerned, and by May a colleague noted both his weakness and his extreme pain,[8] while another prayer request recounted that he was "very frail and thin."[9]

Soon after this, however, he began to improve. In July he reported that, fifteen months after his diagnosis, his bowel and bladder were functioning normally.[10] He reported that he was examined again in May 1946, in a hospital in Luanshya, Northern Rhodesia (now Zambia). There, "further X-ray examination revealed no evidence at all of cancer." He reported that the physicians in Johannesburg deemed his recovery miraculous, and he preserved two sample X-rays—one from the beginning of his condition and one from after his recovery. Although these two surviving X-ray images are not by themselves sufficient to say more today than that his colon was severely impaired in the former picture and healthy in the latter one, the surgeries to place and close the ostomy should have allowed his doctors to make correct assessments. Burton returned to his full schedule and lived until 1971, dying at the age of about eighty-five after decades of effective ministry in Congo, where he reported many miracles, most faster than this one.[11]

Metastasized Cancer of the Hip

By May 1972, twelve-year-old Lisa Larios could no longer walk, and tests showed that she was dying from cancer (more specifically, reticulum cell sarcoma of the right pelvic bone).[12] By the time doctors discovered the hip-socket tumor, a physician notes, it had already "invaded the soft tissues of the interior of the pelvis."[13] Multiple doctors confirmed the diagnosis. Because the cancer had spread so far, doctors grimly warned Lisa's parents that even amputation from the hip down could no longer save her. Although Lisa was expected to live only six more months, her parents had not yet informed her that her condition was terminal. Instead, they took her on various trips, hoping that she could enjoy her remaining months of life.

A neighbor insisted on taking Lisa to a healing meeting, but Lisa's mother, Isabel, was reluctant. Lisa still did not know how sick she was. If they took her to such a meeting, would it frighten her? Although the family was Catholic, they had not even considered the possibility of a miracle. Lisa's father, Javier, however, suggested that they had nothing to lose. So Isabel brought Lisa on July 16.

During the time of prayer for healing, the minister called out that someone in Lisa's section was being healed of cancer. Isabel did not think this was a good time to inform Lisa that she had cancer. Lisa, however, experienced a warm sensation in her stomach. Feeling an overwhelming urge, she abruptly stood up. Then she began to walk up and down the aisle—because she could. Isabel was stunned; the doctor had warned her not to let Lisa put any pressure on the hip bone. "Her hip is just like butter," he had explained.

Lisa still did not know about the cancer, but she knew that she was now able to walk, and she went up on stage with her neighbor. The minister, unaware that there was no hip bone, urged, "Run, honey!" and Lisa ran back and forth across the stage. Isabel still did not know what to make of it and did not want her daughter to have false hope. Nevertheless, they left the auditorium with Lisa walking. When they reached home, Lisa started riding her bike, and Javier realized that she had been healed. Isabel remained more cautious, deciding to wait for the medical results.

The medical results took a little while. The doctors at the hospital were initially confused and gave Lisa every test possible, consulting with more and more physicians. Not only was the cancer gone, but the bone damage that the cancer had caused was gone—a restoration that was impossible naturally. (Richard Casdorph, MD, PhD, a widely published medical school professor, includes the before-and-after X-rays in his earlier-mentioned book, *The Miracles: A Medical Doctor Says Yes to Miracles!*) Lisa's recovery, then, could not have been only on a psychosomatic level, even if she *had* known the nature of her condition.

After carefully examining the medical records, Dr. Casdorph agreed to go on *The Mike Douglas Show* with Lisa and her mother, Isabel, equipped with Lisa's X-rays. After a meeting the night before in one of the hotel's dining rooms, they decided to return to their rooms on the sixteenth floor. Casdorph attests that Lisa eagerly took the stairs all the way up.[14]

Although Casdorph's accounts provide fairly extensive details regarding Lisa Larios's healing, reports of bone restoration after prayer are not unique to this case.[15] For example, in another report, multiple spinal fractures that were evident on a CT scan were, after prayer, no longer evident on MRI reports soon afterward, even though the disease that originally led to the problem had to be treated medically.[16] Another report concerns a four-year-old with an inch-long hole in his skull, where the bone had been eaten away by a tumor; two months later, not only was the tumor gone, but bone had grown and completely closed the cavity.[17]

Pancreatic Cancers

Cancer of the pancreas is one of the deadliest cancers. Even with today's technology, depending on the stage at which the cancer is identified (usually late), the one-year survival rate is 20 percent; the five-year survival rate is 7 percent. On July 2, 2003, the Mälar Hospital in Eskilstuna, Sweden, diagnosed Bengt Eriksson with stage 4 pancreatic cancer, for which the survival prognosis at the time was usually three to six months. Eriksson's pancreas itself contained a four-centimeter tumor, but the cancer had also metastasized to the liver and blocked Eriksson's bile duct. Eriksson's doctors began palliative treatment but warned that he probably would not survive until Christmas.[18]

The clogged bile duct turned Eriksson's skin yellow, and he developed itchy rashes. Because the palliative chemotherapy made him feel worse and was not meant to save his life in the long run anyway, after six weeks he refused further treatment. Because Eriksson was a well-respected leader in his local community, many people were praying for him: pastors, priests, neighbors, and other municipal politicians.

Eriksson was called to the hospital after another CT scan; he went in expecting news of swelling because he had discontinued the chemotherapy treatment. Instead, he reports that his chief physician, Johan Raud, looked uncertain, showing him the plates. "There's no trace of the cancer now," Dr. Raud noted. "You know, Bengt, we doctors can't explain everything." The same, of course, is true for theologians, but sometimes the two forms of discourse can supplement each other.

Eriksson wondered whether his doctors had misdiagnosed him, prescribing the nauseating chemotherapy unnecessarily, but the doctors maintained that the original diagnosis was clearly correct. One of the doctors who had treated him described the healing as a "miracle." Dr. Raud noted that there was no medical explanation. Still, mysteries remain. A few years later, Eriksson's oldest daughter passed away from cancer. After her death Eriksson was sure that she was in heaven, but he could not understand why she had died and he had been spared.

Similarly, at the age of seventy-five, John Margosian was diagnosed in 1984 with an inoperable pancreatic tumor, which had grown around the inferior vena cava and the abdominal aorta. Dr. Dennis Cope, the endocrinologist who first diagnosed Margosian, was a noted professor on the faculty of internal medicine at UCLA. Cope notes that doctors treated Margosian with chemotherapy and radiation only to prevent further growth of the tumor. He was expected to die within three months.

Many people, including inmates at the Chino Prison where Margosian had ministered, were praying for him. Instead of being healed initially, Margosian contracted spinal meningitis, which was expected to kill him or leave him in a vegetative state. He fully recovered, however, and the doctors discovered that his tumor had disappeared. He returned to ministry in the prison and lived till age ninety-one. Dr. Cope concluded that this was "very definitely" a miracle: "There is no human explanation for what happened."[19]

Stage 4B Burkitt's Lymphoma

Brian Wills knew what the Bible said about healing, and he had grown up in a church where he often witnessed healings. But his commitment to that belief was about to be sorely tested. Wills, who had been a skilled college athlete in Missouri, had since become an assistant coach at the University of Richmond. He seemed the epitome of health when sudden pains forced him to undergo medical testing. On February 6, 1987, his despondent doctor had to communicate unpleasant news: "Brian has a mass in his abdomen the size of a golf ball, which has been diagnosed as Burkitt's lymphoma."[20]

Today the survival prognosis for Burkitt's lymphoma is relatively high, but Wills's cancer was much further along than the cases usually diagnosed today, and it was growing rapidly. Only days after the initial diagnosis, Wills reports that the aggressive tumor was nearly ten inches wide. This was not merely stage 4 cancer, but stage 4B. A specialist lamented, "I don't think there's anything I can do for you. You're too far gone."[21] Wills continued to insist that God would heal him, but his cancer metastasized to most of his organs, and even he was shaken when a doctor predicted that he had fewer than ten hours to live.[22]

Yet Wills felt that God spoke to him, instructing him to start by forgiving someone against whom he had harbored anger. A few hours after he did so, the night-shift nurse noticed that his kidney had begun working again. He continued to improve, so the doctor tried a pre-dose of chemotherapy to see how his body would respond. Whether God used the pre-dose or not, something certainly happened in Wills's body. On February 20, less than a month after his diagnosis, his doctor seemed confused. The radiologist report showed no evidence of cancer in any of his organs. The original tumor had completely disappeared. To lower the likelihood of recurrence, a doctor placed Wills and other patients on a harsh experimental regimen—which apparently only Wills survived. Whether God worked through, aside from, or in spite of this regimen, Wills has remained cancer-free.

Brain Tumors

Mathew John reports that he had a six-centimeter brain tumor, revealed by biopsies to be cancerous. It grew behind his left eye until he became mostly blind in that eye. An operation on December 1, 1998, removed two centimeters of the tumor, but the rest was too deeply embedded. After a difficult month of radiation treatment, during which some of his vision returned, he returned to work. Six months later, however, he felt compelled to leave his job and submit to God's different calling for him. As John prepared to board a flight to begin Bible training, his vision suddenly returned more fully, although an MRI shortly afterward showed that four centimeters of the tumor remained. John underwent training and carried on with ministry, and in June 2006, as John navigated another serious health crisis, MRIs revealed that barely any of the tumor remained.[23]

After seven-year-old Tim Nowak suffered an apparent stroke, a CT scan showed an egg-sized tumor on his brain stem.[24] The next day, however, Tim's father, Dave, felt an uncanny assurance that God was taking care of the matter. The MRI that followed found no tumor, malignant or benign, leaving doctors scrambling to figure out what could have caused the stroke. A few days later, one physician confided to Dave, "I've looked at Tim's records, and this is a miracle." But she warned, "You're going to find resistance from the other doctors. They don't believe. They're trying to find something wrong." After six days of futile efforts, however, the staff recognized that nothing was wrong with Tim and sent him home.

The Nowaks' physician in Wyoming, where they moved, examined Tim's forty pages of records from the previous hospital. This doctor, a Christian, concluded that a miracle had taken place. Since his new machine had not been tested yet, he offered to provide another CT scan; this time the radiologist, though unaware of Tim's history, discerned apparent scar tissue in the location of the previous tumor. Ten years after the apparent stroke, Tim remains healthy and active.

Some of my own friends report somewhat similar experiences, although without biopsies to prove malignancy (in some cases because surgery would have been too dangerous). Carol, a colleague at my previous institution, was diagnosed in fall 1998 with a brain tumor the size of a large cherry. After special prayer, the tumor began shrinking and disappeared entirely within about eight months.[25] A science professor I know has also shared his experience of healing from a brain tumor in writing.[26]

Stage 4 Cancer in Ukraine

Frederick Ankai-Taylor, a Ghanaian pastor in Vinnitsa, Ukraine, not only has theological training but also is a medical doctor trained in the former Soviet Union. When his church prays for the sick, they require medical verification of a change in the condition prayed for before allowing persons healed to testify, several months to a year later.

Pastor Ankai-Taylor acknowledges that not everyone prayed for gets healed, but he shared with me various accounts of healings from his church that he could verify on the basis of the documentation provided before testimonies were allowed. He reports the healing of tumors, cancers, endocrine disorders, mental disorders, and other conditions. For example, in 2002 he prayed for a woman from Russia with stage 4, metastatic cancer. She was unable to walk, but when he prayed for her, she walked, completely healed. She lived for ten more years before dying from unrelated causes.[27]

Esophageal Cancer in Minnesota

Minnesota Lutheran pastor Mark Mathews shared with me a number of accounts of healings from advanced stages of cancer. For example, Billy Halme had advanced esophageal cancer, and doctors said there was nothing more they could do for him. He had stopped all treatment in hopes of an improved quality of life for his remaining days. When Mark prayed for him in April 2016, Billy and his wife, Carol, felt God's power. Billy's next CT scan, soon afterward, showed that the cancer had disappeared. His most recent CT scan, on September 10, 2020, continued to show no cancer, although he passed two months later from a stroke.[28]

Healings at Lourdes

Cancer healings have also taken place at Lourdes. A clear case of Hodgkin's disease was cured on May 31, 1950: the pilgrim who was healed felt warmth, and all traces of the disease were gone from his body. The original diagnosis of the disease cannot be disputed, because "the original histological specimens have been repeatedly and thoroughly reviewed."[29]

Repeated X-rays in July 1962 confirmed that a sarcoma had eaten away most of the left hemipelvis of Italian soldier Vittorio Micheli. Histological, radiological, and other evidence was certain. By November, "the left leg was joined to the pelvis by a few sheaves of soft tissue, no bone." Not surprisingly, Micheli could not move the leg. He visited Lourdes on May 24, 1963, still requiring pain medicine and unable to walk. On June 1, he was lowered into the bath and felt that he was healed. He was hungry immediately and did not need pain medicine anymore. Without pain, he began to walk with crutches, though the plaster cast doctors had earlier placed on his leg remained.[30]

In February 1964, when doctors removed the plaster cast, Micheli walked normally, still without pain. Subsequent X-rays showed that "the bony reconstruction of the parts destroyed was progressing steadily"—something that should not happen naturally.[31] That is, his pelvic bone was regenerating. Despite faint scars, the tissue's restoration was even more complete than is usual in patients after surgical interventions.[32] Many orthopedic surgeons were consulted who had dealt with bone cancer; none had "encountered a case of spontaneous cure of a malignant tumour of the bone."[33]

Twelve-year-old Delizia Cirolli was dying from Ewing's sarcoma when she visited Lourdes for four days in August 1976. Unfortunately, no miracle occurred there, and after she returned to Sicily her condition declined further. Her community continued to pray, however, and in December she started recovering. Her condition returned to and remained normal, with X-rays showing her bone repaired. On the basis of specimens from the original biopsy, multiple French experts on bone tumors confirmed the diagnosis of Ewing's sarcoma, for which spontaneous remissions were not known to occur.[34]

Lourdes pilgrim Mademoiselle Delot's cancer was spreading, and physicians had given her up to die. At a point near death, she was instantly cured; even her damaged organs regenerated properly.[35] Similarly, an investigative reporter expresses his confidence in his interview of a woman who had been diagnosed as having "an inoperable malignancy located between her pulmonary artery and her heart" and had been told she had six months to live. She was cured during her second time bathing in the water at Lourdes. She informed the reporter that about sixty cures had been reported in the half year before his visit; one case involved the instant healing of a man whose cancer had eaten away "most of his hip bone," and she showed the reporter the X-rays confirming the full restoration of the bone.[36]

////////////

Doctors can treat many forms of cancer today, and spontaneous remissions are known to occur. They are sometimes estimated as happening in roughly one case out of sixty thousand (depending on the type of cancer).[37] But at advanced stages, when cancer has spread throughout the body, cures are rarer than at early stages. Yet not only do we have random accounts of such cures, but often we see an accumulation of cases from particular circles.[38] The stories above help illustrate what some Christians mean when they claim that God has healed them from cancer in ways beyond normal medical expectations.

Chapter 15

Doctors Cured of Cancer

Psychiatrist Wanda Półtawska had survived imprisonment in a Nazi concentration camp only to discover in 1962 that she was dying of terminal cancer. Her doctor, a personal friend, hoped that surgery could add two or three years to her otherwise-expected longevity of just eighteen more months. Polish bishop Karol Wojtyła, the future Pope John Paul II, meanwhile solicited prayer from a friend, Padre Pio, for this mother of four young girls.

The operation found no tumor. For some time, Dr. Półtawska, not inclined to supernatural explanations, simply assumed that she was among the 5 percent of cancer patients whose tumors were thought to disappear. In May 1967, however, she visited Padre Pio unannounced. He recognized her before she announced who she was. "Are you all right now?" he asked. By 1988, she had concluded that God had graciously healed her and had been patient about waiting for her to realize it.[1]

I focus this chapter, however, on the story of family physician Ruth Lindberg, which she has also made available online.[2] Her blog during her ordeal, also available online, documents her emotions and prayers as she sought healing. In what follows, I condense and adapt her own words from the online version.

Dismal Diagnosis

Ruth became a follower of Jesus when she was a chemistry major at Loyola University Chicago. She and her husband both became family physicians and chose to work especially among particularly needy people, first in an underserved area in Tennessee and then for four years in Nepal. But in October 2013, when they were back in the US, Ruth began to have extreme abdominal pains. A CT scan revealed many abdominal masses and enlarged lymph nodes. Biopsies confirmed cancer, which was spreading so aggressively that her oncologist confessed that her survival appeared uncertain. She was thirty-five years old.

After a month of concerted chemotherapy and prayer, a new CT scan revealed no cancer at all. A few months after Ruth completed chemotherapy, however, endometrial cancer (cancer of the uterus) was discovered, rare as this is among young women. The earlier cancer had apparently resurfaced in another organ. Despite successful surgery in November 2014, cancer again resurfaced in April 2015, this time near her lung. She laments, "This cancer would just not go away. We could not escape. I was scared, confused, and angry at God." This was not a localized cancer but one that had metastasized. Moreover, each time cancer returns after an apparent remission, the odds of a permanent cure diminish. "As a physician," she recounts, "I knew what this recurrence meant for my prognosis. Hope was slipping away."

One of Ruth's pastors felt assurance that she would be healed despite the medical evidence. Sometimes such insistence is merely denial, but the pastor remained adamant. "I sat there, numb and weary," Ruth confesses, "yet reminded by her that all hope was not lost. God was still God." Despite her confusion, she reaffirmed her trust and asked for prayer again. The pastor and another friend anointed her with oil, prayed, and reaffirmed their sense that God had already heard their prayer.

Yet Ruth knew too much about biochemistry and the normal prognosis for her stage of cancer to take their verdict on blind faith, so she quietly asked God for a special encouragement. A few days later she read Jesus's promise in Luke 11:13 that God will give the Holy Spirit to those who ask him. She cried out from the depths of her heart for a deeper experience of the Spirit.

"The Holy Spirit suddenly, unexpectedly knocked me to the ground. It's difficult to explain how it felt, other than that a force outside of myself flipped me onto my back. I had never had an experience like this before, but I immediately knew that this was the sign I had asked God for."

Canceling Cancer

Meanwhile, Ruth's doctors again proposed chemotherapy. Without explaining her experience to them, she requested another CT scan. She did not feel that she could refuse chemo "without having some visible proof (for both my doctors, and to be honest, myself) that the cancer was gone."

Thus in late May 2015 she had another CT scan, just a month and a half after the previous CT scan had revealed the cancer's recurrence. One need not be a radiologist to recognize the clear difference in the two scans, which are now available as a matter of public record.[3] The cancer had vanished.

"My doctors could not explain what had happened, but were all in agreement that no treatment was now necessary, since there was nothing there to treat." Subsequent, follow-up CT scans have confirmed the absence of cancer. Ruth emphasizes that Jesus, who healed throughout Galilee and Judea two millennia ago, "is the same, yesterday, today, and forever." In 2020, she advised me on several cases in this book.

PART 4

"The Blind Receive Their Sight, the Lame Walk, the Lepers Are Cleansed, the Deaf Hear" (Matt. 11:5//Luke 7:22)

Jesus invited eyewitnesses to testify about what God was doing in his ministry: "The blind receive sight, the disabled walk, the lepers are cleansed, the deaf hear, the dead are raised, and the poor are receiving the good news" (Matt. 11:5//Luke 7:22). Why should we suppose that Jesus, now that he has all authority in heaven and on earth (Matt. 28:18), has become any less active where he is welcome? The following chapters treat some of the categories of cures that Jesus listed.

Chapter 16

Do Blind People Still Receive Sight? Witnesses

J esus invited eyewitnesses to testify about what God was doing in his ministry: "Go and let John know what you have heard and seen: The blind receive sight . . ." (Matt. 11:4–5//Luke 7:22). All the earliest Gospel accounts and sources about Jesus attest that he healed blindness, suggesting an accumulation of instances rather than a single case.[1] Remarkable as this seems, such healings continue to be reported today.

Earlier Accounts

Some extrabiblical Christian accounts of healed blindness are very ancient. Augustine and Ambrose, for example, note a public healing of blindness in June 386.[2]

Such accounts continue throughout history, including in the skeptical twentieth century. For example, a number of Anglican bishops around the world, including some who previously doubted that healing occurs today, testified to witnessing healings, including of blindness, when Anglican layman James Moore Hickson prayed. One eyewitness in Calcutta in 1921 reported, "I have seen the eyes of the blind opened immediately; one was an old man, one a child of six years of age born blind."[3] A minister in China observed, "A hospital evangelist, whose eye has for years been unsuccessfully treated by the doctor, was practically healed before the man left the Cathedral."[4] Likewise, multiple witnesses and records attest the restored sight of a blinded, nearly destroyed eye, associated with the ministry of Padre Pio in 1949.[5]

Writing half a century ago, one reporter criticized various faith healers of whom he was skeptical. Then, however, he noted more favorably how Dr. Henry Smith Lieper, previously associate general secretary of the World Council of

Churches, was healed of a medically incurable eye disorder after a Presbyterian pastor laid hands on him.[6]

Nor are healings of blindness uncommon today, although it is sadly true that, at least in most of the world, most blind people who have prayed for healing are still blind. I have surveyed hundreds of reports of healed blindness, including accounts shared with me by eyewitnesses who saw eyes white from cataracts return to a normal color during their healing.[7]

Blindness Healed in Africa

A friend, Dr. Bungishabaku Katho, shared with me his own experience of witnessing a blind woman's healing.[8] Dr. Katho is president of Shalom University in the Democratic Republic of Congo, and we were meeting to discuss other issues for which we shared a passion, such as ethnic reconciliation. But because I was then writing my first book on miracles, I asked him if he had any eyewitness accounts from Congo. His denomination there was affiliated with a Western denomination that is not known for emphasizing miracles.

Nevertheless, he did have an interesting account to share. Sixteen years earlier, he and two of his friends had been sharing Christ in a village dominated by traditional African religious practices. Hearing their message, an older man urged them to pray for his wife. He noted that neither traditional practices nor Western medicine had helped her blindness. "But Jesus is more powerful than a witch doctor!" he confessed. Katho and his friends exchanged glances uncomfortably; none of them had ever prayed for something like this before. After they discussed the matter briefly, however, they decided that this was an opportunity. They had come so that Jesus would be honored, so they began to pray that he would honor his name by healing this woman.

They had been praying for about two minutes when the woman began shouting, "I can see! I can see!" Although she was in her early sixties, she began dancing around while Katho and his friends looked on, amazed. She continued to be able to see for the rest of her life. I happened to be recounting Katho's story during my plenary address on miracles for the Institute of Biblical Research in 2014 when Dr. Katho unexpectedly walked in with another scholar. He was able to confirm the account to anyone there who asked him.

When I wrote my first miracles book, I was teaching at an interdenominational but predominantly Baptist seminary near Philadelphia. Yolanda McCain, an American student from the seminary, visited an international student from the seminary, Paul Mokake, in Cameroon in summer 2006. While there, she was shocked to witness a blind man's sight restored during an exorcism of what purported to be a spirit partly controlling his nervous system.[9]

I now teach at an interdenominational but predominantly Wesleyan and Methodist seminary in Kentucky. One of my students here, Ethan Lintemuth, reported that in March 2017 he was visiting Zambia with some friends, talking and praying with people in villages. In response to a movie they had seen about miracles, Ethan and one of his friends started discussing why they never saw any miracles. As they were expressing their skepticism, a woman came around the corner and called them to follow her. She led them to an old woman who requested prayer because she was blind. Ethan recounts what happened after this:

> Her eyes did look quite dead. So my friend and I prayed for her and we asked if anything had happened, to which they translated "No." So I thought, "Well, okay, time to go to lunch," but then my friend urged us to pray again. So we did. Then when we asked if there was improvement they said "Yes!"—to our surprise. So we prayed again, and they exclaimed, "She can see!" I looked in her eyes and they were whole, full of life. Still in disbelief, I asked, "What color is my shirt?" She answered, "Green!" My friend asked, "How many fingers am I holding up?" to which she said "Three!" Ironically, while the people who prayed for her still had some disbelief, the others were rejoicing over what God had done.[10]

Missionary Shelley Hollis shared with me that she was preaching in a Mozambican village where there were no Christians.[11] A commotion started in the back of the crowd while she was preaching, but she continued preaching until she discovered that a teenage girl had started to hear for the first time. The girl's mother brought her forward and began to testify that her daughter had begun to hear. While they were testifying, the blind right eye of a woman to Shelley's left was suddenly healed. Shelley announced that God was healing people and instructed her listeners to bring the sick. In response, they brought a paralyzed woman on a mat. The woman then got up and began to dance! None of these people, Shelley emphasized, were yet Christians, although before the night was over some five hundred people committed themselves to become followers of Christ, and a church was started the next day.

Bruce Collins is a leader in an international, interdenominational renewal group called New Wine, which was originally based in the Anglican church.[12] He told me of a young orphan in western Kenya, where his group cares for orphans. The boy was perhaps 90 percent blind: he needed to be led around and was unable to see even fingers held up in front of his face. After about ten minutes of prayer, the boy could count all ten fingers even ten meters away; after ten more minutes, he could see them thirty meters away. Bruce witnessed the healing himself, and when he returned to the orphanage that evening, he nearly wept as he saw the boy playing football (soccer) for the first time.

Outside Africa

Korean scholar Julie Ma reports that in 1975 she and some colleagues prayed for a woman in the Philippines named Kapeng Andaloy. Kapeng had previously experienced prayer for her long-term blindness and hearing problems, with no effect, and kept declaring, "There is no God." Finally, however, she allowed prayer again, and this time she was instantly healed of all the conditions. After this, Kapeng and many others in the village became Christians.[13]

Such accounts are not limited to Africa or Asia. The following chapter recounts medically documented cases from Europe and North America. Also, my friend Randy Clark, who has his doctorate of ministry from United Theological Seminary and has taught there in the doctor of ministry track in Christian healing, recounts hearing from a pastor in Goiânia, Brazil, after he took a ministry team there.[14] Despite instructions to pray as quickly as possible for individuals because so many people were seeking prayer, one woman on Randy's team kept praying for four hours for a man blinded fifty years earlier by acid in his eyes. "His eyes were white from about an eighth of an inch thickness of scar tissue that covered the entire pupil and cornea." But while six people were healed of blindness that night, this man was not, and the next day the team returned to the US. Several days later, however, Randy received an excited call from the local pastor. On the third morning after the prayer, the man suddenly awoke "with brand-new eyes and clear vision." The doctors at the hospital kept asking him how this had happened, and the pastor said this was "the greatest miracle in the history of our city!"

(Another disappearance of scar tissue, but one that I do not elaborate on here because it does not deal with eyes and because it was so widely publicized in earlier years, involves the well-known healing of Duane Miller's destroyed vocal cord nerves while he was reading Psalm 103:3: "God heals all your diseases." Miller told me that his non-Christian Jewish doctor regarded the disappearance of the scar tissue as inexplicable apart from a miracle.)[15]

In a recent book, charismatic Catholic Bob Canton shares letters he has received from people for whom he has prayed who experienced healing, in many cases of their eyesight. Tanya Michelle Avendaño from Oregon testifies that she was born blind in her left eye but could see from it after prayer. "The world looks different for me now that I can see with both eyes!"[16] For six years, Tina Sallame could not see well enough to recognize her priest apart from his voice, but after prayer she could see a stop sign a hundred yards away.[17]

Assemblies of God minister Bill Kirsch is a close friend of mine from my time in seminary. Bill shared with me the testimony he had grown up hearing of his mother's healing, and his mother, Alice, graciously shared her account with me. When Alice was about twelve years old, the eye doctor warned that her progressively deteriorating eyesight would lead to blindness. About four years later, she had trouble seeing even with her thick glasses.

When a guest evangelist was praying for the sick during a service in Zion, Illinois, Alice got up to follow others forward for prayer. As she was descending the stairs from the balcony, however, she thought, "It is God who heals, not this minister." Nevertheless, she went forward, but when the minister laid a hand on her head, he declared, "I do not need to pray for you; God has already healed your eyes." Yet as she made her way home, it was obvious to her that her eyesight was no better. The next morning when she got up and donned her thick glasses, however, everything was a blur. So she took them off and realized that she could see perfectly without them. She had in fact been healed.[18]

Cataracts Disappear

I mentioned earlier that in some cases witnesses report cataracts vanishing, something that does not occur naturally without medical intervention. One of these accounts is from my friend Tom Parrish, a Methodist district superintendent.[19] He was visiting a Pentecostal friend, Yohana Masinga, who was ministering in a rural area of Tanzania at the time. Others brought forward a man with a cane whose eyes were white. Masinga paused for a few extra moments to pray for this man and then went on praying for others, until a sudden commotion erupted. The man who had been blind started shouting in his language and running around. As he passed by Tom, he stopped momentarily; Tom, being white, stood out. Tom did not understand the local language, but he did not have to wait for his friends to translate what the man was shouting about. The man's eyes were no longer white, but looked completely normal.

Likewise, a Filipino seminarian, Chester Allan Tesoro, visited a church on the island of Mindanao that was pastored by a friend, where many miracles were being reported. Tesoro told me that he had noticed an older woman whose eyes were completely white; after the service, he suddenly heard her shouting, "I can see! I can see!" Initially she could see only light, but then she began to see color. Tesoro was able to get close enough to recognize that her eyes were no longer white but brown.[20]

Flint McGlaughlin, director of enterprise research at Cambridge's Transforming Business project, shared with me his experience of praying in northern India for a blind man with clouded eyes.[21] Robin Shields, who was also present, separately confirmed Flint's report of what happened next, as well as sharing photographs with me.[22] As the man received sight, he shouted joyfully and ran in circles; the photographs communicate his joy far better than my description could. Later, however, he began to weep as he saw children, and Robin asked why. "Because I've always heard the children's voices," he responded, "but I had never seen their faces!" The healing led to both this man and many others becoming followers of Jesus.

Iris Ministries cofounder Heidi Baker notes the first time when she "saw totally blind eyes, white from cataracts, change color and become normal and healthy."[23] In a 2012 interview with John Lathrop for the *Pneuma Review*, Baker also spoke of a blind girl named Albertina in the village of Mieze. Albertina was about twenty months old, and her eyes were completely white. In front of both local villagers and foreign visitors, "Albertina's eyes turned from white to gray and finally to beautiful dark brown. We sobbed as we watched her actually see her mother for the first time."

Don Kantel, who worked with Rolland and Heidi Baker's ministry and wrote his dissertation about it, told me, "I've seen blind eyes opened."[24] He recounts an example of this in an essay he wrote on development aid. "I was two feet from a blind man and watched his milky pupils change to a solid colour—he could suddenly see clearly."[25]

///////////

While some of these cases occurred too long ago or too far away for investigators like me to obtain medical documentation, other cases do have robust medical documentation.

Chapter 17

Do Blind People Still Receive Sight? Doctors

I begin this chapter with an account from a medical journal of a woman whose twelve years of blindness ended with a desperate prayer. I turn then to another woman whose twelve years of blindness ended with a minister's command of faith. After noting the unexpected outcome of a media investigation in Denmark, I recount briefly the healing of stroke-induced blindness over the course of four successive prayers, and the healing of blindness caused by macular degeneration during a prayer seeking mental purity. Other accounts follow.

After Twelve Years of Blindness

A medical journal recently published a case study of blindness healed during prayer; I condense here the experience recounted there by Clarissa Romez and her colleagues.[1] In 1959, at the age of eighteen, Patience (not her real name)[2] suddenly lost vision in her left eye over a two- or three-day period. About three months later, she experienced the same loss in her right eye. Examination revealed that her sight was now 7/200 (less than 20/400) in each eye, and evidence of organic macular degeneration rules out a purely psychosomatic or psychogenic explanation. "The fundus exam showed . . . a dense yellowish-white area of atrophy in each fovea associated with a central scotoma in both eyes."[3] Doctors concluded that Patience had experienced a severe case of juvenile macular degeneration,[4] a condition that even today is not medically curable.

This condition persisted over the following decade. An examination on January 29, 1971, noted that even with correction Patience's right eye's vision "could

99

be slightly improved" only to 20/400. Lateral deviation in her eyes was consistent with adult loss of vision, so she was enrolled for three months in training for the blind, including in reading braille.

One evening in August 1972, Patience and her husband, who were members of a Baptist church, were praying together before retiring for bed. Although they knew about miracles in the Bible, they were not familiar with anyone who had experienced dramatic healing in their circle of acquaintances. Overwhelmed by the Spirit, however, Patience's husband cried out, while touching his wife, "Oh God! You can restore . . . eyesight tonight, Lord. I know you can do it! And I pray you will do it." Immediately, as Patience opened her eyes, she could see for the first time in nearly thirteen years.

The next medical documentation comes later, in June 1974. Examinations revealed that Patience's sight was now 20/100 in each eye—an "increase of more than 400%." In 2001, when Patience prepared to get new glasses, her eyesight with correction was 20/40 in each eye; another exam in 2013 found the same. The only problems in her eyes were those normal for a woman of her age (seventy-two). "To date," Romez notes, "her eyesight has remained intact for forty-seven years with only common age-related eye problems since the healing."[5]

The article weighs various proposed explanations, finding most of them unsuitable, and concludes with Patience's own perspective:

> What people need to understand is I was blind, totally blind and attended the School for the Blind. I read Braille and walked with a white cane. Never had I seen my husband or daughters [sic] face. I was blind when my husband prayed for me—then just like that—in a moment, after years of darkness I could see perfectly! It was miraculous! My daughter's picture was on the dresser. I could see what my little girl and husband looked like. I could see the floor, the steps.

A Retired White Cane

Although there is nothing special about twelve years per se (despite Mark 5:25, 42), Patience's is not the only recent case of blindness healed after twelve years.[6] Andrea Anderson of Sarnia, Ontario, has experienced many health problems throughout her life. One of them was sudden-onset blindness in both eyes, less than two weeks apart—a complication of her diabetes and the strokes it led to.[7] She remained blind for twelve years.

On Pentecost Sunday morning, May 15, 2016, Anderson was weeping and praying for a health need for her baby great-granddaughter. Yet she also felt unworthy to pray; like many other people who have been molested in childhood, she carried a false feeling of guilt. "How can you love me?" she cried to God.

Anderson normally did not attend an evening church service, but she felt compelled to attend the service that night at her home congregation, Bethel Pentecostal Church. A visiting West Virginia evangelist named Ted Shuttlesworth was speaking. He did not know her, but he felt led to stop and pray for her. Led by the Lord, he began listing some of the sicknesses she had experienced. The church's video captured his fervent command: "You blinding spirit, I command you to go!" Then he instructed her, "Turn around and look at me."

"Well, I can turn around," she reasoned, "but I can't look." When she turned, however, she suddenly could see him, and she began weeping for joy. "If it weren't my own teeth in my mouth," she told me, "I would've dropped them!"

The evangelist led her to the front of the church. Demonstrating her newfound sight, she proceeded to follow all his unspoken motions, as members of her congregation, people who knew how blind she had been, began cheering for God.

As important as this healing was, Anderson tells me that God did another special miracle for her that day. After her healing, Ted Shuttlesworth bent over and announced another message: "God also told me to tell you: he loves you, and it was not your fault." Because of the abuse she had experienced in the past, she had struggled with being afraid of God. But God's love touched her deeply at that moment, and now she delights in the love of her heavenly Father.

When she returned to her eye doctor, he was naturally astonished. "I'm scientific. I don't know what to say." Again, science *as* science is about measurements and data, so he followed appropriate procedures. He examined all his earlier reports, scheduled various tests, and consulted another doctor. The next time he saw her, he announced that he had been telling others about her story. "This is unbelievable," he noted. "But I have to believe it!"

The next time she saw her pastor, Tim Gibb, was in the church lobby, and he celebrated her healing by probing playfully, "How do I look?"

"You're gorgeous," she replied.

His then nineteen-year-old son, Cayden, was walking by. "Andrea says I'm gorgeous," Pastor Gibb declared.

"You better pray for her again," Cayden teased.[8]

Anderson continues to see, and Pastor Gibb keeps her old white cane in his office as a reminder of what God has done. "I have known Andrea for years," he told me. "The miracle that happened that night for her was obvious to all who knew her."[9]

The Backfired Exposé

Danish journalist Henri Nissen reports how TV-2 in Denmark secretly recruited Roger Pedersen, a nonchurchgoer who had chronically impaired vision, to test a visiting Nigerian-born evangelist's ability to heal. Many people in the meeting appeared to be experiencing healing, but producer Thomas Breinholt and his team reasoned that perhaps the evangelist had planted actors merely to pretend healing. The evangelist didn't notice or pray for Pedersen, their own plant, who was sitting in the back. But when Pedersen responded to the call to accept Christ, he found himself healed. When Pedersen went up to thank the evangelist, the latter advised him to thank Jesus instead. The station did not get the story they expected, but they certainly got a story! Nissen reproduces in the book Pedersen's eye charts confirming his healing.[10]

Blinded by a Stroke

Kent Gross from Albany, Oregon, was legally blind from a stroke for four years.[11] The state provided him a legal subsidy because of his disability, and his eye examination from February 21, 2019, clearly states that he is legally blind.

In July 2019, Lee Schnabel spoke at Gross's church, Valley Christian Center, and Schnabel and his colleagues prayed with Gross for the restoration of his sight. His sight improved somewhat after the first prayer, so they prayed again. This was repeated for a total of four times of prayer, and when they finished, Gross's sight was fully restored. His ophthalmologist was surprised by his newfound sight and had to confirm the records with the chief ophthalmologist in the office. Gross then shared with his ophthalmologist that he had been healed during prayer. Gross's September 13, 2019, eye exam shows that he is no longer legally blind, and Gross no longer receives a subsidy for his blindness. He now works for a nonprofit in Eugene, Oregon, that serves disabled persons.

Before, at work, Gross would always have to make sure that people sent him material that could be read aloud to him. His healing made such a difference at work that he no longer needed help, and he advanced to operations manager. At church, he could see all the people that he had been able only to hear formerly. He no longer needed his white cane in public; he had more confidence and far more independence. He could read stories to his grandchildren. His church's way of thinking has also been revolutionized because now people are more open to the reality of healing, not just internationally, but even in the US. This healing of blindness also fits a larger pattern of healings in Lee Schnabel's ministry.

Nor are such healings limited to a single ministry. For example, after submitting the first draft of this book, I learned of another eye healing after a stroke from Methodist pastor Carolyn Moore.[12] Unaware that I was working on a new book on miracles, she mentioned in passing a healing about which I inquired further. When she was doing ministry in Seattle on March 16, 2019, Cheryl Scroggins experienced a deep touch from the Holy Spirit. A stroke roughly half a year earlier, on September 27, 2018, had affected her right side, including blinding her right eye. Her vision had never improved, and the doctor warned her that it would never come back. When Scroggins awoke the morning of Sunday, March 17, however, "I opened my eyes and immediately could see clearly from my affected eye." Her husband tested her sight in various ways for an hour to make sure the healing was genuine, and that morning she shared the experience in church. The church, knowing her prior vision impairment, celebrated with her. The memo from her next appointment, on April 18, says it all: "Absolutely unbelievable. Miraculous. Full recovery from her CVA."

Macular Degeneration Un-degenerates

During his fifteen years in law enforcement focused on narcotics, Greg Spencer was exposed to heavy violence. As a deputy medical examiner as well, he witnessed the bodies of many who had died in road accidents or had been murdered. Hardened on the outside, he was nevertheless deeply disturbed by what he had seen.

Eventually, Spencer left his job in law enforcement and began driving trucks cross-country, but this new career lasted only about six months. His vision began to decline, and medical professionals diagnosed him with macular degeneration, a condition that is irreversible. Tests included mapping the structure of his eyes and revealed a form of permanent mottling in the center of his vision. His vision quickly declined from normal vision to 20/200 in one eye and 20/400 in the other—he was legally blind. Placed on disability, he went through the full training for blindness with the Oregon Commission for the Blind, never expecting to see again.[13]

Soon after this, Spencer met a believer named Wendy, who helped him come to faith in Christ and also became his wife. Still troubled by memories of the awful scenes he had witnessed earlier, he attended a church retreat focused on the healing of his mind.[14] While he was praying for the healing of his mind, he felt that God said, "You are clean." When Spencer opened his eyes, he discovered that God had restored not only his mind but also his vision.[15]

Two witnesses who were present confirm what happened to Spencer next. He rushed outside to learn whether he could really see fully. One of the witnesses, Randy Webb, recounts that Spencer announced to him, "Randy, I've been healed!"

"What?" Webb asked.

"I can see! I can see!"

Webb pointed to some black birds barely visible in the distance. "Can you see those birds out there?" he queried.

"Yeah—I can *see* those birds!" Then Spencer began looking around everywhere and describing all the other things that he could now see. He found that he could read license plates in the distance that even his friends could not read. The rest of the weekend he went around reading license plates to celebrate that he could. On the way home from the retreat, he kept pointing out, "I can see that!" Yet to Spencer, the greatest part of the miracle was the healing of his mind.

Unfortunately for books like this one, when people experience healing they usually celebrate without collecting any documentation for their experience. Spencer did not have that luxury, however, because he now needed to get off disability, and the Social Security Administration could not accept an undocumented claim that macular degeneration had simply disappeared. That was not supposed to happen! Perhaps he had simply faked blindness earlier?

A number of professionals carefully examined him, however, and the documentation is clear: before his experience he was legally blind, but afterward he could see. (For some of the documentation, see Joel Lantz's *Bridges for Honest Skeptics*, from which I have the information about the witnesses of Spencer's healing.)[16] More than three years after Spencer's diagnosis of 20/400 vision, the same specialist confirmed that he had experienced "a remarkable return of his visual acuity," which was now measured at 20/30. Although 20/30 vision is not quite 20/20 vision, it is far better than my own vision.

After finishing its investigation, the Social Security Administration acknowledged that Spencer's eyesight was no longer impaired—that he had been blind but now could see (as in John 9:25). Eighteen years after his healing, now at age sixty-one, Spencer's sight remains normal for his age. Of course, everything has a downside. When your benefits stop, you have to go back to work!

Other Cases

Medical doctor Nonyem Numbere recounts stories from her husband Geoffrey's ministry, including numerous miracles that took place.[17] In one case in May 1973, Geoffrey prayed for a five- or six-year-old girl who had been born blind. Her eyes looked like empty sockets with skin draped over them. She and a blind boy were both healed, leading to the conversion of much of the Nigerian village of Dere.

One could offer many more examples of healings of blindness. An industrial accident left George Orr nearly blind in one eye as a result of irreparable corneal scarring.[18] The state of Pennsylvania therefore provided him with workers' compensation for losing his eye. Two decades later, however, as he listened to a sermon about healing, Orr's eyesight was suddenly healed. The optometrist certified that the scar tissue had disappeared.

Earlier, in chapter 12, I included a doctor's published account of a medical trainee healed of a deadly condition, including of the eye scarring that it had caused.[19] The doctor also notes the case of a schoolteacher blinded by an accident but healed so thoroughly that he did not even need glasses after his healing.

Renay Poirier was an electrician for a three-thousand-employee computer facility in Eau Claire, Wisconsin.[20] At about 9:00 a.m. on October 9, 1990, the power went down at the facility. While the power was off, Poirier was asked to hook up some wires. As he did so, a fireball exploded, hurling him fifteen feet back into a concrete wall. After he regained consciousness, he could not focus with his eyes. "There are some scratches and burns on the cornea," the doctor noted, but he did not expect the effects to be serious.[21] The doctor considered Poirier fortunate to have survived with minimal bruises. The optimism, however, proved premature.

For more than nine years, Poirier was blind, yet he learned how to help others as a physical therapist. In his blindness, he experienced God's grace more deeply. Then, on May 23, 2000, as he was starting work at Sacred Heart Hospital, the most brilliant light that he had seen since the accident flooded his eyes. Was he having a stroke? he wondered. But he could see the cross atop the chapel's roof, and then the trees. Realizing that he could see, he rushed into the chapel, prostrating himself before the altar and crying out his gratitude to God. He shared his experience immediately with Father Edmund Klimek, the chaplain, who had been supportive all along. Now Poirier could actually see the flowers, his coworkers, and the world; he could even read fine print. His supportive boss wouldn't let him stay at work that day. "There must be something in the employee handbook about getting the day off if a miracle occurs!"[22]

That day, Poirier saw his children for the first time in ten years. After putting them to bed with prayer and some Bible verses, he relished the chance to go through photos and catch up on all the family sights he had been missing. Poirier's testimony appeared on *20/20*, *The Oprah Winfrey Show*, the *Today* show, *Larry King Live*, CNN, and PAX TV's *It's a Miracle*.

Other Explanations?

Of course, what a believer calls a miracle a nonbeliever will explain differently. In a 1997 article in *Journal of Religion and Health*, Paul Parker reports,

> When my younger sister was three years old, she walked accidentally into the sword-shaped leaf of a Spanish bayonet yucca plant and punctured one of her eyes. It deflated like a beach ball. The attending physician pronounced her blind and offered what treatment he could. My parents prayed and asked the church to pray. In several weeks, my sister could see again. The church and my family praised God for a miracle. The physician sheepishly objected that he had misdiagnosed the injury and the eye had healed quite naturally.[23]

Misdiagnosis occurs, but many of us would agree with Parker that in many cases, such as this one, a simpler explanation lies close at hand.

Chapter 18

Do Disabled People Still Walk? Reflex Sympathetic Dystrophy

N either Ema McKinley (the primary subject of this chapter) nor Marlene Klepees (the subject of the next chapter) was expected to ever walk again. Their conditions were not limited to inability to walk. Under normal circumstances, both cases would have been physically hopeless, and the second case would have been terminal.

But let's start briefly with another case of the same condition that afflicted Ema McKinley. On December 24, 1993, fourteen-year-old Patricia Zemba was injured while horseback riding near Phoenix, Arizona.[1] Soon after this, Dr. Marilyn Wells testifies, Patricia developed the most serious case of reflex sympathetic dystrophy (RSD) that Dr. Wells had ever witnessed. Although Patricia's parents prayed for her recovery for weeks, a doctor suggested that they would need to institutionalize her. Doctors planned to implant a morphine pump, as they would for terminally ill patients; but the night before her scheduled surgery, on March 11, 1994, the family's prayers were answered in a stunning way.

As Patricia was praying, the pain began to leave her body. A voice said, "Get up." Not surprisingly, she was afraid to believe or try to move, so she said, "God, if that's really you, please give me more confirmation." Then the voice came even more authoritatively: "Get up." The thought seemed impossible to her; she had not walked or even sat up for over three months. But she tried to obey, and when her feet touched the hospital floor, she had no pain. For a moment, she stood transfixed in place. Could this really be happening? Then she walked down the hall. The night-shift nurse, knowing that Patricia was unable to walk, rushed over to her, warning that she should not be out of bed. But Patricia was now convinced that God had performed a miracle, and at 4:00 a.m. she started calling family and doctors: "God has healed me!"

Comparing Patricia's X-rays before and after her healing, Dr. Wells could not find any remaining traces of the source of her condition. Dr. Wells was unaware of any other sudden, spontaneous remissions of RSD in history. When she was interviewed five years later, Patricia reported no recurrence of the symptoms. But she was young and had suffered from RSD only for a few months. What might happen to someone much older who had suffered from it for years?

Ema McKinley's Christmas Eve Surprise

A potentially fatal work accident in April 1993 left Ema McKinley with a concussion, significant hearing loss, and RSD.[2] By January 1995 her disability grew even more severe, and the decline continued that year. Her left hand began to claw in November, and Christmas Eve 1995 was her final complete meal with solid food. She was confined to a wheelchair by February 1996, a wheelchair in which she spent the next fifteen years—all day, every day. Because the top of her body twisted to the left and her head lay far to one side, builders had to expand her home's doors for her to pass through them; even getting her into the transport van was difficult. She required many medicines and depended entirely on fluid intake. Because of pain she was sometimes awake for nearly three days at a time, until exhaustion put her body to sleep.

In 2011, early in the morning of Christmas Eve, Ema was alone in her home when she had another accident. Her wheelchair tipped over, leaving her twisted and in torment on the floor. She describes her agony: "Pain exploded when the curve of my neck slammed the floor, crushing it against the bed. Fire shot through my spine. My crooked foot got pinned somewhere behind my right leg, and my left arm lay trapped beneath me. All I could see of it was my big club fist, looking lifeless and useless in front of my face." The slightest attempt to move "only spiked the pain."[3] She realized that she might soon die in this position.

She could not reach the phone; the only person who could possibly hear or help her was Jesus. For more than eight hours she could do nothing but keep screaming his name through her parched throat.

Suddenly, she heard a roaring wind and felt a bright presence. As her room lit up with brilliance, she saw a glowing robe and wondered whether she was entering another dimension. Jesus's face was too bright to stare into, but his power surged through her. She heard bones crack as he straightened her permanently bent left foot, pinned beneath her. Then he began opening her hand that had been clenched for over sixteen years; the flesh was raw and red, full of sores, but in front of her eyes the flesh healed, and she had the ability to move her own fingers. Finally, he healed her neck and spine, then invited her to take his hands. His presence mattered more than anything, but as she took his hands, he set her on her feet.

Her muscles had atrophied, but it was clear that Jesus now wanted her to walk—so, though wobbly and sore, she began to do so. After the basic tutorial in walking, the sound of the wind and the brightness of Jesus's presence vanished. Nevertheless, Ema began experimenting joyfully with how her body now worked.

Surprises Continue

Ema's sons and grandsons were due to visit that evening. Though still wobbly and practicing coordination, she lit candles herself, laughing gleefully. When the doorbell rang and her family entered, they were stunned to see an empty wheelchair. Before anyone could panic, she walked into the room.

Her son Jason "looked up and then looked again, frozen. Everybody's mouth dropped open." "Are you serious?" Jason exclaimed. He stepped toward her hesitantly. "Mom?"

"Come here," she ordered, and they embraced and broke into laughter together. She turned to her younger son, Jeff, now white-faced and too dumbfounded to speak, and embraced him as well. Finally, she turned to her grandsons, who had never seen her walk or be physically upright before. Young Connor grasped her tenaciously, but fifteen-year-old Brady held back. "Grandma, I'm kinda freaking out right now." She hugged him. "It's okay, honey," she comforted him. "I think we're all freaking out right now."[4]

Connor marveled at the new, smooth skin on his grandmother's hands, though Ema still had some pain in her hands, feet, and back. Although she would continue to use some pain medication, her upper body was now straight instead of bent nearly 90 degrees to the side.

Ema was not done with playful surprises. Soon after Christmas, on January 4, 2012, she surprised Dr. David Bell. Transfixed with astonishment, he gasped, "Please tell me Ema has a twin." As Ema recounted her experience, he hung on every word, celebrating with her.[5] A few weeks later she visited her RSD specialist, Keith Bengston. He had already heard the news but still expressed astonishment at how wonderful she looked. He was particularly amazed to learn that the restoration had been instantaneous.[6]

When, on Valentine's Day, a nurse explained to Dr. Amindra Arora, Ema's gastroenterologist, that Ema was in an examination room, he protested. "She couldn't be in there. She doesn't fit through the door!" As he entered the room, he stood motionless, his eyes wide and his mouth open. He stared from her face to her feet and back. "Wha-what happened? What did you do?" he cried.

"You know that crooked spine and the hand that wouldn't open? And the crooked foot?"

"Yeah, yeah, yeah, I know! What did you do?" He was amazed and grateful to hear the story.[7] And the surprises went on, including surprises for Ema. In 2012, local news in Rochester, Minnesota, covered her well-documented story.

Ema's book includes photographs of her severe condition before her healing, including her frozen left hand and the infected leg, covered with RSD sores, that was nearly amputated.[8] It also includes photos she captured when she surprised her stunned doctors and nurses by walking up to them, healed. A medical report from several months after the healing notes her "extraordinary recovery on Christmas Eve" in connection with an experience she attributes to seeing and feeling God.[9]

Chapter 19

Do Disabled People Still Walk?
Marlene's Cerebral Palsy

Weighing just two pounds at birth, Marlene Klepees from Missouri was born with cerebral palsy.[1] Cerebral palsy is a group of movement disorders originating in childhood; the disease is permanent, but there are varying levels of severity. As will soon be clear, Marlene's case was a severe one.

Marlene became a committed Christian at age eleven, when some Christians in her high school, one of whom had specifically felt led to reach out to her, invited her to a Youth for Christ meeting. An orphan since the age of two, she relished her relationship with God as her Father. Soon after her conversion, she began to pray with words she did not understand, because at such times she experienced feelings of God embracing her. She was as yet unaware of any biblical term for this.

Growing Worse

Marlene took for granted that cerebral palsy was God's plan for her life and remained content. In the years that followed, however, she began to question this assumption, as her condition grew increasingly severe. She lost much of her eyesight and became effectively paralyzed from the neck down. Some of her muscle spasms were so severe that her seizures had broken the bones of those trying to take care of her. She lost control of most of her body, though she retained some control of her eyes and mouth. She never stopped shaking, and her head was always bent to one side. Unable to swallow, she drooled uncontrollably.

Although she still believed that God was sovereign, when she was seventeen, she began to question whether this condition itself was God's ideal plan for her. Although God works everything for our good—even what someone else may intend as evil—God also often desires to thwart that evil.

Finally, after two days of continuous spasms, Marlene became increasingly desperate. Although her intellect was not impaired, those around her began discussing what to do with her. Unable to understand her frantic attempts to communicate, they wrongly supposed that her brain was essentially dead. Yet she felt God assuring her of his love and that he would take care of her, repeatedly subduing her panic.

Happily, she was transferred to the respected Mayo Clinic in Rochester, Minnesota. Doctors at the Mayo Clinic recognized that she actually was fully aware of her surroundings. Unfortunately, they could not offer much hope regarding her condition. After three months of attempted rehabilitation, they informed her that she would need to be placed in a total-care facility. She was now nineteen years old.

The Vision

At this point, Marlene finally became angry with God. Yet she felt not his anger in return but her heavenly Father's comfort. He showed her a vision of her being healed, of a church, and of an impending date: March 29. It took her a few days of attempts to communicate this vision to her hospital roommate, and the roommate, a Christian, believed her. Their faith was encouraged even more when Marlene received as a gift the very T-shirt she had witnessed in the vision. Marlene told staff that she would be healed, but no one else expected it. "Yeah, Marlene," they would say. While hope can provide strength, failed hope yields disappointment, and they had undoubtedly witnessed plenty of dashed hopes before.

By Saturday, March 28, Marlene herself felt disappointed. Her roommate had gone home. There was no one to take her to church, and she had no contact with any local church. As she poured out her heart to God, she felt him speak again, assuring her that he would show her the right church. When a nurse came in to feed her on Sunday morning, March 29, she managed to mouth, "Yellow Pages." Because she was insistent, the nurse brought her a phone book, and Marlene had her open it to the church directory. There the Lord seemed to highlight for her the name of the local Open Bible Church, so she asked the nurse to dial the number for Marlene. The nurse left, disturbed, but finally returned shortly after noon, called the number, and put the receiver to Marlene's mouth.

Scott Emerson, the pastor, answered. Marlene managed to ask whether his church believed in healing. "Yes," he admitted.

"You're the one," she concluded. "You can visit me." It wasn't clear whether the pastor could understand her, so the nurse took the phone again. "Sir, I don't know who you are or where you are, but you'd better get down here." She gave him the room number and then promptly hung up. Then Marlene waited patiently—for four hours. The pastor had the room number, but he didn't know which of the two hospitals had called or the patient's name!

Hesitantly, Pastor Emerson arrived that afternoon. He was taken aback by Marlene's condition. He and his church believed in miracles—but he had never witnessed one like this before. Nevertheless, he listened as she struggled to recount her vision, interpreted to him by a nurse who had learned to understand Marlene. Emerson looked like the pastor she had seen, and he agreed that her description of the church matched what his church looked like. But at first he didn't seem to take the hint to invite her for the evening service.

Finally, however, a Christian nurse helped get authorization, and Pastor Emerson brought Marlene to his church's evening service. It was Sunday, March 29, and there were about seven members there. He explained what the Bible said about healing, then invited his church members to gather around. "I've never prayed for someone like this before," he confessed, not very encouragingly, but then led the group in prayer. After they had prayed, Scott asked Marlene if, by faith, she wanted to try to walk. She did not know what "by faith" meant, but she knew that she wanted whatever God had, so she grunted affirmatively. They released the restraints on her wheelchair and raised her up.

"Suddenly," she testifies, "my feet hit the floor flat, and for the first time I could feel the floor under my shoes! I took a few steps, with others holding onto me. Then, they let go of me."[2] Her feet still pointed inward, but they began to straighten with each step. Every lap she took around the inside of the church she grew stronger and stronger, learning greater motor control, as everyone celebrated with her. Now her eyes felt warm, and she again heard her heavenly Father, this time telling her to take off her glasses. When she took them off, she found that her vision was completely healed—soon certified as better than 20/20.

Pastor Emerson felt that he needn't bother with the sermon that night. The group went out for ice cream to celebrate, and Marlene held and ate an ice cream cone for the first time. As they were leaving, they ran into a worker from the Mayo Clinic. He had seen Marlene's wheelchair sticking out of the back of the pastor's yellow Volkswagen and feared that this meant that Marlene had already died. When instead he then saw Marlene, he asked, stunned, "Marlene—is that *you*?" She recounted the story, and he beat them back to the hospital with the news.

Testimony

When Pastor Emerson brought Marlene back to the Mayo Clinic, the nurse in charge saw her walking in and dropped the telephone he was holding. Marlene soon began entertaining the nurses by demonstrating all the things she could do now. All the professionals were rejoicing with her, except one, who insisted, "We'll see what you're like tomorrow morning." Emerson's wife had worked in a rehab unit, so the pastor could understand the cynicism of repeated disappointment.

On Tuesday the doctors ran tests, and when Marlene walked into the conference room, they stood up and started applauding! Apart from Marlene, no one had expected this outcome, but everyone was pleased. Wondering about her eyesight, someone asked about her vision. Thinking that he meant the vision God had given before her healing, she began recounting it. All of them listened graciously and respectfully, and at the end one doctor, obviously a Christian, blurted out, "Praise the Lord!"

This healing occurred in 1981, and Marlene has remained well in the nearly four decades following. She bicycles and runs a flower shop (Heaven's Scent Flowers) full-time. She also prays compassionately for others, and often they receive healing. One of the better-documented cases is that of Chris Carlson, who suffered for fifteen years from trigeminal neuralgia.[3] Chris and her husband, Dave, had always prayed for the right doctors but had never prayed for God to heal Chris directly. When Marlene offered to pray, Chris protested, "I don't believe in this healing business."

"That's okay," Marlene replied. "I can believe for you. That's not a hard task." She prayed a simple prayer.

Chris felt a warm tingling starting in her neck but brushed it off. "Have a nice trip," she told Marlene as they parted. But the tingling persisted for twenty-five minutes, and when it stopped, Chris's pain was gone. That very night. Permanently. Shaken and reordering their priorities, the Carlsons soon dedicated their lives to God's calling.

After I interviewed Marlene, she prayed a gracious prayer for me. "*Each* of us is special to God," she advised. She recognizes that she does not deserve healing any more than anyone else does. She emphasizes that she did not do anything to merit her healing; it came at the cost of Jesus's suffering for us. Most of all, we need to recognize how loving the heavenly Father is—the heavenly Father who embraced an orphan at age eleven and has been with her ever since.

Chapter 20

Do Disabled People Still Walk?
Bryan's Spinal Injury

D r. Matthew Suh, a surgeon in New York City and regional director of
the Christian Medical and Dental Associations, shared with me healings
that he had witnessed or experienced (some of which appear in chap.
21). In addition, he referred me to his friends Bryan and Meg LaPooh for their
story. And what a story it was.[1]

Officer Down

In 2008, Bryan LaPooh was a New Jersey police officer with nearly twenty years
on the job and a new family. A few days before Christmas, he was directing mo-
torists during a winter storm when, according to witnesses, he slipped on the ice.
The next thing he remembers is waking in the hospital with "a doctor forcing a
tube down my throat."

Doctors performed emergency surgery to stabilize his C4 and C5 vertebrae to
prevent him from being paralyzed, but he nevertheless remained paralyzed on the
right side of his body. Later, doctors discovered more precisely that he suffered
from Brown-Séquard syndrome. Patients often recover in the early stages of this
syndrome, but after years of disability, hope for recovery fades—especially for
a sudden recovery.

Eventually, Bryan's left side also began to lose function, requiring another neck
surgery, a laminectomy. This surgery left Bryan with severe migraine headaches
twenty-four hours a day for four years, requiring heavy doses of pain medicine.
Years into this suffering, he experienced a leg cramp and reached for his crutch,

which he needed to get out of bed to get to his leg brace. Instead, he lost his balance and hit his head on the door. He found himself lying bloodied on the floor for four hours, his neck broken again.

Bryan had been married for just over a year when the first accident happened, and his wife, Meg, who for years had waited on God to send her the right husband, was pregnant. His injury, pain, and frequent despair placed considerable strain on her as well, but she kept nurturing her faith and looking to God to heal Bryan. Some other Christians were not so helpful. When his disability did not respond to their prayers, some shunned him, questioning his faith or suggesting that God wanted to teach him something through his pain. Such suggestions made him feel more distant from God. "I wouldn't bring my kids to the point of killing themselves to teach them something," he retorted.

Take It

In the summer of 2019, Meg urged Bryan to attend one last conference with her, a Global Awakening conference in Pennsylvania. She pleaded that it would count as her birthday gift, her Christmas gift, and her anniversary gift all rolled into one. On the one hand, that sounded to Bryan like a great deal; on the other hand, he was reluctant. He had endured so many people praying for him, with so many disappointments. But for her sake, he acquiesced and went to the conference. This time, though, something was different; a nagging voice inside him was saying, "Take it!" He didn't know what the voice meant, but it seemed to be an encouragement.

At dinner on the second evening of the conference, Bryan felt faith like he hadn't felt before. "I'm going to be healed tonight," he told Meg. During the following service, however, people called out prayers for all sorts of infirmities they believed God was healing, as minute as pain in a finger or a stomachache; they seemed to mention everything *except* Bryan's condition. Bryan was the only one there with a conspicuously visible problem—after all, he was wearing a helpful $100,000 microprocessor-controlled hydraulic leg brace. But nobody had felt led to call out his condition.

Bryan's feeling of faith was dissipating into disappointment and renewed anger; Meg left for the restroom in disgust. Before the minister closed the service, however, he invited forward anyone who might want prayer for something not yet mentioned. Determined not to miss this final chance, Bryan felt compelled to make his way forward.

Some twenty young students, who were learning to pray for the sick, lined the front of the room. Although some were not praying for anybody, Bryan inexplicably veered toward the left and to a young woman whose name he later learned was Julia. As if his need were not obvious, she asked what he needed prayer for. (This does have biblical precedent: Jesus asked the same question of a blind man in Mark 10:51.) Julia Voytovich (now Ososkalo) is a nurse, and she tells me that she asked him, on the basis of observation, if he had had a stroke.[2] "No," he explained. "I have a spinal cord injury. Just pray." So Julia laid her hand on his chest to pray, but he instructed, "You don't need to put your hand on my chest. You need to put your hand on my neck." So she touched his neck, and as she started to pray, he felt heat on the back of his neck—and "then the lights went out."

When he became alert again, he found himself on the floor. Julia asked whether he could move anything. He looked at his always-clutched right hand, as he often did, and demanded, "Move." And this time, for the first time in a decade, it did. First it began to twitch as it came unclenched. He pulled himself over to the altar steps and saw that two young men had joined Julia. One was her cousin Peter; the other was their friend Ruslan, whom she has since married. "I'm taking that brace off," Bryan announced.

"Are you sure?" one of the young men pressed, cautiously.

"Oh yeah, I'm sure," he responded. His hand was working, and he believed his leg could do the same. By this time Meg had returned from the restroom and, confident that God was acting, had begun videotaping the scene. Bryan had depended on leg braces for ten and a half years; he removed his brace only at night to recharge it while he slept.

And on August 23, 2019, after being paralyzed on his right side for ten and a half years, fifty-two-year-old Bryan LaPooh began to walk.

Seeing Is Believing

After three laps around the sanctuary, the last one independently, Bryan carried his brace back to the car. On the drive back to the hotel, the couple remained silent, not knowing what to say. Was this just a dream? By habit, Bryan almost drove to the handicapped parking spot, but then laughed to himself: "After what happened tonight, that would be an abomination!"

Bryan later learned that Julia had had a vision in June that a clutched hand opened when she was praying for it. She and her friends from Syracuse had been sitting behind the LaPoohs during the service; as she looked at Bryan's hand, she remembered her vision. "When we were praying for Bryan," Julia tells me, "that vision came to mind. That increased my faith to believe for healing and restoration."[3] When Julia began praying for Bryan, a man had stepped up in line behind him to receive prayer after him. Thinking that Bryan was going to fall, she had told the man behind him, "I think you're going to need to catch him." The man thought, "He's going to hit the floor. I'm in line for prayer for my shoulder injury!" But as Bryan fell, the man instinctively caught him, laid him gently on the floor—and realized that his own shoulder felt healed. Like Bryan, Julia discovered the man's healing only the next day. "I don't think I ended up praying for him because we were praying for Bryan, and we didn't find out until the next day that his shoulder was healed!" she told me.[4]

Most of the time in the years preceding his healing, Bryan had followed his doctors' insistence that he accept his condition as permanent. Now he was afraid that his doctors would not believe him. Finally, however, he worked up the courage to visit his doctor's office. There he overheard the nurse explaining to the doctor, "Bryan LaPooh is the one who was healed from Brown-Séquard syndrome."

"He must have his brace on," the doctor responded dismissively. But as he examined Bryan—who did not have his brace on—the dumbfounded physician began running tests. Three-quarters of the way through the examination, he left the room to make a call. Finally he confessed, "I believe in God. I don't reject the possibility of miracles. But—I've never seen anything like this." The physician's report, now in my possession, acknowledges some residual problems but affirms that Bryan "regained function of his right upper and lower extremities," "miraculously and quite acutely."[5]

A year later, the LaPooh family are still processing their past years of trauma. Why did God let the accident happen to begin with? Why did God let them suffer for so many years before the healing? Bryan believes that God had been holding out the healing earlier, just waiting for him to "take it." Whatever the case, take it he did, and the family has begun a journey of emotional healing. That profound healing began with a physical one when a young student with a vision prayed.

Chapter 21

Do Disabled People Still Walk? Vignettes

Two stories of disabled persons walking appear in the preface of this book. Here I recount some more. Again, there are far more sample cases than I can include in this book; my previous, longer book includes scores of such healing claims from witnesses, although some are weightier evidentially than others.[1] Other books since then have offered further accounts.[2] For example, after more than eight years of being confined to his wheelchair, Chinh Ha was suddenly healed during a Catholic charismatic conference in California. His son recounts how Chinh Ha then celebrated by pushing around the man who prayed for him in Chinh Ha's own wheelchair.[3] There are also a range of reasons for inability to walk; some of the cases in this chapter include other conditions that also required healing.

Surprises

Some cures are instantaneous and visible. Nevertheless, not all apparent cures are genuine miracles. For example, a person can make it appear that a shorter leg has grown out simply by manipulating (intentionally or unintentionally) the position of the leg. At the same time, there are cases in which shorter legs have actually grown out several inches and ended the need for special shoes or even corrected a lifelong limp.[4] Whatever the physiology of it—loosened muscles or actual bone growth—plenty of such healings happen.

For example, Brandon Hammonds, one of my ThM students, recounts praying for a woman in her mid to late thirties in October 2012 in Medford, Oregon. One of her legs was visibly shorter than the other by about three inches, due to a car accident. Brandon notes that he "asked the Lord to heal her leg, and I, as well as the gentleman standing next to me (possibly her husband, but I am unsure), saw the leg grow and become equal with the other. Both the gentleman and I were amazed. I will never forget him exclaim right after it happened, 'Wow, you are healed!'"[5]

Sometimes such healings prove genuine even when we might have legitimate reasons to be cautious. One scholar friend complained to me about a faculty colleague at Fuller Theological Seminary who used to pray for legs to be lengthened. My friend expressed his skepticism that the legs actually grew. Sometimes the legs did not really grow, and, as in a case he mentioned, the relief was only temporary, and probably imaginary. Yet in 2012, Swiss missionary Marianne Sommer recounted to me how this same minister, whose colleague had been skeptical, had prayed for back problems that had troubled her for the previous ten years, afflicting her since she was fifteen years old. When the minister prayed, she and her children saw her leg spontaneously grow longer. About twenty years have passed, and she has not had any back problems since that time.[6] (At another time she was also permanently healed of long-term epilepsy.)[7]

Healing of inability to walk has continued throughout history, even sometimes in circles that did not believe it would happen now that the Bible was finished. Unlike their Catholic counterparts, some conservative Protestant thinkers in the seventeenth century did not believe that miracles would happen in their own day. Then real life happened (for example, see the story of Mercy Wheeler, recounted in chap. 6).

One widely known mid-twentieth-century testimony was that of William David Upshaw, who was disabled in a farming accident at the age of eighteen. His story is widely known because he spent eight years as a Democratic representative in the US Congress and was the Prohibition Party's candidate for president in 1932. At the age of eighty-four, in 1951, he attended a healing service. At that time he had been disabled for sixty-six years, seven of them in bed and fifty-nine of them on crutches. Although the evangelist who was speaking on that occasion later exaggerated his own role, Upshaw himself publicly claimed healing from his nearly lifelong disability, leaving his crutches at the church. He then sent copies of his testimony to the nation's political leaders.[8]

Miracle in Mongolia

As a surgeon, Matthew Suh often makes medical mission trips to help people in Mongolia. One patient there had broken her hip and possibly injured her sciatic nerve fourteen years earlier. Surgery was unavailable to her at the time, and she had remained bound to a wheelchair since then. Dr. Suh felt led to pray for her in a particular way and then invited her to stand. Initially she needed support, but she found herself able to walk slowly, shuffling her feet.

This was remarkable, considering that she had remained bound to the wheel-chair for so long, but it was not enough. Suh prayed again, and this time she felt an electrical sensation in her legs. This made sense to Suh: if God was going to heal her leg, he would need not only to enable her to move her atrophied muscles but also to heal her sciatic nerve if it was damaged. Apparently, God was restoring her sensory as well as motor nerve function. Now she began walking faster. Four days later he watched as she used her wheelchair as a walker instead of as a wheelchair. Although her muscles remained atrophied from four years of disuse and were only gradually regaining strength, she was clearly no longer paralyzed. Dr. Suh provided me with pictures of the healing and a video of her walking.

This is not an isolated incident. On other occasions, Dr. Suh has prayed for those with impaired mobility in their legs and witnessed immediate changes. This has even happened in the US. In one of those cases, after Suh prayed for a man in his early sixties with serious hip problems, the man began running. When he saw Suh again, he reported that his new MRI, astonishingly, had revealed new cartilage. David Chang, an anesthesiologist who sometimes joins Dr. Suh on trips, also reports witnessing healings of mobility impairment, especially in Mongolia but sometimes also in the US. Some of the people he has prayed for have no longer needed canes or other helps; he also recounts the expressions on the faces of those whose chronic pain has disappeared.[9]

A few years ago, Dr. Suh, a Harvard-trained surgeon, did not believe that God heals in such ways today. He had begun praying for spiritual renewal in his life but was also experiencing a physical problem. Over the course of several months, Dr. Suh's left rotator cuff began causing him increasing pain. An operation would have removed him from his own surgical practice for half a year. But when he heard minister Ken Fish, himself a Princeton University graduate, teaching about the Holy Spirit, Suh heard God clearly speak to him: "I'm going to heal you of your left shoulder pain." Within five seconds, Fish announced that he felt that someone present needed to be healed of pain in the left shoulder. Fish wanted others to learn how to pray for the sick, so he instructed a young woman, about twenty years old, to pray for Dr. Suh. She was not at all sure that anything could happen, but when she prayed, Suh was immediately and permanently healed.[10]

Malformed or Injured Feet

Journalist Tim Stafford writes about a young man named Jeff Moore who had long belonged to Stafford's Presbyterian church.[11] Each week for years, Jeff's father brought Jeff into church in his wheelchair. Multiple operations had restructured Jeff's feet, and some surgeons had suggested further surgeries, but a doctor at Stanford University had warned that further surgeries would not help. Walking was too painful for Jeff.

At another disabled friend's urging, Jeff visited Bethel Church in Redding, California, and experienced healing prayer. Jeff expected nothing to happen, but, unlike his friend, he suddenly found his feet healed. That afternoon, Jeff greeted his shocked parents with "Guess what?" as he walked without his wheelchair. He hopped on the skateboard he had neglected for years and enjoyed his newfound freedom, although the atrophied muscles in his legs left him sore for a few days. Classmates at his junior college the next day bombarded him with questions about why he no longer needed his wheelchair, though some seemed skeptical when he noted that he had been healed in a church. Far from experiencing merely a temporary disappearance of pain, Jeff now proved able not only to walk but even to run.

Randy Clark recounts an incident from 2011 in Saõ Paulo, Brazil.[12] He felt that God wanted to heal someone who had been injured on a motorcycle, and sure enough, a twenty-eight-year-old woman at the service that evening was on crutches because she had caught her heel in the back wheel of a motorcycle fifteen years earlier. It had ripped out muscle and her Achilles tendon, leaving her with a large gash and an inability to walk unaided that surgeries had not been able to repair. After Randy prayed, she walked unaided for the first time in fifteen years, and the hole began to close. "The necrotic tissue turned from dark black dead tissue to pink," and an expected amputation was canceled. "A few years later she came to one of my meetings and danced onstage." Her video testimony, along with photos of the grotesque injury, appear online.[13]

Injured Spinal Cords

Randy mentions another incident that took place when he took a team to Manaus, Brazil, in August 2003.[14] One of his team members, to whom he gives the pseudonym Sam, was a recovering alcoholic who had never yet prayed for anyone to be healed. Because of missed air connections, Sam also hadn't slept in forty-eight hours. Sam thus asked God to send him an easy case to pray for, like a headache. Unfortunately, a twenty-five-year-old man in a wheelchair approached him. A police officer, the man had had his spinal cord pierced by a drunken man's bullet two months earlier, leaving his lower body paralyzed. Sam prayed and nothing happened, so his initially weak faith dissipated into no faith at all.

But Randy had taught his team that he didn't expect them to heal; that was God's business. "But I do expect you to love the people, and to treat them with respect." So, lest he leave the man feeling uncared for, Sam prayed a little longer. Just as Sam was about to fall asleep praying, he recounts, "the young man jumped out of the wheelchair, grabbed me, . . . and wet my shirt with his tears. Then he walked off, pushing the wheelchair." The next day they videoed his testimony.

Biblical scholar Mary Healy, a professor at Sacred Heart Major Seminary, notes healings at Divine Retreat Center in Kerala, South India, where she has also lectured. One case was that of a Sikh woman from the far north of India. The woman's husband had abused her until she had jumped from a balcony and broken her back. Her legs remained paralyzed for twelve years, but hearing of healings performed by Jesus, she traveled to the Catholic retreat center, where she "was instantly and completely healed of her paralysis."[15]

After a truck hit Jermaine Green's car on November 14, 2004, his recovery from a coma seemed swift, but he experienced paralysis on his left side. Although therapy helps some patients overcome this condition, it did not help Green. He did not expect recovery, but he decided that he would serve God no matter what. On Easter Sunday 2007, he was closing a church service in prayer. As he sensed that God was working and called on the congregation to praise God, he got out of his wheelchair and began walking up the aisle—only afterward realizing what had happened as he caught sight of his empty wheelchair. He remains active in ministry.[16]

On June 19, 2000, during a routine operation, a surgeon accidentally scraped carpenter Jimmy Craig's spinal cord.[17] The accident changed Craig's life: a paraplegic, he could no longer walk. Three years later, his son Zach urged his father to visit a service at Zach's California church. To Craig's surprise, the guest preacher, Marc Dupont, was a colleague he had known from work twenty-three years earlier, who had gone into ministry. Because he knew Dupont and trusted his integrity, Craig welcomed prayer. Nothing happened immediately, and while he felt some disappointment, as the service continued he felt his legs growing stronger. Amazed, he stood and started to walk around the back of the sanctuary. Soon, everyone realized what had happened.

Several months later, in January 2004, Craig visited his neurosurgeon for an appointment. When the doctor saw him standing, he was perplexed. He ran another MRI, which showed that Craig's spine remained too damaged for him to walk. While Craig remained in the office, the doctor showed colleagues the results. "This patient is a paraplegic who will never regain any movement," they concluded.[18] Then he introduced them to Craig, who clearly *was* able to walk, without any disabilities.

In some cases in this book, medical documentation attests healing.[19] In this case, by contrast, it attests a continuing condition that conflicts with the other empirical evidence: Craig has full use of his limbs.[20]

Leg Injury

Marisol Ramirez is a home health aide in New York who is originally from the Dominican Republic. Already petite, after several months in a stressful job she had lost a third of her weight, dropping to just eighty pounds. Shortly after this, she injured her leg; photographs show the extensive bruising. When she returned from the hospital, weak and in pain, two EMTs had to carry her up to her apartment on a stretcher. When she walked she needed to lean on a cane in one hand and hold on to her daughter, Linnette Pilar, with the other. After Ken Fish prayed for her, he asked her to stand. She didn't believe that she could, and she didn't want to embarrass herself by falling, but Linnette urged her to try.

As Marisol attempted to stand, she suddenly bolted upright, without pain, and those present emitted a collective gasp. She and her daughter began to weep, but Fish chided, "Let's have her walk before we do the crying!" Marisol started walking, and kept repeating in Spanish, "Oh my God, I have no pain!" She walked out with no problem. Linnette testifies, "I had never seen anything like it," and notes that her mother has been walking ever since.[21] Others unable to walk have also been healed in connection with Ken's ministry, most recently a paralyzed stroke victim who, after ninety minutes of prayer, is seen on video not only walking but even jumping.[22]

Multiple Sclerosis

Dr. Robert Larmer, chair of the department of philosophy at the University of New Brunswick, has published extensively concerning miracles and shared with me some interviews he conducted, including some with Irene MacDonald.[23] MacDonald had thoroughly attested multiple sclerosis, and her condition was declining rapidly; a specialist explained that she did not have long to live. Soon bedridden, she needed spinal injections for pain every ten days. As her decline continued, however, one Friday afternoon a friend assured MacDonald that God was saying that he was going to heal her soon. Given all that she had been through, MacDonald was understandably skeptical of such an encouragement by this point. Nevertheless, a dream and increased strength encouraged her, and on Sunday she asked to be carried into church.

During prayer for her there, feeling suddenly returned to her arm and legs. Instantly MacDonald had full "control of her body and fully regained muscular strength." Although she had long been confined to bed, she walked from the church and returned to all her pre-illness activities. That was more than a quarter of a century ago, and none of the symptoms have ever returned. Dr. Larmer not only interviewed MacDonald but also knows well many of those who witnessed the original healing.[24]

Genetic Disorder

In *Healing Prayer Is God's Idea*, a recent book by Methodist leader Maxie Dunnam and Christian and Missionary Alliance pastor David Chotka,[25] the latter recounts a special occasion in his life. Although David and his wife, Elizabeth, had seen many healings during their ministry, Elizabeth's muscle tissue was gradually degenerating because of her FSH muscular dystrophy, a genetic disorder.

She needed a cane to walk, and after twenty years of suffering they had given up praying for her healing. A Ugandan bishop lecturing at their church, however, suddenly interrupted his lecture and began to describe the precise symptoms of FSH muscular dystrophy. "Whoever has these symptoms," the bishop declared, "Jesus has just healed you!" As the bishop returned to his message, Elizabeth painlessly lifted her hands above her head for the first time in more than three decades, in front of 650 people in their church. It was 11:42 a.m., February 22, 2009. The doctor acknowledged the disappearance of her symptoms,[26] which have never returned, and her muscle tissue grows normally now.

Doctors' Accounts of Mobility Recoveries

Doctors have reported sudden restoration of ability to walk in connection with prayer. In one case, recently married Veronica Lowney fell from a ladder and fractured her spinal column. Doctors expected her paralysis to be permanent.[27] When Dr. Issam Nemeh prayed for her in a church healing service, however, he was sure that God was healing her. Though Lowney was afraid, Dr. Nemeh and his wife, Kathy, encouraged her to walk. Many were present in the church to witness the miracle as she walked, and she soon shocked her father by walking into his home, the paralysis permanently gone.

In Nigeria, a father carried a six-year-old boy who had never been able to walk, seeking prayer. Dr. Chauncey Crandall, a Christian physician cited elsewhere in this book, prayed, and as he was going on to the next person the six-year-old began *running*. The parents fell to the dirt weeping, and about two dozen people who had accompanied them from their village began shouting. Similarly, a drooling man, paralyzed on his right side from a stroke and unable to walk, was also healed as Dr. Crandall prayed.[28] In another meeting, a woman with great faith but apparently little sense insisted that her paralyzed baby had been healed. Crandall, recognizing that the child remained paralyzed on the left side, refused to let her testify. The next day he was shocked to discover that the baby was no longer paralyzed.[29]

In Santiago de Cuba, Mirtha Venero Boza, who is both a doctor and a Baptist evangelist, told me that she witnessed the immediate healing of a twisted leg during one of her evangelistic meetings.[30] A Florida physician with whom I corresponded, Teri Speed Cumpton, reports that she prayed for and encouraged an "incurable" woman who had not been able to walk unaided for fifteen years, whose nerves were degenerating. Dr. Cumpton testifies that despite atrophied muscles, the woman, released from her braces, started walking and then running around the room, and she remained permanently cured.[31]

Professor Michael McClymond shared with me the following story and the medical documentation to confirm it.[32] A woman in the United States was confined to bed for the majority of each day with an incurable, progressive disease.

In fall 2004, when friends in Nigeria called during the night and noted that they had prayed and were convinced that she was healed, she ignored them and simply went back to sleep. The next day, however, she discovered to her astonishment that she was well. New tests confirmed her healing, while trace antibodies in the tests also ruled out any possibility of initial misdiagnosis.

Doctors have reported healings from additional kinds of inability to walk. For example, Dr. Nonyem Numbere attests how a man named Henderson Jumbo, who had a fractured spine, was healed during worship. She provided photographs of him in body casts and skull traction before his healing.[33]

One could fill the entire book with such examples, but I hope these several brief samples can suffice for now.

Chapter 22

Are Lepers Still Cleansed?
Visible Healings

T hird in Jesus's list of cures in Matthew 11:5, after the blind receiving sight
and the disabled walking, is lepers being cleansed. Because I do not live
anywhere near where most leprosy occurs, I do not have enough stories
about cured lepers today to fill a chapter. In any case, what we refer to as leprosy
today (Hansen's disease) differs from most of the skin afflictions called "leprosy"
in the Bible, though it is, if anything, more physically devastating.[1] That I have
only a few accounts of healed modern leprosy to include in this chapter does,
however, leave space to address various other kinds of visible miracles: things
that grow back or disappear.

"Lepers Are Cleansed"

Jesus healed the serious skin condition called "leprosy" in the Bible. Doing so also
liberated the former lepers from the isolation and social stigma of ritual impurity.
Here we survey some modern cases of the usually more physically devastating
Hansen's disease.

One of my former students at Asbury, Ebi Perinbaraj, who went on for his
PhD at Trinity Evangelical Divinity School, shared with me the account of a man
he once worked with.[2] Bari Malto was a village shaman, but after he contracted
leprosy, his village cast him out. A couple of Christians came and prayed for him,
and that night two angels touched his hands in a dream. When Malto awoke the
next day, he was completely healed. He ran into the village and showed the villagers what had happened. As a result, the entire village became followers of Jesus.

Ebi had worked closely with Malto and told me that everyone in the area knew the account. Indeed, by the time Ebi was teaching there, half the region had already become Jesus followers. Along the way, many further healings had occurred, including the raising of thirteen people who were apparently dead.

Professor Jessy Jaison from South India shared with me her eyewitness account of another cure of leprosy.[3] She witnessed this event when she was nine and her father was planting a new church among nonbelievers. Though her father was of high social rank, she watched as he publicly crossed class boundaries by washing a man's leprous foot. Selvan, the leper, was so deeply touched that he wept.

In this case, God touched Selvan's feet as well as his heart. The next day Jessy watched, amazed, as Selvan came to their home and revealed that his leprosy was gone; the skin on his foot looked like baby skin. Selvan, his family, and many of his neighbors chose to follow Christ.

Why Don't Amputated Limbs Grow Back?

A frequent objection of skeptics is that if miracles really take place, we should have reports of amputated limbs growing back. This raises the bar of evidence fairly high, since even the Bible does not report any regrown limbs. There *are* accounts of regrown limbs today, but for whatever reason they are not very frequent. Perhaps in some cases God simply prevents some limbs from being destroyed to begin with. Even where I have encountered reports of limb growth, I rarely have had access to confirming records or direct connections with witnesses. Meanwhile, as noted later in this chapter, other visible miracles, such as the instant disappearance of goiters, lumps, cataracts, and the like, are widely reported.

We do, however, have some examples of something amputated growing back miraculously. Intercultural worker Jim Yost shared an account of an abused woman in Asia whose arm was nearly severed. All the arteries were cut, but the hospital postponed amputation until the next day to allow the woman time to stabilize because of blood loss. That night, Jim's wife prayed for the woman, and the next day the doctor insisted that she must have taken the woman to a different hospital overnight; the bone and blood vessels were reattached. The hospital staff recognized a miracle, and Yost encouraged the woman to share her testimony faithfully.[4]

In one medically documented case, what grew back was an organ far more complex than an arm or a leg. This is the account of thirty-six-year-old diesel mechanic Bruce Van Natta of Wisconsin.[5] One evening when Van Natta was working late, a jack gave way, and a nearly fifty-thousand-pound (twenty-two-thousand-kilogram) truck's massive, half-foot-wide axle crushed his abdomen almost down to the concrete. Blood shot up into his throat, and soon he saw angels holding his body together. The first responders believed that he was dead—for about forty minutes. From his severed arteries, he should have bled to death in ten minutes. His survival in any condition was medically unexpected. "In fact," James Garlow and Keith Wall remark, "subsequent medical studies, drawing on cases from trauma centers around the world, show that he is the *only* person ever known to have survived such injuries."[6]

Despite Van Natta's survival, his abdominal damage was severe. Doctors repaired what they could, but most of his small intestine was dead or dying and had to be removed. His small intestine as a whole had only 121 centimeters left; a small intestine's average length is 600 centimeters. A crucial part of the small intestine, the ileum, is normally 350 centimeters long; after his necessary surgeries, Van Natta had only 25 centimeters of his left.

Unable to digest food properly, he began to decline. His weight dropped from 180 pounds to 125. At this point one of his friends felt strongly led to fly from New York to pray for him. Now with Van Natta in person, the friend commanded his small intestine to grow in Jesus's name. Van Natta felt something like an electric jolt in his body—and was healed.

In an adult, a small intestine can widen but it cannot naturally grow longer. Yet a radiologist confirms that Van Natta's small intestine had more than doubled in length and was now fully functional. (For full documentation and discussion, see Joel Lantz's *Bridges for Honest Skeptics*, available free online.)[7] To do measurements more precisely than this, one would need to actually remove his small intestine and unwind it, which would naturally counter the point of the original miracle (i.e., Van Natta's survival and restoration). But the previous surgeries and the subsequent healing seem plain enough.

I followed up with Van Natta, and he confirms that, years later, he remains healthy. I also mentioned his involvement in Chris Gunderson's gastroparesis healing, which Chris brought to my attention (see chap. 13).

This is a special and extraordinary event, but it is not completely unique, given other accounts of healings—for example, restorations of destroyed bones, as in the cases of Lisa Larios (chap. 14) or at Lourdes (chap. 9). Witnesses also report other cases, although at this remove I often can only mention them. In one multiply attested account, at one large Assemblies of God church in Pomona, California, in the summer of 1972 three individuals were present who had each lost a finger in different accidents. To the surprise of those leading prayer, who had never before seen such a miracle, these fingers each grew back publicly and visibly, complete with joints, over the course of a few minutes of prayer.[8]

Goiters Vanish

Although I have never been around goiters, friends active in goiter-prone areas have attested witnessing a number of large goiters disappear.[9] Dr. David Emmett, now a tutor and lecturer at St. Mellitus College in Liverpool, England, reports a story from his first day as a missionary in Zaire (now the Democratic Republic of Congo) in August 1981. He joined some other missionaries at a rally in Kinshasa where Jacques Vernaud, who soon after this rally hosted Emmett for some time in his home, would be preaching. "I was astounded at the numerous healing miracles that happened that evening," Emmett writes. What struck him most was a woman sitting near him with a huge goiter on the side of her neck. "I saw the huge goitre literally shrink before my eyes."[10]

Testimonies related to Vernaud's ministry, incidentally, could be multiplied. My wife and I both knew the Vernauds before we knew each other. My wife, who is from Congo, recounts that many people were healed when her father prayed, and that this pattern began when his dear friend Jacques Vernaud laid hands on him. I knew the Vernaud family because I attended college with Vernaud's daughter, who had been expected to die from leukemia as a baby but was healed when her father prayed,[11] and who continues to work in Congo today.

Beyond this I will narrate just one account, from my friends Wonsuk and Julie Ma. Both Wonsuk and Julie are highly educated Korean Christians; each has a PhD, has years of teaching experience, and has published extensive research. They have many healing accounts, but here I recount one of my favorites (next to Julie's own medically unexpected, complete recovery after a brain aneurysm in 2010).[12]

One day Wonsuk and Julie prayed for Edna, a woman in the Philippines dying from a toxic goiter. Neither doctors nor local cultic practices had been able to cure the goiter; it had simply grown worse over the course of a year. Already resuscitated once in the hospital, Edna was now in critical condition. Since none of her family's costly spiritist sacrifices had worked, they allowed the Christians to pray for her. "While we were praying," Julie Ma reports, "she felt something in her neck and was able to swallow her saliva, which she could not do before. The goiter disappeared in the sight of many witnesses." Edna and many others became followers of Christ.[13]

I included this testimony when I (with some trepidation) gave one of the plenary addresses for a conference on special divine action at the Ian Ramsey Centre for Science and Religion at Oxford University. Because Wonsuk Ma was at that time the long-standing director of the Oxford Centre for Mission Studies, later that afternoon I walked down the road and shared with Wonsuk and Julie that I had just used their account. Wonsuk chuckled. "That one healing has gone a long way!"[14]

Facial Tumors

From birth, Sean had a benign tumor under his right eye.[15] When he was four years old, his mother, Joan Andrews, brought him to a healing service led by Issam Nemeh, MD, at St. Bernadette Catholic Church in Westlake, Ohio. The tumor was unpleasant in appearance, but because removing it surgically risked even more damage to his face, Cleveland doctors had warned against it. Dr. Nemeh prayed over the tumor and moved on, but when, five minutes later, Joan glanced at her son, she shrieked with astonishment. "Oh my God!" she cried. "It's gone! It's *gone*!" The tumor had disappeared.

Burns

I could give various accounts of instant or near instant healings of severe burns, including an eyewitness testimony shared with me by a medical doctor in Cuba.[16] Here, however, I focus on a case where the eyewitness is a close and trusted friend of mine. Dr. Danny McCain is a religion professor at the University of Jos. I stayed with him and his family for three summers in Nigeria. When I was study- ing healing, I asked Danny whether he had witnessed any significant instances of miraculous healings in Nigeria.

Danny reported that he is suspicious of the sorts of healing claims in Nigeria that involve subjective matters such as improvements in aches (not that any of us enjoy aches). Yet he shared with me a dramatic healing that he witnessed growing up in the United States.[17]

When Danny was eleven or twelve years old, his younger brother Randy, then a toddler, toddled into the family bathroom. The bathtub there, which remains today, was lower than a toilet seat. The family understood that the old-fashioned water heater discharged dangerously hot water, but they mixed it with cold water to adjust it until the water was warm.

Unfortunately, the water at the moment was only hot, and Randy was too young to understand these matters. Perhaps trying to reach something in the bathtub, Randy flipped over into the tub and began screaming. No location in the house was more than ten or fifteen seconds from the bathroom, and their mother, hearing Randy scream, dashed into the bathroom and snatched him from the hot water in the tub.

Randy was so badly scalded that pieces of his skin came off with his shirt. The hospital staff said they could do little to help him, and he cried through the night. In the morning, visitors from the McCains' church came to pray with them. Randy's skin exhibited serious burns, yet during the intense prayers, while Danny was sitting about three feet away from Randy and their mother's rocking chair, Danny noticed that his little brother had stopped crying and was now playing on the floor. Danny stared at Randy in amazement: Randy's skin now looked pink and new, especially in the area that had been burned worst. Their mother examined Randy, and no evidence remained that his skin had ever been burned—not even a blister. Danny emphasizes that the experience was impressed so indelibly in his memory that he would testify to it under oath in court.

Other Flesh Wounds

Tonye Briggs, now a physician in Texas, shared with me a healing that a colleague of his in medical school experienced when an evangelist was praying for the sick.[18] Martin Okokowre's ulcerated arm was scheduled to be amputated the next day, but to even Okokowre's astonishment, it was healed. Briggs noted that the wound had been quite deep and more than four inches wide; because it continually oozed fluids, the bandage had to be changed every night. Overnight, after prayer, the wound closed up and nothing but a small black spot remained on the site. The entire campus recognized the healing and was shaken, and Briggs witnessed the event himself. A number of healing miracles were happening in conjunction with prayer at the time, touching many of his colleagues.

Dr. Chauncey Crandall, a Florida cardiologist, shared with me the full healing of a grapefruit-sized flesh-eating ulcer within perhaps ten days after prayer, averting the scheduled leg amputation. (The story is recounted more fully in chap. 13.)

Restoration of Flesh

In the 1920s, many local eyewitnesses, especially Anglican bishops, commented on those for whom Anglican layman James Moore Hickson prayed. For instance, in one case a "man, whose deep, long-standing wound miraculously filled with flesh during the service," was now able to "walk freely on his formerly lame foot."[19] Likewise, in New Zealand, a witness attested that a person's "calf leg, shrunken, had filled out almost to normal within twelve hours of the service."[20]

Similar reports continued in the later twentieth century. In *Gentle Breeze of Jesus*, written by Indonesian Christian Mel Tari and his American wife, Nona, Mel reports praying for a man with "skinny, shriveled sticks" for legs. The man's legs were also twisted, and bloody and bruised from being dragged around. Mel confesses that he had little faith for a situation like this, but over the next few minutes the man grew stronger and began walking—finally, the man walked home. In a few days, Mel recounts, the man's legs had filled out fully. Mel Tari confirmed this report for me in 2016.[21]

Accounts this dramatic remain rare even in the ministries that report them, but, as the Lord in Scripture encouraged aged parents-to-be, potential mountain-movers, and those needing deliverance, nothing is too difficult for the Lord (Gen. 18:14; Matt. 17:20; Mark 9:23; Luke 1:37).

Chapter 23

Do Deaf People Still Hear?

My undergraduate institution had a program in sign language and a number of deaf students. God blessed and worked through these colleagues just as they were. Most of us have some area of disability or physical weakness and we learn to work around it. Those who have disabilities in any of the nonlethal ways we have mentioned are no exception.

In one way or another, most of us know that one can live a full life despite some limitations. But most of us celebrate when, on occasion, particular limitations prove less permanent than expected. In spring 2021, for example, Joseph Hambrick, one of my MDiv students, shared with the New Testament Introduction class an experience he had in his home city of Newark, New Jersey, in 2014. At the train station, he wrote a note asking an older deaf woman who approached him if he could place his hands on her ears to pray for her healing. She gestured yes, and when he prayed, he commanded her hearing to be restored "in the name of Jesus Christ of Nazareth." As Joseph felt a jolt, she suddenly could hear. They moved ten steps apart "so that we could confirm if she could audibly hear the sound of my voice. As she proceeded to do so, we realized that God had miraculously enabled this older woman to receive her healing. We began to publicly praise God."[1] This was a quick encounter, but, as this chapter should illustrate, it was not an isolated occurrence.

Even the Snoring

Maria Johansson began to lose her hearing in 2012 and eventually reached a point where she needed to read lips and so was unable to talk on the phone.[2]

The condition was organic, and doctors warned that she would lose hearing completely if she did not have a cochlear implant.

On Sunday, August 21, 2016, Johansson and her family went to worship at the Sion Assembly in Flen, Sweden. When people prayed for her, she felt as if a warm blanket had been laid over her. Abruptly and to her astonishment, she noticed that she was hearing the hymn! The next day, she reports, she could hear the gravel beneath her feet. Her children were astounded when she called them, able to talk on the phone. "That night I heard the cars passing by on the road," she recounts. "I heard a fly buzzing against the windowpane, and I heard my husband's snoring. Everything was like sweet music, even the snoring!"

On September 9, she returned to the audiologist. After testing, the surprised doctor concluded, "Now everything with your hearing is within the normal range. Something has happened to your ears that I simply cannot explain. You can call it a miracle!" Johansson notes the audiologist's final comments: "The treble is a little reduced, but it is quite normal at your age. You probably can't hear the crickets anymore." The audiologist, who had been seeing Johansson for a long time, had tears in her eyes as she hugged her and said goodbye.

When author Micael Grenholm interviewed Johansson personally, she had no problems hearing him, even on the phone. Her deafness has disappeared. Her audiologist confirmed to the magazine *Dagen* that Johansson has recovered, and Grenholm's book *Dokumenterade Mirakler* provides the documentation.[3]

It's Not Possible

In his book *Healing Miracles*, Rex Gardner recounts the experience of a nine-year-old girl he calls Rebecca. She was losing her hearing because of significant and confirmed auditory nerve damage; "audiograms and tympanograms showed a hearing loss of 70 decibels in her right ear, and 40 in her left."[4] She began to wear hearing aids on December 3, 1982, but was praying that God would heal her so she wouldn't have to wear them anymore. When one of her hearing aids was damaged at school, however, she needed to procure a new one. She therefore met with the audiologist again on March 8, 1983.

The next night, she suddenly rushed from her bedroom to inform her mother that she could hear. Testing her carefully, her parents discovered that it was true. After thanking God, they called the consultant, who understandably responded, "I don't believe you. It is not possible." He had examined her just a day earlier, after all. But on March 10, 1983, tests revealed that Rebecca's hearing was normal.[5] The dumbfounded audiologist admitted in a report, "*Her hearing returned completely to normal. . . . I was completely unable to explain this phenomenon but naturally, like her parents, I was absolutely delighted. . . . I can think of no rational explanation as to why her hearing returned to normal, there being a severe bilateral sensorineural loss.*"[6]

Even in the large world population such events are fairly rare. Some skeptics respond to this story by citing several other rare cases in which auditory nerve damage has disappeared, even though they lack a ready biomedical explanation for its instant disappearance. Accepting a cure as miraculous only if it has never happened before, however, would exclude any miracles that God has performed more than once. The rare exceptions' spiritual context is not specified and perhaps not known. Often only those who receive the miracle know that it happened in a context of desperate trust in God. Furthermore, sometimes God may show mercy even outside such contexts. This one, however, came by prayer.

Various Cases

In August 2008, Noelle Abbott was fifty years old and had been deaf for about thirty years.[7] When she visited a prayer summit in Ames, Iowa, Pastor Evan Matheson felt that someone present had hearing loss. He prayed for her, and in a moment she began to hear again. Mallory, Noelle's thirty-four-year-old daughter, also was mostly deaf. She asked her mother to take her to the prayer summit in March 2009. Like Noelle, Mallory was healed.

Indiana University professor Candy Gunther Brown notes medical records confirming the healing of "Daisy," who had significant hearing loss. Daisy had worn hearing aids for three decades, and her hearing was degenerating further. During prayer she felt heat, and afterward discovered that she no longer needed hearing aids. Medical documents confirm that she could hear speech normally.[8]

Dr. G. Wayne Brodland, a professor in the University of Waterloo's engineering faculty and a specialist in biomechanics, provided philosophy professor Robert Larmer with his account of his medically documented, progressive hearing recovery. Brodland had suffered from a substantial hearing deficit in one ear as a child, and he became functionally deaf in his late forties because of auditory nerve degeneration. After prolonged prayer from groups that believed in healing, Brodland insisted that his hearing was beginning to improve, despite his doctor's assurance that "nerve damage does not heal." To the audiologist's astonishment, however, tests verified that his ability to hear had indeed improved substantially. Although his hearing was not perfect, he was no longer functionally deaf, and test results revealed that he could hear as well as he had when he had been much younger.[9]

Randy Clark, already mentioned in chapters 16 and 21, shares that in September 2001 God's Spirit touched the deaf section in his ministry meeting and eight of the forty people there were healed without anyone even praying for them.[10] On another occasion, a member of his ministry team announced that God was healing a right ear, and a few seconds later, another member of the team announced that a left ear was being healed. A Brazilian teenager born totally deaf in both ears was present, but she was not seated at a place where she could have read the lips of the speakers. She clasped her right ear as it opened, and then her left, the healing of which quickly followed. The ministry team learned the details only in the ensuing commotion.[11]

On yet another occasion, Randy prayed for a fourteen-year-old boy deaf in one ear, who was then healed. The boy's mother insisted that Randy should be more excited than he was. "I *am* excited," he explained, "but I've seen deaf people healed a number of times before."

"Yes, but have you ever seen a deaf ear healed when there was no auditory nerve?" She explained that tests had shown that her son lacked an auditory nerve for that ear. Needless to say, Randy did get more excited.[12]

Bob Canton's book shares letters from people who report being healed during his ministry trips. A woman in Malaysia recounts that for ten years she was totally deaf without her hearing aids, but since his prayer she no longer needs them.[13] Levy Zindac from New Jersey testifies that his seventeen-year-old nephew, who had been deaf since birth, was astonished to hear noise for the first time. His healing led to many conversions.[14]

Mozambique

As I have already mentioned, the most dramatic healings occur most often on the cutting edge of Jesus's message. More than two decades ago, Rolland and Heidi Baker recognized that God works especially among the broken and the desperate. At the time, Mozambique was the poorest country in the world, so the Baker family moved there, expecting to see God work.

God, however, does not usually work on our schedule. That way, when God does use us, we recognize that what happens is God's doing and not ours. For a long time, Heidi prayed for blind and deaf people, yet no one was healed. Then, suddenly, in one week, three blind women she prayed for in different settings were instantly healed of blindness.

Today thousands of people report being healed of blindness and deafness in Mozambique.[15] Most of these people come from non-Christian backgrounds. Their villages lacked churches and they knew little about Jesus. Yet they and often their villages became followers of Jesus as they experienced and witnessed these miraculous healings. One source told me that she visited this ministry in Mozambique. She was simply preaching in an unchurched village when blind and deaf people began to be healed spontaneously before anyone had prayed for them.[16] God was working in Mozambique!

Hearing these sorts of reports, a team of American investigators, including both Candy Gunther Brown and medical experts, traveled to Mozambique and tested many people in one of these new settings before and after prayer. Their report, published in the September 2010 issue of *Southern Medical Journal*, confirms that people were being healed of blindness and deafness. The results were far beyond any effects documented for psychosomatic cures or hypnotism.[17]

Professor Brown summarizes some of the results in a provocative online article for the *Huffington Post*:[18] "Two of 11 hearing subjects had thresholds reduced by over 50 dBHL [decibels hearing level]." Another person, reported to be "deaf and mute since birth," initially "made no responses to sounds at 100 dBHL." After prayer, however, this person "responded to 60 dBHL tones, imitating sounds in a hoarse, raspy voice. Three of 11 vision subjects improved from 20/400 or worse [legally blind] to 20/80 or better. Before prayer, Maryam could not count fingers from one foot away." After intercessors had prayed for her for one minute, "she was reading the 20/125 line of a vision chart." That is, she went from something like 20/8000 to 20/125 after prayer. These results are simply too significant to be explained as coincidence.

Not surprisingly, critics on the internet were harsh, complaining about the limitations of testing conditions in rural Mozambique. That such conditions are limited is true, but Brown responded to the critics in a chapter in her evenhanded book *Testing Prayer*, published by Harvard University Press.[19] Her account clearly documents people moving from significant blindness or deafness to significant sight or hearing, immediately after prayer.

The only reason I can imagine that some detractors would want to contest such clear evidence is that their worldview cannot acknowledge the possibility that miracles—or at least extraordinary healings during prayer—may occur. Calling fellow scholars liars seems an increasingly steep price to pay merely to hold on to a contested essay by an eighteenth-century philosopher.

PART 5

"The Dead Are Raised" (Matt. 11:5//Luke 7:22)

F ollowing David Hume, one philosopher concludes, "If anyone were to tell you that a man had died and come back to life," it would be more rational to disbelieve him than to believe him.[1] One may question, however, whether deeming all witnesses liars or fools (Hume's approach) is the best explanation for multiple, independent accounts of raisings.[2]

Whatever other maladies might be considered psychosomatic, we do not ordinarily speak of someone being psychosomatically dead. For this reason, the hundreds of reports of raisings in the contexts of prayer or mission today are particularly significant. Other scholars have published a number of reports; I cite many of them in my 2011 book *Miracles* and in a 2015 academic article.[3] Even since the publication of *Miracles*, I have received accounts of raisings fairly often, from friends working in various parts of the world. The stories I include here are samples only.

Of course, no one will say that these things happen all the time; everywhere in the world, the vast majority of people who die stay dead. We consider some extraordinary events miracles, or *special* divine action, precisely because they do *not* happen all the time. To speak somewhat tongue in cheek, if dead people were raised on a regular basis we might have a significant problem with overpopulation, and thousand-year-olds (a different sort of "millennials") might dominate most public affairs. The point in recounting such stories is not to imply that they happen all the time but to point out that they do happen sometimes, and to suggest that God has a message for us in their happening. (I return to this message later in the book.)

Too many witnesses have recounted reports of raisings to narrate all of them in this book. In an effort to narrate at least a few, I have divided this section on raisings into several chapters: accounts from earlier history (chap. 24), accounts from Africa (25), accounts from Asia (26), accounts from the West that make the news (27), accounts from the West that do not make the news (28), accounts from doctors who have witnessed raisings (29), accounts from friends I know personally (30), and an account from within our family (31).

Chapter 24

Are the Dead Still Raised? History

When witnesses lack advanced medical means to verify death, individuals they deem to be dead might later be considered to have been merely in a coma—or not *very* dead. Sometimes in these cases I will use language such as "apparently" dead—that is, dead so far as anyone could tell. In most of these cases, however, the body has grown stiff and cold, and there are no signs of respiration, pulse, or heartbeat. In such cases, for all practical purposes, the person is generally considered *fairly* dead![1] (With the exception of Lazarus, this is also the case for resuscitations reported in the Bible.) Sudden recoveries are not typical in such cases, especially if this state continues for very long.

Church Fathers' Reports

Reports of divine resuscitations from death are not new.[2] For example, the early second-century bishop Quadratus reported that some people whom Jesus had raised remained alive into Quadratus's own lifetime.[3] Similarly, an apparently second-century source reports that the first bishop of Arbil in Mesopotamia was converted through witnessing the Syrian evangelist Addai raising a man from the dead in the year 99.[4]

In the late second century, Irenaeus, a church father in what is now France, argued that God was with true followers of Jesus rather than with quasi-Christian cults that misrepresented Jesus. One of Irenaeus's arguments[5] was that cultists could not cure the blind, the paralyzed, or the demonized, as some members of the true church could. Nor did these cultists even recognize the power to raise the physically

139

dead, as Jesus and the apostles had. By contrast, Irenaeus insisted, the dead are often raised through the prayers and fasting of true Christians in some locations:

> And so far are they [the sectarians] from being able to raise the dead, as the Lord raised them, and the apostles did by means of prayer, and as has been frequently done in the brotherhood on account of some necessity—the entire church in that particular locality entreating [the boon] with much fasting and prayer, the spirit of the dead man has returned, and he has been bestowed in answer to the prayers of the saints—that they do not even believe this can possibly be done, [and hold] that the resurrection from the dead is simply an acquaintance with that truth which they proclaim.[6]

Augustine and other leaders of the ancient church cite eyewitness reports of raisings through prayer.[7]

Medieval and Early Modern Reports

Such accounts have continued throughout history; I could elaborate at length[8] but offer here merely a few examples. Although medieval Christians often invoked saints, they ultimately hoped for their prayers to reach God. In one medieval account, a girl drowned in a pond in the early afternoon and was discovered face-down after sunset, "her face and body . . . so badly bloated as to be unrecognizable." Firsthand witnesses noted that the father had to use a knife to pry open her mouth to put her tongue back in, and then the mouth would not close. Forty people prayed together till midnight; her recovery in the morning was attested by various witnesses, including herself.[9]

Similarly, Welshman William Cragh had been hanged for hours before he was cut down; firsthand witnesses described his face as black, with his mouth bloody, his black and swollen tongue hanging out, and his eyes protruding from their bloody sockets. That is, most observers would have considered him genuinely dead. Nevertheless, witnesses claimed that Cragh returned to life after bystanders prayed.[10]

Some readers who are inclined to underline the frequent credulity of medieval witnesses might be less apt to dismiss a firsthand account from Oxford fellow and Anglican minister John Wesley, founder of the Methodist church. In his journal, he recounts an experience on December 25, 1742. According to Wesley, a man named Mr. Meyrick appeared to be dead until Wesley and others prayed. At that point Meyrick opened his eyes and called for Wesley, afterward recovering gradually from his sickness. Although this account is now centuries old, it is an eyewitness report recorded on the day of the experience.[11] Firsthand accounts also surround the ministry of nineteenth-century German Lutheran pastor Johann Christoph Blumhardt.[12]

How dead were these people? That is, were they clinically dead by modern standards? None of these reports, including those in the Bible, include heart monitors or analyze brain activity; these are inevitable limitations in dealing with historical reports. But most are associated with prayer, some are associated with reported afterlife experiences, and in some eyewitness accounts the body in question was bloated, blackened from cell death, and so forth.

Twentieth-Century Reports

With the emphasis on healing in the early twentieth century, accounts of raising from death proliferated, often accompanied by dramatic recoveries. Most of these accounts are now available only in the popular Christian periodicals that reported them at the time, all witnesses being now long deceased. Mike Finley, however, helped me trace one such report back to the records of earlier witnesses, including the attending physician, which were cited in local newspaper articles—some published within days of the event.[13]

A majority of the reports published and thus surviving from this period appear in the United States, but they do appear elsewhere as well. Thus, for example, on September 7, 1930, a woman named Kuzuwa apparently bled to death in her village in what is today the Democratic Republic of Congo. A visiting evangelist, Pelendo, associated with the Evangelical Free Church, prayed for her. When he said, "Amen," Kuzuwa reportedly repeated the amen and sat up, wondering what had happened to her. Throughout the region, the village remained identified by this event for years afterward.[14]

In Memphis, Tennessee, Elouise Jordan suffered for many years from throat cancer before she finally died in 1949. Learning of her death, her daughter left work and arrived at Elouise's home in time to see the expected hearse and a crowd gathered. Yet she also witnessed something utterly unexpected: her mother, Elouise, was now not only alive but celebrating. Their pastor, Bishop C. H. Mason, founder of the largely African American denomination Church of God in Christ, had prayed over her mother's body.

Moreover, Elouise was not only now alive but also completely healed of throat cancer, and she lived healthily for thirty-three more years. I first learned her story from Eric Greaux, a colleague in my Duke University PhD program who was friends with the family. I learned further details and received the photographs from Elouise's daughter and granddaughter.[15]

But such accounts did not stop in the mid-twentieth century. For example, during my visit to Cuba in August 2010, Iris Lilia Fonseca Valdés, a nurse, told me that her infant had died the preceding year. She had prayed for perhaps an hour, until the child revived. I was not present at the child's death, but the child's life I can certify: Fonseca Valdés had the child with her as we spoke.[16]

////////////

The next few chapters offer further examples of raisings from death in Africa, Asia, and the contemporary West, as well as from doctors and from witnesses I know firsthand.

Chapter 25

Are the Dead Still Raised?
Africa

Eyewitness accounts of resuscitations from death seem more common in Africa[1] than in the West, not least because in Africa there is often less access to medical technology that could prevent many deaths. Two decades ago, Assayehegn Berhe, then the general secretary of Evangelical Churches Fellowship of Ethiopia, is quoted as reporting that raisings were "considered normal" in Ethiopia.[2]

A Family Friend in Cameroon

When I was giving some lectures in Cameroon in 2013, I met a humble and self-effacing pastor named André Mamadzi.[3] Although I got to know Pastor André in person only over the course of a week, two respected contacts had introduced me to him, both insisting that they knew he had reliable accounts of healings in his ministry. One was Dr. Daniel Yoon, president of Faculté de Théologie Évangélique du Cameroun; the other was my own brother-in-law Aimé Moussounga, who teaches New Testament at that seminary and had worked for a long time with Pastor André.[4]

Among Mamadzi's accounts was one of a resuscitation. A six-year-old girl named Olive had died in the morning, and doctors had insisted that she could not be revived. Lacking any other means to help their daughter, the desperate parents finally carried her body to Mamadzi's church, which was known for prayer, and laid her on a table in his office. Mamadzi and his assistant, Samuel, were preparing for the midweek prayer meeting and asked them to remove the girl's body, but as Mamadzi saw the broken parents weeping, he decided that it was better to at least pray rather than simply send these visitors away.

"We don't have time," Samuel protested, but they began to pray. Soon it was time to begin the prayer service—6:00 p.m.—so Mamadzi urged Samuel to go out and start the service by himself. "I'll be out soon," he assured him.

As Mamadzi continued praying, he felt increasing faith and heard a clear voice, like someone speaking in his ear. "Do you remember what Jesus did with Lazarus? Call the girl's name." He had forgotten her name, but the voice reminded him. He called out, "Olive." Nothing happened. He called a second and third time. The third time, her eyes opened. A few minutes later, Samuel looked on aghast as Mamadzi did indeed join him in the service. Walking hand in hand with him into the sanctuary were Olive's parents—and Olive herself, alive.

At the time that I interviewed Pastor André, five years had passed since Olive's raising, and she remained fine. I asked whether her parents had joined the church after Olive's raising. "Of course!" he laughed. Meanwhile, my translator turned to me, amused. He had heard this same story before, but not from Pastor André. He was friends with Samuel, who had confessed his bewilderment on seeing Olive walk into the prayer service alive.

A Medical Student's Account

In 2017 a medical student and former nurse in Boston shared with me a raising that he experienced in his home country.[5] Ifeanyichukwu Chinedozi, from southeast Nigeria, certainly does not oppose God's activity to medicine. He believes that medicine is an extension of God's healing power for people around the world. He and his family were originally steeped in traditional African religion, but when he was eight years old a man dressed in white kept appearing to him in dreams. Afraid, his family went to a nearby church to get help from the Christians, and the entire family soon became Christians.

While Ifeanyi was in high school, he was a leader of the Fellowship of Christian Students. One day when he was preaching, he became aware that a woman was outside crying. He asked what was wrong, and she replied, "My mother was pronounced dead after spending a week in the hospital. I'm not here for comfort," she insisted, "but I believe that God will use you to raise my mother." Ifeanyi was taken aback; he had tried that once before, without the Spirit's leading, and it hadn't worked. But he felt as if God wanted him now to just act in obedience, so he told the woman to get olive oil. When she brought it, he and the other Christian leaders at the school prayed that God would raise the mother up according to the daughter's faith. He handed the oil back to the woman and instructed her to pour it on her mother's body.

Ifeanyi was not sure what to expect when the woman approached him three days later. "I poured the oil on my mother," she reported, "and my mother came back to life." Even the daughter had been shocked, and when she screamed, others had rushed into the room.

Ifeanyi and his fellow student leaders were delighted, and the family now brought them to a celebratory feast they had prepared. There they introduced Ifeanyi to the mother and explained, "This is the man of God who woke you up from the dead."

Ifeanyi protested immediately. "That's not right. Did you even see me by your bedside? It was *Jesus* who woke you up!"

Other African Raisings

Dr. David Emmett, whom I have mentioned before (chaps. 14, 22), recounts an event from the Democratic Republic of Congo. Around 1984, Dave heard a nearby clap of thunder and then, for some time, the sound of crying, wailing, and people praying. Lightning had struck a secondary school student "very near to my house in Kipushya." She was the daughter of an elder in the local church whom Dave knew. People carried her body to the maternity building of the local clinic, about two hundred yards behind Dave's house. Nyembo Lukama, the nurse who filled all medical roles in the area, declared her dead. As local Christians prayed for her, however, she returned to life, and Dave heard the sound of wailing shift to shrieks of delight and quickly learned the story. He has subsequently confirmed his memory by checking with others who were present at the time.[6]

Elsewhere in this book I have noted various conversions through healings, including raisings. Sometimes the conversions include the person who had died. Swidiq Kanana was an imam in folk Islam in Rwanda, but he began to be persuaded that Christianity was true after God healed him. The cost of conversion was high, however—potentially death—and he refrained from fully committing himself to Christ. Later, after a long illness (unrelated to his previous healing), he died. He found himself facing a dangerous eternity without Christ, but he was rescued and yet confronted by Christ and then found himself back in his body— waking during his funeral. He was now not only alive but fully healed. Barely dressed but knowing better than to conceal what he knew any longer, Kanana began preaching Christ at his own funeral. A local Anglican priest who was present for the funeral joined him in preaching, and their message, along with the miracle, immediately led many of his fellow nominal Muslims to follow Jesus.[7]

Kanana is now an Anglican priest himself and has replaced his first name, Swidiq, with the name Cedric. Benjamin Fischer, who has a PhD from the University of Notre Dame and teaches at Northwest Nazarene University, initially considered Kanana's account hard to believe, but during his sabbatical in Africa he met many of the people who had experienced the events narrated in the story, including members of Kanana's family and the local Anglican bishop. "Most interesting," Dr. Fischer shared with me, "has been walking with Cedric in Kigali and meeting several people from his Muslim school days, who had come to faith in Jesus because of the events told in the book" that Fischer afterward helped him write.[8]

I will return to African raisings in chapters 30 and 31, where I recount incidents that happened to people I knew before I heard their stories. Some of them, in fact, I met after they had died.

Chapter 26

Are the Dead Still Raised? Asia

I have surveyed scores of accounts of raisings from around the world, many of those today from highly respected sources.[1] For example, the renowned Anglican canon Andrew White, the former "vicar of Baghdad" often interviewed on international news, reports raisings through prayer in Iraq. When some women from his church found a mother weeping for her dead baby, they went with her to the mortuary and prayed for a few minutes until the baby revived.[2]

Canon White shared a more recent account when he visited my local church in 2014.[3] There he mentioned instructing a man to call on the name of Jesus when the man went to visit his daughter in the hospital. Although the man was Muslim, he kept repeating Jesus's name on his way to the hospital; in the Islamic faith, of course, Jesus is a great prophet and miracle worker. In contrast to some folk Muslims unfamiliar with Jesus in the Qur'an itself, educated, orthodox Muslims respect him. When the man reached the hospital, the workers informed him sadly that his daughter had just died. Devastated, he threw himself on her body, weeping, but still crying, "Jesus! Jesus! Jesus!"

She immediately sat up. "I'm hungry," she said.[4]

"Don't worry," Canon White says he assured the man afterward. "We've seen this before." A former anesthesiologist, Andrew White is well qualified both medically and theologically to recognize healing miracles.

Indonesia Rising

Two of my students shared with me their accounts during a week in 2015 in which I was giving some lectures in South Sulawesi, Indonesia. Kornelia Makani told about the raising of her baby sister in West Timor,[5] whereas Sifra Ndawu told about herself.[6]

Here I will summarize only Sifra's experience, which she shared with me only because she had a question she did not understand. (Some of the details, of course, she got from her parents and her doctor since she was not conscious during a key part of the story.) She had suffered from breast cancer that spread rapidly through her body over a period of months. Finally, on December 25, 2013, the doctor at the hospital, Dr. Made, pronounced her dead, unable to revive her. The staff disconnected the equipment and laid a cloth over her body.

Her family, who had been praying for her, grieved but accepted this outcome as God's sovereign will—whereupon suddenly she moved. She explains that a figure had hugged her and told her that she had not yet completed her task: "I want you to be my witness. Whatever you experience now will be a testimony that you will tell others." The cancer that had killed her was now gone, but she was alive.

As she spoke with us, Sifra exuded only sincerity, without the slightest evasion, deceit, boastfulness, or anxiety. But now came her question for me as a Bible teacher: Why did God let her suffer with cancer and let her parents suffer grief before he raised her and healed her? I had to simply admit that I did not know. Sometimes our testimony comes at a high price.

As I recount the following stories, keep in mind that, even if a person can be revived, after six minutes with no oxygen, irreparable brain damage begins to occur. Yet brain damage is not reported or evidenced in these cases.

Extremely Dead

In May 2005, Sri Lankan Assemblies of God pastor Noel Fernando experienced a heart attack.[7] He returned home after treatment but suffered another heart attack a month later, and his wife found him slumped and unconscious. He briefly regained consciousness in the hospital, complaining that he could not breathe. After he lost consciousness again, a doctor tried valiantly to revive him but could not, breaking three of his ribs in the process.[8] Finally the doctor put him on a ventilator and went home.

Other pastors and Noel's associates at the Bible college came to pray for him, but the other doctors gave them no hope, explaining that his heart had failed. Noel's wife, Shanthi, explains, "We stood outside and prayed for many hours with tears. When the doctors noticed this, they said, 'The patient inside is not breathing and once the doctor who admitted him comes we will remove the ventilator.' They asked us to go and make the necessary arrangements for the funeral."

The admitting doctor had not returned to sign the release for the morgue, however, so the believers kept praying. "Suddenly," Shanthi explains, "after nearly 30 hours there was movement in the body. The heart started beating. The doctors who insisted that there was no hope were amazed." She adds, "My husband said that during those hours when his heart had failed, he felt the presence of God and that God showed him many faces of foreigners and requested him to serve them. God had told him that he was going to use him as a mightier witness than at present."

Because there was little privacy in the hospital, not only doctors and nurses but also many patients were aware of Noel's death. Other workers and patients in the hospital, who belonged to various religions, all recognized this as a miracle; some even laid food at the foot of his bed as offerings, in accordance with their traditions. Noel's one remaining problem was three broken ribs.

Contrary to predictions, Noel had no brain damage. He fluently and regularly interpreted three languages; before I had more direct access to his testimony, I learned it from a US missionary for whom he regularly translated. She testified that everyone in the Bible college knew the story. Noel went on to have a great ministry of healing for others, until he passed away again some years later.

India Rising

India offers many examples of reports of raisings from the dead.[9] One dissertation recounts, for example, the incident that sparked a movement among the Nishi tribal people to faith in Christ. When a Nishi government official's son died, he learned of "the Christian God, Jesus," who had raised Lazarus. After he prayed to this God, his son revived.[10]

In another location in India, two Western sociologists interviewed local witnesses, among them a Hindu village elder, concerning a dead woman who had revived after several hours of a pastor's intercession. The sociologists also researched another incident, reported by local newspapers, in which a pastor prayed for half an hour over a corpse with worms in its nose. The girl then revived and recounted her afterlife experience.[11]

A pastor in Mumbai shared with me that at a camp in May 2007 "one of our young people noticed a young boy lying motionless at the bottom of the pool." The boy, Vikram, belonged to a Hindu family visiting the resort. Jaya, a trained nurse who was part of the church, found no pulse, breathing, or other signs of life, so Jaya, with Suneeta, an intercessor, took the boy and his father in an auto-rickshaw to find a doctor. The first doctor said the boy was dead and offered no help; when they found another, he tried and failed to resuscitate him. The Christians kept praying, and an hour and a half later, as the rickshaw was returning, Vikram returned to life. He explained that he had heard the name "Jesus" and then was rescued. His Hindu parents were astounded, explaining that previously he "had never heard the name of Jesus!" The family joined the Christians in their worship service.[12]

Resuscitation Saves Other Lives

I mentioned Professor Jessy Jaison in chapter 22. In addition to the story that she shared with me about the healing of a leper, she told me about a woman named

Leelamma.[13] When Jessy was a child, a Hindu family close to Jessy's household became followers of Jesus, but the mother in that family, Leelamma, was not very committed to her new faith. One day a poisonous snake bit Leelamma; as the poison spread, her body began turning black and blue. Some of the local people believed that their gods had judged her for worshiping only one God, and they blamed the church for bringing this about. After her body was brought back to her house, the local people summoned the pastor, Jessy's father, who in turn called other believers to join him in prayer.

Leelamma's body had turned black, and she was already nearly dead. The local militants surrounded the believers, ready to attack. "This is your fault!" one charged angrily. "You must revive her!" After Jessy's father had prayed for a few minutes, everyone was certain that Leelamma was dead. Nevertheless, he kept praying, and after a few more minutes she began coughing and then vomiting black fluid. After this, she was fine. Jessy knows Leelamma and her family well; later Leelamma's son Rejeesh even stayed for several years with Jessy's family.

China Rising

Many accounts of raisings circulate in China. Rather than repeating those noted in my earlier book,[14] I will briefly note a more recently published set of accounts. Paul Hattaway recounts that in Nanyang in 1992, an eighteen-year-old Christian died after weeks of fever. Two days after the death, the family's doctor was passing through the area and noticed mourners at the house. After checking the body, he provided a death certificate. The next day, as the funeral was about to begin, Elder Fu came and requested that they open the coffin. After they did, he and his companions worshiped God for three hours and then began to pray for her raising. The young woman sat up, alive. "Subsequently, the parents took their daughter and her death certificate and traveled around the border area between Henan and Hubei provinces, testifying that Jesus Christ had raised her from the dead. Six entire villages, numbering more than 6,000 people, repented and turned to God."[15] The Nanyang region remains a major center of Christian faith in China.

Brother Timothy was a poor farmer and a church leader, also in the Nanyang area. In 1993, people invited him to pray for a wealthy Communist Party official who was dying from mouth cancer.[16] By the time Timothy gained access to him, Mr. Chang had died. Shocked but wishing to honor the request, Timothy asked to be allowed to pray over the body in the refrigeration unit. As he did so, workers gaped, entertained by the simple farmer's faith. Nothing happened, and, remembering the biblical story about Lazarus, Timothy promised to return to pray the next day.

When he came back, more than twenty gathered, laughing, to entertain themselves at his expense. "As I laid hands on the corpse," Timothy recounts, "I leaned forward and whispered, 'Mr. Chang, if you are unable to talk, then I command you to move your eyes in the Name of the Lord Jesus Christ.' I looked closely and it appeared his eyes twinkled a little!" Nothing further happened, however, so he prayed aloud the message of the gospel and said that he would return the next morning at 10:00 a.m. to pray one final time. As he arrived, the stairs and basement morgue were full of staff wanting to watch. He prayed again, nothing happened, and he left. But soon after, he heard the news: "About 20 minutes after I left, Mr. Chang suddenly sat up and started coughing."[17] Word spread through the hospital, bringing many to faith in Christ; Mr. Chang and his family became believers, and he lived many more years. But as Timothy notes, in that period of revival, miracles were occurring regularly, with thousands coming to Christ. "Miracles were not something we focused on. They were merely evidences that confirmed the message we were preaching about Jesus was true."[18] Today it is estimated that more than three million committed Christians live in the Nanyang Prefecture.[19]

Unfortunately, some Western critics, like Hume, discount stories from other parts of the world. Yet such experiences also happen at times in the West.

Chapter 27

Raised in the West?
Cases in the News

Sometimes people in the West speak as if events such as the dead being raised happen only "overseas"—that is, outside their own potential sphere of experience. But these events sometimes occur in the West as well. Some of these accounts include medical intervention because accounts involving physicians are usually the ones that we can medically document. Some are more dramatic than others; all are simply samples.

Raising Reports in the Media

Media reports provide a massive number of stories, sometimes attested by doctors. For example, in 2012 British footballer (soccer player) Fabrice Muamba collapsed during a game, and his heart was restarted only after seventy-eight minutes. Although his recovery was gradual after he returned to life, it should have been impossible. Muamba, who suffered no brain damage, expressed gratitude to God and testified that God had done a miracle for him.[1]

Some of these reports include afterlife experiences with Jesus. For example, doctors were ready to pronounce Texas teenager Zach Clements dead after he went twenty minutes without a heartbeat, but he returned to life, reporting his experience with Jesus during the interim.[2] One of the best-known accounts, popularized through the film *Miracles from Heaven*, involves Annabel Beam, who reported an experience of heaven and the healing of her prior chronic, debilitating condition.[3] A film was also made about the account of Baptist pastor Don Piper, who was killed in a vehicle collision; although the rest of his physical recovery was gradual, his return to life was immediate after his experience of heaven and another minister's prayer.[4]

He Drew Me Out of Many Waters

One case that made widespread news was the 2015 resuscitation of twenty-two-month-old toddler Gardell Martin after more than one hundred minutes of CPR.[5] Gardell was playing with siblings when he fell into a swollen creek and was swept nearly a quarter of a mile downstream. There a neighbor found him close to half an hour later, facedown in the creek but caught in a tree branch as water raged around him. This was a cold-water drowning, which is sometimes survivable, as in this case; but oxygen deprivation had driven Gardell's blood acid level to a pH of 6.5, the time without oxygen had been too long, and brain damage seemed certain. Nevertheless, the outcome defied normal expectations.

As Gardell's mother, Rose Martin, points out, his family and local church groups were banding together to pray for him at the very time his pulse returned. Frank Maffei, the physician who oversaw Gardell's early hours in the pediatric intensive care unit, testifies to his delight that Gardell was conscious and answering questions just eight hours after his pulse started again. Dr. Maffei considered the rare collocation of factors that preserved the child miraculous.[6] A week after Gardell's resuscitation from death, a CNN video shows him running around playfully; even his parents were astonished at the recovery.[7]

Breakthrough

Another case that made widespread news,[8] and one that I shall elaborate more fully here, is that of fourteen-year-old drowning victim John Smith. This story also became a major motion picture, *Breakthrough*, released near Easter 2019. Based on Joyce Smith's book *The Impossible*,[9] *Breakthrough* movingly recounts the experience of Joyce's son John. In 2015, John fell through lake ice on a frigid January day. When his two friends tried to pull him out, the ice broke under them as well. They managed to escape, but John was now submerged.

Providentially, the local fire rescue team had been trained in ice rescue—actually, just the week before. But John was underwater for fifteen minutes, and his heart remained stopped for the following forty-three minutes as emergency personnel performed CPR. As one medical resident and experienced kayaker notes in a different context, "Fatal neurological injury normally occurs within 5 to 7 minutes of submersion, and almost always occurs following 12 to 14 minutes," with survivors experiencing a range of disabilities. "Submersion time over 5 minutes makes intact survival unlikely."[10] He goes on to note that, despite half a million fatal drownings per year, "miracle cases" are rare, with just forty-three documented cases altogether "of survival with near normal functionality" after more than four minutes underwater, all of them concerning individuals smaller than John.[11]

As noted, cold-water drownings often allow resuscitation after a longer period of time than normal drownings. But while the water temperature beneath the ice was only forty degrees, it was above freezing and unfortunately not cold *enough*, given the other factors noted below, for the outcome John experienced.

Emergency room doctor Kent Sutterer and his team valiantly tried to revive John, but after exhausting all possible resources, Dr. Sutterer allowed John's mother to say goodbye to her deceased child. Instead, she screamed a desperate prayer— and the heart monitor abruptly and spontaneously sprang to life. Astonished, the medical team jumped back into action, preparing to transfer John to Cardinal Glennon Hospital in nearby St. Louis. But while Dr. Sutterer and his colleagues all publicly acknowledged the resuscitation during prayer as a miracle,[12] he believed that it would take another miracle even to get John to the hospital still alive.

Nor, once John arrived there alive, did the specialists at Cardinal Glennon give John much of a chance of making it through the night. Although John was now alive, he had been dead for over an hour. His lungs were full of contaminated water that had infected his entire system. He experienced heart failure, liver failure, acute pancreatitis, and ischemic bowel necrosis: "Every organ was in catastrophic failure."[13]

Dr. Jeremy Garrett, an expert on drowning, had rescued many drowning victims only to have them never awake from comas; John's brain, like his other organs, had been oxygen-starved for too long to recover. "Although there are many stories of cold water drowning with surprisingly good outcomes, those require a special combination of factors—none of which were present for John except the cold water," Dr. Garrett explains, and even that, as mentioned, wasn't cold enough for someone of John's size.[14] Apart from some basic brain stem function, John lacked brain activity, and Dr. Garrett did not expect him to survive the first night, nor, when he did so, to survive succeeding nights. In fact, his survival was virtually impossible. "Damage to John's organs and tissues was so severe," Dr. Garrett reports, that "his muscle cells were literally breaking open and dumping their contents into his bloodstream."[15]

Yet John's mother and his pastor, Assemblies of God minister Jason Noble, had already seen enough to trust that God had a plan and would restore John fully. "During the first night we prayed over John and saw awesome miracles in his room," Pastor Jason notes. "After that I walked out and told Joyce that John was going to walk out of the hospital. I didn't know when exactly, or how, but he was. We agreed and that's what we stood on. I was completely confident that he would walk out."[16]

Dr. Garrett notes that within two days of reaching the hospital, "John began opening his eyes," and soon could answer complex questions. Sixteen days after John entered the hospital, he walked out of it carrying his basketball and was soon back to playing sports. Apart from initial physical therapy for fine motor movements with his hands, John's brain function "was otherwise entirely normal" at the time of his discharge.[17]

Touched by John's experience, many of his peers committed their lives to Christ. John himself was initially resistant, but in time he recommitted himself to Christ. Today he is a student at North Central University, and he travels many weekends to recount his story. Although John was initially unhappy about the way *Breakthrough* was going to portray his story, he grew to appreciate the movie and now sees it as a game changer. Despite some of the sorts of adaptations scripts make, he feels that actor Marcel Ruiz captured him perfectly. Most importantly, John tells me that now he "wouldn't change [what happened to him] for anything."[18]

His healing might seem a mere anomaly, but it fits a wider context of other healings in his church circle—a pattern for those willing to recognize it.[19] Pastor Jason's ministry includes a number of other dramatic healings,[20] including what appear to be a couple of other raisings from death in response to prayer.[21]

Angels Watching Over Me

Moreover, the context of John's healing was one of prayer and divine guidance. When John's pastor, Jason Noble, prayed beside John's bed, he reports that he saw two angels.[22] Pastor Jason shared with me the full story:

> It was the day of the accident and we had been told that there was a 99 percent chance that John wouldn't make it; if he did make it he would most likely be a vegetable. Every one of John's organs was in catastrophic failure with the brain and the lungs being the most injured. So I went into the room with a group of pastors and we began to pray. We prayed first for John's lungs that God would breathe the same breath that he breathed into Adam to give him life.
>
> It was at that moment that I turned around and saw in my mind's eye two angels in the room that stood from floor to ceiling. I had seen the same two angels four years before that, in Port Angeles, Washington. That was in an ICU unit when I was called in to pray for an eighty-five-year-old lady who had been given about fifteen minutes left to live. She had never given her life to Jesus. I got down by her ear and said, "You are on the edge of eternity. Now is your time to give your life to Jesus and make a decision for him. If you want to do that squeeze my hand." She did, and, as she squeezed my hand, I turned around and saw the same two angels in her room. Within fifteen minutes you could see the color come back into her grey body, from her feet to her head. Within an hour she woke up. When she woke up, she said, "I gave my life to the Lord." The next day, she went home healed.
>
> I turned back to John after I saw the angels and his eye opened and he over breathed his respirator, and his shoulder came off the bed. It was like at that moment that God had definitely breathed new life into John. We then continued to pray that God would restore John's brain and "recreate" it. Over his head in my mind's eye I saw a million colors coming down from heaven, almost like electricity, knitting his brain back together again. After that prayer you could feel the power and presence of God in the room. John again opened his eyes, and his shoulders came off the bed. I looked into his eyes and saw life.
>
> The accident happened on Monday. By that Friday, we got a call from a lady who asked, "Were there angels in John's room on Monday night?" We said yes. She said, "I saw them in his room. Those were the same angels that I had seen in my room when I was fifteen years old dying." She was fifty-six at this point.[23]

I hope skeptics will pardon my (hopefully gracious) skepticism about what appear to me as excessive degrees of skepticism.

Chapter 28

Raised in the West?
Cases That Don't Make the News

M ost resuscitations don't make the news. Because ER technicians and doctors have to resuscitate patients often, cases are deemed newsworthy only when the person or setting is deemed noteworthy or if the outcome is particularly extraordinary. Some of the following cases are more extraordinary than others. Some reflect a better-than-expected outcome; some appear impossible apart from special divine action.

Dead in Church

I met Charlotte Pridgen-Randolph, a United Methodist pastor, when I was speaking about healing at a Methodist conference in July 2016. Pastor Charlotte and her husband, Lavergne Randolph, shared with me a shocking incident from her church in New England. While some New Englanders joke about spiritually dead churches there, this apparent case of death in church was more material.[1]

And Pastor Charlotte should know: she was a registered nurse before she felt called to pastoral ministry. "My background was medical intensive care, psychiatric nursing and administration," she explains. "I know what physical death looks like. I spent four years caring for people in life and death situations."

One Sunday in 2011, about an hour after congregants stood for the Scripture reading, Pastor Charlotte closed the morning service. One member of the congregation, however, a widowed, older usher named Mrs. E, remained in her seat. Pastor Charlotte tells me what she witnessed as she approached Mrs. E: "She was an ashen color and a blue ring had formed around her lips. I touched her hands, and they were cold." She found no pulse. Barely able to speak, Pastor Charlotte glanced at those standing around and mouthed, "Call 911."

She kept praying under her breath, "Lord, please don't take her like this. It's almost Christmas. And please don't take her in the sanctuary!" She was angry that death had dared enter the sanctuary, and she began crying out to God. She asked everyone to leave the sanctuary quickly without blocking the entrance because an ambulance was on the way.

The ambulance, however, took twenty minutes. Meanwhile, Pastor Charlotte attempted to take Mrs. E's pulse again, both at her carotid and her brachial. There was still no pulse. Still praying under her breath, but thinking it was better to lay the body down, Pastor Charlotte crossed the woman's legs and gently lifted them.

Suddenly Mrs. E bolted upright. "I'm all right! I'm all right!" she insisted.

The members standing around looked at Pastor Charlotte, whose eyes traveled from them back to Mrs. E. Mrs. E was still a chalky white, with a pronounced blue line around her lips indicating that she had been deprived of oxygen. "Okay," the pastor admonished, "just take it easy."

Just then the paramedics burst in. "Why did you call us?" one asked. They looked at Mrs. E, who was still insisting that she was fine. "Well, if you're feeling all right, there's no need to go to the hospital."

"No way," the pastor and former nurse blurted out. "You're taking her to the hospital! The line around her lips shows that something happened to her and she needs to be cleared." Pastor Charlotte accompanied them to the hospital, where the emergency room kept Mrs. E for about two hours. They did tests, had her walk, stand on one leg, and explain what happened. Mrs. E could not tell them; she just kept looking at her pastor and winking.

Finally Pastor Charlotte took Mrs. E home. Once they reached her home, Mrs. E explained, "I saw my deceased husband, and told him it's not my time yet." Then she winked again and added, "I always feel most alive in the sanctuary."

"On my way home," Pastor Charlotte recounts, "I broke down in my car and wept. I knew beyond a shadow of a doubt what God had just done. I was beside myself. I had been crying out for God to reveal his presence in New England the same way people were experiencing him in other parts of the world. But I never thought it would happen on my watch so dramatically."

Mrs. E still attends Pastor Charlotte's church. She has grown frailer, and one of the church families has adopted her because her adult children live out of state. She still likes to light the altar candles, and she greets everyone who enters with a loving hug.

Bringing a Nurse to Church

Technicians shocked Jeff Buchanan twenty times after he went into cardiac arrest on the evening of Monday, February 14, 2011.[2] With no normal heartbeat for ninety minutes and no oxygen to his brain for roughly fifteen, he was expected to be a vegetable if he survived. Nevertheless, the medical staff labored diligently and chilled his body to reduce brain damage. Oklahoma Heart Hospital nurse Don Payne notes that he marveled at the bold faith with which Jeff's family and friends prayed. Jeff's heart stopped again on Wednesday evening, but after he was stabilized the medical team began to bring him out of his medically induced coma. Jeff's wife, Erica, spoke to him and he responded, and the nursing staff began posing other tests, delighted at his responses.

When staff removed the ventilator on Thursday, Jeff breathed without it. CT scans revealed no brain damage. The hospital sent him home on March 2, sixteen days after his bout with death. And Don Payne, the nurse, ended up joining Jeff's church.

In Jeff's case as in Mrs. E's, although the outcome was unexpectedly positive, God worked through skilled medical personnel. What would happen in a Western setting with less medical technology available?

Raised in Eastern Europe

One Western account comes from Polish minister Józef Bałuczyński, the father-in-law of my friend Rob Starner.[3] The time and setting and the limitations of the medical assistance available do not allow for medical documentation in this case, but Bałuczyński's years of faithful witness as a member of a persecuted minority and the knowledge of the story within his family argue for its trustworthiness.

Forced to work in Nazi labor camps, Bałuczyński survived the Second World War only to fall prey to suppurative pneumonia. Although he recovered temporarily from the pneumonia, he remained in St. Lazarus's Hospital in Kraków and succumbed to it again. There he found himself paralyzed and soon afterward saw his body from outside it. He then found himself in Jesus's presence. He had never experienced anything more beautiful, but he quickly found himself returning to his body, and back, fittingly, in the hospital named for Lazarus. A nurse beside his bed asked what had happened to him, noting that his heartbeat and breathing had stopped for a time.

Bałuczyński certainly recovered, and he continued ministry as a pastor through the ensuing decades of Communist repression of religion in Poland. I cherish the kind note that this faithful pastor wrote to me in 2015—roughly seven decades after this experience.

Converted through a Raising

A more recent and detailed Eastern European account comes from Charlie and Florentina Mada in their moving book *Raised!*[4] I interviewed this couple at length; their excitement over what God has done in their lives is contagious.

Their story starts on August 6, 1991. Living in Romania and not yet believers, the Madas found their sixteen-month-old son, Marius, their only child, submerged in an open pipe. After fishing his lifeless body out of the water in front of many witnesses, they rushed Marius to a hospital, where the staff found no signs of life. Because the staff found no heartbeat or reflexes, they administered no medical help. Nevertheless, they allowed the desperate parents to work through their grief beside the body. Yet Charlie and Flori slowly began to realize that, as Dr. Maria Coman at the hospital kept telling them, only God can make a miracle.

Seven hours later, the moment Charlie showed kindness to another person, the cold, gray, bloated body returned suddenly to life, restoring Marius fully. Several witnesses have also provided affidavits attesting to what they saw. The after-the-fact discharge notice suggests that the lifeless state was a stage 4 coma, but in Romania at the time this stage included brain death with no hope of recovery.[5] The language was phrased less technically before Marius began breathing again; witnesses' affidavits agree that the doctors reported the child dead, without pulse, respiration, or eye or muscle response.

This event started the entire family on a new path of faith that culminated in becoming committed followers of Christ. Nor was this the last wonder the family experienced. Marius later experienced an unexpected healing of his hip, for which his parents provided me with medical documentation. I interviewed them at length over many details. Today, Marius is a well-adjusted young man.

///////////

One could multiply such accounts,[6] but I hope you get the idea. Unexpected resuscitations happen more often than many of us suppose. But doctors have a better sense of what to expect than most of the rest of us do. Do any of them provide eyewitness reports of raisings?

Chapter 29

Doctors Who Witness Raisings

I have received accounts from doctors who witnessed raisings in the context of prayers of faith, and many over the years have published their observations of such occurrences.[1] Naturally, settings that include doctors' observations, unlike many that I have recounted, presuppose medical intervention; most of my accounts of resuscitations that lacked medical intervention did so only because it was not available. Doctors who were present and didn't intervene medically would have been acting irresponsibly. Normally we do what we can do, and trust God to do what we cannot. But as in cases such as that of John Smith, recounted in chapter 27, some doctors (in that case, Dr. Sutterer and Dr. Garrett) report witnessing outcomes beyond what their best procedures could achieve.

Published Accounts

One recent collection by doctors includes a thirty-page section of doctors' testimonies about extraordinary resuscitations,[2] although not all the examples are equally relevant. "After [patients were] pronounced dead, or presumed to be brain dead," the editor notes, "the miracles began."[3] Here I summarize one of these accounts.

Dr. Michael Fleischer recounts a patient's fatal experience with an amniotic fluid embolism, in which amniotic fluid leaks into a pregnant woman's bloodstream. Doctors did their best to resuscitate their patient, a young mother named Ruby, but after she had no pulse for forty-five minutes, they allowed the family to enter the operating room to say their goodbyes. Dr. Fleischer describes as "heart-wrenching" their loud pleas with God not to take her, and he quietly joined them in prayer.

Afterward, recognizing the futility of further attempts at resuscitation, the medical team stopped chest compressions. The heart monitor "showed some type of vague background electrical activity, although no true beats." But Dr. Fleischer continues: "Then the impossible happened. . . . Somehow, Ruby's heart started to pump on its own, now with a normal rhythm. And just as impossibly, her blood pressure was suddenly normal."

Still, after forty-five minutes without a heartbeat, she would surely have brain damage and other organ failure. But soon after attempts to revive her stopped, she opened her eyes and pointed to heaven. The next day, Dr. Fleischer was able to explain to her what had happened. She had no damage to her organs, including her brain; indeed, not even her ribs were broken or her chest bruised, "despite all the pounding" during CPR. "Defying all the statistics and all the textbooks," Fleischer notes, "three days later Ruby went home with her healthy baby and entire family."

In another book, Dr. Dave Walker recounts his experience with Andrew, a four-year-old boy lifeless for more than twenty minutes before CPR even began.[4] This was a drowning, but not a cold-water one. Even after Dr. Walker's team was able to start Andrew's heart, his dilated pupils did not respond to light and his body began stiffening, his "head back in the posture of severe brain damage."[5] Once Dr. Walker knew how long the brain had been deprived of oxygen, he realized that it could not survive.

Andrew's parents rallied their friends to pray; Dr. Walker also prayed, but, given his knowledge of normal medical expectations, he did not pray with much faith. Yet when he saw the child the next day, the boy was able to converse with him. The following day Andrew was sitting upright and playing with toys. Doctors treated his chest infection, but he suffered absolutely no brain damage. This experience shifted Dr. Walker's understanding of what God might do in answer to prayer.

In Jesus's Name!

Dr. Mervin Ascabano was a local health officer in charge of a primary care clinic in the Philippines.[6] He shared with me that on January 7, 2009, he was meeting with the mayor when the mayor's assistant suddenly burst in, breathless. "There's an emergency at the clinic," the assistant reported. Even as he raced toward the clinic, Dr. Ascabano could hear pandemonium, and he rushed in to find a patient already apparently dead. She was lying stiff "on the floor, eyes half-opened, grayish in skin color and not moving, with saliva all over her face."

Because the facility was simply an outpatient clinic, it lacked resuscitation equipment, and no ambulance was available. The patient lacked heartbeat or pulse and had reportedly been unresponsive for two or three minutes already; she was also cold to the touch, which suggests that two to three minutes may have been an underestimate. Because her companion, who was embracing her and weeping, would not get out of the way, it took another minute to get her onto the bed. As Ascabano desperately tried to administer CPR, the midwife noted that the patient's pants were already full of urine. As far as the midwife was concerned, the patient was already too far gone to revive without medical equipment.

At this point Dr. Ascabano began shouting, "In Jesus's name!" while pumping her chest. On the third shout, about thirty seconds after he began CPR and some five minutes after her pulse and heartbeat disappeared, "the patient . . . began to cough out fluids, moved her arms and her skin turned pink." To the doctor's shock, "she then began to open her eyes and tried to get up," so he had to make her lie flat. His nurse and midwife went with her to the hospital, but Dr. Ascabano reports that "the patient was already moving freely as if nothing happened! And when they arrived at the hospital, the patient was almost not admitted because her vital signs were all normal! Her blood pressure, pulse rate, respiratory rate and heart rate were all normal."

Although resuscitation within this time frame is possible, especially with CPR, such full and especially immediate restoration is unusual. Normally under such circumstances a patient would require a significant period in the hospital; odds of survival even then would normally be "on the order of 5–10% from reported literature and then usually with serious neurologic and physical impairments."[7] Usually restarting the heart without equipment requires a pounding harder than mild chest compression and often results in broken bones; Dr. Ascabano's thirty seconds of CPR was probably insufficient. Also, subsequent tests should reveal that a patient's organs had been oxygen-deprived for several minutes when that was the case. Yet this woman, pulseless and breathless for some five minutes, showed no signs of having been oxygen deprived.[8] For himself, Dr. Ascabano was so convinced that a miracle had taken place that the event convinced him to join another helping profession: he became a pastor.

I asked an old friend from Duke University, Arthur Williams, now an emergency room doctor, about this experience. He responded that he understands. He often prays for patients and sees immediate results. But he also recounted an occasion when his team had labored at length to resuscitate a patient to no avail. Finally they had to give up, their faces sweaty and their hearts disappointed. Suddenly, even though a sheet was now draped over the patient's head, "the monitor starts to beep and the patient's heart miraculously starts to beat." "There are many cases like this one but no one gets to hear just how [great] God is and how miracles are still prevalent."[9]

Cases like the one Dr. Ascabano experienced may not be typical, but it's also true that irreparable brain damage may not start before five or six minutes without a heartbeat. While the experience in his clinic was sufficient to convince Dr. Ascabano, some readers may want further accounts. Happily, doctors do report extraordinary resuscitations after significantly longer periods of time.

Second Chance

I have already recounted some of Dr. Chauncey Crandall's testimonies, but the one that drew the most attention was the account that follows. On a day in early autumn 2006, physicians in a Florida emergency room labored for almost forty minutes to try to revive Jeff Markin, following all the American Heart Association protocols. Despite shocking Markin seven times, they were unable to revive him. As a cardiologist, Dr. Crandall confirmed that Markin was beyond resuscitation, and Markin was declared dead shortly after 8:00 a.m.

Crandall wrote his assessment and then started to return to his rounds, when, he reports, he felt an unusual prompting from the Holy Spirit to return to the body, which the nurse was then preparing for the morgue. Markin's eyes were fixed and dilated, and his face and extremities had turned black with cyanosis; he was unquestionably dead. Crandall did not feel much faith that day, but he obeyed the prompting.

Dr. Crandall prayed aloud for God to resuscitate Markin, giving him a second chance to know the Lord. Then he urged his colleague, the emergency room doctor, to shock Markin one more time. The colleague was reluctant, given their consensus that Markin could not be resuscitated, but he acquiesced out of respect for Crandall's request and shocked him. Suddenly the flat line on the monitor jumped to a normal heartbeat—which does not normally occur even when the heart stops for a short time. "In my more than twenty years as a cardiologist," Crandall notes, "I have never seen a heartbeat restored so completely and suddenly."[10] With no help, Markin started breathing immediately, and in just a few minutes his extremities were moving and he was speaking.

Although even six minutes without air leaves irreparable brain damage, Markin had neither that nor problems with his other organs. After this experience he visited regularly with Dr. Crandall, and he did indeed come to know the Lord. Dr. Crandall even sent me a photo of them together at Markin's subsequent baptism as a Christian.

Journalists interviewed witnesses and checked records; their report circulated widely.[11] Crandall's reputation as a cardiologist was already well established, and he had no desire to risk it by seeking a questionable notoriety with a controversial raising claim.[12] (I can identify: I am well aware that my research on miracles tends to weaken skeptical academic colleagues' respect for my work rather than strengthen it. I speak out only because of conviction, certainly not out of convenience.) Nevertheless, the experience encouraged Crandall to pray for more miracles. He has since seen further extraordinary results, some of which have been noted in patient interviews broadcast on local television. Some were mentioned in chapter 13.

Are Doctors Themselves Ever Raised?

On October 24, 2008, Dr. Sean George was driving home from running a medical clinic in Western Australia.[13] Suddenly, about thirty miles from his home in Kalgoorlie, he began experiencing chest pains. As a consultant physician at Kalgoorlie Hospital, he understood the possible dangers, although at thirty-nine years old he considered himself surely too young to be having a heart attack. Accompanied by his intern (who had been traveling with him), he checked himself into a local clinic run by a friend of his, Dr. Rao. While Dr. Rao was at lunch, nurses administered an electrocardiogram—which revealed that Dr. George was indeed experiencing a heart attack.

Eleven minutes after this diagnosis, Sean went into full cardiac arrest while the clinic staff and his intern labored desperately to revive him. Yet, as Sean himself points out, "When the blood supply is interrupted to the brain for three minutes the cells begin to die," and "after 20 minutes the organ is completely dead." That is why, after half an hour, workers normally give up, but for nearly fifty-five minutes, his friends struggled in vain to revive him. They administered some four thousand chest compressions during that period and shocked him thirteen times, leaving burns on his abdomen.

Notified of his condition, his wife, Sherry Jacob, also a medical professional, and emergency room doctors from Kalgoorlie Hospital reached the clinic. Sean's body was now cold; by this time he had been dead for an hour and twenty-five minutes. His colleagues from Kalgoorlie sized up the situation. The senior physician reluctantly counseled Sherry to go in and say goodbye to her husband. Instead of saying goodbye as expected, however, she took Sean's hand and offered a simple prayer for God to grant them more time together. "Sean is just 39, I'm just 38, and we have a 10-year-old boy. I need a miracle!" she cried. Immediately, his heart began beating.

Though moved by Sherry's devotion, one of his colleagues recoiled. "This is the worst thing that could happen," he thought. "Sooner or later his wife will now have to decide when to disconnect life support." Though an unexpected hailstorm delayed Dr. George's emergency flight to Perth, doctors there were finally able to clear his blocked artery. Nevertheless, his survival seemed uncertain, as Steve Dunjie and other doctors who were present now testify. Sean already had acute kidney and liver failure, as records subsequently made available to the public clearly show, and doctors were certain that he would have irreparable brain damage.

Three days later, however, he awoke with full brain function and began talking. He had not experienced loss of memory, and he began reading his own medical charts. Two weeks later he was discharged from the hospital, and within three months he was back to working full-time. As Pravin Sulya Shetty, consultant physician at Kalgoorlie Hospital, puts it, "To come out of a situation where all your organs needed some kind of support and despite three days of being in a coma, your brain functions were not compromised—I must say that it's not possible to explain this in medical terms." Three of the doctors who witnessed Sean's death were Christians, but two others were Hindus and one was a Muslim. All recognize the miracle their colleague experienced.

Aware of the significance of his experience, Sean kept the medical records, including the original defibrillator logs. Sean subsequently made available on his website the medical details and documentation, as well as his testimony and some articles about his extraordinary recovery.[14] Sean is head of the Department of General Medicine at Kalgoorlie Health Campus (previously Kalgoorlie Hospital).

///////////

Dead for more than an hour under clinical conditions. Sudden restarting of the heart after prayer. No brain damage. Isn't there something noteworthy about cases like Dr. George's? But while clinical conditions are not available every-where, such resuscitations after prayer are not unique. Trustworthy witnesses with something to lose (that is, people who meet one of Hume's chief criteria for witnesses) report events like this around the world—and usually in settings where, unlike in most of the cases recounted in this chapter, medical technology is not available to help in the recovery.

Chapter 30

Friends Who Used to Be Dead or Met Those Who Had Been

It's one thing to read records, and another to hear an account from trusted friends. As of early 2021, I haven't witnessed or prayed for a raising myself. But I do know plenty of people who have. Strangely, though, if I hadn't asked friends about healing, I usually wouldn't have heard these accounts, since we all had plenty of other, more current subjects to talk about. Sometimes we even forget to celebrate past miracles we have witnessed or experienced.

But I soon discovered that many of my friends have such accounts. Here I leave aside those whom I first met because of their testimonies, although I could include many more of those. I focus here only on people in my or my family's immediate circle, friends or colleagues we knew *before* hearing their testimonies. Limiting the testimonies in this way allows me to screen out unstable or attention-craving witnesses; it also indicates that these testimonies are only samples. These are merely the accounts that flourish in my own family's circle, which is only a tiny slice of global Christian experience.

Although I recount stories from various locations, a disproportionate percentage are from Africa because that is where I have spent most of my time outside the US. (In the US I am obliged to stay at my desk most of the time!) Inside the US, medical interventions are much more commonly available to resuscitate persons than they are in most of Africa, and nonemergency personnel tend to have less access to corpses.

Scholars Discuss

Being excited about my discoveries concerning Majority World miracle reports, I shared some of them in a scholars' meeting in 2009. Because this was a meeting for scholars from a range of religious perspectives, I did not call the experiences miracles. I simply recounted them and suggested that taking these experiences seriously could help us hear more sympathetically the reports of miracles in the Gospels. Not surprisingly, some debate ensued, although, perhaps more surprisingly, everyone on every side of the issue remained respectful, as good scholars should.

But after a few minutes of discussion, Professor J. Ayodeji Adewuya, who now teaches in the United States, stood up and explained an experience that had informed his own perspective on such matters. On January 1, 1981, in Nigeria, his son was pronounced dead at birth. Those who were present banded together in prayer, and after thirty minutes of prayer the infant began to breathe. Ayo's son did not sustain brain damage, and at the time of the meeting where Ayo shared this story, his son had recently earned his master of science degree at the University of London. I know Ayo well and was grateful for his testimony.

Friends in Nigeria

Firsthand reports of miracles count most heavily, and among those, I weigh most heavily reports I receive from people whose trustworthiness I know personally. What surprises me, then, is how many friends in my own circle or my family's circle have accounts of raisings.

During parts of my first three summers in Nigeria, I worked with a Nigerian missions organization called Capro. One of my friends there was Capro's research officer, Leo Bawa, who now has a PhD from the Oxford Centre for Mission Studies. When I was doing research for my academic book on miracles, it occurred to me to ask Leo whether he had seen any.

Leo and I had never discussed the topic before, and he apologized at the beginning of his response that he did not have much to share. Then he provided seven pages of testimonies, including an account that involved a dead child in a village in Adamawa State, where he was doing research. His host's neighbors brought the child to him. After his initial dismay, he prayed for the child for a few hours. Afterward, he explains, the child revived, and Leo handed him back to his parents alive.

Timothy Olonade was another friend and leader in Capro whom I knew from those summers in Nigeria. Although I had noticed the large keloid scar on his neck, I had never asked him about how he got it. Later, however, a mutual friend who was a physician told me the story,[1] as did another mutual friend,[2] so I followed up and interviewed Timothy in person.[3] On one Friday in December 1985 he discovered two flat tires on his car, so he decided to travel to the next city by taxi. Around 6:00 p.m., he was the sole passenger in a taxi that collided head-on with a pickup truck.

Since that was the last event he remembers from that day, it was other people who later filled in for him the following details. Both the taxi driver and someone in the truck lost their legs, but two people lost their lives—and one of them was Timothy. By the time the police learned of and reached the accident, it was 9:40 p.m. They were adamant that Timothy had neither pulse nor heartbeat. They reached the hospital around 10:30, and doctors there quickly sent him to the mortuary, while word was sent to his parents to start preparing for the funeral.

About 2:00 or 3:00 a.m., however, a worker trying to make more room in the mortuary found him moving.[4] At first the worker's colleagues, certain that Timothy was dead, accused their coworker of hallucinating. The blood had baked on Timothy's skin. They had pricked him with needles, some of the marks from which he still has on his arm today. But when they found he had a pulse of twenty-four beats per minute, they immediately sent him back to the hospital.

When Timothy started quoting Scripture instead of giving his name, the doctor concluded that he would be a vegetable and thought it fruitless to try to save his life. The university hospital proved more helpful, however. There Dr. Adekeye, a surgery professor who had also practiced in the United States for many years, worked on him and recounted afterward that there was no medical explanation for his survival. Although his full recovery was not instantaneous, X-rays soon attested the rapid healing of his skull fractures, except for one on his jaw; this made no sense to the younger doctors. Their professor reminded them, "I told you, this one is beyond medical explanation." A journalist for a Christian newspaper who wanted to disprove the account ended up convinced of it instead.

Since then, Timothy has had a significant ministry in the Nigerian missions movement. Today he is a senior Anglican priest and the global mission leader for the Anglican Province of Jos, Nigeria.

A Western Nurse in Congo

Medical documentation is usually not available for healings in rural Africa. Indeed, often people suffer precisely because they lack access to adequate medical help. Still, sometimes medical documentation does exist in Africa, even for raisings.[5] Somewhat more often there is testimony from medical personnel.

One of my wife's close friends, who also has visited us in the United States, is Sarah Speer, a Canadian nurse working in a mission hospital in the Republic of Congo.[6] She told us about treating a mother who had experienced protracted and finally failed labor. The baby's arm stuck out, but the mother was unable to deliver him, and she was transported ten hours over rugged dirt roads to the hospital where Sarah serves. Seeking to save the mother's life, the medical team had to rupture her uterus to remove the infant. They found him dead, however, with no heartbeat or respiration, so they continued their surgery on the mother.

Meanwhile, one of the more persistent nurses refused to give up on the baby and held him while her husband prayed. Twenty minutes after he had been removed, during which time he showed no signs of breathing, he suddenly began to cry. The entire medical team, Sarah reports, "knew that God had worked a miracle."

Congolese Friends in Congo

Because my wife is from the Republic of Congo, I was able to interview family friends who have accounts of raisings there. These come from my wife's denomination, which is the mainstream Protestant church in her country, and the stories include the raising of the son of the evangelical church's former president, Dr. Patrice Nsouami.[7] Rather than try to recount all of them, I will focus on several.

My brother-in-law Emmanuel Moussounga, who passed away in 2020, was well educated. He earned a PhD in France and became a beloved professor of chemistry at the University of Brazzaville in the Republic of Congo, where he supervised many doctoral students and published cutting-edge scientific research. He was present on one occasion when Jeanne Mabiala (known locally as Mama Jeanne), a deacon in his church, prayed for a woman who was believed to be dead and she revived. My wife's family knows Mama Jeanne well. She was among their fellow refugees during the civil war of the 1990s and was known for her effective prayers. Emmanuel knew not only Mama Jeanne but also the woman who was apparently raised.

When I interviewed Mama Jeanne, she shared three raising experiences. Since I have published these accounts before (in *Miracles* in 2011),[8] I will recount only one of them in detail here.[9]

Mama Jeanne had training as a midwife from the World Health Organization, and so she helped deliver some babies during the country's war. Toward the beginning of the war, a young woman named Flore went into labor and delivered a baby who had apparently died in the womb a number of hours earlier. The infant's body was white, with the umbilical cord wrapped around her neck. The Protestant mother and her Catholic friend were weeping, but Mama Jeanne felt led to urge them to turn their strength to prayer. Soon the baby opened her eyes and mouth, and after Mama Jeanne started patting her, she cried.

Meanwhile, Flore's father, a carpenter, had gone away to build a coffin. When he returned, he was dumbfounded: the child was now fine. "This child is a thousandfold grace!" he declared. Flore and her family named the girl Mille Grace (a thousandfold grace). She is now attending school.

Raised Baptist in the Philippines

While more of my stories are from Africa, they are not limited to Africa.[10]

For example, Elaine Panelo lives in the Philippines.[11] I got to know her because she helped arrange my schedule when I was lecturing in a seminary for which she works there. Because I was researching for my first book on miracles, I asked whether any of the students had witnessed any; many shared their accounts with me. Elaine held back because she was afraid to say anything, since she had once been thrown out of a church to which she belonged when she had shared her story. But timidly, and with urging from a close friend who knew the story, she shared it with me.

After living for two years with untreated liver cancer, in 1984 Elaine was brought to a hospital, pronounced dead, and sent to the morgue. When her friend's Baptist pastor prayed over her an hour and forty-five minutes later, Elaine suddenly became conscious. I asked her why a Baptist pastor had prayed over her when she was dead.

Elaine responded, "I don't know. I heard about the prayer only after I revived. Remember, I was dead!"

"Yeah, sorry," I apologized.

Her swelled abdomen had also returned to normal size, and subsequent examination showed that the cancer itself was gone. Her complete healing led to the conversion of the same physician who had informed her that her death was imminent. More than thirty-five years later, Elaine remains well, and we keep in touch periodically.

Neighbor from Indonesia

After I moved to Asbury Seminary, one of my closest neighbors for a time was a humble man of prayer from Indonesia named Yusuf Herman.[12] My next-door neighbor, who also liked to pray with Yusuf, urged me to ask Yusuf about a story he had recounted. Yusuf then not only offered me the story but helped me interview his friend Dominggus, who had had an experience of heaven during a time that he was, so far as anyone could tell, dead. I watched the video taken from the evening news in Jakarta, Indonesia, where Dominggus's dead body lay in a pool of blood, his neck sliced wide open. I watched as health workers carelessly transported his body to a vehicle, plainly assuming he was dead.

Dominggus says that when the doctors at the hospital were preparing to send him to the morgue, he managed to squeak out, "I'm alive." That he could speak at all shocked the doctors, as you might imagine, but they immediately and dutifully began working on him. He did need medical attention, not least to sew up his neck, but he recovered fully. He still has the neck scar to show for his experience, perhaps not unlike Jacob's limp in the Bible (Gen. 32:31).

New Testament Colleague

Such accounts are not limited to my friends in the Majority World. One of this book's informants that I know particularly well is a former colleague from Eastern University's Palmer Theological Seminary, Professor Deborah Watson.[13] At the PhD level she studied with the renowned scholars James Dunn and John Barclay at Durham University, and she and I co-taught some classes, including an intensive

January-term Greek class. (I am very much a night person, so this class, which started early in the morning, seared itself indelibly and painfully in my memory.)

Debbie grew up in the northeastern United States, where her father was a Baptist minister. After sharing her account with me, she connected me with her father, who supplied many more details. When Deborah's younger sister Gloria was an infant, forty-five years earlier, Gloria fell from a high location faceup onto the hard floor of a washroom. She was motionless, and as her father, James, tried to lift her up to rush her to the nearby doctor's office, it felt as if the back of her skull was crunching in his hand. It continued to feel that way as he carried her unmoving form into the doctor's office and explained to the doctor about her skull.

After about five minutes, however, the doctor seemed puzzled and asked where James had felt the skull crushed. James felt the back of her head again, and now it felt solid. Deborah explains that Gloria "was better right away," without subsequent repercussions.

Student Testimonies

Some students in seminaries where I have taught also have shared with me experiences that they construe as raisings.[14] In one case, an Asbury student's father-in-law was without a pulse after an accident until the student prayed for him.[15] In another, a leader from the Malagasy Lutheran Church, doing doctoral work at Asbury, recounts the raising and full restoration of a baby after he and his wife prayed, leading to widespread conversions and the confession of those who had killed the baby to begin with.[16] In yet another, an Asbury ThM student offers his firsthand account of the restoration to life through prayer of a friend who had fallen some forty to fifty meters to his death.[17]

When I taught at Palmer Theological Seminary just outside Philadelphia, one of my students, Margufta Bellevue, on one occasion casually mentioned her own experience in Port-au-Prince, Haiti. Her mother had told Margufta that she (Margufta) had been raised from death as an infant in 1979. At my subsequent request, she provided further details, which I quote directly:

> I was one year old with a high fever. The doctor told my mom that I would not make it. Within a few hours, I was pronounced dead by the doctor and they tried to take me to the mortuary, but my mom refused. My mom picked up my lifeless body and went to the church where the old saints prayed day and night in those days. They laid me down and prayed for hours as they kept singing nothing is impossible with God. One of the prayer intercessors took a deep breath and breathed on me. A few seconds later, I sneezed, opened my eyes, and started crying. God brought me back to life after being pronounced dead for over five hours.[18]

Again, most people who die are not resuscitated. But many of us today, including those to whom Margufta ministers, are grateful that she was.

Chapter 31

Raised in Our Family

A lthough I have never been present during a raising, medically assisted or not, I have been noting friends who have. These testimonies extend even to members of my near and extended family: the parents of one of my former sisters-in-law, and even my own mother-in-law.

My In-Law In-Laws

Albert and Julienne Bissouessoue were close friends of my wife's family when I first interviewed them;[1] afterward they actually became relatives, since my brother-in-law married their daughter. This led me to joke that they were my in-law in-laws. Like Jeanne Mabiala, Albert was a deacon at my brother-in-law Emmanuel Moussounga's church. I did not know him nearly as well as Jeanne Mabiala, but he did share with us accounts of his experiences and try to help us personally.

Albert recounts that he was a school inspector in the town of Etoumbi, northern Republic of Congo, in the 1980s when, at around three in the afternoon, he found a large group of people gathered at his house. They had brought him the corpse of a five-year-old girl who had died some eight hours earlier. The relatives had paid six local shamans, hoping to revive her. Despite sacrifices to spirits and the blood smeared in her ears, nose, and mouth, she did not revive; desperate, they now were ready to try the Christian God.

"Why did you try the Christian God last of all?" Albert reproved them. "You need to turn from all these other spirits to follow the one true creator." He took the girl aside to his normal place of prayer. He tells us that, after half an hour of prayer, "Jesus performed his first miracle in Etoumbi through me by bringing

171

this little girl to life." Many of the town's residents became followers of Jesus, abandoning many ancestral religious practices.

Later, the local clinic manager's daughter died, and all attempts to revive her failed. Knowing about the earlier raising, people went looking for Albert, but he was out of town inspecting schools elsewhere. One of Albert's young children agreed to come in his place, but, naturally being afraid, she decided that she was not ready for this situation. By this point, however, they had located Albert's wife, Julienne.

After singing a song about Lazarus, Julienne led the people in prayer. When she concluded, she reports, "the girl opened her eyes and moved." Once she had revived, they were able to treat the rest of her condition medically. Meanwhile, Julienne herself was astonished at what had just happened; the Lord gave her the courage she needed in the moment she needed it. These are the only two times Albert or Julienne prayed for someone who was dead; this was just something special that God wanted to do at that time and place.

I met the Bissouessoues in person just once and, given the language and geographic barriers, communicated with them thereafter largely through my brother-in-law. I do, however, have a family story closer than that of in-law in-laws.

My Wife's Family of Origin

God gifted my father-in-law, a deacon in Congo's evangelical church, in praying for healing. Many people were healed when he prayed, though the prayers he offered were concise and simple. Indeed, my wife and her brother were instantly healed through his prayers. Their youngest sister was once dying of cerebral meningitis and not expected to live through the night, but she, too, was healed through her father's prayers. During my time in Congo, I met people who testified about being healed when he prayed for them.

At the time this next story took place, however, my father-in-law was out of town in his work for the railroad. I first heard the story from my wife but learned the details only when I was able to visit Congo and interview in person the witness, Antoinette Malombé, locally known as Madame Jacques.[2] One day when her daughter, Thérèse Magnouha, was two years old, Madame Jacques took some food to a neighbor. Madame Jacques returned to discover that her daughter had been bitten by a snake. Most snakes in the area were very poisonous, so Madame Jacques panicked. Her daughter had stopped breathing, and there was no medical help available in the village.

Lacking other means to help her child, Madame Jacques strapped the lifeless toddler to her back and ran to a nearby village, where family friend Coco Ngoma Moïse was doing ministry. Coco Moïse prayed for Thérèse, who then started breathing again; the next day Thérèse was fine, playing as if nothing had ever happened.[3]

Although I had heard this account before from my wife, she did not know details such as how long Thérèse was believed to be dead. So I asked Madame Jacques how long Thérèse was not breathing. She apparently had never considered this question before; she probably did not even understand why it mattered to me. I watched as she calculated how long it took to get from the first village to the second, with the hills in between. "About three hours," she concluded, and I was aghast. Three hours was shorter than many other reports, but this was my first time hearing of a raising after such an extended period of lifelessness from someone so close to me.

You see, Madame Jacques (Antoinette Malombé) was my mother-in-law, and Thérèse is my wife's big sister. Here was a report of a raising within my own family, and not after just a few minutes. As I have noted, after six minutes with no oxygen, irreparable brain damage starts in, even if the patient can be revived. Thérèse, however, had no brain damage. In fact, at the time we were visiting Congo, my wife and I were helping to support Thérèse as she was finishing her master's degree in a nearby country. Our big sister now does ministry back in Congo.

Not to question one's mother-in-law, but we also did confirm the story with the other witness, Coco Moïse.[4]

Coincidence?

Coincidences happen often, but some skeptics treat the power of coincidence as almost unlimited. What is the probability that death gets misdiagnosed very often? Periodically, cases of such misdiagnosis make the news. Some of these may be the unexplained and extremely rare phenomenon that medical literature sometimes calls the Lazarus syndrome—though some of these cases involve drugs and some (or potentially all) of them might themselves represent special divine action. In any case, skeptics hearing one account of a resuscitation during prayer could well suggest that this particular prayer for a raising simply *randomly* coincided with an occasion when someone had been misdiagnosed as dead.

Yet such a coincidence can hardly be expected to happen often, unless we are burying an excessive number of people prematurely. But just in case, I asked some of my informants how often they had prayed for people to be raised. After all, if they've prayed over apparently dead bodies thousands of times, they might get lucky like this once or twice. The Bissouessoues prayed only twice for anyone to be raised, and both times it happened. Leo Bawa prayed only twice—the other was for his best friend—and one of the people was raised. What does that say about the odds? Why do so many cases cluster in circles of people known for prayer, so often in conjunction with prayer for a person to be raised?

How often are people being pronounced dead prematurely? Some experienced emergency room doctors who witnessed extraordinary resuscitations such as those I have recounted have noted that they had never seen anything similar in their years of practice. This sort of resuscitation after a significant period of time is rare among doctors in Africa, just as it is rare in the West. So what are the odds—were we to try to offer an educated guess—that any given family would know someone misdiagnosed as dead? From 1982 to 2017, there were thirty-eight reported cases (many not well documented) of the Lazarus Syndrome from sixteen countries, thus averaging a bit more than one per year. During those thirty-five years, there were more than eighty million deaths in United States *alone* (not counting the other fifteen countries), so reported cases of the Lazarus Syndrome were far fewer than one case in every two million reported deaths. If we estimate (I think generously) that on average ten people directly witnessed each unaided resuscitation as it occurred, we might then generously estimate one chance in two hundred thousand of someone being a witness to such an incident. If we estimate, certainly very generously, that my wife and I together have one thousand fairly close friends (a grossly exorbitant estimate; the real number might be closer to one-tenth of that), that gives us a one in two hundred chance of knowing a witness. But for the sake of argument, let's be even more generous and estimate one chance in one hundred.

But my wife and I have *ten* fairly close friends on three continents who have witnessed—or in some cases experienced—this rare phenomenon (not all recounted in this short book). I refer here only to those who were friends before we heard their accounts. The odds of this being merely a natural coincidence might appear to be one chance in $100^{10} = 10^{20} = 100,000,000,000,000,000,000$, or one chance in one hundred quintillion. But because some of the friends were in locations where the phenomenon might be underdiagnosed, even though in each of those cases the apparent death lasted for hours, we might estimate *super*-generously a figure of just one chance in ten (instead of one hundred) of having a close friend who witnessed or experienced the phenomenon. For ten friends, that would still be one chance in 10^{10}, which is a much lower figure: one in 10,000,000,000, or just one in ten billion. (By way of comparison, however, at the time of writing the world's population is only about eight billion.) And I just happened to be writing a book on miracles, for unrelated reasons?[5]

If this is coincidence, it is not a single coincidence but a coincidental cluster of lots of coincidences! Can an event that happens once in ten billion times be a coincidence? Certainly. But if a one-in-ten-billion chance is the best explanation skeptics can offer, they should not claim that their explanation is very probable. I believe that a much simpler explanation exists—especially for those who already recognize that one true God exists.

Nature Miracles

Although the accounts in this book focus primarily on healings, which also form a majority of miracle accounts in the Gospels and Acts, God is not limited to acting on human bodies. As accounts in the Bible illustrate, God also sometimes acts in other parts of nature, whether to protect his people (e.g., Mark 4:38–39), to provide for them (6:41–44), to enable them to fulfill their mission, or simply to reveal himself (6:48–50).

Part 6 recounts some modern reports of nature miracles. These include not only more general accounts from the nineteenth and twentieth centuries (chap. 32) but also some accounts from witnesses whom I know firsthand (chap. 33).

Chapter 32

Do Nature Miracles Still Happen?

I f no one will call raisings from the dead psychosomatic, neither will anyone consider storms psychosomatic. Stilling storms, turning water into wine, and walking on water are not ordinarily explained in such terms!

Of course, God does not always protect us in the most conspicuous way. In Luke 8:24–25, Jesus stilled a storm; in Acts 27, by contrast, a storm continued, yet the survival of all 276 passengers on Paul's ship demonstrated God's power in a different way. Nevertheless, we do have some accounts of conspicuous nature miracles today.[1]

Stirring or Stilling Storms in the Nineteenth Century

In Africa in the 1840s, when a drought ended after missionary W. J. Davis's public prayer, "the first [known] Bantu church" began.[2]

An account from a visitor to the church of German Lutheran pastor Johann Christoph Blumhardt records the visitor's temporary annoyance with the pastor. Blumhardt, concerned for the needs of the congregation's farmers, briefly interrupted the liturgy to pray that God would stop an impending hailstorm. The visitor testifies that his annoyance turned to astonishment as "in an instant it grew light and in a few minutes we had blue skies and bright sunshine."[3] Such accounts about Blumhardt's ministry are attested in letters and journals from the time in which they occurred.

Other figures in the nineteenth century such as George Müller, Hudson Taylor, and those associated with them reported experiences that could be understood as weather miracles.[4] Historian Paul King cites primary sources. George Müller reports in his diary for November 20, 1857, that workers needed to repair the boiler at an orphan house in Bristol, England, to provide heat. Unfortunately, that also meant that the children would lack heat until the boiler was fixed. Bristol's night temperature in late November and December can be in the forties (Fahrenheit). It had been cold, so Müller prayed for a change to warm weather, which came and persisted until the day that the boiler was able to again provide heat.[5] Similarly, "in 1865 hurricane-force winds damaged the orphan houses, causing twenty holes in the roofs," so Müller and his colleagues prayed for protection, and "the wind and rain ceased" until the necessary repairs were made.[6]

Likewise, Hudson Taylor, a British missionary to China, prayed in 1853 as the ship he was traveling on careened toward deadly rocks; suddenly the wind shifted and the ship evaded destruction. Later in the voyage there was a lack of favorable winds, and the current was driving the ship toward reefs. Taylor prayed briefly and then instructed the captain to put up the sail. To others' astonishment, the wind came, and "in only minutes they were plowing through the sea at nearly seven knots."[7]

Stirring Storms in the Twentieth Century

Unlike Chinese evangelist John Sung, mentioned earlier, Watchman Nee (1903–1972) was not known primarily for miracles. (Nor does my citation of his or others' miracle accounts entail endorsing all their views or practices on every subject.) Nevertheless, in his book *Sit, Walk, Stand*, Nee recounts his experience with a nature miracle in the early twentieth century.[8] Nee and six friends were preaching about Christ in the village of Mei-hwa, but their detractors mocked them. The local god had ensured that it never rained on the day of the god's festival—for 286 years. Enthusiastic young Li Kuo-ching, one of Nee's colleagues, responded that this year it would rain on that day.

When Li informed Nee and his other companions about this challenge, they were horrified. Even if the local god was powerless, half the villagers were fishermen who were quite skillful at predicting the weather. Now if it did not rain on the scheduled day, no one would listen to their preaching. Then again, no one was listening anyway, so the seven believers prayed and felt God's assurance that God would indeed send rain on the scheduled day.

The appointed day began as usual, but soon the streets flooded as a result of the greatest rainstorm in years; the elders carrying the god's statue stumbled, injuring themselves and chipping the statue. In the face of this unexpected incident, the local priests decided by divination that they had picked the wrong day this time and so rescheduled their festival for a few days later. This time, now confident in their hearts that God would act, Nee and his colleagues promised rain on that day also. The next few days were dry, but at the time appointed for the procession on the newly designated day, rain again gushed down in torrents. Many of the people of Mei-hwa became followers of Jesus.

Also in the early twentieth century, the Congolese evangelist Pelendo experienced an apparent nature miracle when villagers in Mondongo, in the Democratic Republic of Congo, took away his drum.[9] This was the drum that he used to call people to hear God's message, but the local residents wanted to use it for their dancing and drinking party one night. Pelendo warned that God would punish them for this abuse. As they were celebrating, a bolt of lightning unexpectedly struck, burning some homes and the other drums but leaving Pelendo's drum untouched. From then on, members of the village listened to Pelendo's message.

Stirring or Stilling Storms Today

During my first visit to Jakarta, Indonesia, Rev. Dr. Mangapul Sagala shared with me some accounts of nature miracles. For example, one time when he and colleagues planned to hold an evangelistic meeting in a stadium during the rainy season, clouds shrouded the sky. Dr. Sagala and his colleagues knelt, prayed, and confessed that they needed a miracle; people would not come if it rained. Just before they began preaching, the rain stopped and the sky cleared; moonlight brightened the stadium. After the meeting, as Sagala and his colleagues were on the way back home, rain poured down again.[10]

As a recent convert to Christ from a radically anti-Christian ideology, Sai Krishna Gomatam of India wanted to attend a one-week InterVarsity leadership camp in his region.[11] His mother, under social pressure from others in the community, forbade him from attending this camp because of its Christian focus. After he pleaded his case, she insisted, "You can't go unless your God can bring down rain today." It was May, when, in his region, it does not rain. Nevertheless, he responded, "My God can do anything." There was a downpour that day, and he went to the InterVarsity camp. I got to know Sai Krishna when he was a PhD student at Trinity International University, where I was researching this book.

In the United States, Randy Clark (noted already in chaps. 16, 21, and 23) shared with me an experience he had when he was nineteen years old. He was camping with three other Baptist friends, all teens except one who was about twenty-four: "[We] had spent all summer canvassing every home in the town of 3,000. We were doing a tent meeting in my hometown of McLeansboro, Illinois. A terrible storm came up and we prayed hard for the storm not to touch us. It rained all around us but it didn't rain on the tent; you could see the stars above the tent."[12]

David Chotka of the Christian and Missionary Alliance Church received his doctor of ministry degree from Gordon-Conwell Theological Seminary. On September 2, 2007, Chotka was part of a team ministering to fifty thousand people in Uganda, many of them refugees from nearby countries. A storm cloud began hovering above the stage, starting to drop rain and threatening to ruin the electrical equipment and disperse the crowd. David felt led to command the storm to leave, at the top of his lungs, "in the name of the Lord Jesus Christ." Meanwhile others, including colleague Lisa Plunket, were also interceding. The storm retreated, but twenty minutes later began to return. Five times over the next three hours, David and his colleagues prayed, and five times the storm retreated. During this time, the area directly above the meeting, in contrast to the rest of the sky, remained bright. That evening, after a Ugandan minister preached, three thousand people gave their lives to Christ, with no rain to dampen their commitment.[13] Two of the other witnesses involved in the event, Fred Hartley and Michael Plunket, confirmed the event;[14] the latter also wrote about it in his dissertation.[15]

Multiplied Food

Although much rarer than healing claims (including in the Gospels), stories of multiplied food also continue to appear. The scale is normally not the same as in the Gospels—that is, the feeding of five thousand (or even four thousand)—but something that is naturally impossible by currently known laws normally does not become more possible by simply reducing its scale.[16] Accounts of multiplied food appear both for earlier[17] and for more recent times;[18] for example, they occur in the early Jesus People movement.[19]

Karen Schmidgall recounts that in early 1968 her new church in Naperville, Illinois, invited members of the community to a potluck. Unfortunately, while many in the community showed up, Schmidgall was the only person who brought food—by itself enough to feed six people. Yet people treated themselves to seconds, and Schmidgall was astonished to discover enough food left over at the end for another meal. Over the following years, she and her husband, Bob, the pastor, found great encouragement in this memory of God's provision, as the church eventually grew to an attendance of about seven thousand.[20]

Catholic charismatic New Testament scholar Mary Healy shares the testimony of her friend Butch Murphy, who witnessed counted food supplies multiply when he was involved in distributing them to economically poor residents in Mexico City.[21] Likewise, when New Testament scholar Grant LeMarquand was Anglican bishop of the Horn of Africa, about a hundred refugees sheltered temporarily at an Anglican center in Gambella, Ethiopia, on January 30, 2016. Scrambling to provide some food for these guests, LeMarquand and his colleagues found only some bread and peanut butter crackers, enough to feed maybe twelve people. Yet they kept distributing the food and even provided multiple helpings, until everyone was satisfied. "It was weird," he told me. "We couldn't see the food multiplying, but it just didn't seem to run out. We're pretty sure it was a multiplication miracle."[22]

Rolland and Heidi Baker, who serve orphans, refugees, and other desperately needy people in Mozambique, testify to witnessing food multiplied among the poor on multiple occasions.[23] Early in their years of ministry there, they took in large numbers of street children. A crisis arose when they refused to give up prayer and worship, and consequently some hostile authorities expelled them from their property and started beating the children when they tried to sing. Perhaps a hundred now-homeless children followed the Bakers to the flat they used as an office, fifteen miles away on foot from their former location. There was not enough room for everyone, but neither could the Bakers bear to turn them away.

Some of the children reminded Heidi that she had said that God would always provide. Sometimes our words to children come back to challenge us. How could the Bakers feed all these children or, for that matter, even their own? Their birth daughter Crystalyn began crying from hunger; it had been several days since the Bakers themselves had eaten. Just then, someone who worked at the US embassy visited them, bringing enough chili and rice for the family: Rolland, Heidi, and their two children. Heidi opened the door, exposing children packed wall to wall and looking in from the patio. "I have a big family," she noted.

The gracious worker was horrified. There was enough food only for the four! But Heidi asked her to pray and then began serving the food on plastic plates. She was too exhausted to consider backup plans if God did not make this work; she simply gave each child a full serving, as she normally would. "But all our children ate, the staff ate, my friend ate and even our family of four ate. Everyone had enough."[24] Imagination or exaggeration could account for stretching a meal for four to perhaps ten—but to a hundred? This was a clear miracle.

Dr. Brandon Walker, who worked with the Bakers' ministry, shared with me his own eyewitness experiences of food being multiplied.[25] So did Don Kantel, who wrote his dissertation on their ministry.[26] In the essay that I mentioned in chapter 4, Kantel notes, "In his goodness, God has supernaturally multiplied food on at least four occasions in Mieze," a town of some twenty thousand inhabitants in northern Mozambique. On three of these occasions, Kantel witnessed God multiply food for the scores of children gathered; he did not understand why God acted on these specific occasions and not all the time when desperate need pervaded the entire region. During the ongoing desperate refugee crisis at the time of my writing, Rolland also shared with me, "We have already seen God multiply emergency food packages. Once we had around 500 packs, but over 1,000 received a pack. . . . We don't know how!"[27] That's not the kind of story you would make up if you were trying to convince people to donate more food packages! (As the husband of a former refugee, I must add that we should contribute sacrificially for refugees. Again, God normally works through natural means that he has already provided.)

Prayers for Rain

In the Bible, God raised up not only explicit preachers but also servants of his purposes in public administration, such as Joseph, Daniel, and Nehemiah, artists such as Bezalel, warriors such as David, and so forth. Today, Kenyan Charles Mully (also spelled Mulli) cares for thousands of mostly abandoned children, applying his past skills in business to serve the neediest in his community. Those who have watched the documentary about his life (*Mully*) may recall that during a life-threatening drought, God showed him where to drill a new well. No one had reason to believe water would be found there other than what Mully thought God said, but he insisted that they break even through bedrock, and, sure enough, they found abundant water to supply their entire community.[28]

Such experiences are not limited to Africa, however. Richard Holcomb is a real estate developer and shared with me his experiences of praying for rain in a dry land.[29] (Nothing grows, of course, without water.) In 1994, he bought five thousand acres in Texas, including a dry creek. He estimated that he needed about five inches of rain to fill the creek and the lakes to be produced by the dams he was building there. He felt that God invited him to specify the day in prayer. It was then July, so he prayed for the rain by September 21. "On the night of September 19 and morning of September 20, we got 5–6 inches of rain and all my lakes made by the new dams were filled."

Later, drought was afflicting the hill country, and on June 1, 2002, Holcomb felt God spurring him to pray again for rain—for at least 17.1 inches in June and July. June and July were normally two of the driest and hottest months of the year. But the church joined him in prayer, and rain came almost every night when they prayed together. "The USDA recorded 5.16 inches for June and 19.07 inches for July." Holcomb explains that "the July amount is the most recorded rain *ever* for the month of July" since 1931, when records for the area began.

Nature Miracles in Indonesia

During the West Timor revival in 1960s Indonesia, German scholar Kurt Koch heard reports of dramatic miracles taking place there.[30] Although he believed that God could perform miracles, he questioned the possibility of modern miracles on the scale of water being turned to wine. Deciding to investigate, he personally traveled to Indonesia during the height of the revival. Koch was uncomfortable with charismatics, but in West Timor he found himself especially among Reformed Christians. To his astonishment, he reported witnessing water turned to wine multiple times. He then collected reports from many other witnesses to guard his own reputation against skeptics when he would recount these events in the West.

Some reported walking on water in the context of evangelism.[31] It's fitting that such reports come from Indonesia, a nation with lots of water. In 2014, I interviewed Mel Tari, who in the 1970s wrote two popular-level books about the recent Indonesian revival.[32] He knew his own firsthand stories best, but given the American tendency for celebrity worship, he tried to avoid mentioning himself more than necessary. (I understand that; in some earlier books I told my own stories anonymously in the third person to keep from talking about myself too much.) Miracles are good, and it is natural to be excited about them, he conceded, but he emphasized that our focus should be on Jesus. Most of the miracles occurred when believers were risking everything to share Jesus with groups of people who did not know anything about him.

"I wish I'd known I was walking on water when I did it!" Tari commented, laughing. On one of the occasions when an evangelism team walked on water, he explained, he was part of the team of seven or eight people. This was team 36, which included his sister and was led by his brother-in-law. Although it was rainy season, the Lord directed them to share the message about Jesus in a particular area a couple of days' walk away, but when they reached the Mina River (Noel Mina), it was too swollen to cross. During the rainy season the river, more than one hundred yards across at this point, is deep and the current is dangerously strong. When the river is this swollen, it carries even trees, boulders, and any water buffalo that slip into its grip downstream toward the ocean.

The team thus planned to wait till the water receded, but while they were praying they felt that the Holy Spirit was telling them to cross now. Meanwhile, local Christians and polytheists warned them not to attempt this, so they began discussing the matter. After some hesitation, one of Tari's cousins, who was often the boldest member of the group, stepped into the water. Seeing that it did not pass his ankles, he proceeded further and invited the others to follow. His companions saw that the water came no higher than his knees even in the middle of the river, where it should have been some thirty feet deep, so they joined him. Apparently the water where they were crossing was not as deep as they had assumed, and the Lord simply knew that when he directed them to cross.

Thinking no more of it, they went and preached the gospel in the mostly polytheistic villages on the other side of the river. The results were astonishing. Invited to a funeral, for example, the team felt led to gather around the decomposing body of a man dead for two days, and while they sang, the man revived. Needless to say, thousands of people in the region became Christians.

On the way back, roughly a month after their crossing, they reached the village next to the river. There the local pastor, one of Tari's relatives, informed them, "You know you walked on water." They asked him what he was talking about. "After we saw you walk across the river, we decided that maybe the water was now shallower than we thought. So some of our people tried to follow the path we saw you take through the river, but after the first step or two they almost drowned." The water was still twenty-five or thirty feet deep when the team crossed.

"People ask, 'What was it like to walk on water?' I tell them I don't know, because we didn't even know we were doing it when we did it. Whether God raised the bottom of the river or lowered the top or whatever, we didn't know,"

Tari concluded. They had not been looking for a miracle; they were just trying to follow the Lord.

When I was in Indonesia, Dr. Christin Kalvin shared with me her own recent story of accidental water-walking.[33] On December 26, 2014, she preached at a Christmas service at Bittuang in Toraja. Some of her non-Christian coworkers joined her because, three months earlier, they had seen a paralyzed person walk after she prayed. But it was raining heavily, and the local people warned her that a river they would need to cross on the six-hour journey back was now flooded. Because it was already dark and she had a preaching engagement elsewhere the next day, however, she decided that they needed to forge ahead.

When they reached the river, her colleagues waded in up to their chests. They found that they had to lock arms together to keep from being swept downstream. Because Kalvin knew that it dishonored local custom for modest women to lock arms with men, she decided that she would need to cross separately, by herself. She did not want to offend local believers from the region who had attended the service and were now also waiting at the edge of the river, unable to cross.

She prayed with the local believers for the water to grow calm, but they urged her not to try to cross. When the river flooded, crocodiles and snakes were also in the water. Because the rest of her team was now across, however, she felt that she had no choice. Yet she noticed that the water had now grown calm, just as she had requested in prayer, so she stepped in. The water seemed quite shallow, and she walked across. It was her team on the other side that informed her that she had walked on water. (One of them even took a photograph, though in the dark it did not come out very well.) By then, another believer had followed her across. Her non-Christian colleagues became Christians that night.

Chapter 33

Do You Know Any Witnesses to Nature Miracles?

I have some relationship with some of the miracle witnesses mentioned in the previous chapter, but here I focus on those whom I know fairly well but who are usually not so well known to others. That is, my accounts here are from my own circle, reducing the likelihood of coincidence and eliminating thirdhand reports.

A Precipitating Event

Emmanuel Itapson, whose PhD is from Hebrew Union College in Cincinnati, was for a number of years my colleague at Palmer Theological Seminary, and he was the best man in my wedding. Emmanuel grew up witnessing the ministry of his father, Anana Itap, a Nigerian church planter, and shared with me accounts of various miracles that he witnessed. One was the following story.

Itap and his family had just moved to a new community. He was getting a roof on his new dwelling, and completing the roof would take about four more days. Some residents of the village mocked Itap's mission and presence in the village, noting that it was the rainy season and everything he had would be ruined before he could get a roof up. Unfortunately, Itap lost his temper, declaring, "It's not going to rain one drop of rain on this village until I have a roof on my dwelling!" His critics laughed as they walked off, and Itap, realizing what he had done, fell on his face before God. "What have I done!" he cried, dismayed.

For the next four days, however, the village remained dry while rain fell all around it. After this event only one person in the village remained non-Christian, and residents to this day recount that incident as what precipitated the village's conversion.[1]

Massive Hailstorm Stops

One of my brilliant PhD students, now Dr. Kevin Burr, is also a Church of Christ minister. Churches of Christ are not known for their Pentecostal proclivities, and neither is Kevin. But one day in early April 2006, Kevin and some friends were driving in three vehicles to Harding University. Near Augusta, Arkansas, they ran into a major hailstorm. The following account draws on the testimonies of Kevin and, independently, each of his four friends who were present on the occasion.[2]

The sky looked green, suggesting tornado weather. Kevin pulled off to the right side of the road as pea-sized pellets of ice began pounding his windshield. Gradually, the hailstones increased in size until, as large as baseballs, they were bouncing from the ground. One dented Kevin's 2005 Ford Ranger, which by the end of the storm had suffered what would amount to $3,200 worth of hail damage. Hail shattered the windshield of the vehicle driven by Bridget Lindsay, another member of the group. Lindsay agreed with other witnesses that some of the hailstones now falling were as large as softballs; she called it "the biggest hail I've ever seen in my life."

Nevertheless, maneuvering on a gravel road, the caravan made it to a sort of pole shed or tractor port. There the students dove for cover, horrified to see softball-sized hail flying horizontally outside—consistent with an F2 or F3 tornado.[3] Kevin yelled that they should pray; they huddled and closed their eyes. Because the wind was howling loudly, he had to shout his concise prayer so they could hear. As soon as he concluded with "Amen," the wind died and the sun suddenly emerged. When the friends looked up, they saw that a rainbow now spanned the eastern horizon, the first time that some of them had seen a rainbow from one end of the horizon to the other. Jonathan Lindsay, who was then a photographer for Harding University, snapped a photograph of the rainbow, a photo that also shows the terrain still littered with golf ball–sized hailstones.[4]

The Christian T-Shirt

While sitting in on one of my courses, Asbury Old Testament PhD student Brian Shockey shared an experience from January 1999.[5] When he was studying in Australia, he stopped for a week in Fiji, starting on January 17. The next day he traveled by boat to a small island. He had not checked the weather forecast and was not aware that part of Cyclone Dani (Jan. 15–22), which at its peak was 115 mph (185 km/h), was approaching Fiji.

Especially since Brian just wrote a dissertation, I'd better let him describe his own experience:

The company operated a boat service from Nadi on the main island to the small island on a daily schedule. It was supposed to be a short, easy trip to the island. About thirty minutes into the trip we encountered a storm. The waters became very dangerous with large waves, heavy rain, and strong wind. The captain of the boat sent one of his staff outside to ride on top of the boat and spot the waves for him. At one point the storm was so great that the movement of the boat caused the captain's chair to break and fall to the floor.

The passengers, including Brian, began to fear that the boat would sink. "At this point," Brian continues, "the captain pointed to a young woman seated in the back of the boat who was wearing a Christian T-shirt. He motioned her to the front, pointed to the floor next to him, and instructed her to pray. Shortly after she began praying, the waters calmed and the rain stopped, allowing us to continue our journey to the island without any further problems." The sun came out and they arrived safely, though still extremely tense from the experience.

Once they disembarked on the small island, the captain immediately rushed his vessel back to the main island. That was the last boat to leave the main island for several days, leaving Brian and his fellow tourists stranded that week. When they were finally able to return to the main island, they discovered that, though Cyclone Dani's winds had not lashed the island, its outer bands had dumped heavy rains that led to flooding.

One moral of the story might be to check the weather forecast before your outing. A bigger moral of this story, however, is: Don't wear a Christian T-shirt unless you are ready for someone to ask you to pray.

Missionaries, Miracles, and Mechanics

My previous book included several stories of stranded missionaries who needed unexpected help with vehicles.[6] More recently I learned that my friend and fellow Bible professor Scott Ellington was once stranded on a Mexican desert highway with his family after their main radiator hose burst. "We had a spare," he notes, "but not enough water to refill the radiator," so they prayed. There in the Sonoran Desert, a sudden rainstorm kept their engine cool for the next six or seven miles until they could get water to refill the radiator, whereupon the rain stopped.[7]

Eugene and Sandy Thomas were long-term missionaries in Republic of Congo and worked closely with my wife, Médine. They helped encourage our early relationship, and until they passed away they treated us like members of their family. They were not charismatic, but they were afraid to recount in the United States some of their supernatural experiences for fear that people would not believe them. (That can be a serious situation when you depend partly on Christians in the United States for your support.)

Sandy told us of one occasion in the 1970s when they were baking thousands of bricks for a building project. The bricks had to be baked for three days yet protected from rain; when heated, the bricks would explode if they got wet. Because it was the rainy season, the missionaries constructed a roof to protect the baking bricks. On this occasion, however, the roof burned, leaving them no option but to pray that the rains would not come as the vulnerable bricks were baking. In fact, the rains did come; it rained for more than an hour. While it rained on either side of the brick kiln, however, no water fell on the kiln itself. The Thomases' son was running in and out of the rain, and Sandy reported that the workers could not believe what they saw.[8]

On another occasion, as Sandy and Eugene were returning by boat from Bangui in the Central African Republic, their forty-horsepower outboard motor burned up, perhaps 150 miles from their destination. Faced with overwhelmingly hot sun, Sandy insisted on praying. Her husband opened the motor and showed her the burned parts. "I generally have a lot of faith," he said, "but this time, if you want us to pray, you're going to have to lead the prayer."

After Sandy prayed, confident that God would help them, she insisted that they push out into the water and pull the rope on the motor. "Well, we have nothing to lose," Eugene conceded, so he pushed out and pulled the rope. The motor suddenly sprang to life. "I have no idea how this is working," he admitted, "but I'm very happy that it is!" The motor took them the remainder of their journey until it died about fifty feet from the shore of their destination, never to work again. When their Bible school students examined the motor, they pointed out that it was burned out inside; hence, this could not have been how they returned. Nevertheless, the burned motor had worked.

On various occasions I have been present when God answered prayers for vehicles that were not working. If he is a healer of something as complex as the human body, how much more is he able to repair simpler mechanical problems? This is good news for my own family; the temporary restoration of a dying car saved the life of my brother-in-law Dr. Emmanuel Moussounga during war in Congo.[9]

A Faith Drill

When Shivraj Mahendra was a PhD student at Asbury Seminary, he recounted the following story to me at my home, nearly three and a half years after the events occurred.[10] More than ten years after his conversion to Christ from a strongly non-Christian background, Shivraj was visiting his Christian uncle in the village of Telgara (in Chhattisgarh, central India), where Shivraj had been born. He was on a family vacation, just planning to spend a couple of days there. But by the next day word had gotten around that a man of prayer had come to the village.

Early in the morning, therefore, on December 26, 2012, a Hindu man knocked on his uncle's door and requested prayer for an urgent matter. All week long six or seven workers had been trying to drill for water, but the area was harder than they expected, preventing their success. "The ground is like rock everywhere. The borewell machine quits after just a couple of feet down." The workers believed that some of the village deities were causing them trouble, so they decided to request prayer at the only Christian home in the village, the uncle's home. Perhaps Christian prayer could solve this problem.

The visitors wanted Shivraj to go with them and pray at the spot where they were getting ready to drill afresh. He did not dare refuse, but he accompanied the workers reluctantly. What if God did not decide to make the drill work? And what might happen to him if it did not work? Before his conversion, Shivraj himself had helped persecute a relative who was associating with a Christian, and after his conversion he had to elude some militant former friends. He feared that if his Christian prayer was not answered, some of the villagers who shared that militant perspective might take out their frustrations on him.

When he reached the field where the drill was, he felt so vulnerable that he prayed quietly first. "Lord, you know what's going on here; I just ask that you take care of this situation for your name's sake." He then offered one loud but brief public prayer: "Dear Jesus Christ, you are the Lord of the earth and water. The land is yours and you are able to do anything. These people are looking to you for help, so please give them water. In your name, let this be so."

He concluded with "Amen," took some water from a cup, and sprinkled it on the marked spot, like the biblical Elijah, who poured water on the sacrifice before asking God to answer by fire. He glanced at the giant drilling machine, a challenge to his simple faith. "All right," Shivraj suggested. "Try it now." Then he ran back to his uncle's house as quickly as he could.

About an hour later, workers showed up again at the door, which Shivraj answered warily.

"We got water," they announced. "Your God is great!" Although they had tried drilling in three or four places before, they found water immediately after Shivraj's prayer, and they did not even have to drill deep. The workers, the uncle's family, and the neighbors were all witnesses. And Shivraj was very relieved.

Colleagues, Students, and Myself

Professor Ayo Adewuya publicly recounted that he witnessed a colleague confront a shaman by announcing that the expected rain would not fall that day, but it would fall the next day at 4:00 p.m. It happened accordingly.[11] My Cameroonian student Paul Mokake shared with me multiple eyewitness accounts of nature miracles, including one in which a heavy storm receded before his team as they approached one resistant location to proclaim Christ.[12] When one of my students, Benjamin Ahanonu, was an undergraduate in Philadelphia, rain was pouring down on the day that he and his friends had planned an outreach. After they prayed, the rain stopped precisely in their part of the city, allowing the outreach and astonishing a non-Christian witness. One of Benjamin's friends who was present at the incident also confirmed it for me.[13]

Dame Simanjuntak, a Lutheran PhD student at Asbury Seminary from North Sumatra, Indonesia, recounted to me a time when she was on a beach with friends from another faith. Something like a small tornado seemed to be forming on the ocean and heading toward them, so her companions scattered for shelter. While the others watched her from cover, Dame lifted her hand toward it and prayed for about two minutes, and then it fizzled and disappeared into clouds.[14]

Lest someone accuse me of giving too much credence to students and colleagues, let me recount an occasion when I myself was a witness and participant.

I was then teaching at Hood Seminary, associated with Livingstone College in Salisbury, North Carolina.[15] Some students from a campus ministry at another historically African American college, North Carolina A&T State University in Greensboro, were visiting to help students from Livingstone's campus ministry with an outreach event that day. The outreach seemed likely to be dampened, however, by a serious storm that had lasted for a couple of hours and was predicted to continue for much of the day. A sophomore biology major from the other campus led us in prayer for the rain to stop. No sooner had we said "Amen" than the heavy rain slackened to drips and then stopped, like a bathroom faucet that has been turned off. Within a few minutes, the sky cleared and the sun came out for the rest of the day. This, by the way, is no mere distant recollection; I recorded it in my journal on the day that it happened.[16] Yes, once in a while even this introverted scholar has witnessed something for himself.

───────────── PART 7 ─────────────

Kingdom Mysteries

G od continues to act in our world; I have experienced his action myself. But sickness, sin, and death remain in this world. The "already" signs of the kingdom nurture hope for its "not yet" consummation. Nothing is impossible for God, but the time of full restoration that banishes sin and its effects will also banish unrepentant sinners, making delay as well as consummation an act of God's kindness. Living between the already and the not yet still requires faith that has yet to become sight (2 Cor. 5:7). That means that miracles—what theologians call "special divine action"—remain special. Until the consummation, suffering and death still happen in this world.

Chapter 34

A Firsthand Witness?

I f the universe is a miracle written too large for those who are spiritually nearsighted to recognize it, God also works in some details that many people consider too small to recognize. What one recognizes depends on what glasses one wears. Because these smaller acts are recognized only by those who already have some faith, I struggled with whether they were appropriate to even mention in this book.

Nevertheless, some readers may consider a mere scholar whose expertise lies in historical and literary disciplines unqualified to write a book on miracles. Although my research skills came in handy (along with my high school major in journalism), I recognize some validity in this criticism. To some extent, I am an outside observer doing research. There are indeed people far more qualified to recount miracles, either because, on account of their particular ministry gifts and spheres, they see many more than I do, or because they are medical doctors (or meteorologists) far more qualified to evaluate the reports. Certainly many people are far more qualified than I am to share practical insights regarding how to facilitate health and healing; they are the people from whom I as a researcher seek to learn.

I welcome and even plead for more documented resources from these voices. Some of those I know who are more qualified have not gotten around to writing such books, however, and even when they have, some people who do not typically read those types of books read mine for other reasons. I write this book to fill a niche, but it is not meant to fill all the niches for books about miracles.

More to the point of the rest of this chapter, some may object that even when I cite witnesses I have interviewed or know personally, these are secondhand to me and thus thirdhand to my readers. So before I turn to a frequent question—why miracles seem less common in the West—I offer a brief sample of a few of my more extraordinary firsthand experiences (thus secondhand, rather than thirdhand, to you). I do not regard them as meeting exacting scientific standards for incontrovertible proof, but they may at least help explain to skeptics why it remains reasonable for me, even from my own experience, to take miracle reports seriously enough to consider them. I am, to this extent at least, what social science researchers call a participant observer.

Until I began writing my first book about miracles, I, like most other people, never thought of collecting medical documentation. My personal examples, unlike some cases recounted in this book, are thus of limited evidential value. Still, they are firsthand, and if I had space to record them all somewhere they might appear to be an extraordinary number of coincidences coincidentally accumulated around the author of this book.

Most individual cases may not seem to bear mentioning—for example, when my doctor preliminarily diagnosed me with ischemic colitis in my large intestine. That night our small group prayed; the next day the urgent CT scan showed that I was completely normal.[1] My doctor, who is a believer, said that either he had misdiagnosed me or God had healed me.[2] I have plenty of examples like this one but little reason to elaborate on them, since misdiagnosis does happen and, through God's gift in creation, the body does often heal itself.

Physical Blessings

But, having transitioned from being an atheist to being a follower of Jesus, I did notice that some sorts of things happened frequently after my conversion, when I prayed, that hadn't happened before, when I didn't. I focus especially on the earliest years of my Christian life because that was when, as a recent convert from atheism, I found them most shocking and memorable. In my first couple of years as a Christian, I tended to pray loudly and so had to look for less-inhabited places to pray. In summer, I often prayed in the woods and found my arms plastered with mosquito bites. I would keep praying, trying to ignore them, and when I remembered to look half an hour later, they were gone. That had never happened to me in my pre-Christian days even with a single bite or two, but now it happened without fail.

During those early years I twice contracted the flu. In previous years, having the flu had always led to vomiting as well as fever. I really hated vomiting; I prayed for my indigestion to get flushed out the other, more natural direction. On both these occasions as a new Christian, I bent over the toilet, ready to disgorge, when faith arose to rebuke the flu in Jesus's name. Not only was I suddenly no longer sick at all, but whatever was coming up was gone and I didn't throw up at all. It was, in fact, close to four decades before I threw up again. (I do, however, still often suffer indigestion!)

My ankles have always been as weak as my stomach, and during one cross-country season I twisted my ankle, after which a visible bulge formed on the back of it. I limped through the rest of the week, so when the next race came, on discouragingly hilly terrain, the coach urged me to just finish the race, even if I had to hobble my way through it. I felt God declare my healing when the starting gun went off, and that turned out to be the only race I ever took first place in.

Perhaps the weakness of my ankles relates to my feet turning inward when I was born so that I wore foot braces for a while. In one case, though, when I was twenty-two or twenty-three years old, I apparently broke my ankle. I say "apparently" because I was then a penniless graduate student and I could not afford to see a doctor. Though the swelling went down and I was eventually able to walk again, the ankle failed to heal properly. After some months I could walk without a noticeable limp, but if I tried to run, after just a few yards the pain became unbearable and I found myself limping again. This condition persisted for two years.

After two years, my ankle was still not getting any better, and I was still a penniless graduate student. But after a summer of doing ministry on the streets of New York City, my faith felt very strong, and I felt confident that God would heal my ankle when I prayed about it now. I promised God that if he healed my ankle, I would not take the blessing for granted but would exercise regularly. At that moment, I felt that he healed me, so I tried out the ankle immediately. The next day I was at a multistory building and so took the bolder opportunity to run up six flights of stairs to celebrate my ability to do so. I returned to regular, vigorous exercise, which in turn has naturally benefited the rest of my health.

Of course, I have also witnessed other healings. Within my first year of being a Christian, an evangelist prayed for someone I knew from church who had back trouble, and though the evangelist merely held a hand motionless under one of the man's legs, the leg abruptly and visibly spurted out a couple of inches, restoring the man's back. The same evangelist also prayed for a woman in our church who could hear only with the help of a hearing aid. Afterward this woman was conversing with me and lamenting, "I wish I weren't deaf," before I noticed that she had forgotten to put her hearing aid back in.

People around me have also been healed when I joined in prayer for them at times. (This is only because God hears prayers offered in the name of Jesus; I mention a couple of examples only so readers who presume that *everybody* should see healings may be satisfied that, yes, even a staid scholar may see them at times.) In the early years of my faith, an ear cyst vanished immediately when I prayed for it; after a friend and I prayed for one woman whose kidneys were failing, she reported the medical verdict that her kidneys were now functioning again.

When I was working in maintenance at some apartments for older adults during college summer break, a resident named Mabel Cooper told me that she had been coughing up blood and her doctor thought she had lung cancer. On my lunch break, I stopped at her apartment and prayed for her, led her to faith in Christ, and incidentally encouraged her to give up smoking. "My doctor told me to give up smoking too," she said, as if she regarded that advice as surprising. She did not cough up any more blood, her doctor determined that she must be fine after all, and she continued living in that apartment for the next fifteen years. My grandmother, who later occupied the apartment above her, noted that Ms. Cooper was a very kind woman.[3]

Many other such examples are possible, but these are really others' experiences to tell. Moreover, I make no pretense that God has removed all my maladies: I have attention deficit hyperactivity disorder, am nearsighted, often have digestive problems, often have sleep problems (sometimes related to the digestion, sometimes to my writing schedule), and so on. I joke more freely about my male-pattern baldness. Not least, I can't run as fast at sixty as I could at twenty.

Beyond Health

But the biggest changes after my conversion were spiritual. These spiritual experiences do not precisely fit the narrower parameters of this book's subject; including many such experiences in this book would have defeated my intention to keep it fairly concise. Nevertheless, my spiritual encounters help keep me respectful of unusual experiences associated with God.

Two days after my conversion from atheism, I felt so overwhelmed by God's presence that I began praising him in a language that I didn't know; as the wording was flowing out of me, I was listening intently, trying to decipher the syntax. I had no idea that there was a biblical name for this experience.[4] Yet I was experiencing an intense, ecstatic joy unlike any I had ever known before. Having been a Christian just two days, I had not yet read about this experience in the Bible or heard of it before.

I have continued to experience God's presence in ways utterly foreign to my preconversion life. While my own hearing of God can be very subjective when emotions are involved (it seemed quite ambiguous when I was looking for a spouse), other cases tend to be more accurate. Rather than describe my own experience of hearing God, let me recount here another's. One Ethiopian man of prayer, who did not know that I was a writer, prophesied accurate information about two of my forthcoming books that I myself did not yet know (or at the time believe).[5]

I could recount multiplied experiences that individually might be explained as luck but that have been too frequent in my life to readily fit that explanation. For example, one time when I was an undergraduate, I was trying to explain a biblical point to a new believer. She was distracted, however, because my college roommate was then driving us during an unexpectedly heavy storm. We could barely see beyond his windshield because the windshield wipers didn't work, and he suddenly realized we were going down a one-way street at the right speed but in the wrong direction. Annoyed with the distraction, and without thinking first, I commanded the windshield wipers to work "in the name of Jesus." Instantly they sprang into action, and our friend, the new believer, started screaming with astonishment. Now she was distracted by the wipers working, and I never did get to finish that Bible study. Other incidents include broken cars working after prayer, dogs that had been pursuing me retreating after a command in Jesus's name, and the like, always in the context of working for the Lord.

Provision is not the focus of this book, and God is not in the business of counterfeiting money. Still, provision is another area of my life that has helped shape my faith. Without these incidents, neither this book nor my thirty-two others would have happened. From a nonbeliever's perspective, my experience in this regard might be merely a random survivor's tale; yet it may at least help a nonbeliever sympathize with why I trust divine activity.

In 1991, I was accepted into Duke University's PhD program, but without funding. My temporary work at that time was ending, and at one point I got down to literally a single dollar. At that point someone who did not know my situation knocked on my door, feeling led to give me some money. That allowed me to buy food. Then, the day before I was going to call Duke and explain that I couldn't come, a family member who had not provided money for my master's work and did not yet know my situation offered to sponsor my PhD work. I tried to refuse her offer, but to no avail. Had it come one day later, I could not have started a PhD that year. Although people do get money unexpectedly, this experience was particularly meaningful for me. By allowing me to become a scholar, it shaped my subsequent life.

During my final year of PhD work, I diligently wrote to one or two hundred schools, looking for work for when I finished. Neither those schools (most of which lacked openings) nor any actually posted job openings materialized; it was a time when many religion departments had closed down and even many experienced professors were looking for work. (Even today, competition for jobs in New Testament is very stiff in the Western world.)

During the summer after I completed my PhD, it became increasingly clear that I would not have a teaching position for the fall. I prayed and tried to maintain courage, but after estimating one night how much money I would need to live on in the following year, I gave up in despair. I did not need much room to sleep, but a fast-food or unskilled maintenance job might not support even an efficiency apartment large enough for my research files. (This was in the days before you could fit gigabytes of data on a flash drive.)

The next day an editor from InterVarsity Press called to say that IVP was excited about my proposed *Bible Background Commentary*. Welcome as this news was, it wasn't enough to raise my spirits. *How can I write a commentary if I'm living on the street?* I thought. My two previous books, written during the last year of my PhD, received royalties only after their publication, and these were certainly not enough to live on. But the editor went on to say that IVP had also decided to offer me an advance. It was to the dollar what I had calculated the night before. I was stunned. That year I worked on the commentary, to provide cultural background for the New Testament; the next year I had a teaching position.

I have had many other experiences like these, any of which by themselves might be explained as coincidence. Together, however, they help explain why I am able to work as a scholar today. These are mere samples of what I believe are my fairly frequent personal experiences with a God actively involved in my life.

Although I see God's hand in all these events, they would not fit typical definitions of miracles. Nor do I present them as models for everyone; they fit God's larger purposes, with which my own needs at those points coincided. I include them, and the other stories in this chapter, not to convince skeptics but to explain my own heart. I am confident of God's action in the world not least because I believe that I have experienced it.

Chapter 35

Why Don't We See More Miracles in the West?

Christians in the West often ask why we don't see more miracles here. If you have read this far in the book, you know that events that most people would call miracles do happen here. Think, for example, of the accounts in previous chapters of Chris Gunderson, Marlene Klepees, Bryan LaPooh, Ema McKinley, Greg Spencer, and Bruce Van Natta. Naturally, *fewer* miracles occur within the US than outside the US, because the US contains less than 5 percent of the world's population. North America as a whole has roughly 8 percent of the world's population.

But there are also some other factors. For example, when miracles happen here, our antisupernatural mindset often renders them invisible to us because we grasp at other explanations. Since miracles are therefore less meaningful to us, they are also less likely to happen (Mark 6:5–6). But miracles are also less often necessary here than in some other places. We may begin to be open to more of what God may have for us if we start by being more grateful for the gifts that God has already provided for us.

General and Special Providence

When Father Karl went into full cardiac arrest, he happened to be doing hospital visitation. Likewise, he happened to be in an elevator that opened on the same floor as the cardiac care unit and that deposited his body at the feet of an experienced cardiac surgeon who was about to board. Had Father Karl collapsed anywhere else, he might have suffered irreparable brain damage before he could be revived. As it was, however, this beloved priest was revived medically in an incident that the surgeon considered miraculously serendipitous.[1]

Sometimes we want to see miracles to prove that God (or we) can do what is *super*natural versus what is merely "natural." Although Jesus used his authority to heal people in need, he kept his identity secret from the public for as long as possible. Jesus refused when the devil, even quoting Scripture (Ps. 91:11–12), wanted Jesus to show off his power by jumping off the pinnacle of the temple (Matt. 4:5–7//Luke 4:9–12). Ignoring works that God has already done, then asking God to prove himself just to get what we want, is faithlessly testing him (Ps. 78:18–20; John 6:26, 30–31).

God especially provides supernaturally when there is no other way, not simply to entertain us or show off. (I sometimes joke that when I stepped on a frozen puddle to try to practice for walking on water someday, the ice cracked.) When natural means exist, God often works through them. There were no grocery stores for Israel in the wilderness, so God provided manna for forty years. But the manna stopped once the Israelites could eat the fruit of the land (Josh. 5:12).

Jesus taught us to pray for our daily bread (Matt. 6:11//Luke 11:3), but it is not unbelief to go out and earn a living (1 Thess. 4:11–12; 2 Thess. 3:6–12). When sufficient food was unavailable by natural means, Jesus multiplied food to feed thousands of people. Afterward, however, he told his disciples to gather the fragments that remained (John 6:12). He fed the crowd when they needed a miracle, but the disciples' next few meals would not require any new miracles.

Can you imagine how silly the disciples would have been to throw away the leftovers because they were praying for daily bread? Why should we neglect natural means of healing any more than we neglect natural means of eating? The fact that God does a miracle sometimes does not mean that we should expect him to do it every time. Both in Scripture and in accounts of genuine miracles today, God often likes to surprise us. The fact that Psalm 91:11–12 speaks of God's protection does not mean we should jump off the high point of the temple.

Medicine and Miracles

There is no necessary conflict between what we call natural and what we call supernatural means, which can often work together. Thus Joshua was sent by God (Josh. 8:1–2) but used a military strategy (8:4–9) given by God (8:2). God defeated peoples hostile to the Israelites (Pss. 135:10–12; 136:17–22), but the Israelites understood that God would do this work through them rather than exempting them from responsibility to act (e.g., Num. 21:21–25, 33–35). The ways our bodies often recover naturally are no less a gift of God than the times when he acts more dramatically. When God cures us through doctors, it is no less an answer to prayer than when he does it without them. Jesus gave thanks and then multiplied food to feed five thousand people; we call that a miracle.

But when he told the disciples to gather up the fragments that remained, that was provision for their next meal, and they would give thanks for that meal also (1 Tim. 4:3–5).

The ways that God provided for humans to learn about medicines and the human body, though imperfect, generally allow us to enjoy far better health and longevity today than was possible in the past. (As noted earlier, faith led many founders of modern science in scientific inquiry; the supposed historic war between faith and science rests on propaganda, not solid history.)[2] God provided these means in nature, and societies with access to them have much lower mortality rates than societies that do not, even when God often provides exceptional miracles in the latter. Ancient medicine was not as helpful as modern, empirical medicine, but prophets could use what they had. Isaiah applied a fig poultice to Hezekiah's boil (Isa. 38:21). Paul instructed Timothy to drink some wine for his stomach's sake (1 Tim. 5:23), even though this might offend the legalistic false teachers (4:3–4).

The Vatican rejects healing claims from those who shun medical help "to rely solely on faith."[3] Most Protestants likewise respect empirical medicine. Everett Cook, a Pentecostal church planter who mentored me early in my ministry, told me many stories about how God answered prayers for his family over the decades. But once he also told me about his recent encounter with a Christian who had a growth on his nose.

"You'd better see a doctor," Everett warned.

"I'm healed!" the man insisted, apparently believing that if he insisted on it enough, God would make it happen.

The next time Everett saw him, the growth was larger. "You really ought to see a doctor," Everett suggested.

"No, I'm healed, bless God!" the man insisted.

The third time Everett saw him, the growth was quite large. This time the man admitted, "Maybe I *should* go see a doctor."

Everett's point in recounting this story to me was that God heals, but he also expects us to use common sense. "God provided me a job and health insurance so I can go to the doctor," he explained. "That's no less God's blessing than direct healing is."

Most of my African friends, including my wife, contend that life in Africa is a miracle. "In the West," they emphasize, "you have medical technology, and this is God's gift." God doesn't do miracles for our entertainment; he usually works through natural means that he already created when they are available. Yes, there are many miracles in Africa. But in many places in Africa, death in childbirth is still ten times as frequent as it is in Western hospitals.

God usually performs dramatic signs either when people desperately need them or when he is getting people's attention for the good news of Christ's love in a special way. As African Christians who have witnessed miracles often tell me, "You don't need them as much in America. Your medical system works better!"

Most doctors naturally gravitate toward regions that can enable them to pay off their loans from medical school. Some estimate that only 2 percent of the world's doctors serve in Africa, the world's second most populous continent, with one doctor for every ten thousand people. Because of inadequate health care in Africa, despite some miracles, some two hundred thousand women die in childbirth annually and some 9 percent of children born die before age five. Of the trillions of dollars spent globally each year on health care, the vast majority is spent in the wealthier nations. If we care about what the Jesus of the Gospels cares about, we need to work to provide wider health care in needier areas, and provide moral and economic support for physicians, nurses, and other health care workers who choose to serve there. Miracles are not meant to be a panacea for the world's problems, as if there were nothing more for us to do. In fact, they show us how much God cares about people's health, and that we should care about it too.

Earlier I mentioned Heidi Baker's interview with the *Pneuma Review*. At the conclusion of that interview, Heidi notes, "I hug lots of people every Sunday, people in wheelchairs who don't get out of them. As many blind people as we see healed, we also have homes for blind people who aren't healed. We have cottage industries for blind people. It's all about God and giving His love to others. Love accomplishes God's will even if a supernatural miracle doesn't happen. The biggest miracle is love."

Miracles do not, and are not intended to, resolve every problem in this world. Miracles are foretastes of a better future, and they show us what God cares about. Jesus miraculously healed the sick, delivered those afflicted by spirits, fed the hungry, and protected his followers from lethal storms. God cares about people's health, hunger, and safety. This means that when God is *not* doing a miracle, those who care about what God cares about should use whatever natural means at our disposal to meet the same kinds of needs.

Signs versus Gifts of Healings

In this book, like the larger one, I use the designation "miracles" because that is the term with which people today are familiar in English. The biblical term usually translated as "miracles," however, means something more like "acts that show power," and it often refers to what some parts of the Bible call "signs" or "wonders."[4] Technically speaking, a majority of the examples in this book function for most people as extraordinary signs rather than as more everyday blessings.

But something does not need to be extraordinary to be God's gift. When Paul speaks of gifts of healings (1 Cor. 12:9) or James speaks of healing in answer to prayer (James 5:14–16), these passages do not specify that healings must be dramatic. If God heals gradually, quietly, or through medical technology and skill or healthy lifestyles, God is still answering prayer. Admittedly, sometimes the difference between healing and a sign may be a matter of degree as well as of function.

But whereas the main purpose of healing in 1 Corinthians and James is to help believers, the main biblical purpose of signs is to draw attention to and—for those with eyes to see—to invite faith in God's message. God can testify to the message of his grace with signs and wonders (Acts 14:3), and early Christians could even pray that God would continue to grant his servants boldness to preach in conjunction with healing, signs, and wonders (Acts 4:29–30; compare 4:9–10, 13).

In the New Testament, the majority of signs are healings. Like other healings, they benefit the people healed. But they also get attention and point to something beyond themselves. Jesus tells us that his signs point to the promised future kingdom. Other kinds of healing may be less conspicuous.

God often does dramatic miracles to get nonbelievers' attention when he is breaking new ground in a region or a sphere (Rom. 15:18–19). Earlier in the book I noted Ebi Perinbaraj's testimony about how the healing of a leper and subsequent miracles stirred much of an entire people group to follow Christ. After those events, however, dramatic miracles became less common, and the main gift needed among the new converts was teaching. Another friend who spent years in Mongolia made the same observation about the church there: although signs helped to birth the movement, these declined once the church was started.

As good news about Christ continues to reach new villages in Mozambique, miracles keep happening, perhaps partly because new ground continues to be broken with each new village. God does dramatic works to open up resistant people groups to his kindness to them. This may be especially true among groups that are particularly impressed by such signs, where these signs draw attention to and confirm the message preached. (Sometimes these take the form of what missiologists call "power encounters," where God shows his power to be greater than that of local religious claimants, as he sometimes does in the Bible—e.g., Exod. 7:11, 22; 8:7, 18–19; 9:11; 1 Kings 18:24–39; Acts 8:9–11; 13:6–12.)

That does not mean that God is not at work where we see fewer signs; sometimes God's work is simply less dramatic, though no less real. This does not mean, of course, that God *never* does signs elsewhere. It just means that fewer of his works need to be dramatic. We do not seek drama for drama's sake; we seek signs to honor Christ. Nevertheless, in some unevangelized or post-Christian spheres today even in the West, signs may still get people's attention.

Chapter 36

Spiritual Factors and Miracles

S ometimes miracles flourish in special seasons of revival; such seasons are
not always predictable, but they often follow prayer for the outpouring of
God's Spirit. Often, too, signs flourish in areas of groundbreaking evangelism for the sake of getting attention for the liberating message of the Lord Jesus.
Miracles also tend to predominate where there is more faith for them, although
we should remember to trust Christ himself, not our faith. All these factors are
sometimes related. But as leaders in some revival movements, as in Indonesia and
Mozambique, emphasize, miracles follow those who seek Jesus and his purposes,
not those who seek miracles.[1]

Special Seasons of Revival

God chooses to work in different ways and at different times. Sometimes this
variation corresponds to the spiritual state of his people, and sometimes it is just
because God has chosen to work differently, so we learn to trust his sovereign
wisdom.

In the time of faithful Abraham, God sends angels to deliver Lot (Gen. 19:7–11)
and provides a ram to sacrifice in place of Isaac (22:12–13). By contrast, in the
spiritually dark and chaotic period of the judges, no ram replaces Jephthah's
daughter (Judg. 11:34–40) and no angels deliver the Levite's concubine (19:25–28).
The ordinary course of events continues without God stopping them. Such narratives fit many of the unspeakably tragic realities that occur around our world
daily, summoning us to work for justice with all ordinary means available to us. In
a time of foreign oppression, Gideon has reason to wonder where all the miracles

of the exodus are (Judg. 6:13). God goes on to give Gideon a great victory, but without any pillar of fire or parted waters.

Sometimes differences in the ways God works just reflect his choice to reveal himself in different ways through different people (compare Matt. 11:18–19// Luke 7:33–34; Rom. 12:4–8). John the Baptist expected Jesus to baptize in fire, and Scripture shows that he someday will. But when John heard that Jesus was just healing people and not pouring out fire, he doubted Jesus's identity. When Jesus does not act the way we expect him to, we, like John, may be tempted to stumble over him (Matt. 11:6//Luke 7:23).

The first of the plagues in Exodus was water turned to blood; the first of Jesus's signs was water turned to wine. The last of the plagues was the death of the firstborn; in John's Gospel, the last of Jesus's signs before the cross was the raising of Lazarus. God had chosen to act in a new way.

Moses's miracles in Exodus humbled a mighty empire, taking back the prosperity earlier given through Joseph.[2] The many miracles in the Gospels and Acts occurred on a less grand scale. They did not bring down the Roman Empire. But over the next few centuries, through the compassionate and faithful witness of Christians willing to care for the poor, pray and care for the sick, and die martyrs' deaths, they converted much of that empire. Eventually the emperor himself claimed to become a Christian! God worked in a more subtle way—yet the glory of the new covenant is incomparably greater than the glory of the previous covenant (2 Cor. 3:7–11). The one glory was obvious yet brought death; the other could be seen only with the eyes of faith to behold resurrection power in Jesus's cross and his apostles' suffering. Yet that glory brings life (2 Cor. 2:15–16; 3:6).

God does not fit in any box. He deserves our trust, whether he does what we think he should or not. Some details we will understand only in the light of eternity, when we can view the larger picture of God's plan. But for those with eyes to see, God is already at work in our world. And he welcomes us to pray for outpourings of the Spirit, for times of revival when the extraordinary becomes more common (see, e.g., Luke 11:13; Acts 4:29–31; compare Acts 1:14 with 2:1–4). Revivals vary considerably in some of their effects, but healing is often among the effects.[3]

Revivals or outpourings of God's Spirit often come in the ways we least expect. After a series of visions, Elena Guerra, Italian founder of the Oblates of the Holy Spirit, privately urged Pope Leo XIII to renew emphasis on the Holy Spirit.[4] Toward the end of the nineteenth century, therefore, Catholics were praying for the outpouring of the Spirit. The same was true of radical evangelicals, the holiness-oriented Christians who were praying for divine healing and power to evangelize the world.[5] (A. J. Gordon, A. B. Simpson, and others were part of this interdenominational, intercontinental evangelical movement.)

On January 1, 1901, Pope Leo dedicated the twentieth century to the Holy Spirit. On roughly the same day (allowing for time zone differences), holiness evangelical Agnes Osmond began worshiping in tongues in a small Kansas Bible school. This was the beginning of the movement that led to the 1906 Azusa Street Revival, which has since touched some half a billion people (more on diverse revivals below). God began answering the prayer in a place and a manner that many of those who were praying initially would not have expected.

Humility

The Lord is not impressed with what impresses mortals (1 Sam. 16:7; Luke 16:15).

- Psalm 34:18: "The Lord is near the brokenhearted, and rescues those crushed in spirit."
- Psalm 138:6 (NIV): "Though the LORD is exalted, he looks kindly on the lowly."
- Isaiah 57:15 (NRSV): "For thus says the high and lofty one . . . : I dwell . . . with those who are contrite and humble in spirit."
- Habakkuk 2:4 (NRSV): "Look at the proud! Their spirit is not right in them, but the righteous live by their faith."
- Matthew 23:12//Luke 14:11; 18:14: "Whoever exalts themselves will be humbled, and whoever humbles themselves will be exalted."
- 1 Corinthians 1:28–29: "God chose those things that the world deems base and disdains, things that are not, in order to nullify the things that are, so that no one could boast before God."
- James 4:6–7 (NIV): "But he gives us more grace. That is why Scripture says: 'God opposes the proud but shows favor to the humble.' Submit yourselves, then, to God."
- 1 Peter 5:5–6: "Now *all* of you: clothe yourselves with humility, since God 'stands against the arrogant, but bestows grace on the humble.' So humble yourselves under God's powerful hand, so that he may exalt you at the right time."

Miracles tend to occur especially among the humble—not among those who won't appreciate them. Humility is knowing who God and who, correspondingly, we are. Humility comes from the fear of the Lord (compare Prov. 15:33).

Whether Jesus heals visibly and dramatically or more quietly and ultimately, his healings express his heart: compassion (Matt. 14:14; 15:32; Mark 8:2; Luke 7:13–15). A common human tendency, widespread even well before valuable scientific understandings of contagious viruses, has been to avoid the sick or distressed (Job 6:21; Ps. 38:11). Yet Jesus acted counterculturally in this regard. He did not associate with powerful people in his society in order to gain their favor; he invited ordinary and even despised people to be his disciples; and he healed the most powerless. Even though the religious elite might consider him lax regarding purity laws, Jesus touched the ritually impure to heal and so purify them (Mark 1:41; 5:41). Even before Jesus died, Matthew says that he bore our sicknesses (Matt. 8:17), because by serving the least he had already started on the road to the cross. We should remember that any healing or any other gift that Jesus gives us cost him everything.

Most revivals in modern history began among the poor and the marginalized, or among youth not yet set in their ways.[6] Consider, for example, some of the various revivals that broke out in the first decade of the twentieth century. Many of those first touched by the 1904–1905 Welsh revival were hardworking coal miners. Reports of this revival stirred spiritual hunger elsewhere.[7] In 1905, another major revival broke out at the Mukti Mission in India, where Pandita Ramabai took in young widows and orphans.[8] In 1906, revival broke out in Los Angeles at the Azusa Street Mission led by William Seymour, an African American holiness preacher whose parents had been born in slavery.[9] Within years this revival movement began to spread globally. One could multiply examples of revivals that began among the marginalized. For example, toward the end of the twentieth century, we might note revivals among repressed Christians in China and orphans in Mozambique.[10]

None of these movements first took hold among elites. Some revivals have risen among the more privileged, but these revivals sometimes followed in the wake of suffering or prepared for greater suffering to come. The businessmen's revivals of the 1850s preceded the terrible suffering of the US Civil War, just as the Welsh revival presaged World War I.

Some revivals started among college students, such as the two major revivals at Asbury College,[11] or the missions movement that began with the so-called Haystack Prayer Meeting.[12] Yet even most of these revivals began among those who were desperate for God—not those who just thought that it would be nice to experience more of God, but those who knew they could not live without this experience. The Nigerian revival that began with students in Scripture Union in Nigeria commenced in the wake of the devastating Nigerian civil war of the 1960s.[13]

The God who is near the lowly and brokenhearted shows himself most often among those who are desperate for him. Usually even there, however, he shows himself in ways we don't quite expect. Laws of nature may predict natural processes that God established, but they do not dictate his workings with humanity. What remains consistent is his nature of justice and compassion and his patience in working out his purposes in his time rather than ours.

To Believe or Not to Believe

Another reason we may see fewer miracles in the West is that Humean skepticism has shaped so much of our thinking here. While some skepticism is necessary to prevent gullibility (see Prov. 14:15), we should become skeptical of our skepticism to the extent that faith's object has proved reliable. That is, those of us who know God should not trust all untested claims people make, but we can surely start by trusting that God sometimes does act outside the expected course of nature.

The Gospels connect faith with healings quite often (Matt. 8:10, 13; 9:2, 6–7, 22, 28–29; 15:28; Mark 2:5, 11–12; 5:34, 36; 9:23–24; 10:52; Luke 5:20, 24–25; 7:9; 8:48, 50; 17:19; 18:42; John 4:50; 11:40; compare also Mark 16:17–18; Acts 3:16; 14:9). Similarly, they connect many other answers to prayer with faith (Matt. 14:28–31; 21:21–22; Mark 11:23–24; Luke 17:6; compare also Mark 16:17–18). Sometimes a shortage of healings may reflect a culture of disbelief (Matt. 13:58; Mark 6:5–6; Luke 9:41) or the disbelief of Jesus's agents (Matt. 17:20; compare Mark 9:29; Luke 9:41). Jesus often chides his disciples for their limited trust, since after his many miracles they should have seen enough to trust him (Mark 4:40; Luke 8:25; 12:28; compare also 17:5), a point especially prominent in Matthew's Gospel (Matt. 6:30; 8:26; 14:31; 16:8; 17:20).

Jesus's frequent association of divine action with faith may sometimes make us uncomfortable because we misunderstand what faith is. For some, faith is make-believe, a matter of wishing very hard until something happens. But that is not what faith means in Scripture. Biblical faith is the kind of trust you have in someone whom you know to be trustworthy. That trust also grows in time as part of a continuing relationship.

Sometimes that does not feel like what we think faith should feel like. Although faith may sometimes be expressed serenely (which is certainly welcome when it happens), Scripture often portrays it as a decision of the will in the face of obstacles. In Scripture, faith sometimes expresses itself in desperate acts—acts driven by Jesus being our only hope. The Bible recounts that the woman with the flow of blood forced herself through the crowd to touch Jesus. It was against the rules for someone in her condition to touch people, but she was desperate; only Jesus could help her (Mark 5:27–29).

Others were desperate enough to tear up a neighbor's roof to get their friend to Jesus; Jesus calls their determination faith (Mark 2:5; though presumably they were expected to help fix the roof afterward). The Syrophoenician woman would not give up petitioning until Jesus granted her petition (Mark 7:26–30); Jesus refers to her persistence and self-humbling as faith (Matt. 15:28). Jesus lets her overcome his objection and make her case, as God welcomed Abraham, Moses, and a bold widow to persist in intercession (Gen. 18:23–32; Exod. 32:11–14; 34:9; Luke 18:1–8). Sometimes the answer "no" is an invitation to persevere, to show faith, until the answer becomes "yes." Standing firm in stubborn faith, continuing to call on Jesus's name rather than simply giving up without a fight, is biblical.

But what happens when the answer is no—period?[14] That was the Father's answer to his own son in Gethsemane. In the Lord's Prayer, we pray, "Your will be done," thinking of God's kingdom values that include healing and restoration (Matt. 6:10). But when Jesus prayed, "Your will be done," the Father's will for him was the cross (Matt. 26:42), needed for the greater good. The world's condition of rebellion against our creator was too serious for anything less to remedy it. Even in that case, however, God's ultimate answer was a yes (Heb. 5:7–9)—in the resurrection. No matter what we may suffer in the present, the assured past event of Jesus's resurrection is the promise of eternal life with him when God also transforms our bodies someday. We celebrate God's power over sickness and spirits, but the greatest cause for celebration is eternal life with Jesus (Luke 10:20).

Faith in the Faithful One

Faith—that is, recognizing God's trustworthiness—is essential. But not all miracles start with our faith. God sometimes does signs to invite basic faith (Exod. 4:8–9), although this faith must persevere and mature to discipleship (Num. 14:11). Basic faith (along with increased hostility from those who reject signs) often *follows* signs (especially in John's Gospel: 1:50; 2:11, 23; 4:39, 48, 53; 7:31; 11:15, 42, 45, 48; 12:11; 14:29; 16:30; 20:30–31; compare also 9:35–38; 10:25; Acts 13:12). God is thus not *limited* to our faith. Certainly it was not Moses's faith that made the burning bush burn (Exod. 3:2); God acted because he saw the suffering of his people (Exod. 2:23–25). He heard their groaning (Exod. 2:23–24), as he also hears that of his children today (Rom. 8:23). Jesus's ministry itself was God's initiative; God "sent" his Son (Mark 12:6; John 3:17; Rom. 8:3; Gal. 4:4). God has taken the initiative in our lives.

Faith is missing in some accounts of Jesus's miracles (Matt. 8:14–15; 14:14; Mark 1:30–31; Luke 7:12–15; 13:11–13; John 5:6–9; 9:4–7) and, more to the point, Jesus sometimes acts *despite* some participants' *lack* of much faith (Matt. 8:26; 14:17, 26; 16:8–10; Mark 4:40; 6:49; 8:4, 17–21; 9:24, 26; Luke 2:9; 5:4–9; 8:25; 11:14–15; especially Luke 1:20).

Faith is important because God is not magic; he invites us into a relationship with him, and the more intimately we grow to trust him, the more he can trust us not to abuse his gifts. It is not so much faith *that* (faith *that* God will give us something) as faith *in* (relying on the reliable one, faith in the faithful one, trust in the trustworthy one). Dr. David Kimberlin testifies that, grateful as he was for his patient Casey's miraculous recovery, he was particularly touched by her family's confidence that, if God did *not* heal her, they would reunite with her in heaven (see chap. 13).[15] Sifra Ndawu was restored to life when her grieving parents, recognizing her death, relinquished her to God (see chap. 26). In many of the other cases reported in this book, however, God acted when someone refused to quit praying, and God counted this persistence as faith. Faith is not expressed in a formula of action we can simply repeat; that would be magic. Faith is a *relationship* with God.

The problem with Israel in the wilderness was not that the people could not work up a feeling of faith. Their problem was that they kept acting faithlessly even though God kept showing himself faithful.

Not Make-Believe

We often get the cart before the horse with the make-believe version of faith. We end up putting faith in our own faith, as if that is what makes God work, like some magic formula. I learned about that the hard way many years ago. I was still a fairly young Christian, and I thought that if I had enough faith I would always get healed. One day in college I passed out in class from coughing too much. The nurse and a colleague carried me back to my room and told me that I had to see a doctor. I protested in prayer that (according to my misplaced theology at the time) God should heal me directly. But I felt that God said, "What if I *want* to heal you through a doctor?" Lying on my bed, I acquiesced weakly. "Okay, Lord, but I don't have any money to go to a doctor. So I need you either to heal me or to provide me with money to go to the doctor." Then he healed me.

But I still hadn't learned my lesson. In my next year of college I passed out because of blood loss from a different condition. This time I was taken to a doctor even though I protested that I had no money. The doctor diagnosed the bleeding problem (and since then I have learned that I pass out more easily because of my low blood pressure), and the bill was sent to my parents. I felt ashamed because I had told my parents, who were not yet Christians, that God often healed people when I prayed for them. Now here I was, in need of a doctor!

I was now better physically but annoyed emotionally. At the time, I was helping at a street mission that fed homeless people. Praying in the upper room of the mission, I protested in immature words that I now shudder to recall: "God, how could you let this happen to me? I thought you loved me!" And suddenly I heard him very clearly: "I let this happen to you *because* I love you." He didn't need to say any more because the point struck home immediately. I had begun an intimate relationship with him a couple of years before, but it had become stale as I began treating him like a formula that I could make work for me. God is not subject to my formulas. He is my creator. And I had forgotten what I needed most: the intimacy with him for which I was created. "It was good for me to be afflicted so that I might learn your decrees" (Ps. 119:71 NIV; see also 119:67, 75).

Growing the Mustard Seed

Sometimes we're afraid of biblical invitations to trust God because we think that we do not have enough faith. But Jesus said that even a mustard seed—the tiniest amount—of faith can move mountains (Mark 11:23). We should not focus on how big our faith is. We should focus on how big is the God in whom we have faith. That is what biblical faith is about. Trusting God is not so much a leap in the dark. It is a step into the light, deliberately choosing to depend on the God who is truly dependable. It is not believing *in spite* of what is true; it is *recognizing* that God is true and reliable.

Someone once introduced the famous faith missionary Hudson Taylor as a very great man. When Taylor got up to speak, he corrected the introduction: "God must have been looking for someone small enough and weak enough for Him to use, so that all the glory might be His."[16] We should not think that we are too small spiritually for God to hear us. The Bible says that he is far from the proud but nearest the broken and the lowly. Genuine faith is realizing our need to depend on God and recognizing his absolute dependability.

We should thank God for gifts such as medical technology in the West, while also beginning to exercise our spiritual muscles for faith when the occasion arises. Faith includes trusting God to work *through* these other gifts, as well as beyond them. Faith means trusting God for the impossible, when we have sufficient reason to believe that God has promised something (Matt. 17:20; Mark 9:23; 11:23). And faith means that God is still trustworthy whether or not a specific miracle we pray for happens.

Some people known for ministries of healings, such as John Wimber and Heidi Baker, initially prayed fervently for healings for months and saw no one healed. Nevertheless, they persisted, refusing to give up, on the basis of their stubborn trust that God wanted them to keep praying for healing. Eventually they experienced breakthroughs, after which they saw healings regularly. In the case of Heidi Baker, she suddenly saw three women healed of blindness in the same week.

Whereas even most ministers accustomed to praying for the sick see fewer than 10 percent healed, especially when they pray over large groups of people, some seem to experience or develop a particular gifting to trust God in this area and see much higher proportions healed (especially in particular settings). Not everyone has the same gift of healing or the same frontline calling, but all believers in Jesus have spiritual gifts to share with others, motivated by trust that God will enable them to do this (Rom. 12:3–8, esp. faith in 12:3, 6). All of us can join others in prayer.

It takes faith to press through the disappointments—to trust God that miracles can still happen. Because sometimes they do! Yet sometimes, no matter how much some of us may pray, they don't.

Chapter 37

When Healing Is Temporary

One of the downsides of living is that we eventually die—though any life at all is ultimately a gift. No healing in this life is permanent, if only because this life is not permanent. That is true even for those resuscitated from death. Jesus raised Lazarus, but Lazarus is no longer among us. In the early second century, Quadratus declared that some whom Jesus raised had lived into his own generation; but we do not hear of them remaining any later. Our fullest physical hope is ultimately the resurrection of our bodies when our risen Lord returns. Present healing is just a foretaste of that future promise.

Healing today does not guarantee permanent health, although some of those who are healed do enjoy health and long life. Sometimes cancer, malnutrition, contaminated water, or another cause of the original problem remains. Sometimes the genetic predisposition to a sickness remains, so that years later a person may experience the same problem, requiring treatment or healing again.

Nevertheless, even temporary remissions are a blessing. C. S. Lewis married Joy Davidman in a civil ceremony in 1956 so she could stay in England, but because she was divorced, despite biblical grounds, the local bishop refused to grant them a church marriage. They thus were living separately when, on March 21, 1957, Davidman collapsed, her body full of cancer. Medical tests showed that not only did she have malignant breast tumors, but "her bones were riddled with cancer."[1] She was expected to live only a matter of weeks.

Anglican priest Peter Bide, known for prayers for healing, anointed her with oil and performed a Christian marriage ceremony. To the doctors' amazement, Davidman quickly recovered, regaining full health without signs of sickness. She and Lewis enjoyed three of the happiest years of Lewis's life. Then in spring 1960 the cancer suddenly returned, and in July, Davidman died. Lewis, who had finally let down his rational guard for love, was now shattered by grief.[2] Marital bliss, like any other blessing, is temporary; yet it is still a gift to be enjoyed while one has it. In retrospect, Davidman's remission was a gift to both of them; but it was at best only a shadow and reminder of the perfect healing that awaits.

Healings That Last a Long Time

Some skeptics demand medical documentation for healings while also demanding that researchers verify that the healings have lasted for a long time. It can sometimes be difficult to meet both of these conditions because hospitals often have not kept older medical records, and patients themselves often never thought to acquire the records when they were healed. Other cases, though, are like that of "George," reported by Candy Gunther Brown. Healed of a medically untreatable brain tumor solely through prayer, George clearly remained healed when he was examined more than a decade later.[3]

It is more difficult to trace the effects of a healing over the course of decades, but this, too, has sometimes been done. For example, historian Wayne Warner, curious about the long-range effects of the cures he read about in old newspaper articles and Christian publications, decided to track down some of the people who had claimed healing.[4] One of these cures was that of Louis Romer, who had been instantly healed of chorea as a boy. Warner found him at the age of eighty, and Romer confirmed that his healing remained.[5] Sixty-one years after Benjamin Denton was healed of bloody tuberculosis of the lungs in 1917, his healing remained.[6] Examples of such long-term cures could be multiplied, and, among those that occurred sufficiently long ago to be tested, they are the majority recounted in this book.

Long-Term Extension

Sometimes my students ask for a week's extension on their papers, but I have yet to have a student request a nine-year extension. Sometimes, though, God grants an inexplicable remission linked with prayer that provides relief for many years.

One case was sufficiently significant to warrant a recent journal article. Parkinson's is a neurodegenerative disease involving progressive decline in motor and cognitive abilities. At an advanced stage, it is not known to reverse course, especially suddenly, yet this was what happened in a case of advanced Parkinson's disease in the Netherlands. One of the study's coauthors was the physician whose patient experienced the cure. A medical assessment team at the Amsterdam University Medical Centre reports what they consider the "remarkable" case of a woman with rapidly progressing, advanced Parkinson's disease.

The patient, Corlien, had been both a nurse and a psychotherapist, but chronic arthritis made her work difficult. She came from a cessationist Reformed background, but in 2006, out of desperation, she accepted her friends' invitation to a healing service. To her astonishment, she was healed. But Corlien had experienced other infirmities, and more awaited her, including an unexpected but treatable recurrence of breast cancer. Not everything, however, would prove medically treatable.

In September 2009, Corlien visited a neurologist after experiencing difficulty writing with her right hand, along with general stiffness in the right side of her body. The neurologist diagnosed Parkinson's, a disease that had also afflicted Corlien's mother and grandfather. By early 2012, she had lost facial expressions and much of her verbal ability, and could walk only short distances, even with medication. She increasingly needed to use a wheelchair because shaking and stiffness made any controlled movements difficult. Her husband had to care for her, and she anticipated imminent death.

Then, on April 6, 2012, Corlien attended an Easter conference, hoping simply to share a final Easter with her family in church. At the conclusion of the service, however, the pastor unexpectedly invited prayer for the sick. When someone Corlien did not know began praying for her, she felt a cloud of heat settle over her. As something that felt like a net around her brain vanished, she rose from her wheelchair, finding herself no longer disabled.

She experienced 90 percent healing instantaneously, enough to return to normal life. The few remaining symptoms progressively decreased. Her husband, who had been caring for her, watched with amazement over the next month; she was now caring for herself. When she consulted her neurologist twelve days after the prayer, he was shocked by her improvement. The change was too sudden and dramatic to be attributed to the placebo effect. Although this experience fit Corlien's Christian worldview, it shocked her too. The debilitating symptoms were gone and did not recur, and she returned to full capacity in her professional work and day-to-day life.

By 2015, with very few possible signs of the disease remaining, doctors suspected a prior misdiagnosis, but further tests ruled out this possibility. The study's authors note that "the clinical course was extraordinary, contradicting data from imaging studies as well as the common understanding of this disease." The only comparable case they found was the cure of a French nun after intercession by French and Senegalese Catholics.

About nine years after Corlien's healing experiences, Parkinson's symptoms began to surface again, and Corlien has continued to experience other physical problems, including cancer in her other breast. At the time of this book's writing, the medical outcome regarding her Parkinson's symptoms is uncertain. Nevertheless, her sudden restoration from Parkinson's, which granted her many years of renewed ability, gave her a new sense of God's love and faithfulness. For her, this puts everything else in perspective.[7]

The Second Time Around

Healings are not always long-term. Healings do not confer immortality, and not all remissions are permanent. Occasionally we have medical documentation for an initial healing without medical treatment precisely because the person healed received a medical diagnosis but refused treatment. Under normal circumstances, refusing available and effective treatment is unwise; God's mercy in extending our life is not meant to teach us to refuse his healing through other means. On occasion a person who experienced a remarkable recovery later succumbs to the same illness.

My friend and historian Kimberly Ervin Alexander provided me with the account of Terry Schalk's cancer and healing. A cancerous lump appeared on the side of Schalk's neck in 1996. Although his non-Hodgkin lymphoma was treatable, he did not expect a long-term cure medically. Except for the lump, he seemed to remain stable. Although he did not see a problem with others having medical treatment, he determined for himself to depend solely on prayer.

But one week in 1999, Schalk's neck suddenly swelled so much that he could not eat. By the end of September, the tumors on his neck had more than doubled it in size, and tumors began to break out all over his body. Alexander shared with me numerous graphic photographs documenting his terrible condition. Clearly, the cancer had metastasized; now he continually felt as though he was choking. One day, he began to bleed from pores throughout his body; when his wife returned from work, she found him covered in blood. Tumors the size of melons formed in his stomach. His pain became unbearable; although for biblical reasons he would not consider suicide, he understood well why some cancer sufferers did. After he lost consciousness, his family took him to the hospital, where tests found his body full of cancer, especially in his lungs. He remained on life support throughout October; his kidneys shut down, and doctors daily gave him about two hours to live. He did not enjoy proving them wrong.

Finally, on October 31, Schalk's doctor put him on pain medicine and sent him to hospice care. Two weeks later, however, the cancer began to go away, and he began to be able to walk. After two more months, only the original lump remained, and finally even that vanished. Schalk had experienced a remarkable recovery and, starting in early 2000, had several years of successful ministry. I have a copy of the medical report from August 24, 2004, declaring no "evidence of active disease" and an "excellent" prognosis. This is a case of medically documented remission without medical treatment.

In 2006, however, the cancer returned, and this time Schalk quickly died. The extra years of ministry were a blessing, but they were not forever.

Similarly, in 1977, doctors diagnosed college professor Bob Neff with malignant melanoma. Although he did not oppose medical treatment, he felt that God wanted him to depend on Jesus alone, and for the next six years he did not undergo any treatment or take any medicine. After the first few months, he began to feel pain throughout his body, and he struggled for several years. In the end, though, he found himself healed without medical intervention.[8]

In January 2012, well over three decades later, I found myself living just a few houses down the street from Neff. I trudged through the snow and joined a gathering in his basement as various people he had touched over the years testified about how they had been healed through his ministry. Neff noted that his melanoma had just come back, but he was going to fight it in faith again.

This time, however, Neff died. Some might suggest that the melanoma had remained dormant in his body for three decades, rare though this is. I am more inclined to think that whatever genetic disposition he had to melanoma resurfaced under similar conditions. In any case, he ultimately died from the same disease he had overcome decades before. In the meantime, though, he spent three fruitful decades helping others.

Such a recurrence seems to be the exception rather than the rule; cancer that does not resurface after five years is usually considered cured. Yet in a sense, whatever we are healed from, the healing is temporary because all human life in this age stands under the sentence of death. No finite being can live forever apart from an infinite being bestowing eternal life. Nevertheless, the Bible portrays healings as kingdom samples. Such signs in this life are a foretaste of a greater future to come, when sickness, sorrow, and death will be no more.

Chapter 38

When Miracles Don't Happen

This is not a book about the problem of suffering, but that problem persists in miracles' shadow. This chapter does not offer evidence for miracles; it simply acknowledges that evil continues in the present world, but that the Bible offers believers hope in the face of it. Even in the West, most of us do not need additional evidence for the reality of suffering, though sometimes we need to pay more attention to that reality.

Many of those I interviewed regarding healing had great faith, though only a few felt absolute assurance during the entire period of testing. Some were surprised by God's acts that transcended their faith. Often those who expressed faith before healing trusted God specifically for healing; in many other cases, they simply trusted God no matter what. All experienced healing as an act of God's love, and almost all believed that they were not more deserving of healing than others who did not experience it.[1] Some of those I interviewed expressed the belief that anyone *can* be healed in this life; others expected healings to be less common. Everyone, however, recognizes that not everyone *is* healed in this life, and no one I interviewed taught that there was something spiritually deficient in those who were not healed.[2]

Sickness and death are a natural part of this world, and when God does *not* act otherwise, directly or indirectly, we often experience their effects.

Nabeel

I have known few young men who appeared to have as much potential for God's kingdom as Nabeel Qureshi seemed to have.[3] I have also known few who were as passionate and eager to learn. When we met at academic conferences, he would ask me and our other friends many questions, soaking in all the knowledge he could. He was so humble that he did not realize that God had given him an even wider audience than most of us from whom he was learning. Nabeel had been converted through his friend David Wood's consistent reasoning and witness, in addition to a dream and a vision he had experienced, and he listened eagerly as I talked about my discoveries regarding miracles, the reliability of the Gospels, and so forth.

When I learned that Nabeel had stage 4 stomach cancer, his health became a top priority on my prayer list. The five-year survival rate for stage 4 stomach cancer—as Nabeel, himself a medical doctor, knew—was about one in twenty-five; most patients did not survive the first year. I and others shared with him testimonies of healing, though we could not guarantee what would happen in his case. Still, *logically*, it seemed hard to fathom why God *wouldn't* heal our friend. Various friends whose prayers for healing God often answers prayed for Nabeel, on the phone or even after traveling to visit him. They too had a vision of what Nabeel could do for the kingdom, along with sympathy for him and his young wife and daughter. During these prayers, Nabeel often felt something, and sometimes had a temporary remission in his symptoms. He didn't experience full healing, but it was clear that God was hearing prayers.

At one conference in Texas I had dinner with Nabeel and another friend, Alex Blagojevic. Alex was so committed that he was fasting a day every week for Nabeel's healing. After dinner I prayed for Nabeel, and he again felt the Spirit and experienced some relief. We went for a walk, and he asked me again about healing, sharing encouraging signs others had given him. I agreed that these signs nurtured expectation, and I was praying with that expectation. Yet I also confessed that, for whatever reasons, healing does not always happen in this life. While encouraged by what he shared, I could not add further assurances to what some others were telling him.

Another friend with stage 4 stomach cancer, for whom I was also praying, was undergoing an (ultimately successful) experimental treatment, and the possibility of Nabeel trying that treatment intrigued him. But we weren't sure it would be available to him; he didn't have the same kind of insurance and access. Toward the end of his mortal life, Nabeel suffered terribly. A hurricane in Houston flooded his neighborhood, a tube that came loose in his throat caused profuse bleeding to which no one in the hospital was available to attend, and Nabeel realized that he was dying.

Although it is not really biblical and I should not have done it (nor was my wife happy that I did it), I even prayed that God would take me rather than Nabeel. I felt that I had already accomplished enough for one life, if need be, whereas Nabeel had many years of fruitful ministry ahead of him. Thousands were praying for Nabeel, Christians (and occasionally Muslims) with diverse theologies of healing. If prayer, faith, and fasting are guaranteed to heal someone physically in this life, Nabeel would surely have experienced healing. But on September 17,

2017, I learned that my friend had died at the age of thirty-four, not much over a year after his diagnosis.

Nabeel touched more people in his short life than many of us touch in long ones. God does not weigh the value of a life's work by its length. After all, Jesus himself completed his earthly mission at around the age of thirty (Luke 3:23). As I prayed after Nabeel's death, I felt that God was saying we would understand this matter someday. It is beyond me to understand now, but I trust that God does know and understand much more than I do.

Early in the writing of this book, my friend Brittany Buchanan Douglas, whose zeal and sacrifice for the kingdom I esteemed very highly, passed away from illness. During the editing of this book, my friend Corneliu Constantineanu, an active Romanian scholar and seminary dean in Croatia, passed from COVID-19, as did my beloved uncle, Duane High. In recent years some other godly friends passed from sickness, such as Caritha Clarke, a former student and woman of prayer. I hadn't known that the people I have just mentioned were sick until I received word of their passing, but they were people whose love for God I respected. While two students I was close to survived a car crash in 2019, another, Aaron Nickerson, did not. And the day that I turned in the first draft of this book to the publisher, my Congolese brother-in-law and compassionate friend Emmanuel Moussounga died suddenly and without explanation, with no resuscitation following. Those who are healed in this life aren't superior to those who aren't. Sooner or later, all of us will meet the Lord, and what matters most is that we have already welcomed him as our Savior.

The Mysterious *Other* Side of Healing

One journal article dispassionately comments, "The observed effects of prayer vary widely, from no apparent effect to remarkable improvement in conditions that are not medically expected to improve."[4]

When Jesus says that we will have whatever we ask for in his name (John 14:13–14; 16:23–27), "in his name" qualifies the asking: acting in his name means acting as his agent, led by him (compare 14:11–12, 15–18; 15:7; 1 John 5:14). There is an element of hyperbole, then, when Jesus succinctly promises, "Ask, and you shall receive" (Matt. 7:7–11//Luke 11:11–13). Although the contextual objects of the kingdom (Matt. 7:13–14) and the Spirit (Luke 11:13) are certain, sometimes God's greater plan differs from the details that we envision. Paul requested three times for Jesus to remove his "thorn" (2 Cor. 12:7–8, evoking Num. 33:55), which I believe at least included persecution (2 Cor. 12:10).[5] Yet Jesus's greater purpose in Paul's life meant that he kept the thorn so that he could also keep the blessings that went with it (2 Cor. 12:9; compare 12:1, 7; also Ps. 119:67, 71, 75).

Prayer in God's will might mean that a team we are playing or rooting for will do its best. But it does not mean that our favored team will win. It does not mean that because I am a Duke University alumnus, I can pray in confidence that God will make Duke win the national championship this year. (That would be true even if they weren't called "Blue Devils." I'm still happy when they win.)

When James and John request that Jesus do for them "*whatever* we ask" (Mark 10:35), Jesus first queries, "*What* is it you're requesting?" (10:36). Their request is for their own benefit at the expense of others (10:37), so Jesus corrects them with a lesson on servanthood (10:38–45). By contrast, Jesus soon asks Bartimaeus, a blind man, what his request is. Bartimaeus pleads for Jesus to restore his sight, and Jesus restores it (10:51–52). Unlike the request of James and John, requests for healing do not come at someone else's expense; God's power to heal is not limited. Nevertheless, genuine trust in one who is absolutely trustworthy cannot depend beforehand on whether we achieve a particular outcome that we desire, no matter how noble.

I recounted in chapter 29 how God raised Jeff Markin when Dr. Chauncey Crandall prayed for him. But the backstory is important. Before Crandall prayed for God to raise Markin, Crandall had prayed for God to raise his own son Chad. Despite years of prayer, Chad died from leukemia. Crandall valiantly prayed for an hour and a half that God would raise his son, but Chad remained dead. At that point Crandall had to determine whether he would lose heart or would continue trusting God no matter what. He determined to keep trusting, and when God later moved him to pray for Markin, he was ready.[6]

Likewise, in the context of missions, the child for whom Leo Bawa prayed for a few hours was raised (see chap. 30). Yet when Leo prayed for his own best friend, the friend was not raised.

Danny McCain, who testified to the healing of his toddler brother's burned skin (see chap. 22), also recounted to me that Danny's own first son, Nathaniel, contracted spinal meningitis at the age of four months. Many people prayed for Nathaniel, but five days later the child died. Why did God heal one child dramatically and let the other die? Quoting Job, Danny responds, "The Lord gives and the Lord takes; blessed be the name of the Lord."[7]

I recounted how Anthony Wainaina Njuguna's son Adiel was miraculously healed (see chap. 7). Yet every other infant in the same neonatal intensive care unit at that time died. As Anthony recognizes, surely many of these babies, too, had families who prayed for them. In Scripture, God preserved his long-range purpose against injustice by sending the holy family away before Herod's massacre in Matthew 2:14, but he mourned rather than prevented Herod's brutal killing of baby boys (2:16–18).

Many people in many cultures want children, but for some cultures, such as my wife's African culture, women often feel a need to bear children as part of their identity. God protected our son David through many life-threatening circumstances (recounted at points in our book *Impossible Love*) and answered years of prayer in uniting us with our daughter Keren. We are delighted beyond words with the family that we have. As far as genetic children for us as a couple, however, we suffered seven successive miscarriages. There is no question in my mind that we exercised firm faith in the Lord. The God who gave Sarah and Elizabeth children in their old age could do the same for us. But no one will suppose that any of the seven miscarriages, now many years ago, will be reversed in this life. My wife notes that she is the mother of many children—most of them already in heaven.

Yet God merits our trust even when we feel disappointed or shattered. Faith in God is more than faith *that* God will do a particular thing we ask for.

Those who work in hospice care see death more often than miracles. Those who work in Western cancer wards see prayers for miracles more often than they see miracles. Perhaps in the West this is partly because many of those whom God will heal, God heals through medical means. But I cannot blame many Christians who work in such settings if they develop a certain cynicism toward miracles after witnessing so much suffering. What we call miracles are still the exception rather than the rule.

Nevertheless, those exceptions are a gift to all of us because they point to a future hope for all of us. They remind us of God's promise of resurrection life.

Chapter 39

What Does the Bible Say about Non-healing?

I n a time of both empire-wide plague and persecution, the early third-century North African bishop Cyprian wrote before his martyrdom,

> It disturbs some that the power of this Disease attacks our people equally with the heathens, as if the Christian believed for this purpose, that he might have the enjoyment of the world and this life free from the contact of ills; and not as one who undergoes all adverse things here and is reserved for future joy. It disturbs some that this mortality is common to us with others; and yet . . . until this corruptible shall put on incorruption, and this mortal receive immortality, . . . whatsoever are the disadvantages of the flesh are common to us with the human race.[1]

Drought and suffering are alike to all (compare Matt. 5:45; Luke 13:2–5; Rom. 8:35–36), but "these are trainings for us, not deaths: they give the mind the glory of fortitude; by contempt of death they prepare for the crown."[2] Death is alike to all who live in the state of mortality, but whereas Christ's enemies die to face the second death, "the righteous are called to their place of refreshing"; death frees them from further suffering and brings them to glory.[3] Under Cyprian's leadership, Christians risked their lives to nurse back to health not only suffering Christians but even their persecutors. Their care for the sick functioned as a precursor of later hospitals.[4]

In the late nineteenth century, it was especially John Alexander Dowie who promoted the idea that people would *always* be healed if they had enough faith.[5] Dowie was a man of incredible faith and spiritual gifting, and many dying people were dramatically healed through his ministry. At the same time, gifts of healing and teaching are distinct gifts. Dowie was opposed to medicine,[6] and some people died because they followed his teaching against it.[7] Many early Alliance and Pentecostal missionaries died because they were unwilling to take medicine against malaria, until finally the survivors decided that live missionaries on medicine were more helpful than dead missionaries without it.[8] Before passing on his questionable teaching, Dowie's own views degenerated further. Dowie declared that he was the end-time Elijah, and he became so heavy-handed that his own church deposed him.

Death Ends Mortal Life until Life Ends Death

Every moment of biological life is a gift; but, apart from special divine action, createdness, finiteness, and biological physicality ultimately entail death. Biblically, God's plan for humanity was eternal life, a plan marred by our human resistance to God and to one another. At the greatest cost to himself, God made eternal life available as a further gift to those who are willing to accept it.

The Bible naturally highlights the reminders we need most, the miracles that show us God's special care for us in this age. But as for life in this present age, the Bible doesn't need to tell us that some people stay sick or that most dead people aren't raised; we know that from ordinary experience. In fact, when the Bible speaks of sickness or death without healing, it seems to take for granted that this is the ordinary course of nature (e.g., 2 Kings 4:1; 13:14). The Bible takes for granted that death remains in this age; consider the repetition of "and he died" in the various generations of Genesis 5:5, 8, 11, 14, 20, 27, 31, with only Enoch excluded.

When Paul speaks to other Christians about Christians' deaths, he says nothing about the need to raise them in this age.[9] He focuses instead on the ultimate resurrection to come (see, e.g., 1 Cor. 15:6; 1 Thess. 4:13–14). Death is still an enemy (1 Cor. 15:26), but it remains part of our mortal condition until our mortality puts on immortality (1 Cor. 15:53–54; 2 Cor. 4:16–5:5).

In this life, both kind and evil people suffer and receive blessings (Eccles. 9:1–3; Matt. 5:45). If God healed all Christians, most people would become Christians, but without a genuine, mature, tested relationship with God. Some might explain even this pervasive healing naturalistically, as something inherent in Christian practice rather than in the Lord in whom Christians are to trust.[10] As it is, Christians who share others' sufferings are better placed to speak to them (2 Cor. 1:4), just as Jesus shared our humanity and our sufferings (e.g., Heb. 2:14). Christians aren't better than others; we just know the gracious God who is ready to show grace to whoever seeks him.

In chapter 35 I mentioned church planter Everett Cook, who lived through the early days of the Pentecostal revival. He was usually accurate in sensing God's voice. One day he confided in me that he was going to live only one more year. I protested, but he responded, "No, the Lord told me to get things ready." Within the year, he was diagnosed with cancer. His wife stayed by his side as his strength declined and reported to us, astonishingly, that he had no pain, but that this was just the Lord's way of taking him home. She told us that she saw his spirit leave his body when he died.

Whether or not you agree that God might use something as horrible as cancer, the Lord does have a plan that includes our eventual homegoing (compare Deut. 31:14; 34:4–5; 1 Sam. 26:10; 1 Kings 2:1). This was true even in the case of our Lord's own mission (Matt. 26:18; Mark 14:36; John 12:27; 13:1; 18:11). God may build some flex room into that plan on the ground (Isa. 38:1–22), but Jesus's followers can remain confident that our lives are in our loving Father's hands (Matt. 10:28–31//Luke 12:4–7).

The Bible promises physical immortality only when Christ returns and our bodies are made like his (Phil. 3:20–21; 1 Thess. 4:15–17). None of the noted nineteenth-century heroes of the faith, such as George Müller or Hudson Taylor, remain alive. None of the original apostles, no matter how great their faith, remain alive either. Ever since God excluded sinful humanity from the tree of life for our own good (lest we perpetuate our guilt indefinitely), death remains part of this life. Jesus's resurrection promises us a better future, but until his return all healing—even resuscitation from death—is at most temporary.

So far, only Jesus has been resurrected to *eternal* life, the firstfruits and proof that God will do the same with us someday. (God provided plenty of evidence for *Jesus's* resurrection, not least a vast number of witnesses ready to stake their lives on it.)[11] So while the Bible focuses on how Jesus came to help us, it also assumes that we already know we live in a world full of suffering and death.

When Healing Did Not Happen in the Bible

> In the time of Elisha the prophet, many people had leprosy, but none of them was cured except for Naaman the Syrian. (Luke 4:27)

> When you throw a party, invite those who are destitute, disabled, lame or blind. (Luke 14:13)

Jesus knew that many people had leprosy in Elisha's day because, two chapters after the cure of Naaman, four Israelite lepers were at Samaria's city gate (2 Kings 7:3). God used them to make known a miracle that God performed, fulfilling a prophecy of Elisha (7:9–10), but they themselves remained lepers.

In the Bible, David became physically weak, declining with old age. Indeed, this previously ambitiously polygamous king did not have any intimate relations with the young woman his attendants brought to keep him warm (1 Kings 1:1–4). In contrast to Moses, the prophet Ahijah was physically blind in his old age—yet so spiritually sighted that he could reveal who had just come to his door (1 Kings 14:6–14). We learn in passing that the prophet Elisha died of a sickness (2 Kings

13:14), even though his bones remained so full of God's power that a corpse thrown on top of his bones came back to life (2 Kings 13:21). Obviously, Elisha's sickness is not a negative comment about God's power in his life.

The apostle Paul said that he preached to the Galatians because of a bodily sickness or weakness (Gal. 4:13). This experience fits the experience of Jesus's missionaries in facing not only hunger, thirst, travel, and imprisonment for Jesus but sometimes conditions leading to sickness as well (the likeliest meaning of Matt. 25:35–36).[12]

When Epaphroditus was sick and close to death after a difficult voyage, Paul did not say, "We guaranteed his health." Instead he celebrates, "God had mercy on him" (Phil. 2:27); by God's grace, Epaphroditus recovered. Paul left Trophimus sick at Miletus (2 Tim. 4:20) and does not feel the need to offer any justification. Nor does he offer a rationale for not urging (further?) prayer for healing when he instructs Timothy to use healthier means to take care of his digestive issues (1 Tim. 5:23).

God often heals, but sometimes we stay sick for a short or long while, and that does not mean that something is wrong with our faith. The Bible teaches us much more about healing than non-healing, not because we are always healed but because most of us need our faith encouraged to believe for healing. We do not need much encouragement to believe in sickness.

Signs as a Foretaste of the Kingdom

Part of the genesis of this book was the request that I speak for the 2014 annual conference of the Society of Vineyard Scholars. The organizers asked me to speak about "suffering and the kingdom," including why miracles often do not happen. I had often wrestled with and briefly lectured about the question before, but now I needed to gather all my notes in one place.

We do not receive every aspect of the kingdom now; what we have now is a foretaste. Earlier I mentioned Canon Andrew White's testimony of people being raised from the dead. Yet more than a thousand of Canon White's church members in Iraq were killed, many in random or sectarian violence and most for being Christians. As he points out in *Faith under Fire*, "From the time of the resurrection of Christ to His second coming, God's kingdom exists alongside the kingdom of darkness"[13] (compare Matt. 13:29–30, 47–49; Rom. 9:22–23).

When John the Baptist is facing impending death in Herod's prison, he hears that Jesus is healing people. This is obviously the work of God, resembling the activity of earlier prophets, but it isn't what God has shown John about the coming one. John's expected kingdom-bringer will baptize in the Holy Spirit and fire (Matt. 3:11//Luke 3:16), and John has not heard of any fire. So John sends messengers to Jesus to ask whether he really is the coming one as John had originally thought, or whether John had it wrong (Matt. 11:2–3//Luke 7:18–20).

John's messengers see the healings, and Jesus makes their eyewitness experience part of his message: the blind see, the lame walk, lepers are cleansed, the deaf hear, the dead are raised, and good news is preached to the poor (Matt. 11:5// Luke 7:21). Using this language, Jesus appeals to John's knowledge of Scripture. The coming restoration, the time of the kingdom, will include such blessings: the blind will see, the deaf will hear, the lame will walk (Isa. 35:5–6), and the Lord's anointed will preach good news to the poor (Isa. 61:1).

The fullness of the kingdom will bring the expected healing and restoration of God's people and indeed of all creation (Isa. 35:1–2, 10; 61:4, 11; 65:17–19). In the meantime, though, Jesus is doing *kingdom* works. Healing and bringing good news to the disenfranchised is a genuine foretaste of the kingdom. Jesus is saying, "Yes, John, I *am* the kingdom-bringer." But everything would be in its own time. The kingdom comes first like a tiny seed before it comes like a massive bush or tree (Matt. 13:31–32//Mark 4:31–32//Luke 13:19).[14] It comes first like yeast concealed before it becomes the kingdom banquet (Matt. 13:33//Luke 13:21).

Likewise, Jesus warned his opponents that his widespread deliverance of the needy from evil spirits meant that the kingdom had come upon them (Matt. 12:28//Luke 11:20). The kingdom has invaded the world, and Satan is not able to supplant it, though he continues to rage until his final removal (Rev. 12:12).

After the Second World War, scholars began comparing this already–not yet character of God's kingdom to the difference between D-Day and V-E Day. Once the Normandy invasion succeeded (D-Day), the outcome of the war was clear; the Nazi regime's defeat was just a matter of time. But battles continued and soldiers kept dying until the final collapse of the Nazi regime (V-E Day). We, too, live between the times of the spiritual D-Day and the final V-E Day, continuing the war but now with full knowledge of the outcome.

We are not yet in the fullness of the kingdom, although that is what we strive for as we seek kingdom purposes in the present and work against this world's evils. Nevertheless, the works of the kingdom in the present remind us that God has not forgotten his promise. As Delia Knox's sister Enid testifies about Knox's healing (see chap. 8), after twenty-two years of disability, Enid was thinking that Delia might be healed only in heaven. But since Delia has been healed, Enid sees it as a piece of heaven on earth.[15]

We may not individually receive every miracle that we would like, but anyone else's miracle is also a gift to the rest of us. Any miracle is an encouragement to all of us to trust the future that God has promised, when God will bring streams in the desert (Isa. 35:6) and renew the heavens and the earth (Isa. 65:17; Rev. 21:1). In that day, war will be no more (Isa. 2:4; Mic. 4:3). There will be no more sickness, no more suffering, and no more death, and the Lord will wipe away every tear (Isa. 25:8; 49:10; Rev. 7:16–17). Indeed, these promises resound in some of the final verses of the Bible: "He will wipe every tear from their eyes. Death will be no more; mourning and crying and pain will be no more, for the first things have passed away" (Rev. 21:4 NRSV), because the Lord God will dwell among us in fullness. The miracles God does in this world are a foretaste, evidence that gives courage in present suffering and kindles expectation for the consummation of God's promises.

The Price

Life is a gift; the air we breathe is a gift. These are gifts of the first creation. God did not owe us any of these things; our very existence is a gift. But the gift of the new creation is greater, and present salvation is a foretaste of that gift. Whatever blessing we receive as a foretaste now, such as healing, and whatever gift we expect for the future, such as a renewed creation, we should be grateful because it cost something for God to give it to us.

Jesus fulfilled the servant's mission in Isaiah 53:4–5: "Surely he carried our sicknesses and bore our pains. . . . By his wounds healing has come to us." The prophets often apply illness language figuratively for spiritual sickness, and that is certainly paramount in Jesus's mission (1 Pet. 2:24). But the larger restoration context of Isaiah also involves physical restoration (e.g., Isa. 35:5–6). Thus Matthew 8:17 applies Isaiah 53 to Jesus healing people physically during his ministry. When we receive gifts such as healing in this life and, ultimately, the glories of the world to come, we must remember what it cost Jesus to make any of these gifts available for us: everything. That's how much your ultimate well-being matters to him.

Signs Point to Jesus

In the Bible, signs do not convert people. Sometimes they even make opponents of the faith more angry. Signs instead get people's attention so that they can hear the message. The signs reported in this book may have gotten your attention. They do not guarantee that God will do every miracle we want. They do, however, promise a marvelous future with no more suffering, injustice, or conflict for those faithful to God. They also point us to the one in whom we can begin to live that future life.

When seventy-two of Jesus's disciples returned from their first mission, excited that they could heal the sick and drive out demons (Luke 10:17), Jesus acknowledged that he had commissioned them as his agents with this authority (10:18–19). But he also reoriented their thinking: "Don't celebrate that the spirits are subject to you. Instead celebrate that your names are recorded in heaven" (10:20).

The Gospel of John reports seven signs before Jesus's resurrection. At the climax of the main part of his Gospel, John says, "Jesus performed many other signs in front of his disciples, signs that I haven't written about in this book. But I wrote about these signs so that you may believe that Jesus is the Christ, God's Son, and so that by believing you may have life in his name" (John 20:30–31).

If you want to begin sharing that eternal life that the Bible promises, Jesus tells you the way. This is how God loved the world: He gave his one and only Son on the cross. Because of this sacrifice, whoever depends on him will not perish. Instead, they will experience the life of the coming world (my paraphrase of John 3:16). If you want to begin that relationship with him, you have only to ask him for it, and he will grant it.

Probably most people who choose to read this book already have a relationship with God; so did most of the first hearers of John's Gospel. For them, the signs John recorded were meant to strengthen and encourage their faith. Wherever your faith started when you began this book, I pray that it is even stronger now.

Although this book is about miracles, the Gospels tell us something deeper than miracles. Miracles are signs of God's love for us, a foretaste of the future. But the Gospels also recount the message of the cross. Jesus's first disciples were excited about the miracles, but they were terrified by the cross. Yet the cross ultimately shows us that, no matter how deep the darkness, the injustice, the agony—when God seems silent in the face of our pain—God is at work even there—indeed, especially there. Because an empty tomb declares that the cross is not the final word.

Chapter 40

Closing Personal Thoughts

I have not usually been a person of great faith when it comes to praying for healing. My public spiritual gift is especially providing scholarship for the church, a form of the gift of teaching. I do try to follow the Holy Spirit's leading, but I have needed to grow a lot regarding healing.

For example, one time in college I sensed during prayer that I was supposed to walk to a particular dormitory hallway on campus and pray for healing for someone I would meet there. (This was a Christian college, so in principle this should not have been a controversial activity.) When I reached the hallway, only one person was walking there, so I caught up with him and asked him if he needed to be healed of anything.

"Well, my back hurts a lot," he admitted. "I've already had people pray for it, and nothing's happened. But hey, if you want to pray for it, go ahead."

As I started to pray, I suddenly became conscious of the fact that I did not know how I was supposed to pray for his healing. My only instructions were to come pray for healing for someone I would meet there. I did not feel any particular faith or anointing. I had begun praying but did not know what I would do if this took a long time and I ran out of words. So I stalled, praying with whatever words I could think of.

A few moments into the prayer, however, the young man straightened up and started shouting, "I'm healed! My back is healed!"

I stared at him, dumbfounded. "Wait, God!" I wanted to protest. "I'm not ready yet!"

One does not need a special gift of healing (nice as that is) for God to answer prayer. You would think that, with all the healing testimonies I have heard and some that I have experienced, I would not be surprised by miracles. Yet I have found myself astonished over and over again by God's generous wonders to us. He's the healer, and he's the one who gets any credit for healing.

This book contains only a few samples of the hundreds of millions of miracle claims reported around the world today, many of them similar to the kinds of accounts I have offered in this book.

I have focused here partly on accounts close to me, and (in a majority of cases) on accounts not already provided in my academic book *Miracles: The Credibility of the New Testament Accounts* (Grand Rapids: Baker Academic, 2011), which contains hundreds of other accounts. Accounts that appear for the first time here are based especially on my interviews with the people in question or on works that provide good evidence for trusting them.

I have addressed some of these matters on a more academic level also in the following articles and chapters: "A Reassessment of Hume's Case against Miracles in Light of Testimony from the Majority World Today," *Perspectives in Religious Studies* 38 (3, Fall 2011): 289–310; "Miracle Reports: Perspectives, Analogies, Explanations," in *Hermeneutik der frühchristlichen Wundererzählungen: Historiche, literarische und rezeptionsästhetische Aspekte*, ed. Bernd Kollmann and Ruben Zimmermann, WUNT 339 (Tübingen: Mohr Siebeck, 2014), 53–65; "'The Dead Are Raised' (Matt. 11:5//Luke 7:22): Resuscitation Accounts in the Gospels and Eyewitness Testimony," *Bulletin for Biblical Research* 25 (1, 2015): 55–79; "Miracle Reports and the Argument from Analogy," *Bulletin for Biblical Research* 25 (4, 2015): 475–95; and "Luke's Acts, Miracles, and Historiography," in *Faszination der Wunder Jesu und der Apostel: Die Debatte um frühschristliche Wundererzählungen geht weiter*, ed. Ruben Zimmermann (Göttingen: Vandenhoeck & Ruprecht, 2019), 31–48. I cite some other key works in "Miracles," in *The Oxford Encyclopedia of Bible and Theology*, ed. Samuel E. Balentine, 2 vols. (New York: Oxford University Press, 2015), 2:101–7, though that essay addressed the biblical theology of miracles; and in "Miracles," in *Dictionary of Christianity and Science*, ed. Paul Copan et al. (Grand Rapids: Zondervan, 2016), 443–49.

My more popular-level articles on the subject appear in *Catalyst: Contemporary Evangelical Perspectives for United Methodist Seminarians*, *Charisma*, *Christianity Today*, *Good News*, *Huffington Post*, and *Slate*. During the period that I was speaking on this topic, I gave invited lectures on the subject for a scholarly forum at Oxford University, as well as at Adventist, American Baptist, Assemblies of God, Catholic, charismatic, Evangelical Free, Free Methodist, interdenominational, Missionary Church, Pentecostal, Reformed, Southern Baptist, United Methodist, Uniting Church, Vineyard, Wesleyan, and secular academic institutions.

Lee Strobel also interviewed me for chapters 4–6 of his book *The Case for Miracles*.[1] And Lee, like me, ended his book by addressing the subject of when miracles don't happen in this life. Miracles are signs, reminders that God has not forgotten his promise. They are temporary, but they point us to a hope that is eternal. Jesus will come to reign, and then he will wipe away every tear from our eyes. The public resolution to the question of suffering remains future—but God has given us enough sparks of the future in the present to give confidence to anyone willing to trust him.

Appendix A

Did Prayer Make Things Worse?

As all scholars recognize, not all evidence is of equal weight. A controlled study is ideal in science, but in some other disciplines, such as history, this is not possible. Because each miracle is a one-off event, a case-study approach is usually more suitable than a controlled study, or at least the one noted in this appendix.

And case studies do sometimes provide compelling evidence. Because obtaining complete evidence depends on both complete existing records and the willing cooperation of all involved parties, which is often not available (at least to me), I have sometimes cast the net more widely. At other times, however, available medical evidence seems quite strong, and sometimes fairly bulletproof; cases confirmed by the Medical Bureau at Lourdes and those processed by Global Medical Research Institute, for example, are limited to healings with complete documentation and usually concern conditions not known to be cured naturally.

Wish You Hadn't Prayed

But what happens when research suggests that prayer makes things *worse*? One massive study of prayer for coronary patients found that patients who received distant intercessory prayer actually fared *worse* rather than better after surgery. Yes, you read that right: they fared worse. The study's designers, who themselves had expected a different outcome of the study, concluded that such prayer did not affect surgical outcomes either way.

Nevertheless, it was widely noted that many of the people in the control group for this study probably had relatives and friends praying for them, intercessors who were more committed than those recruited for the study. Moreover, from a

Christian perspective there was a serious flaw in the study's design. Most of those recruited as intercessors were not orthodox Christians from groups known for praying in faith for healing. The study's "Protestant" representatives belonged to Unity, a New Thought movement that began in the nineteenth century. Unity provides benevolent encouragement and does much good work, but the movement's beliefs differ from traditional Protestantism. According to its website, members "believe every person is an expression of God and our thoughts have creative power."[1] For many intercessors in Unity, prayer is not "supplication to a personal deity outside the self but . . . an exercise of the divine and human power of the mind."[2]

This massive, expensive study, which some critics claimed disproved once for all the value of prayer,[3] rested on the debated premise that there is no difference among various religious groups.

Testing God?

The study may also have been fundamentally misconceived in another way. It depended on the premise that God would participate as an actor in a prayer study by favoring, if ever so slightly, the generalized prayer of distant petitioners over the desperate pleas of those close to the patients,[4] just to prove himself to those putting him to the test.

This may have been the only test design possible given usual testing frameworks—apart from the caveat that the lead participant's informed consent was not obtained before the study began. This observation is not meant to minimize the integrity or intellect of the scholars who designed the study. But one's epistemic approach must fit the subject studied. Just as experimental designs useful in certain kinds of controlled studies will not work in history, so some experimental designs do not fit the ways that Scripture declares that God will reveal himself.

Sometimes God does address the questions humans put to him. Disillusioned by Jesus's death, his disciple Thomas refused to believe others' testimony of the resurrection unless he met the risen Christ himself (John 20:25). But Thomas hadn't given up on the community of believers, and while he was with them, Jesus showed up (20:26). While Jesus granted this request made by his friend and disciple, he invites the rest of us to believe because of reliable testimony (20:29–31) of both the human eyewitnesses and God's own Spirit (15:26–27). God granted Gideon confirmation (Judg. 6:17–18, 36–40) when he commissioned him to a radical task (6:14, 25; 7:2–9), but again, Gideon lacked much prior evidence (6:13), and one sign was offered without Gideon's request (7:10–15). God offers no guarantee that he will always work this way.

Two thousand years ago, some scholars ignored the signs that Jesus had already been doing and sought from him an acceptable, more "spectacular," perhaps cosmic, sign, at their personal request. The Gospel writers warn that these scholars did so "to test" Jesus. In that setting, he replied, "No sign will be given to this generation" (Matt. 12:38–39; 16:1, 4; Mark 8:11–12; Luke 11:16, 29–30). Refusing the signs God offers and demanding signs on our own terms is testing God, who will not subject himself to such examiners (Ps. 78:18–20).[5] He veils his signs (compare Deut. 29:29; Isa. 45:15) from those who test him; such unbelief may be a factor in fewer visible signs in the West. Those who proclaim that God is *obligated* to supply them evidence on their own terms mistake God's kindness for weakness and mistake around whom the world really revolves. It is incumbent on us to look for signs where God has promised to offer them, not to act like consumers stipulating our own custom-designed expectations.

After refusing the demands from the scholars of his day, Jesus continued healing the sick. He still cared for their needs and revealed God's kingdom to those ready to accept lower-key signs among the lowly. But his signs were for those open-minded and humble enough to follow him and witness healings in their native setting. He does not jump through our hoops or submit to our tests for him, but he remains available to those who, drawn by the signs that he does offer, will dig deeper and learn more.

Appendix B

Some of Hume's
Other Arguments

ume's essay concerning miracles includes a number of subsidiary points. Here I address two of them: his complaint that miracle reports stem only from "ignorant and barbarous" peoples, and his idea that miracle reports in various religions cancel each other out.

Hume's Ethnocentrism

The first argument is disturbing today even for those who do not believe in miracles. In his effort to reduce the pool of witnesses, Hume dismisses all testimony from nonwhite, non-Western witnesses. This prejudice is unfortunately characteristic of Hume, some of whose other writings display his racism and anti-Semitism. There he goes so far as to deny that nonwhite peoples have produced any inventions, works of art, or the like. He supports the slave trade of his day. He dismisses the poetry of a Jamaican by comparing him to a parrot.[1]

Although most scholars who reject miracles today would not dare utter such charges, I have met some who share this prejudice against non-Western testimony. Never mind that witnesses in non-Western societies often live closer to sickness and death, recognizing their signs more clearly, than do most Westerners.

Nevertheless, plenty of people in the West believe in and claim to have witnessed miracles. As noted in chapters 3 and 4, polls consistently show that a strong majority of people in the United States believe in miracles, and a substantial minority claim to have witnessed them personally.[2] As also noted earlier, nearly three-quarters of doctors in the United States believe in miracles, even though their scientific training naturally leads them to look for ordinary causes first. (That is appropriate, although in Scripture itself God himself most often uses the collocation of ordinary causes in nature to achieve a miraculous outcome: remember the crossing of the sea.) The majority of physicians surveyed report having seen miracles. So who says that only "ignorant and barbarous" peoples believe in miracles?

Competing Religions?

Hume's argument about miracles in other religions is also problematic. His error is not in noting that multiple (albeit not all) religions claim miracles; spiritual healing does appear in non-Christian religious contexts. (Contrary to the complaints of a few reviewers who critiqued my previous book on miracles without actually *reading* it, I did include a section on this topic.)[3]

Against Hume, it is not true that the claims of all religions about miracles at their founding cancel each other out. First, not all religions claim these equally, though these claims predominate in traditional religions.[4]

Second, even if all religions displayed genuine supernatural activity, that would undermine Hume's nonsupernatural approach. It would raise other questions that those religions would want answers to, but it would not show that all religions *falsely* claim supernatural activity.

Third, God does not care about or answer the prayers only of Christians. As a Christian writing from a Christian perspective, I can give an example from my own family. My wife's parents grew up in African traditional religions before they became Christians and before Christianity became widespread in their country. When my mother-in-law was a girl, she was crossing a river on a log but slipped and fell into the river. As she was drowning, she felt a hand lift her and set her back on the log. She thought that a mighty spirit had protected her. When she became a Christian, she realized that the one who had saved her was God, giving her a chance to someday live for him. Similarly, a friend who spent years among Palestinians in the 1980s told me that many Muslim Palestinians would pray in the name of the prophet Isa—Jesus—because they found that God often healed that way. My friend's view was that God was reaching out to them to honor his Son. (The Qur'an already recognizes Jesus as a virgin-born prophet and miracle worker.)

Fourth, believing in one God also does not preclude recognizing that there are other spiritual forces at work in the world. Jesus's miracles were mostly benevolent signs of God's compassion, such as healing, deliverance, protection, and provision. In many cultures, however, people seek to send curses,[5] a practice that lacks positive biblical precedent.[6] That is, Christians can also acknowledge the activity of other spiritual forces at work besides that of God.

Converted by a Witch Doctor

I address power encounters more generally in my 2011 book on miracles;[7] here I offer just one example of something related but not included there. Fasil Wolde-mariam, from Ethiopia, is one of my PhD students. When a medical doctor was unable to cure his younger brother's sickness, Fasil's biological mother took the boy to a well-known witch doctor (Fasil's phrase). Though she was spending all her money for treatment, her son was not recovering. Angrily, she publicly confronted the witch doctor and kicked over some of his paraphernalia.

The witch doctor, now angry in turn, cursed her. "You will die on Monday," he declared. She was afraid, but then she remembered that the witch doctor had told her why he was so often sick himself: "When the Pentecostals pray," he lamented, "I get sick." So she quickly joined a Pentecostal church. Not only did she not die on Monday, but she remains a follower of Christ.[8]

I discuss false signs in appendix C.

Appendix C

False Signs

In the West, a key question, to which this book primarily responds, is whether God acts in our world. In many other parts of the world where I have lectured, such as Ethiopia, India, Indonesia, and Nigeria, the key question about apparent miracles is how to distinguish acts of God from acts of other spiritual forces.[1] (I leave aside cases of fraud, misinterpretation, and so forth, which I and others have explored elsewhere.)[2]

Biblical accounts take for granted that hostile spiritual powers can imitate divine signs, although they are subordinate to God's agents when conflicts occur.[3] Such confrontations appear with Pharaoh's magicians (Exod. 7:11, 22; 8:7, 18–19; 9:11), with Elymas Bar-Jesus (Acts 13:6–12), and in a different way with Simon the sorcerer (Acts 8:5–24).

Beyond Jesus and his first followers, some other Jewish people practiced exorcism (Matt. 12:27//Luke 11:19; Acts 19:13–14), without all knowing exactly what they were dealing with (Acts 19:15–16). Although Scripture does not fully explain these cases, perhaps spirits sometimes cooperated with existing magical systems to keep people enslaved to them (see Matt. 12:43–45//Luke 12:23–26). Unlike typical exorcists of his day, however, Jesus needed no magical formulas or rituals, but cast out spirits by his mere command (Matt. 8:16).[4]

Scripture also speaks of false prophets who work signs (Matt. 24:24; Mark 13:22; 2 Thess. 2:9; Rev. 13:13). In ancient Israel, spiritual leaders, including prophets, often committed immorality and prophesied blessings despite immorality, making up their own messages (Jer. 23:11–30). (Nevertheless, the prophet Jeremiah is careful to emphasize that counterfeit prophets do not invalidate true ones; see 23:28.) Some prophets just told people what they wanted to hear (Jer. 6:14; 8:11; 2 Tim. 4:3–4). Such false prophets are often outside the church (Rev.

16:13), but they can also appear among believers to trick them (Matt. 7:15; 24:11, 24; 2 Pet. 2:1; 1 John 4:1).

Scripture invites God's people to discern prophetic voices partly by their message (compare Rev. 13:11). Prophets are false (even if their prophecies prove otherwise accurate) if they, for example, call us to untrue gods (Deut. 13:1–5), or if a spirit denies that Jesus is the Messiah (1 John 2:22), rejects that he came in the flesh (1 John 4:2–3), or insists that he is accursed (1 Cor. 12:3). Prophets are false if they promote immorality (Rev. 2:14), turning grace into an excuse to sin freely (Jude 4).

In a book about miracles, it is important to remember Jesus's teaching that we recognize prophets not by their gifts but by their *fruits* (Matt. 7:16, 20)—that is, by whether they obey God (7:17–19). Some alleged prophets exploit God's people for their own profit (Mic. 3:11; 2 Pet. 2:1–3). Gehazi was Elisha's genuine understudy, but he sacrificed his future calling for profit (2 Kings 5:26–27). (In fact, although prophets might depend on offerings—e.g., 1 Sam. 9:7–8—early Christians were taken advantage of so often that they quickly passed a rule that if prophets ask for money, they're false prophets!)[5]

Some prophets start well as God's servants but go astray (1 Sam. 10:9–10; 15:17–19; Acts 20:28–30). Someone who is disobeying God may still have a remnant of anointing for a time, like Samson (Judg. 16:1–3), but Samson eventually lost this blessing and regained it only at a terrible cost (Judg. 16:17–31). Sometimes God's Spirit uses someone simply because the Spirit is strong among others in a place (1 Sam. 19:20–24). My wife tells me about a man in Congo who prophesied very accurately, but then started becoming inaccurate and was finally found to be sexually exploiting young women he had recruited as workers. It is possible for apparently Christian leaders to prophesy, drive out demons, and perform miracles in Jesus's name—yet be lost because they do not follow him (Matt. 7:21–23). Sadly, our own generation has witnessed the moral failure of some gifted ministers, not always followed by genuine repentance. Some may have even fallen so far because of the inappropriately high pedestals on which we placed them.

One key criterion is whom prophets genuinely exalt: the Christ who came in the flesh—in other words, the Christ of the Gospels—or themselves. False teachers seek for people to follow after them rather than after the chief shepherd, Jesus Christ (Acts 20:29–30).[6] When miracles occur, God's servants must humbly seek Christ's honor alone (Acts 3:12; 14:14–17; compare also Gen. 41:16; Dan. 2:28–30).

Notes

Acknowledgments

1. Craig S. Keener, *Miracles: The Credibility of the New Testament Accounts*, 2 vols. (Grand Rapids: Baker Academic, 2011), hereafter cited as *Miracles* (2011).

2. Craig S. Keener, "'The Dead Are Raised' (Matthew 11:5//Luke 7:22): Resuscitation Accounts in the Gospels and Eyewitness Testimony," *Bulletin for Biblical Research* 25 (1, 2015): 55–79.

Preface

1. My younger brother Christopher Keener, now a PhD in physics, also witnessed the event I'm about to describe, though his then middle-adolescent recollection is less detailed than mine (personal correspondence, Jan. 30, 2009; Feb. 8, 2009).

2. Much of the following is from Barbara Cummiskey Snyder, phone interview, Dec. 5, 2015; personal correspondence, Dec. 13, 2015; July 11, 2016; Jan. 16, 2020. Thanks to Dwight Crowell for informing me about Barbara (Nov. 21, 2015) and making the initial connection (Nov. 26, 2015). For a video interview with her, see "Lee Strobel: *The Case for Miracles*," YouTube video, posted by Woodlands Church with Kerry Shook, March 26, 2018, 38:05, https://www.youtube.com/watch?v=y3VSIWHZtOI (accessed Aug. 31, 2020), starting at 26:25.

3. Harold P. Adolph with Mark D. Williams, *Today's Decisions, Tomorrow's Destiny* (Spooner, WI: White Birch Printing, 1999), 48–49.

4. Scott Kolbaba, *Physicians' Untold Stories: Miraculous Experiences Doctors Are Hesitant to Share with Their Patients, or Anyone!* (North Charleston, SC: CreateSpace, 2016), 115.

5. Barbara Cummiskey Snyder, personal correspondence, Jan. 16, 2020.

6. Kolbaba, *Physicians' Untold Stories*, 121.

7. Adolph, *Today's Decisions*, 49.

8. Barbara Cummiskey Snyder, phone interview, Dec. 5, 2015; personal correspondence, Dec. 13, 2015; July 11, 2016; Jan. 16, 2020.

9. Kolbaba, *Physicians' Untold Stories*, 122.

10. Adolph, *Today's Decisions*, 49.

11. Richard Tison, phone interview, June 8, 2019; personal correspondence, July 23, 2019.

12. Personal correspondence, Dec. 6, 2015.

13. Phone interview, Dec. 10, 2016. Dr. Kolbaba has continued to provide me some guidance regarding some cases for this project.

Introduction

1. Craig S. Keener, *Miracles: The Credibility of the New Testament Accounts*, 2 vols. (Grand Rapids: Baker Academic, 2011).

2. One online critic, reading not the book but an interview that showed my wife is from Republic of Congo (Congo-Brazzaville), launched an ethnocentric attack against Democratic Republic of Congo (Congo-Kinshasa), saying they kill child witches there. Aside from the fact that my wife's circles try to save lives rather than harm them, the ill-informed assault confused the two Congos, which are separate nations.

3. Craig S. Keener and Médine Moussounga Keener, *Impossible Love: The True Story of an African Civil War, Miracles, and Love against All Odds* (Bloomington, MN: Chosen Books, 2016).

4. Lee Strobel, *The Case for Miracles: A Journalist Investigates Evidence for the Supernatural* (Grand Rapids: Zondervan, 2018).

5. E.g., notably, J. P. Moreland, *A Simple Guide to Experience Miracles* (Grand Rapids: Zondervan, 2021); Eric Metaxas, *Miracles: What They Are, Why They Happen, and How They Can Change Your Life* (New York: Dutton/Penguin, 2014). For books addressing Jesus's miracles in the Gospels academically, see, e.g., David Wenham and Craig Blomberg, eds., *The Miracles of Jesus* (Sheffield, UK: JSOT Press, 1986); Graham H. Twelftree, *Jesus the Miracle Worker: A Historical and Theological Study* (Downers Grove, IL: InterVarsity, 1999); Wendy J. Cotter, *The Christ of the Miracle Stories: Portrait through Encounter* (Grand Rapids: Baker Academic, 2010); Vern S. Poythress, *The Miracles of Jesus* (Wheaton: Crossway, 2016); Luke Timothy Johnson, *Miracles: God's Presence and Power in Creation* (Louisville: Westminster John Knox, 2018), 167–273; Metropolitan Hilarion Alfeyev, *The Miracles of Jesus*, trans. Nicholas Kotar (Yonkers, NY: St. Vladimir's Seminary Press, 2020).

6. See, e.g., accounts of healings (with photographs of those healed) in Daniel Kolenda, *Impact Africa: Demonstrations of the Real Power of Jesus Christ Today* (Orlando: Christ for All Nations, 2015), including healings of blindness (124–25, 222, 262, 286–89, 322–23), deafness (181, 228, 312–13), and sickle cell anemia (324–25). See also the healing of deafness shared in Daniel Kolenda, "Miracles—Deaf Muslim Finds Jesus," YouTube video, June 12, 2017, 5:19, https://www.youtube.com/watch?v=SI5C9v_LJ1s; and the raising attested in Daniel Kolenda, "Miracles—Risen from the Dead," YouTube video, June 8, 2017, 5:23, https://www.youtube.com/watch?v=vqmT9by86cA. I have interviewed some ministers who recount large numbers of healings, including Vineyard minister Ken Fish (Jan. 22, 2020) and Nazarene minister Dan Bohi (Jan. 24, 2020).

7. See Keener, *Miracles* (2011), 1:242–49.

Chapter 1 What *Is* a Miracle, Anyway?

1. For some sample approaches, see, e.g., Robert A. Larmer, *Water into Wine? An Investigation of the Concept of Miracle* (Kingston, ON: McGill-Queen's University Press, 1988), 5–15; Richard Swinburne, "Introduction," in *Miracles*, ed. Richard Swinburne (New York: Macmillan, 1989), 2–10; J. Houston, *Reported Miracles: A Critique of Hume* (Cambridge: Cambridge University Press, 1994), 103–4; Richard L. Purtill, "On Defining Miracles," *Philosophia Christi* 3 (2, 2001): 37–39.

2. See esp. Paul Gwynne, *Special Divine Action: Key Issues in the Contemporary Debate (1965–1995)* (Rome: Gregorian University Press, 1996).

3. See references to Epictetus and others in the notes to chap. 3.

4. Compare discussion in, e.g., *Intelligent Design: William A. Dembski and Michael Ruse in Dialogue*, ed. Robert B. Stewart (Minneapolis: Fortress, 2007); John Polkinghorne and Nicholas Beale, *Questions of Truth: Fifty-One Responses to Questions about God, Science, and Belief* (Louisville: Westminster John Knox, 2009), 13, 44–45, 99–116; Alister E. McGrath, *A Fine-Tuned Universe* (Louisville: Westminster John Knox, 2009), esp. 111–26 (for the fine-tuning of chemistry necessary for biology to function, see 127–42); Michael Peterson and Michael Ruse, *Science, Evolution, and Religion: A Debate about Atheism and Theism* (New York: Oxford University Press, 2017), 62–65; Jason Waller, *Cosmological Fine-Tuning Arguments: What (If Anything) Should We Infer from the Fine-Tuning of Our Universe for Life?* (New York: Routledge, 2019); Stephen C. Meyer, *Return of the God Hypothesis: Three Scientific Discoveries That Reveal the Mind behind the Universe* (New York: HarperOne, 2021).

5. This point is noted unhappily but respectfully by atheist Quentin Smith, "The Metaphilosophy of Naturalism," *Philo* 4 (2, Fall/Winter 2001): 195–215.

6. See discussion in John Leslie, *Universes* (New York: Routledge & Kegan Paul, 1989); Paul Davies, *The Mind of God: The Scientific Basis for a Rational World* (New York: Simon & Schuster,

1992), 220; Polkinghorne and Beale, *Questions of Truth*, 13. The economy-of-logic principle is called "Ockham's razor."

7. Brian Miller (PhD in physics, Duke University), personal correspondence, March 28, 2020; Meyer, *Return of the God Hypothesis*, chaps. 16–18 (esp. chap. 16, pp. 326–47).

8. See Veritas Forum, "[Official] Miracles: Is Belief in the Supernatural Irrational? With John Lennox at Harvard," YouTube video, March 10, 2012, 1:23:35, https://www.youtube.com /watch?v=2Kz4OgXsN1w (accessed Jan. 26, 2020).

9. For varied Christian approaches to DNA, see Francis Collins, *The Language of God: A Scientist Presents Evidence for Belief* (New York: Simon & Schuster, 2008); Fazale Rana, *The Cell's Design: How Chemistry Reveals the Creator's Artistry* (Grand Rapids: Baker Books, 2008); Stephen C. Meyer, *Signature in the Cell: DNA and the Evidence for Intelligent Design* (New York: HarperOne, 2009); Thomas Woodward and James P. Gills, *The Mysterious Epigenome: What Lies beyond DNA* (Grand Rapids: Kregel, 2011). (Francis Collins, who led the Human Genome Project and won the Templeton Prize, has served as director of US National Institutes of Health under presidents Obama, Trump, and Biden.)

10. For the principle, albeit applied in different ways, compare Eccles. 11:6; Matt. 13:47–48; Mark 4:4–8. Some supposedly superfluous elements may simply reflect God designing a creation that would develop and life that would propagate itself.

11. In *Improbable Planet: How Earth Became Humanity's Home* (Grand Rapids: Baker Books, 2016), Christian astrophysicist Hugh Ross suggests that an enormous amount of mass was necessary in the universe to provide the raw materials for life to form (pp. 24–25). For his design argument, see *Creator and the Cosmos: How the Latest Scientific Discoveries Reveal God*, 4th ed. (Covina, CA: RTB Press, 2018).

12. Compare Ambrose, *Concerning the Mysteries* 1.3: "If God invariably listened to every supplicant equally, he might appear to us to act from some necessity rather than from his own free will" (*Mark*, ed. Thomas C. Oden and Christopher A. Hall, Ancient Christian Commentary on Scripture, New Testament 2 [Downers Grove, IL: InterVarsity, 1998], 96).

13. I have addressed historical evidence, my own sphere of expertise, in some other books, such as *The Historical Jesus of the Gospels* (Grand Rapids: Eerdmans, 2009); *Acts: An Exegetical Commentary*, 4 vols. (Grand Rapids: Baker Academic, 2012–2015), 1:51–422; *Christobiography: Memories, History, and the Reliability of the Gospels* (Grand Rapids: Eerdmans, 2019); *Acts*, New Cambridge Bible Commentary (Cambridge: Cambridge University Press, 2020), 1–51.

Chapter 2 Why Do Some People Assume That Miracles Don't Happen? Worldviews

1. There are also some safe spaces for respectful dialogue. I am grateful, for example, to Justin Brierley's *Unbelievable?* radio show in 2012 (and grace toward my grogginess that day); to the Ian Ramsey Centre for Science and Religion, Oxford University (which hosted the conference on special divine action in July 2014); and to the Atheist and Christian Book Club on Feb. 4, 2021.

2. This can function in effect as the skeptical equivalent of a theistic God-of-the-gaps argument. Some critics have appealed instead to a psychic force emanated by spiritual humans apart from the activity of a deity (compare, e.g., Robert H. Thouless, "Miracles and Psychical Research," *Theology* 72 [1969]: 253–58; Hugh Montefiore, *The Miracles of Jesus* [London: SPCK, 2005]; hypothetically, Caryle Hirschberg and Marc Ian Barasch, *Remarkable Recovery: What Extraordinary Healings Tell Us about Getting Well and Staying Well* [New York: Riverhead, 1995], 144)—though that should make outcomes more controllable and predictable.

3. Jacalyn Duffin, *Medical Miracles: Doctors, Saints, and Healing in the Modern World* (Oxford: Oxford University Press, 2009), 189 (compare also 113, 132–34, 186–87).

4. Jesus depicts as committing an unforgivable sin those who so twist divine evidence that they render their hearts incapable of ever accepting truth (Matt. 12:28, 32; Mark 3:29–30). Those who subsequently repent, of course, logically demonstrate that they have not gone so far.

5. On this skepticism, and the importance of believers reembracing a biblical worldview, see Luke Timothy Johnson, *Miracles: God's Presence and Power in Creation* (Louisville: Westminster John Knox, 2018), esp. 46–64, 286; consider also Craig S. Keener, *Spirit Hermeneutics: Reading Scripture in Light of Pentecost* (Grand Rapids: Eerdmans, 2016), 153–204, esp. 200–204.

6. He may have also viewed some of the plagues as mere amplifications of Egypt's ecosystem; see esp. Terence E. Fretheim, "The Plagues as Ecological Signs of Historical Disaster," *Journal of Biblical Literature* 110 (1991): 385–96. From various perspectives, see, e.g., Robert R. Stieglitz, "Ancient Records and the Exodus Plagues," *Biblical Archaeology Review* 13 (6, 1987): 46–49; Ziony Zevit, "Three Ways to Look at the Ten Plagues," *Bible Review* 6 (3, 1990): 16–23, 42, 44; H. M. Duncan Hoyt, "The Plagues of Egypt: What Killed the Animals and the Firstborn?," *Medical Journal of Australia* 158 (1993): 706–8; Colin Humphreys, *The Miracles of Exodus: A Scientist's Discovery of the Extraordinary Natural Causes of the Biblical Stories* (New York: HarperSanFrancisco, 2004). I am grateful to Craig Bartholomew for the last reference.

7. Although etic (external) approaches provide means for comparison, going beyond describing emic (indigenous) views, etic approaches are best used heuristically rather than, as in an earlier phase of anthropology, imposing structures on the data that sort the results by interpreters' grids without sufficient sensitivity to patterns that may emerge by inductive examination of the collected data.

8. Amy K. Hall, "Why Science Does Not Disprove Miracles," *Stand to Reason*, June 28, 2018, https://www.str.org/w/why-science-does-not-disprove-miracles#.Wz4MTn4nZPM (accessed May 16, 2020).

9. See, helpfully, Ian H. Hutchinson, *Can a Scientist Believe in Miracles? An MIT Professor Answers Questions on God and Science* (Downers Grove, IL: InterVarsity, 2018). Hutchinson is a professor of nuclear science and engineering at MIT.

10. For a discussion exposing the false narrative of a war between science and religion, see, e.g., Ronald L. Numbers, ed., *Galileo Goes to Jail and Other Myths about Science and Religion* (Cambridge, MA: Harvard University Press, 2009); on a philosophic level, see, e.g., Alvin Plantinga, *Where the Conflict Really Lies: Science, Religion, and Naturalism* (New York: Oxford University Press, 2012).

11. John Polkinghorne, *Quarks, Chaos, and Christianity: Questions to Science and Religion*, 2nd ed. (New York: Crossroad, 2006), 100.

12. Regarding the possibility of discussing some divine action within history, see esp. Brad S. Gregory, "The Other Confessional History: On Secular Bias in the Study of Religion," *History and Theory*, theme issue, 45 (4, Dec. 2006): 132–49.

13. Compare my comments, e.g., in *Acts: An Exegetical Commentary*, 4 vols. (Grand Rapids: Baker Academic, 2012–2015), 1:539–41, 780–83, 880–82; more focused in Keener, *Gift and Giver: The Holy Spirit for Today* (Grand Rapids: Baker Academic, 2001), 89–112 and (in the 2020 afterword) 212–14; reiterated in "Are Spiritual Gifts for Today?," in *Strangers to Fire: When Tradition Trumps Scripture*, ed. Robert W. Graves (Tulsa: Empowered Life, 2014), 135–62.

Chapter 3 Why Do Some People Assume That Miracles Don't Happen? David Hume

1. See David Hume, *Of Miracles* (La Salle, IL: Open Court, 1985). For much fuller documentation, see Keener, *Miracles* (2011), 1:107–208.

2. Stanley Jaki, *Miracles and Physics* (Front Royal, VA: Christendom, 1989), 23.

3. See, e.g., Richard Price, "*Four Dissertations*: Dissertation IV, 'On the Importance of Christianity and the Nature of Historical Evidence, and Miracles,'" in *Hume's Abject Failure: The Argument against Miracles*, by John Earman (Oxford: Oxford University Press, 2000), 157–76; J. B. Mozley, *Eight Lectures on Miracles Preached before the University of Oxford in the Year M.DCCC.LXV, on the Foundation of the Late Rev. John Bampton*, 3rd ed. (New York: Scribner, Welford, 1872), 130; William Sanday, "Miracles and the Supernatural Character of the Gospels," *Expository Times* 14 (1902–1903): 62–66 (65); A. E. Taylor, *David Hume and the Miraculous* (Cambridge: Cambridge University Press, 1927). See, further, John Stewart Lawton, *Miracles and Revelation* (New York: Association Press, 1960), 62–80; Robert M. Burns, *The Great Debate on Miracles: From Joseph Glanvill to David Hume* (Lewisburg, PA: Bucknell University Press, 1981), 176–246, esp. 181; Colin Brown, *Miracles and the Critical Mind* (Grand Rapids: Eerdmans, 1984), 89–91, 144–46; William Lane Craig, *Reasonable Faith: Christian Truth and Apologetics*, rev. ed. (Wheaton: Crossway, 1994), 134–38.

4. See John Earman, "Bayes, Hume, and Miracles," *Faith and Philosophy* 10 (3, 1993): 293–310 (305); Earman, *Hume's Abject Failure*, 24–25; Earman, "Bayes, Hume, Price, and Miracles," in *Bayes's Theorem*, ed. Richard Swinburne (Oxford: Oxford University Press, 2005), 91–109; Philip Dawid

and Donald Gillies, "A Bayesian Analysis of Hume's Argument concerning Miracles," *Philosophical Quarterly* 39 (1989): 57–65 (58); Barry Gower, "David Hume and the Probability of Miracles," *Hume Studies* 16 (1, April 1990): 17–32 (17–18); Elliott Sober, "A Modest Proposal," *Philosophy and Phenomenological Research* 68 (2, March 2004): 487–94 (487). See also Timothy McGrew, "The Argument from Miracles: A Cumulative Case for the Resurrection of Jesus of Nazareth," in *The Blackwell Companion to Natural Theology*, ed. J. P. Moreland and William Lane Craig (Malden, MA: Blackwell, 2009), 593–662; McGrew, "Miracles," *The Stanford Encyclopedia of Philosophy* (Spring 2019 Edition), http://plato.stanford.edu/entries/miracles/ (accessed Sept. 12, 2020).

5. Earman, *Hume's Abject Failure*, 25; Dorothy Coleman, "Baconian Probability and Hume's Theory of Testimony," *Hume Studies* 27 (2, Nov. 2001): 195–226 (196).

6. Charles Babbage, *The Ninth Bridgewater Treatise: A Fragment* (London: John Murray, 1837), esp. 118–32 (compare 133–42). See also John King-Farlow, "Historical Insights on Miracles: Babbage, Hume, Aquinas," *International Journal for Philosophy of Religion* 13 (4, 1982): 209–18 (209, 212–14); Michael R. Licona, *The Resurrection of Jesus: A New Historiographical Approach* (Downers Grove, IL: IVP Academic, 2010), 149–50.

7. The idea of divine design already appears among most ancient philosophers (e.g., Diodorus Siculus 12.20.2; Cicero, *On the Nature of the Gods* 2.32.81–82; 2.54.133–2.61.153; *Tusculan Disputations* 1.13.30; Cornutus, *Greek Theology* 20, §37.4), including Socrates (Xenophon, *Memorabilia* 1.4.5–6; 4.3.12–13), Plato and Aristotle (Helen King, *Greek and Roman Medicine* [London: Bristol Classical Press, 2001], 54; Vivian Nutton, *Ancient Medicine*, 2nd ed. [New York: Routledge, 2013], 117, 240–41), and esp. Stoics (e.g., Epictetus, *Discourses* 1.6.7, 10; 1.16.8). Detractors such as Epicureans were the minority (Dio Chrysostom, *Orations* 12.36–37). Scripture also assumes divine design: for God forming creation through his Word or designing it by his Wisdom, see, e.g., Gen. 1:3–29; Pss. 33:6–9; 119:90–91; 148:5–6; Prov. 8:22–31; John 1:3; compare Ps. 147:15.

8. John Hedley Brooke, "Science and Theology in the Enlightenment," in *Religion and Science: History, Method, Dialogue*, ed. W. Mark Richardson and Wesley J. Wildman (New York: Routledge, 1996), 7–27 (9). See also Brooke, *Science and Religion: Some Historical Perspectives* (New York: Cambridge University Press, 1991), 118; John C. Sharp, "Miracles and the 'Laws of Nature,'" *Scottish Bulletin of Evangelical Theology* 6 (1988): 1–19 (11); James E. Force, "The Breakdown of the Newtonian Synthesis of Science and Religion: Hume, Newton, and the Royal Society," in *Essays on the Context, Nature, and Influence of Isaac Newton's Theology*, ed. James E. Force and Richard H. Popkin (Dordrecht: Kluwer Academic, 1990), 143–63 (146–50); Lorraine Daston, "Marvelous Facts and Miraculous Evidence in Early Modern Europe," *Critical Inquiry* 18 (Autumn 1991): 93–124 (113; consider also 114–23); Stephen C. Meyer, *Return of the God Hypothesis: Three Scientific Discoveries That Reveal the Mind behind the Universe* (New York: HarperOne, 2021), 19-49.

9. John Polkinghorne, *Quarks, Chaos, and Christianity: Questions to Science and Religion*, 2nd ed. (New York: Crossroad, 2006), 100; Polkinghorne, *The Way the World Is: The Christian Perspective of a Scientist* (Louisville: Westminster John Knox, 2007), 56; Polkinghorne, *Quantum Physics and Theology: An Unexpected Kinship* (New Haven: Yale University Press, 2007), 34.

10. See, e.g., Ivan Tolstoy, *James Clerk Maxwell: A Biography* (Chicago: University of Chicago Press, 1981); Linda McMurry Edwards, *George Washington Carver, Scientist and Symbol* (New York: Oxford University Press, 1982); David Lindberg and Ronald Numbers, eds., *God and Nature: Historical Essays on the Encounter between Christianity and Science* (Berkeley: University of California Press, 1986); Charles Hummel, *The Galileo Connection* (Downers Grove, IL: InterVarsity, 1986); Brooke, *Science and Religion*; Ian G. Barbour, *Religion and Science: Historical and Contemporary Issues* (San Francisco: HarperSanFrancisco, 1997), 24–29, 64–65; John Hedley Brooke with Geoffrey Cantor, *Reconstructing Nature: The Engagement of Science and Religion* (Edinburgh: T&T Clark, 1998); David N. Livingstone, D. G. Hart, and Mark A. Noll, eds., *Evangelicals and Science in Historical Perspective* (New York: Oxford University Press, 1999); Dava Sobel, *Galileo's Daughter* (New York: Bloomsbury, 1999); Nancy K. Frankenberry, *The Faith of Scientists in Their Words* (Princeton: Princeton University Press, 2008); David Lindberg, *The Beginnings of Western Science*, 2nd ed. (Chicago: University of Chicago Press, 2008); Ronald L. Numbers, ed., *Galileo Goes to Jail and Other Myths about Science and Religion* (Cambridge, MA: Harvard University Press, 2009); Michael C. W. Hunter, *Boyle: Between God and Science* (New Haven: Yale University Press, 2010); Frank A. J. L.

James, *Michael Faraday: A Very Short Introduction* (New York: Oxford University Press, 2010); Matthew Stanley, *Huxley's Church and Maxwell's Demon* (Chicago: University of Chicago Press, 2015).

11. John William Draper, *History of the Conflict between Religion and Science* (London: Henry S. King, 1875); and Andrew Dickson White, *A History of the Warfare of Science with Theology in Christendom*, 2 vols. (New York: D. Appleton and Company, 1896). See discussion in Keith Thomson, "Introduction," in *The Religion and Science Debate: Why Does It Continue?*, ed. Harold W. Attridge (New Haven: Yale University Press, 2009), 1–3, 6–7; Ronald L. Numbers, "Aggressors, Victims, and Peacemakers: Historical Actors in the Drama of Science and Religion," in Attridge, *Religion and Science Debate*, 31–33; Numbers, *Galileo Goes to Jail and Other Myths*, passim; Brooke, *Science and Religion*, 34–36; most recently and forcefully, Derrick Peterson, *Flat Earth and Fake Footnotes: The Strange Tale of How the Conflict of Science and Christianity Was Written into History* (Eugene, OR: Cascade Books, 2020).

12. See esp. the thorough treatment in Burns, *Great Debate on Miracles*, esp. 70–95, 141. This book is based on Burns's Princeton University PhD dissertation.

13. Some early deists did not deny even that (Burns, *Great Debate on Miracles*, 83; see also 247).

14. Burns, *Great Debate on Miracles*, 12, 19, 47–69.

15. See David Johnson, *Hume, Holism, and Miracles* (Ithaca, NY: Cornell University Press, 1999), 19; J. Kellenberger, "Miracles," *International Journal for Philosophy of Religion* 10 (3, 1979): 145–63 (149); Brown, *Miracles and the Critical Mind*, 243; Robert A. Larmer, *Water into Wine? An Investigation of the Concept of Miracle* (Kingston, ON: McGill-Queen's University Press, 1988), 37; Terence L. Nichols, "Miracles in Science and Theology," *Zygon* 37 (3, 2002): 703–15 (703–4).

16. See Paul Gwynne, *Special Divine Action: Key Issues in the Contemporary Debate (1965–1995)* (Rome: Gregorian University Press, 1996), 184–87; William P. Alston, "Divine and Human Action," in *Divine and Human Action: Essays in the Metaphysics of Theism*, ed. Thomas V. Morris (Ithaca, NY: Cornell University Press, 1988), 257–80; Brian Hebblethwaite and Edward Henderson, eds., *Divine Action: Studies Inspired by the Philosophical Theology of Austin Farrer* (Edinburgh: T&T Clark, 1990); Arthur Peacocke, "The Incarnation of the Informing Self-Expressive Word of God," in *Religion and Science: History, Method, Dialogue*, ed. W. Mark Richardson and Wesley J. Wildman (New York: Routledge, 1996), 321–39 (332); C. Stephen Evans, *The Historical Christ and the Jesus of Faith: The Incarnational Narrative as History* (Oxford: Clarendon, 1996), 145–46.

17. Peter Byrne, "Miracles and the Philosophy of Science," *Heythrop Journal* 19 (1978): 162–70 (165–66); John A. Cramer, "Miracles and David Hume," *Perspectives on Science and Christian Faith* 40 (3, Sept. 1988): 129–37 (136–37); Gwynne, *Special Divine Action*, 172; Nichols, "Miracles in Science and Theology," 705.

18. Nichols, "Miracles in Science and Theology," 705.

19. See Francis J. Beckwith, *David Hume's Argument against Miracles: A Critical Analysis* (Lanham, MD: University Press of America, 1989), 28–32; Evans, *Historical Christ*, 154; Rodney D. Holder, "Hume on Miracles: Bayesian Interpretation, Multiple Testimony, and the Existence of God," *British Journal for the Philosophy of Science* 49 (1, March 1998): 49–65 (57); Larmer, *Water into Wine?*, 36.

20. See Hume, *Of Miracles*, 44–48; Brown, *Miracles and the Critical Mind*, 71; Richard Swinburne, *The Concept of Miracle* (London: Macmillan, 1970), 16; Beckwith, *David Hume's Argument against Miracles*, 51. Hume revised a deist argument regarding Huguenots with the easier target of Jansenists (Burns, *Great Debate on Miracles*, 74–75).

21. Burns, *Great Debate on Miracles*, 174.

22. See, e.g., Swinburne, *Concept of Miracle*; J. Houston, *Reported Miracles: A Critique of Hume* (Cambridge: Cambridge University Press, 1994); Johnson, *Hume, Holism, and Miracles*; Earman, *Hume's Abject Failure*. Compare also Beckwith, *David Hume's Argument against Miracles*; Robert A. Larmer, "C. S. Lewis's Critique of Hume's 'Of Miracles,'" *Faith and Philosophy* 25 (2, 2008): 154–71; Larmer, "Interpreting Hume on Miracles," *Religious Studies* 45 (3, 2009): 325–38.

23. See, e.g., C. S. Lewis, *Miracles: A Preliminary Study* (New York: Macmillan, 1948), 102 (often cited to this effect); Taylor, *David Hume and the Miraculous*, 15; Johnson, *Hume, Holism, and Miracles*, 18–19; Larmer, "C. S. Lewis's Critique," 163–64, 167; Rick Kennedy, "Miracles in the Dock: A Critique of the Historical Profession's Special Treatment of Alleged Spiritual Events," *Fides et Historia* 26 (2, 1994): 7–22 (17–18); Evans, *Historical Christ*, 153–54.

24. Luke Salkeld, "We Don't Do Miracles: Power of Prayer Helps Woman to Walk Again . . . Yet Officials Refuse to Stop Her Benefits," *Daily Mail*, Dec. 11, 2007, M5. Andrew Wilson shared this article with me.

25. The average in central and eastern Europe is about 60 percent; in Latin America, 91 percent; in sub-Saharan Africa, 74 percent; and in the US, 79 percent. See Travis Mitchell, "3. Religious Beliefs," in *Religious Belief and National Belonging in Central and Eastern Europe*, Pew Research Center, May 10, 2017, https://www.pewforum.org/2017/05/10/religious-beliefs/ (accessed Jan. 27, 2020). Compare earlier statistics in Robert Wuthnow, *After Heaven: Spirituality in America since the 1950s* (Berkeley: University of California Press, 1998), 122; Kenneth L. Woodward, *The Book of Miracles: The Meaning of the Miracle Stories in Christianity, Judaism, Buddhism, Hinduism, and Islam* (New York: Simon & Schuster, 2000), 21; Judith L. Johnson and Nathan D. Butzen, "Intercessory Prayer, Group Psychology, and Medical Healing," in *Medical and Therapeutic Events*, vol. 2 of *Miracles: God, Science, and Psychology in the Paranormal*, ed. J. Harold Ellens (Westport, CT: Praeger, 2008), 249–61 (249).

26. Dieter Ising, *Johann Christoph Blumhardt, Life and Work: A New Biography*, trans. Monty Ledford (Eugene, OR: Cascade Books, 2009), 222–23 (compare 93–94). German New Testament scholar Rainer Riesner shared with me an oral tradition from within his own family about a healing through the prayers of Blumhardt's son Christoph (personal correspondence, Aug. 14, 2020). Ironically, Strauss proved quite interested in preternatural subjects; see Thomas Fabisiak, *The "Nocturnal Side of Science" in David Friedrich Strauss's "Life of Jesus Critically Examined,"* Emory Studies in Early Christianity 17 (Atlanta: SBL Press, 2015).

27. Henry F. May, *The Enlightenment in America* (New York: Oxford University Press, 1976), 123; Mark David Hall, "Were Any of the Founders Deists?," in *The Wiley Blackwell Companion to Religion and Politics in the U.S.*, ed. Barbara A. McGraw (Malden, MA: Wiley & Sons, 2016), 51–63 (52).

28. Ethan Allen, *Reason the Only Oracle of Man; or, A Compendious System of Natural Religion* (New York: G. W. and A. J. Matsell; Philadelphia: Wm. Sinclair, 1836; orig. 1784), 46.

29. See, e.g., Kimberly Ervin Alexander, *Pentecostal Healing: Models in Theology and Practice* (Blandford Forum, UK: Deo, 2006), 15. Historian J. D. King, author of a work on Allen, notes that "his hometown obituary from 1903" claims this (personal correspondence, July 22, 2020). The obituary is reprinted from the *Springfield Republican* (Jan. 1903) in William T. MacArthur, *Ethan O. Allen* (Philadelphia: Parlor Evangelist, n.d. [possibly 1920s]), 18–19, but King notes that scholars dispute the connection. See, further, Ethan Otis Allen, *Faith Healing*, ed. J. D. King (Lee's Summit, MO: Christos, 2020). Historian Glenn W. Gohr notes that although the chronology would work, Ethan O. Allen's father's name is not the name of any of the earlier Ethan's children (personal correspondence, July 23, 2020).

30. Rudolf Bultmann, *New Testament Mythology and Other Basic Writings*, ed. Schubert Ogden (Philadelphia: Fortress, 1984), 4 (see further 5–9).

31. See Ronald A. N. Kydd, *Healing through the Centuries: Models for Understanding* (Peabody, MA: Hendrickson, 1998), 42n40. Contrast favorably Karl Barth, *Letters 1961–1968*, trans. Geoffrey W. Bromiley (Grand Rapids: Eerdmans, 1981), 251; Ising, *Blumhardt*, 420; others cite Karl Barth, *Church Dogmatics*, vol. 4.3, *The Doctrine of Reconciliation* (Edinburgh: T&T Clark, 1961), 165ff. Note also Jürgen Moltmann, "The Blessing of Hope: The Theology of Hope and the Full Gospel of Life," *Journal of Pentecostal Theology* 13 (2, 2005): 147–61 (149).

32. See the copious documentation in Ising, *Blumhardt*.

33. Ismael Laborde Figueras, interviews, Aug. 7–8, 2010.

34. Justo L. González, *Acts: The Gospel of the Spirit* (Maryknoll, NY: Orbis Books, 2001), 84–85.

35. Hwa Yung, *Mangoes or Bananas? The Quest for an Authentic Asian Christian Theology; Biblical Theology in an Asian Context*, 2nd ed. (Oxford: Regnum, 2014), 6; also personal correspondence, Sept. 22, 2014.

36. Hwa Yung, "A 21st Century Reformation: Recover the Supernatural," *Christianity Today*, Sept. 2, 2010, https://www.christianitytoday.com/ct/2010/september/yung.html.

37. Philip Jenkins, *The Next Christendom: The Coming of Global Christianity* (New York: Oxford University Press, 2002); Jenkins, *The New Faces of Christianity: Believing the Bible in the Global South* (New York: Oxford University Press, 2006); Jenkins, "Reading the Bible in the Global

South," *International Bulletin of Mission Research* 30 (2, April 2006): 67–73. Compare also examples in Mark A. Noll and Carolyn Nystrom, *Clouds of Witnesses: Christian Voices from Africa and Asia* (Downers Grove, IL: IVP Books, 2011), 30, 74–75, 158–59, 172, 192, 219, 224–25.

38. Cephas Omenyo, *Pentecost outside Pentecostalism: A Study of the Development of Charismatic Renewal in the Mainline Church in Ghana* (Zoetermeer, Netherlands: Uitgeverij Boekencentrum, 2002); Omenyo, "New Wine in an Old Bottle? Charismatic Healing in the Mainline Churches in Ghana," in *Global Pentecostal and Charismatic Healing*, ed. Candy Gunther Brown (Oxford: Oxford University Press, 2011), esp. 242–45; Mark R. Gornik, *Word Made Global: Stories of African Christianity in New York City* (Grand Rapids: Eerdmans, 2011), 76.

Chapter 4 Are There Many Witnesses of Miracles?

1. Ken Fish, phone interview, Jan. 22, 2020. In personal correspondence on May 31, 2021, he sent me a video of a paralyzed woman who, three days earlier (May 28), was healed and began walking, right after his team prayed for her.

2. For the materials that translate into these statistics, see esp. "Spirit and Power: A Ten-Country Survey of Pentecostals," Pew Research Center, Oct. 5, 2006, https://www.pewforum.org/2006/10/05/spirit-and-power/#executive-summary (accessed Jan. 27, 2020).

3. Christiaan Rudolph De Wet, "Signs and Wonders in Church Growth" (MA thesis, Fuller School of World Mission, Dec. 1981), 119–21.

4. Pew Forum on Religion & Public Life US Religious Landscape Survey, May 2007; see, e.g., https://www.reuters.com/article/us-usa-divinehealing-life/a-third-of-americans-report-divine-healing-pew-idUSN2042499020080623.

5. "Most Americans Believe in Supernatural Healing," Barna Research poll, released Sept. 29, 2016, https://www.barna.com/research/americans-believe-supernatural-healing/.

6. Lee Strobel, *The Case for Miracles: A Journalist Investigates Evidence for the Supernatural* (Grand Rapids: Zondervan, 2018), 30, citing a Barna survey Strobel commissioned.

7. See "Science or Miracle? Holiday Season Survey Reveals Physicians' Views of Faith, Prayer and Miracles," *Business Wire*, Dec. 20, 2004, https://web.archive.org/web/20201111190541/https://www.businesswire.com/news/home/20041220005244/en/Science-Miracle-Holiday-Season-Survey-Reveals-Physicians (accessed Jan. 27, 2020).

8. Margaret M. Poloma, *The Assemblies of God at the Crossroads: Charisma and Institutional Dilemmas* (Knoxville: University of Tennessee Press, 1989), 57; Jacalyn Duffin, *Medical Miracles: Doctors, Saints, and Healing in the Modern World* (Oxford: Oxford University Press, 2009), 131.

9. See, e.g., Karl R. Popper, *Conjectures and Refutations: The Growth of Scientific Knowledge*, 3rd rev. ed. (London: Routledge & Kegan Paul, 1969), 21; Robert Wuthnow, "Teaching and Religion in Sociology," in *Religion, Scholarship, Higher Education: Perspectives, Models, and Future Prospects*, ed. Andrea Sterk (Notre Dame, IN: University of Notre Dame Press, 2001), 184–92 (187); Richard L. Gorsuch, "On the Limits of Scientific Investigation: Miracles and Intercessory Prayer," in *Religious and Spiritual Events*, vol. 1 of *Miracles: God, Science, and Psychology in the Paranormal*, ed. J. Harold Ellens (Westport, CT: Praeger, 2008), 280–99 (284–85); Michael R. Licona, *The Resurrection of Jesus: A New Historiographical Approach* (Downers Grove, IL: IVP Academic, 2010), 171n119. See also criticism of Hume in George I. Mavrodes, "David Hume and the Probability of Miracles," *International Journal for Philosophy of Religion* 43 (3, 1998): 167–82 (168); John Earman, *Hume's Abject Failure: The Argument against Miracles* (Oxford: Oxford University Press, 2000), 33. For eyewitness testimony in science specifically, compare Stanley Jaki, "Miracles and Physics," *Asbury Theological Journal* 42 (1, 1987): 5–42; Keith Ward, "Miracles and Testimony," *Religious Studies* 21 (1985): 131–45 (133). For discussion of the typical sufficiency of core memories, despite their imperfection, see sources cited in Craig S. Keener, *Christobiography: Memories, History, and the Reliability of the Gospels* (Grand Rapids: Eerdmans, 2019), 365–501.

10. Although, for the record, I have not found compelling reason to affirm intelligent alien life (apart from Christian belief in angels and demons), such a belief would not be irrational if sufficient evidence supported it. It is, in fact, often noted secular scientists such as Carl Sagan and Francis Crick who have proposed panspermia from other worlds or who search the universe for signs of alien life. For

Richard Dawkins hypothesizing about design by intelligent aliens, compare comments in Stephen C. Meyer, *Return of the God Hypothesis: Three Scientific Discoveries That Reveal the Mind behind the Universe* (New York: HarperOne, 2021), 264–65.

11. Stuart Appelle, Steven Jay Lynn, and Leonard Newman, "Alien Abduction Experiences," in *Varieties of Anomalous Experience: Examining the Scientific Evidence*, ed. Etzel Cardeña, Steven Jay Lynn, and Stanley Krippner (Washington, DC: American Psychological Association, 2000), 253–82 (255–56, esp. 256).

12. Pew Forum on Religion & Public Life US Religious Landscape Survey, May 2007.

13. Roger Walsh, *The World of Shamanism: New Views of an Ancient Tradition* (Woodbury, MN: Llewellyn, 2007), 169.

14. Paranormal beliefs seem less common among the religiously committed (James McClenon, *Wondrous Events: Foundations of Religious Belief* [Philadelphia: University of Pennsylvania Press, 1994], 21; consider also Andrew M. Greeley, *The Sociology of the Paranormal: A Reconnaissance* [Beverly Hills, CA: Sage, 1975], 15), and even if most of the 22 percent of the US population who believe that space aliens have visited earth (Appelle, Lynn, and Newman, "Alien Abduction Experiences," 258) overlap with those who believe in divine miracles, which is highly improbable, perhaps half the US population (some 150 million people) would remain who believe in miracles but not in space aliens.

15. See, e.g., Harold Remus, *Jesus as Healer* (Cambridge: Cambridge University Press, 1997), 109.

16. See Remus, *Jesus as Healer*, 109; Herbert Benson with Marg Stark, *Timeless Healing: The Power and Biology of Belief* (New York: Scribner, 1996), 49.

17. On psychosomatic cures, see, e.g., Morton T. Kelsey, *Healing and Christianity in Ancient Thought and Modern Times* (New York: Harper & Row, 1973), 243–77; Louis Rose, *Faith Healing*, ed. Bryan Morgan, rev. ed. (Baltimore: Penguin, 1971), 119–34, 176. Psychosomatic cures are allowed for by all those who pray for healing surveyed in James A. Tilley, "A Phenomenology of the Christian Healer's Experience" (PhD diss., Fuller Graduate School of Psychology, 1989), 565. For emotions' effects on the immune system and health, see Bernie S. Siegel, *Law, Medicine, and Miracles: Lessons Learned about Self-Healing from a Surgeon's Experience with Exceptional Patients* (New York: Harper & Row, 1986), esp. 65–124 (though he may overestimate cure rates); Daniel E. Fountain, *God, Medicine, and Miracles: The Spiritual Factor in Healing* (Wheaton: Harold Shaw, 1999), 71–82; Sidney M. Greenfield, *Spirits with Scalpels: The Culturalbiology of Religious Healing in Brazil* (Walnut Creek, CA: Left Coast Press, 2008), 18, 180, 201; also Esther M. Sternberg, *Healing Spaces: The Science of Place and Well-Being* (Cambridge, MA: Harvard University Press, 2009), 169–80, 198–99, cited in Bernard François, Esther M. Sternberg, and Elizabeth Fee, "The Lourdes Medical Cures Revisited," *Journal of the History of Medicine and Allied Sciences* 69 (1, Jan. 2014): 135–62. In a religious context, see Harold G. Koenig, *Medicine, Religion, and Health: Where Science and Spirituality Meet* (West Conshohocken, PA: Templeton Foundation Press, 2008), 82–95. But some Christian healings occur in which the healed people lacked expectation of healing (Randy Clark, *Eyewitness to Miracles: Watching the Gospel Come to Life* [Nashville: Nelson, 2018], 122).

18. For fake paranormal experiences, see, e.g., Matthew Tompkins, "The Two Illusions That Tricked Arthur Conan Doyle," *BBC Future*, Aug. 29, 2019, https://www.bbc.com/future/article /20190828-the-two-bizarre-hoaxes-that-tricked-arthur-conan-doyle.

19. David Hume, *Of Miracles* (La Salle, IL: Open Court, 1985), 27, 29, 32, 34, 36–39, 43, 52–55 (esp. 38), considers them all liars or deceived fools. Compare the observation of John A. Cramer, "Miracles and David Hume," *Perspectives on Science and Christian Faith* 40 (3, Sept. 1988): 129–37 (136–37). Such a priori suspicion regarding any antecedently improbable information would undermine ordinary communication; see George Schlesinger, "The Credibility of Extraordinary Events," *Analysis* 51 (1991): 120–26 (121), as followed by Ruth Weintraub, "The Credibility of Miracles," *Philosophical Studies* 82 (1996): 359–75 (360).

20. See Duffin, *Medical Miracles*, 132–35 (compare 90, 97–99). Early fundamentalist critiques of "faith healing" also associated faith healing with feminine "hysteria" (James Opp, *The Lord for the Body: Religion, Medicine, and Protestant Faith Healing in Canada, 1880–1930* [Montreal: McGill-Queen's University Press, 2005], 168; Craig Keener, *Miracles* [2011], 1:400–401). On the history of the sexist diagnosis of hysteria, see Donald Capps, *Jesus the Village Psychiatrist* (Louisville: Westminster John Knox, 2008), 15–22, 111–12; on nineteenth-century expectations of female frailty, see Heather D.

Curtis, *Faith in the Great Physician: Suffering and Divine Healing in American Culture, 1860–1900* (Baltimore: Johns Hopkins University Press, 2007), 38–50.

21. Walter Wink, "Write What You See," *Fourth R* 7 (3, May 1994): 3–9 (4, 6).

22. Hume, *Of Miracles*, 29; Lloyd F. Bitzer, "The 'Indian Prince' in Miracle Arguments of Hume and His Predecessors and Early Critics," *Philosophy and Rhetoric* 31 (3, 1998): 175–230; Michael J. McClymond, *Familiar Stranger: An Introduction to Jesus of Nazareth* (Grand Rapids: Eerdmans, 2004), 83; A. E. Taylor, *David Hume and the Miraculous* (Cambridge: Cambridge University Press, 1927), 8–10; Robert A. Larmer, *Water into Wine? An Investigation of the Concept of Miracle* (Kingston, ON: McGill-Queen's University Press, 1988), 39; Earman, *Hume's Abject Failure*, 34–35.

23. Hume, *Of Miracles*, 34.

24. I.e., like many of us, they have grown theologically. Most of us acknowledge that we have more to learn beyond where we started.

25. E.g., Rolland Baker and Heidi Baker, *Always Enough: God's Miraculous Provision among the Poorest Children on Earth* (Bloomington, MN: Chosen Books, 2003); Baker and Baker, *Expecting Miracles: True Stories of God's Supernatural Power and How You Can Experience It* (Bloomington, MN: Chosen Books, 2007). Journalist Tim Stafford heard many such reports from witnesses when he visited Mozambique (Stafford, *Miracles: A Journalist Looks at Modern-Day Experiences of God's Power* [Minneapolis: Bethany House, 2012], 151–59).

26. Wendy J. Deichmann, "Lessons from Mozambique," *Good News Magazine*, Jan. 2015, 20–22, https://goodnewsmag.org/2014/12/lessons-from-mozambique/; supplemental information from personal correspondence, May 27, 2016.

27. Personal correspondence, Dec. 9, 2011; May 27, 30, 2016.

28. Don Kantel, "Development Aid as Power Evangelism: The Mieze Model," in *Supernatural Missions: The Impact of the Supernatural on World Missions*, ed. Randy Clark (Mechanicsburg, PA: Global Awakening, 2012), 375.

29. Kantel, "Development Aid," 370–73, 377–81; personal correspondence, May 28, 2016.

Chapter 5 Do Only Christians Report Christian Healings?

1. J. P. Moreland, *Kingdom Triangle: Recover the Christian Mind, Renovate the Soul, Restore the Spirit's Power* (Grand Rapids: Zondervan, 2007), 166–67. For an earlier example, see Christiaan Rudolph De Wet, "Signs and Wonders in Church Growth" (MA thesis, Fuller School of World Mission, Dec. 1981). For some examples after these sources, see, e.g., Jerry Trousdale, *Miraculous Movements* (Nashville: Nelson, 2012), 13, 135, 160, 173; Tim Stafford, *Miracles: A Journalist Looks at Modern-Day Experiences of God's Power* (Minneapolis: Bethany House, 2012), 148–60.

2. Douglass Paul Norwood, "A Reconciliation Colloquium for Church Leaders in Suriname" (DMin project, Assemblies of God Theological Seminary, 2001), 24–26; interview, Philadelphia, June 6, 2006; interview, Wynnewood, PA, Jan. 14, 2009; further details from personal correspondence, July 15, 19, 20, 22, 2016.

3. Claudia Währisch-Oblau, "God Can Make Us Healthy Through and Through: On Prayers for the Sick and the Interpretation of Healing Experiences in Christian Churches in China and African Immigrant Congregations in Germany," *International Review of Mission* 90 (356/357, Jan.–April 2001): 87–102 (92–93); Gotthard Oblau, "Divine Healing and the Growth of Practical Christianity in China," in *Global Pentecostal and Charismatic Healing*, ed. Candy Gunther Brown (Oxford: Oxford University Press, 2011), 307–27 (313).

4. Edmond Tang, "'Yellers' and Healers—Pentecostalism and the Study of Grassroots Christianity in China," in *Asian and Pentecostal: The Charismatic Face of Christianity in Asia*, ed. Allan Anderson and Edmond Tang (Oxford: Regnum, 2005), 467–86 (481). Compare also Oblau, "Divine Healing," 313; David Aikman, *Jesus in Beijing: How Christianity Is Transforming China and Changing the Global Balance of Power* (Washington, DC: Regnery, 2003), 76, 85, 273–74; Candy Gunther Brown, "Introduction: Pentecostalism and the Globalization of Illness and Healing," in Brown, *Global Pentecostal and Charismatic Healing*, 3–26 (14). For a more general treatment, see Gotthard Oblau, "Pentecostal by Default? Contemporary Christianity in China," in Anderson and Tang, *Asian and Pentecostal*, 411–36 (414).

5. Accounts from China and some other countries are unfortunately underrepresented in this book; a large number appear in my *Miracles* (2011), but I did not wish to reuse too many of them.

6. Interview, Bangalore, India, Jan. 13, 2016.

7. R. R. Cunville, "The Evangelization of Northeast India" (DMiss diss., Fuller Theological Seminary, 1975), 156–57, as cited in De Wet, "Signs and Wonders," 110–11.

8. For many non-Christians coming to churches only for healings and not remaining, see Michael Bergunder, "Miracle Healing and Exorcism in South Indian Pentecostalism," in Brown, *Global Pentecostal and Charismatic Healing*, 287–305 (298); compare John 6:26.

9. Michael Bergunder, *The South Indian Pentecostal Movement in the Twentieth Century* (Grand Rapids: Eerdmans, 2008), 233.

10. S. Israel, personal discussion with notes, Wynnewood, PA, Nov. 2, 1997; May 6, 1998. Other accounts from India could be multiplied: e.g., then seminarian Manohar James, interview, Nicholasville, KY, Sept. 4, 2011.

11. Sai Ankem, Feb. 8, 2020, interview followed by his written testimony (which I have condensed but followed verbatim at some points).

12. Phone interview, April 15, 2019; personal correspondence, April 21, 25, 2019; April 30, 2020.

13. Donald A. McGavran, "Divine Healing and Church Growth," in *Signs and Wonders Today: The Story of Fuller Theological Seminary's Remarkable Course on Spiritual Power*, ed. C. Peter Wagner, rev. ed. (Altamonte Springs, FL: Creation House, 1987), 71–78 (75).

14. Various students have also shared with me that this was how their families in the US became Christian: e.g., Marilyn P. Turner, "Spiritual Autobiography" (Virginia Union University, Jan. 2011); Nathaniel Dean, personal correspondence, Dec. 12, 2013 (regarding his in-laws).

Chapter 6 Is Healing Just a New Thing?

1. Amanda Porterfield, *Healing in the History of Christianity* (Oxford: Oxford University Press, 2005), 3.

2. I use "pagan" not in the modern (sometimes pejorative) sense but in the sense in which it applied in the late Roman Empire, often even as a self-designation, for gentile polytheists.

3. See, e.g., *t. Hullin* 2:22–23; *b. Sanhedrin* 43a; *y. Abodah Zarah* 2:2, §3; Ephraim E. Urbach, *The Sages: Their Concepts and Beliefs*, trans. Israel Abrahams, 2nd ed., 2 vols. (Jerusalem: Magnes Press, 1979), 1:115–16; R. Travers Herford, *Christianity in Talmud and Midrash* (Clifton, NJ: Reference Book Publishers, 1966), 103–11, 115–17; Ray A. Pritz, *Nazarene Jewish Christianity: From the End of the New Testament Period until Its Disappearance in the Fourth Century* (Jerusalem: Hebrew University; Leiden: Brill, 1988), 96–97; Roland Deines, "Religious Practices and Religious Movements in Galilee: 100 BCE–200 CE," in *Life, Culture, and Society*, vol. 1 of *Galilee in the Late Second Temple and Mishnaic Periods*, ed. David A. Fiensy and James Riley Strange (Minneapolis: Fortress, 2014), 78–111 (100).

4. Origen, *Against Celsus* 1.46, 67, in Morton T. Kelsey, *Healing and Christianity in Ancient Thought and Modern Times* (New York: Harper & Row, 1973), 136.

5. Reginald Maxwell Woolley, *Exorcism and the Healing of the Sick* (London: SPCK, 1932), 29–30. Compare Kelsey, *Healing and Christianity*, 151; Kilian McDonnell and George T. Montague, *Christian Initiation and Baptism in the Holy Spirit: Evidence from the First Eight Centuries* (Collegeville, MN: Liturgical Press, 1991), 314.

6. Athanasius, *On the Incarnation* 48.3, cited in Woolley, *Exorcism and the Healing of the Sick*, 47. These reports differ from the sort of "imperial miracle" stories examined in H. A. Drake, *A Century of Miracles: Christians, Pagans, Jews, and the Supernatural, 312–410* (New York: Oxford University Press, 2017).

7. See R. J. S. Barrett-Lennard, *Christian Healing after the New Testament: Some Approaches to Illness in the Second, Third, and Fourth Centuries* (Lanham, MD: University Press of America, 1994), 44–86, 277–323; Gérard Godron, "Healings in Coptic Literature," in *The Coptic Encyclopedia*, ed. Aziz S. Atiya, 8 vols. (New York: Macmillan, 1991), 4:1212–13.

8. See some of Gregory's accounts in Raymond Van Dam, *Saints and Their Miracles in Late Antique Gaul* (Princeton: Princeton University Press, 1993), 70; Amanda Porterfield, *Healing in the*

History of Christianity (New York: Oxford University Press, 2005), 67–69; compare Andrew Cain, "Miracles, Martyrs, and Arians: Gregory of Tours' Sources for His Account of the Vandal Kingdom," *Vigiliae Christianae* 59 (4, 2005): 412–37.

9. Bilinda Straight, *Miracles and Extraordinary Experience in Northern Kenya* (Philadelphia: University of Pennsylvania Press, 2007), 135–37.

10. See *Confessions* 9.4.12 and esp. *City of God* 22.8. This often receives comment: e.g., Nathan M. Herum, "Augustine's Theology of the Miraculous" (MDiv thesis, Beeson Divinity School, 2009).

11. See Barrett-Lennard, *Christian Healing*, 89–135.

12. Tertullian, *To Scapula* 4, in Kelsey, *Healing and Christianity*, 136–37. For further discussion on exorcism in Tertullian, see Woolley, *Exorcism and the Healing of the Sick*, 20–21 (citing *Idolatry* 11; *To His Wife* 2.5; *The Crown* 11; *The Shows* 26; *Prescription against Heretics* 41). Woolley, *Exorcism and the Healing of the Sick*, 21, and Kelsey, *Healing and Christianity*, 150, note that *Acts of S. Eugenia* 10–11 tells how Eugenia would cast out demons; Minucius Felix, *Octavius* 27, also notes Christians casting out demons.

13. Ramsay MacMullen, *Christianizing the Roman Empire* (New Haven: Yale University Press, 1984), 61–62. See also W. H. C. Frend, *The Rise of Christianity* (Philadelphia: Fortress, 1984), 566–67; Frend, "The Place of Miracles in the Conversion of the Ancient World to Christianity," in *Signs, Wonders, Miracles: Representations of Divine Power in the Life of the Church; Papers Read at the 2003 Summer Meeting and the 2004 Winter Meeting of the Ecclesiastical History Society*, ed. Kate Cooper and Jeremy Gregory (Rochester: Boydell & Brewer, for the Ecclesiastical History Society, 2005), 11–21.

14. See, e.g., Kenneth Scott Latourette, *A History of Christianity* (San Francisco: HarperSanFrancisco, 1975), 1:344; Ian Finlay, *Columba* (London: Victor Gollancz, 1979), 173; William Young, "Miracles in Church History," *Churchman* 102 (2, 1988): 102–21 (115).

15. Sean C. Kim, "Reenchanted: Divine Healing in Korean Protestantism," in *Global Pentecostal and Charismatic Healing*, ed. Candy Gunther Brown (Oxford: Oxford University Press, 2011), 267–85 (268–74); Mark Shaw, *Global Awakening: How 20th-Century Revivals Triggered a Christian Revolution* (Downers Grove, IL: IVP Academic, 2010), 44–45. Consult also Young-hoon Lee, *The Holy Spirit Movement in Korea: Its Historical and Theological Development* (Eugene, OR: Wipf & Stock, 2009), 41–47, 111, 113, 134.

16. Christiaan Rudolph De Wet, "Signs and Wonders in Church Growth" (MA thesis, Fuller School of World Mission, Dec. 1981), 92.

17. See, e.g., Hwa Yung, "The Integrity of Mission in the Light of the Gospel: Bearing the Witness of the Spirit," *Mission Studies* 24 (2007): 169–88 (173–75).

18. Compare 2 Kings 13:21. Other incidents took place while the person was alive: Luke 6:19; 8:46; Acts 5:15; 19:12.

19. This is reflected, e.g., in Chrysostom and Augustine. See Ramsay MacMullen, *The Second Church: Popular Christianity A.D. 200–400* (Atlanta: Society of Biblical Literature, 2009), 29, 65, 90, 108. Ambrose claims to be an eyewitness (90). On relics generally, see James Bentley, *Restless Bones: The Story of Relics* (London: Constable & Company, 1985).

20. O. Föller, "Martin Luther on Miracles, Healing, Prophecy, and Tongues," *Studia Historiae Ecclesiasticae* 31 (2, Oct. 2005): 333–51 (342–46).

21. Bentley, *Restless Bones*, 133–34, 138–42.

22. Bentley, *Restless Bones*, 177.

23. Colin Brown, *Miracles and the Critical Mind* (Grand Rapids: Eerdmans, 1984), 39–40; B. Robert Kreiser, *Miracles, Convulsions, and Ecclesiastical Politics in Early Eighteenth-Century Paris* (Princeton: Princeton University Press, 1978), 70–71.

24. See, e.g., Rex Gardner, *Healing Miracles: A Doctor Investigates* (London: Darton, Longman & Todd, 1986), 81–89; Kelsey, *Healing and Christianity*, 234–35; Rosemary Moore, "Late Seventeenth-Century Quakerism and the Miraculous: A New Look at George Fox's 'Book of Miracles,'" in Cooper and Gregory, *Signs, Wonders, Miracles*, 335–44 (335). For earlier accounts, see William Young, "Miracles in Church History," *Churchman* 102 (2, 1988): 102–21 (115–16).

25. Thomas S. Kidd, "The Healing of Mercy Wheeler: Illness and Miracles among Early American Evangelicals," *William and Mary Quarterly* 63 (1, Jan. 2006): 149–70 (149–50, 157, 161). Not

antisupernaturalists, Puritans believed that nothing was by accident and that God was active in the details of daily life and in history.

26. Quoted in Kidd, "Healing of Mercy Wheeler," 162.

27. Kidd, "Healing of Mercy Wheeler," 152, 155–57, 169–70; Thomas S. Kidd, *The Great Awakening: The Roots of Evangelical Christianity in Colonial America* (New Haven: Yale University Press, 2007), 163.

28. Kidd, "Healing of Mercy Wheeler," 161, 163, 170.

29. Kidd, "Healing of Mercy Wheeler," 157–58. They expected God to work in their day *through* nature, though they made exceptions for some *biblical* miracles.

30. See Dieter Ising, *Johann Christoph Blumhardt, Life and Work: A New Biography*, trans. Monty Ledford (Eugene, OR: Cascade Books, 2009).

31. Marcus Dods, "Jesus as Healer," *Biblical World* 15 (1900): 169–77 (174); A. J. Gordon, "The Ministry of Healing," in *Healing: The Three Great Classics on Divine Healing*, ed. Jonathan L. Graf (Camp Hill, PA: Christian Publications, 1992), 119–282 (213–19); Robert Bruce Mullin, *Miracles and the Modern Religious Imagination* (New Haven: Yale University Press, 1996), 89; Ronald A. N. Kydd, *Healing through the Centuries: Models for Understanding* (Peabody, MA: Hendrickson, 1998), 142–53.

32. See Rimi Xhemajli, *The Supernatural and the Circuit Riders: The Rise of Early American Methodism* (Eugene, OR: Pickwick, 2021).

33. For Gordon, Murray, and Simpson, see, conveniently, Graf, *Healing*.

34. For healing in the nineteenth and early twentieth centuries, see also, e.g., James Robinson, *Divine Healing: The Formative Years, 1830–1890* (Eugene, OR: Pickwick, 2011); Robinson, *Divine Healing: The Years of Expansion, 1906–1930* (Eugene, OR: Pickwick, 2014); Paul Gale Chappell, "The Divine Healing Movement in America" (PhD diss., Drew University Graduate School, 1983); Mullin, *Miracles and the Modern Religious Imagination*; Jonathan R. Baer, "Perfectly Empowered Bodies: Divine Healing in Modernizing America" (PhD diss., Yale University, 2002); James Opp, *The Lord for the Body: Religion, Medicine, and Protestant Faith Healing in Canada, 1880–1930* (Montreal: McGill-Queen's University Press, 2005); Kimberly Ervin Alexander, *Pentecostal Healing: Models in Theology and Practice* (Blandford Forum, UK: Deo, 2006); Heather D. Curtis, *Faith in the Great Physician: Suffering and Divine Healing in American Culture, 1860–1900* (Baltimore: Johns Hopkins University Press, 2007). See also the wider, more popular survey in J. D. King, *Regeneration: A Complete History of Healing in the Christian Church*, 3 vols. (Lee's Summit, MO: Christos, 2017). For a brief account, see Tony Cooke, *Miracles and the Supernatural throughout Church History* (Shippensburg, PA: Harrison, 2020).

35. See James Moore Hickson, *Heal the Sick*, 2nd ed. (London: Methuen, 1924), which includes testimonial letters from the various Anglican bishops present at his meetings. Consult discussion in Stuart Mews, "The Revival of Spiritual Healing in the Church of England, 1920–26," in *The Church and Healing: Papers Read at the Twentieth Summer Meeting and the Twenty-First Winter Meeting of the Ecclesiastical History Society*, ed. W. J. Sheils (Oxford: Blackwell, 1982), 299–331.

36. See, e.g., Shang-chieh Song, *The Diaries of John Sung: An Autobiography*, trans. Stephen L. Sheng (Brighton, MI: Luke H. Sheng, Stephen L. Sheng, 1995); Song, *The Diary of John Sung: Extracts from His Journals and Notes*, ed. Levi Sung (Singapore: Armour, 2011); Ka-Tong Lim, "The Life and Ministry of John Sung: Sowing Seeds of Vibrant Christianity in Asian Soil" (PhD diss., Asbury Theological Seminary, 2009); Lim, *The Life and Ministry of John Sung* (Singapore: Armour, 2011).

37. See esp. Jacalyn Duffin, *Medical Miracles: Doctors, Saints, and Healing in the Modern World* (Oxford: Oxford University Press, 2009); and discussion in Shelley McKellar, "Making a Case for Medical Miracles," *Canadian Medical Association Journal* 182 (6, 2010): 595–96, https://doi.org/10.1503/cmaj.091943; Ruth Cranston, *The Miracle of Lourdes: Updated and Expanded Edition by the Medical Bureau of Lourdes* (New York: Image Books, 1988).

38. Will Oursler, *The Healing Power of Faith* (New York: Hawthorn, 1957), 78–82.

39. C. Bernard Ruffin, *Padre Pio: The True Story*, 3rd rev. ed. (Huntington, IN: Our Sunday Visitor, 2018), 371–90. Healings with medical attestation include uterine disease (378), a heart disorder (378–79), severe diabetes insipidus (380–81), and inability to walk (382–83).

40. Quoted in Ruffin, *Padre Pio*, 383 (see also 384).

41. Dan Doriani, personal correspondence, Jan. 1, 2013; June 1, 2016.

Chapter 7 Baby Pics

1. These are merely samples; for another account of a baby miracle, see the testimony of Evangelina Garza from Houston in Dean Merrill, *Miracle Invasion: Amazing True Stories of the Holy Spirit's Gifts at Work Today* (Savage, MN: BroadStreet, 2018), 56–63.

2. Malia Wiederhold, phone interview, Feb. 15, 2020; personal correspondence, Feb. 17, 20, 2020; April 27, 2020; June 20, 2020. I am grateful to Ken Fish for referring me to Malia.

3. Valerie Fillar, personal correspondence, April 27, 2020.

4. Valerie Fillar, personal correspondence, April 27, 2020.

5. Received Feb. 20, 2020.

6. Medical consultant David McCants, personal correspondence, Feb. 20, 2020.

7. Mija, short for "mi hija," affectionately means "my daughter."

8. Peter Edwards, "Miracle at Hemet Hospital: Baby Resurrected," *Message of the Open Bible*, March 2007, 7; Edwards, personal correspondence, May 22, 2020; Manuel Hernandez Jr., "A Father's Inspirational Prayer," *Guideposts*, Dec. 1, 2007, https://www.guideposts.org/faith-and-prayer/prayer-stories/answered-prayers/a-fathers-inspirational-prayer (accessed June 12, 2020); Merrill, *Miracle Invasion*, 147–50. I am grateful to Dean Merrill and Peter Edwards for facilitating these connections.

9. Manuel Hernandez Jr., phone interview, May 22, 2020; personal correspondence, June 11, 15, 2020.

10. Video on flash drive received June 12, 2020. The videos are now available online as "Baby Siara Miracle Testimony," four YouTube videos (see especially part 3), posted by Blue Magic, June 19, 2020: "Part 1," 19:58, https://www.youtube.com/watch?v=f0oAb4jRIec; "Part 2," 18:37, https://www.youtube.com/watch?v=d9WnHFpUopI; "Part 3," 18:37, https://www.youtube.com/watch?v=nW75BuWMhLg; "Part 4," 4:06, https://www.youtube.com/watch?v=Q-vgyYhl_sE.

11. Anthony Wainaina Njuguna, interview, Deerfield, IL, Feb. 17, 2020; plus subsequent correspondence (including May 18, 2020). Anthony and Edwina introduced me to Adiel the evening before our interview (Feb. 16).

12. Elliott Nesch, personal correspondence and medical documentation, Feb. 6, 2020, plus Elliott's earlier report from Dec. 7, 2017.

13. Fred Ankai-Taylor, WhatsApp interview, Aug. 31, 2020.

14. Daniel Fazzina, *Divine Intervention: 50 True Stories of God's Miracles Today* (Lake Mary, FL: Charisma House, 2014), 176–79. Fazzina includes medical documentation for Sandra on p. 222.

15. Jeff Durbin, April 23, 2020. I am grateful to Julio Rodriguez for facilitating my connection with Jeff.

16. In personal correspondence, Aug. 9, 2020, and March 5, 2021, Jeff Durbin provided me with some supporting medical documents, including one from a Phoenix obstetrics clinic, dated Nov. 21, 2019.

17. Jeff Durbin, personal correspondence, Oct. 17, 2020.

18. Medical documentation, Feb. 23, 2020; Kathleen Bratun, interview, Feb. 25, 2020; personal correspondence and further documentation, Feb. 29, 2020.

19. I have drawn both from Korene Sturtz, *A Mother's Prayer and God's Miraculous Answer* (n.p.: Worldwide Publishing Group, 2015), which also includes many photographs and Madison's testimony, and from Christian Broadcasting Network, "Miraculous Cure for Incurable Deadly Disease," *The 700 Club*, YouTube video, March 23, 2018, 6:52, https://www.youtube.com/watch?v=OHN6jJxMrTw (accessed July 14, 2020), which shows some of the medical tests.

20. Syam Jeevan Babu, interview, Jan. 15, 2016, Dehradun, India. Shivraj Mahendra also shared with me an account (interview, Wilmore, KY, April 8, 2016, regarding an experience some six years earlier).

21. See Kelley Nikondeha, *Adopted: The Sacrament of Belonging in a Fractured World* (Grand Rapids: Eerdmans, 2017), 60, 88–92: a baby named Emma tested positive for HIV and was declining from AIDS, but then was healed at just the time needed to be able to bring her to the US for adoption. Although a possible naturalistic explanation is that the first test was a false positive because of the mother's antibodies, the healing corresponded with what the adoptive mother felt God had spoken to her, and the change in test status happened right when it was needed. See also Daniel Kolenda, *Impact Africa: Demonstrations of the Real Power of Jesus Christ Today* (Orlando, FL: Christ for All

Nations, 2015), 134–35: a man reports that he was dying from AIDS, but after prayer and retesting he was HIV-negative (the negative test is shown).

22. See Robert Canton, *Miracles Never Ending* (Stockton, CA: Aimazing Publishing & Marcom, 2015), 238–39. A letter reproduced in Canton's book claims that the writer's daughter-in-law's sonograms and other tests showed that a four-month fetus was dead, but the day after prayer for restoration, just before the scheduled dilation and evacuation, a heartbeat was detected, and five months later the healthy girl was born. Retired Ohio pathologist Narciso Albarracin favorably reviews *Miracles Never Ending*.

Chapter 8 Do Healings Ever Get Captured on Video?

1. Online videos showing the healing abound; for a particularly complete testimony, with scenes from the beginning of the healing and afterward, see "Paralytic Woman Bound to Wheelchair for 22 Years—Healed by Jesus Christ! Caught on Tape!," YouTube video, posted by Jon George, March 19, 2013, 43:34, https://www.youtube.com/watch?v=8qqONI5WMTs.

2. Note, e.g., sight restored at an Ohio meeting related to the Mobile, Alabama, Bay Revival, led by John Kilpatrick and Nathan Morris, in May 2011: "Blind Girl Begins to See @ Bay Revival, Ohio," YouTube video, posted by Bay Revival, May 24, 2011, 3:30, https://www.youtube.com /watch?v=MaSd9Me6ZO8 (accessed Jan. 20, 2020).

3. This is common in healings, including those that are otherwise inexplicable. See, e.g., Maura Poston Zagrans, *Miracles Every Day: The Story of One Physician's Inspiring Faith and the Healing Power of Prayer* (New York: Doubleday, 2010), 124; Caryle Hirschberg and Marc Ian Barasch, *Remarkable Recovery: What Extraordinary Healings Tell Us about Getting Well and Staying Well* (New York: Riverhead, 1995), 113–15. Compare also Ruth Cranston, *The Miracle of Lourdes: Updated and Expanded Edition by the Medical Bureau of Lourdes* (New York: Image Books, 1988), 136.

4. Bob Tice, interview, Rochester, NY, June 21, 2016; personal correspondence, June 24, 2016; Feb. 14, 2020; Aug. 5, 2020.

5. Tommy Reid, phone conversations and interviews, July 8–9, 2016; Aug. 29, 2016; further phone interview, Feb. 27, 2020.

6. Gregory Helsinki, conversation, July 22, 2016; personal correspondence, July 31, 2016.

7. Marguerita Cooley, conversation, Nov. 10, 2017.

8. Enid Mojica-McGinnis, phone interview, Aug. 5, 2020.

9. See, e.g., videos of Robby Dawkins and many of Todd White: "Todd White—God Restores Eyes at a Basketball Game (Anyone Can Represent Well)," *Lifestyle Christianity*, YouTube video, May 19, 2017, 11:15, https://www.youtube.com/watch?v=YzqaZHfak0k; "Todd White—Radical Healing of Ears in Jesus' Name," *Lifestyle Christianity*, YouTube video, June 3, 2016, 6:36, https:// www.youtube.com/watch?v=VDKLYFYc40Q; "Todd White—Poor Vision Restored While Touring at Capernaum," *Lifestyle Christianity*, YouTube video, April 16, 2018, 3:29, https://www.youtube.com /watch?v=x8QTPbl4f44. See also Pete Cabrera Jr., "Get Up and Walk Out of That Wheel Chair in Jesus Name," Royal Family International School of Ministry, School of Identity and Lifestyle, YouTube video, May 17, 2016, 4:14, https://www.youtube.com/watch?v=2e1woYu1HbU. Even more numerous than credible video healings are credible video testimonies, including testimonies about healings of long-term blindness, a child's resuscitation through prayer after paramedics declared her dead, and healings of some other health problems. See, e.g., "Eyewitness to Miracles," Global Awakening, accessed June 10, 2020, https://globalawakening.com/eyewitnesstomiracles. For testimony about the healing of deafness and inability to walk, see Damian Stayne and Cor et Lumen Christi Community, "Healing Miracles—Hearing Aids, Walking Frame and Wheelchair," YouTube video, Nov. 17, 2016, 2:11, https://www.youtube.com/watch?v=ijKDln0zEHE (accessed July 21, 2020).

10. Here is just a single example: the healing of student Jonathan Pollard. I watched the video and followed up with personal correspondence, May 15–16, 19–20, 22, 2010; July 16, 22, 2010. I also received some medical documentation. The incident was attested also by my and my wife's friend Lauren Mason, who witnessed it (Lauren Mason, personal correspondence, May 3, 5–6, 8, 2010; interview, June 3, 2010).

Chapter 9 Medically Attested Catholic Cures

1. See Jacalyn Duffin, *Medical Miracles: Doctors, Saints, and Healing in the Modern World* (Oxford: Oxford University Press, 2009), 7.

2. Nor do I share all the theology associated with all apparitions (e.g., in Albert E. Graham, *Compendium of the Miraculous* [Charlotte: TAN Books, 2013], 43–64). But Catholics, like Protestants, do affirm that God's revelation of himself in Jesus is the final public revelation before Jesus's return, albeit a revelation subject to development in clarity (Graham, *Compendium*, 13–14; cf. Peter Toon, *The Development of Doctrine in the Church* [Grand Rapids: Eerdmans, 1979; Eugene, OR: Wipf & Stock, 2017], 1–16), and that private revelation, while helpful, differs from public revelation in Scripture (Michael O'Neill, *Exploring the Miraculous* [Huntington, IN: Our Sunday Visitor, 2015], 21; compare 31).

3. Robert Bruce Mullin, *Miracles and the Modern Religious Imagination* (New Haven: Yale University Press, 1996), 100; compare 181, 206, 219.

4. Benedict Heron, *Channels of Healing Prayer* (Notre Dame, IN: Ave Maria, 1992), 142–43.

5. Ruth Cranston, *The Miracle of Lourdes: Updated and Expanded Edition by the Medical Bureau of Lourdes* (New York: Image Books, 1988). Compare the briefer treatment in Christopher J. Wilson, "Modern Miracles as the Foundation for a Renewal Apologetic" (PhD diss., Regent University School of Divinity, 2017), 141–59. In general, openness to miracles at Lourdes correlates positively with religious sentiment and cannot be correlated with psychological deficits (Anne Schienle et al., "Belief in the Miracles of Lourdes: A Voxel-Based Morphometry Study," *Brain and Behavior* 10 [1, 2020]: e01481, https://doi.org/10.1002/brb3.1481).

6. See Duffin, *Medical Miracles*, esp. 8, 113–43.

7. Duffin, *Medical Miracles*, 142–43.

8. Mullin, *Miracles and the Modern Religious Imagination*, 117.

9. Kenneth L. Woodward, *The Book of Miracles: The Meaning of the Miracle Stories in Christianity, Judaism, Buddhism, Hinduism, and Islam* (New York: Simon & Schuster, 2000), 370; Duffin, *Medical Miracles*, 139.

10. Heron, *Channels of Healing Prayer*, 123–24.

11. Heron, *Channels of Healing Prayer*, 142. Testimonies from other Catholic healing ministries today, most not traced elsewhere in this book, include "Testimonies," Cor et Lumen Christi Community, accessed March 2, 2021, http://www.coretlumenchristi.org/testimonies.php; "Healing Testimonies," Miracle Healing Ministry, accessed March 2, 2021, http://www.miracle-healing-ministry.org/healings.html; "New Testimonies," Robert Canton Ministries, accessed March 2, 2021, http://www.robertcantonministries.org/testimonies.html.

12. Victor Agbeibor, phone interview, Aug. 30, 2020.

13. Travis Jon Dichoso, "Lourdes: A Uniquely Catholic Approach to Medicine," *The Linacre Quarterly* 82 (1, 2015): 8–12, https://doi.org/10.1179/2050854914Y.0000000034. Dichoso highlights the positive spiritual experience there.

14. Terence L. Nichols, "Miracles in Science and Theology," *Zygon* 37 (3, 2002): 707–8. See also Cranston, *Miracle of Lourdes*, 39. Many of the cures leave "some vestige to show that the original illness existed, e.g., scars or a bone in a slightly different position" (Cranston, *Miracle of Lourdes*, 119). Compare Gen. 32:25, 31–32; Lev. 13:23, 28. Note also another case (that of Pierre De Rudder) in which scarring marked the injury site but new, whiter bone tissue had connected what had been considered a medically incurable fracture (Will Oursler, *The Healing Power of Faith* [New York: Hawthorn, 1957], 71, noting on 72 that twenty-eight physicians were involved in certifying this cure). In one account, however, a physician admits that he would refuse to accept a cure as miraculous if he found a scar—and he found none (Duffin, *Medical Miracles*, 137).

15. Jim Garner, "Spontaneous Regressions: Scientific Documentation as a Basis for the Declaration of Miracles," *Canadian Medical Association Journal* 111 (Dec. 7, 1974): 1254–63 (1259). Nearly half the confirmed cures until 1948 involved tuberculosis, partly because this was a common and then not really curable disease that drew many pilgrims to Lourdes (Cranston, *Miracle of Lourdes*, 281). Cases of healed tuberculosis have also been verified at Lourdes in more recent times (284–85, 292–93, 300–302).

16. Cranston, *Miracle of Lourdes*, 180–84 (including the report of an astonished agnostic physician, 182–83). The case of Jeanne Fretel (209–16, 269), cured Oct. 8, 1948, is also noteworthy.

17. This cure was recognized as a miracle in 1949 (Patrick Marnham, *Lourdes: A Modern Pilgrimage* [New York: Coward, McCann & Geoghegan, 1981], 189). See also Cranston, *Miracle of Lourdes*, 233–39, which includes Cranston's interviews with Pascal and his family.

18. D. J. West, *Eleven Lourdes Miracles* (London: Gerald Duckworth, 1957), 6.

19. Cranston, *Miracle of Lourdes*, 236–37.

20. Cranston, *Miracle of Lourdes*, 42–44, 227–33.

21. Marnham, *Lourdes*, 190 (for more on Bigot, see 192–94; Cranston, *Miracle of Lourdes*, 293–95). Bigot happens to have been captured on film just before and after her cure (Cranston, *Miracle of Lourdes*, 295).

22. Marnham, *Lourdes*, 197; Cranston, *Miracle of Lourdes*, 307–8.

23. Marnham, *Lourdes*, 197–98.

24. Cranston, *Miracle of Lourdes*, 295–96.

25. See, e.g., F. A. Gasquet, "The Catholic Church and the Lourdes Cures," *British Medical Journal* 2 (Aug. 20, 1910): 465–67 (466), https://doi.org/10.1136/bmj.2.2590.465. Gasquet notes that the cures were normally required to be virtually instantaneous.

26. Heron, *Channels of Healing Prayer*, 142–43. Only a minority of cures pilgrims believe they have experienced are even reported to the Medical Bureau (see Bernard François, Esther M. Sternberg, and Elizabeth Fee, "The Lourdes Medical Cures Revisited," *Journal of the History of Medicine and Allied Sciences* 69 [1, Jan. 2014]: 135–62 [accessed at https://www.ncbi.nlm.nih.gov/pmc/articles/PMC3854941/, June 11, 2020], citing Ruth Harris, *Lourdes: Body and Spirit in the Secular Age* [New York: Penguin, 1999]; and personal communications with Bernard François).

27. Allen Spraggett, *Kathryn Kuhlman: The Woman Who Believes in Miracles* (Cleveland: World, 1970), 31–32.

28. Spraggett, *Kathryn Kuhlman*, 32 (compare also Kuhlman's meetings, with unbelievers healed on 165 and infants healed on 171). Healings include those who denied the supernatural (until the cure) and also Muslims and Jews at an extension site (Garner, "Spontaneous Regressions," 1257).

29. François, Sternberg, and Fee, "Lourdes Medical Cures Revisited." The earlier cures appear in *Annales de Notre-Dame de Lourdes* (1868–1944); those from the 1920s forward exclude potentially functional disorders, though these had been a minority to begin with. Better records were kept after 1928, and stricter methods of verification were used after 1947. Some recent cures announced in *Bulletin du Bureau des Constatations Medicales de Lourdes* include cures of Hodgkin's disease, multiple sclerosis, and sciatica (François, Sternberg, and Fee, "Lourdes Medical Cures Revisited"). Some demands for verification became almost impossibly strict: Cardinal Lambertini's canons, originally established in the eighteenth century, are too narrow to accept many certified cures today, not least because the dismissal of cases that had received curative treatment excludes nearly anyone today who also has medical documentation of a condition.

30. Oursler, *Healing Power of Faith*, 72; Nichols, "Miracles in Science and Theology," 706.

31. Nichols, "Miracles in Science and Theology," 706.

32. Nichols, "Miracles in Science and Theology," 707; Cranston, *Miracle of Lourdes*, 35.

33. Carrel's publications and a letter cited in the conclusion of François, Sternberg, and Fee, "Lourdes Medical Cures Revisited."

34. Malcolm L. Diamond, "Miracles," *Religious Studies* 9 (3, 1973): 307–24 (311–12).

35. Diamond, "Miracles," 313.

36. Diamond, "Miracles," 312. For the cures of children at Lourdes, see Cranston, *Miracle of Lourdes*, 227–46.

37. Diamond, "Miracles," 314–15, 323.

38. God may work through natural causes even in highly extraordinary cases, but attributing the most extraordinary cases exclusively to natural factors autonomous from guiding intelligence seems analogous to explaining a paragraph in this book as a random collection of letters.

Chapter 10 A Few Vignettes of Brain Recovery

1. Dan Van Veen, "From Tragic Death to Miraculous Life," Assemblies of God, May 5, 2020, https://news.ag.org/en/Features/From-Tragic-Death-to-Miraculous-Life (accessed May 19, 2020).

2. Dina Cafiso, personal correspondence, March 4, 12, 17, 2020; Maria Cafiso, personal correspondence, March 16, 2020, with notes from her journal from the time of the incident; medical documentation (June 11, 2014, discharge summary, which includes the ten-minute, full cardiac arrest). Dina Cafiso was referred to me by her professor, Bryan Darrell.

3. The CBN interview includes Dr. Diez and others: Christian Broadcasting Network, "Natalie's Easter Miracle," *The 700 Club*, YouTube video, April 21, 2011, 4:12, https://www.youtube.com/watch?v=dohEP8L35sY (accessed July 15, 2020).

4. Valerie Paters and Cheryl Schuelke, with Kay Farish, *Heaven Is a Breath Away: An Unexpected Journey to Heaven and Back* (New York: Morgan James, 2015). See also a summary at Christian Broadcasting Network, "Woman Comes Back to Life with a Message," *The 700 Club*, YouTube video, April 17, 2018, 7:24, https://www.youtube.com/watch?v=zOjxlv_jj_E.

5. A. J. Atkinson, "The Miracle Continues: Chillicothe's Reissig Overcomes Adversity to Play Sport," *Chillicothe Gazette*, Sept. 19, 2013, 1–2B (sports section).

6. Malachi Reissig's name also appears online on Chillicothe honor roll records.

Chapter 11 Back from Virtual Brain Death

1. CNN, "Real-Life Miracles and Unexplained Events," *Larry King Live*, June 11, 2002, transcript at http://transcripts.cnn.com/TRANSCRIPTS/0206/11/lkl.00.html (accessed April 10, 2020).

2. Regina Pullum, phone interview, May 20, 2020; Wayne Pullum, phone interview, May 20, 2020; Dallas Pullum, phone interview, May 22, 2020.

3. The images of the scans shown on *It's a Miracle* (now available on DVD) are the actual images from the hospital. Dallas told me that when *It's a Miracle* researched his case, it was his own first time seeing the scans and hearing the doctor discuss them. Regarding this case, Dr. David McCants advised me (Aug. 9, 2020) that brain death is considered medically and legally indistinguishable from death from cardiac arrest. In *Miracles* (2011), 1:354–55, I noted another remarkable multiply attested brain recovery, that of Baptist minister Margarita Campos in Chile; my student Alberto Bonilla-Giovanetti has subsequently attested her continued health (personal correspondence, Sept. 19, 24, 2018).

Chapter 12 More Medically Attested Twentieth-Century Cures

1. John White, "Young Lady, Old Hag," in *Power Encounters among Christians in the Western World*, ed. Kevin Springer (San Francisco: Harper & Row, 1988), 69–86 (72–73). The cured woman recounts the same story in Loretta White, "Laying Aside Regrets," in Springer, *Power Encounters*, 175–85 (177).

2. Antarctica lacks permanent residents; to my knowledge, the opinion of its few yearlong residents on this topic has not been surveyed.

3. Micael Grenholm, *Dokumenterade Mirakler: Vetenskap, Helande och Guds Existens* (Örebro, Sweden: Sjöbergs, 2019), 121–40. I follow Grenholm's accounts close to word for word at many points, except in English.

4. Grenholm, *Dokumenterade Mirakler*, 135–37.

5. In Grenholm, *Dokumenterade Mirakler*, this document is reproduced in figure 7.3.

6. Grenholm, *Dokumenterade Mirakler*, note 46; personal correspondence, May 19, 2020. Pär-Ola and his wife joined in the book release and appear in the related video: Micael Grenholm, "Bokrelease för Dokumenterade Mirakler," YouTube video, May 31, 2019, 1:05:14, https://www.youtube.com/watch?v=T8Hzdi4q0iI, esp. 16:20–30:10.

7. Sofi Berggren and Ingela Ronquist, "Gudomligt Helande" (graduate project work in medicine, Sahlgrenska akademin, supervised by Johan Holmdahl och Lennart Thörn, 2003), treated in Grenholm, *Dokumenterade Mirakler*, 126–28.

8. The book's back cover identifies Gardner as "a Fellow of the Royal College of Obstetricians and Gynaecologists, and of the Association of Surgeons in East Africa. He served as Examiner to the University of Newcastle-upon-Tyne, as Vice-President of the North of England Obstetric and Gynaecological Society, and as President of the Newcastle and Northern Counties Medical Society." See Rex Gardner, *Healing Miracles: A Doctor Investigates* (London: Darton, Longman & Todd, 1986).

9. Gardner, *Healing Miracles*, 77 (noting many eyewitnesses). The story is also reported in Rex Gardner, "Miracles of Healing in Anglo-Celtic Northumbria as Recorded by the Venerable Bede and His Contemporaries: A Reappraisal in the Light of Twentieth-Century Experience," *British Medical Journal* 287 (Dec. 24–31, 1983): 1927–33 (1931).

10. Gardner, *Healing Miracles*, 104–6 (partly through prayer, partly at Lourdes).

11. Gardner, *Healing Miracles*, 20–21; Gardner, "Miracles of Healing," 1929.

12. Gardner, "Miracles of Healing," 1932.

13. Gardner, *Healing Miracles*, 165.

14. H. Richard Casdorph, *The Miracles: A Medical Doctor Says Yes to Miracles!* (Plainfield, NJ: Logos, 1976), 25–33; Casdorph, *Real Miracles: Indisputable Evidence That God Heals* (Gainesville, FL: Bridge-Logos, 2003), 21–32.

15. Casdorph, *Miracles*, 37–45; Casdorph, *Real Miracles*, 34–47.

16. Casdorph, *Miracles*, 49–57; Casdorph, *Real Miracles*, 44–61.

17. Casdorph, *Miracles*, 61–72; Casdorph, *Real Miracles*, 63–80.

18. Casdorph, *Miracles*, 77–86; Casdorph, *Real Miracles*, 83–97.

19. Casdorph, *Miracles*, 91–100; Casdorph, *Real Miracles*, 98–113.

20. Casdorph, *Miracles*, 105–16; Casdorph, *Real Miracles*, 115–33.

21. Casdorph, *Miracles*, 121–32; Casdorph, *Real Miracles*, 134–52.

22. Casdorph, *Miracles*, 137–43; Casdorph, *Real Miracles*, 154–64.

23. Casdorph, *Miracles*, 147–57; Casdorph, *Real Miracles*, 165–80. See also Delores Winder with Bill Keith, *Surprised by Healing* (Shippensburg, PA: Destiny Image, 2009). For video testimony, see "The Greatest Healing-Miracle of the 20th Century," YouTube video, posted by Ian Francis, March 16, 2018, 24:17, https://www.youtube.com/watch?v=mz_xkcxbEtQ (accessed Aug. 7, 2020).

24. They are named in Casdorph, *Miracles*, 9–10; Casdorph, *Real Miracles*, 10–11.

25. Trousdale, who later passed in 1990, reportedly built more than twenty-five thousand homes in Southern California.

26. Casdorph, *Real Miracles*, 171.

27. On Owellen and Kuhlman, see also Eleanor Blau, "Evangelist Draws the Sick and Anguished," *New York Times*, Oct. 20, 1972, 45; Gary Settle, "Kathryn Kuhlman, Evangelist and Faith Healer, Dies in Tulsa," *New York Times*, Feb. 22, 1976, 48.

28. Jamie Buckingham, *Daughter of Destiny: Kathryn Kuhlman . . . Her Story* (Plainfield, NJ: Logos, 1976), 185. Allen Spraggett (*Kathryn Kuhlman: The Woman Who Believes in Miracles* [Cleveland: World, 1970], 120) interviewed Dr. Titus, who attested that he had personally witnessed this instant healing.

29. Spraggett, *Kathryn Kuhlman*, 59–60, 64, 111–12.

30. Noted in Buckingham, *Daughter of Destiny*, 185.

31. Buckingham, *Daughter of Destiny*, 187; see also Spraggett, *Kathryn Kuhlman*, 6–7.

32. Buckingham, *Daughter of Destiny*, 185. Dr. Owellen's testimony appears also in Candy Gunther Brown, "Healing Words: Narratives of Spiritual Healing and Kathryn Kuhlman's Uses of Print Culture, 1947–1976," in *Religion and the Culture of Print in Modern America*, ed. Charles L. Cohen and Paul S. Boyer (Madison: University of Wisconsin Press, 2008), 271–97 (278).

33. Buckingham, *Daughter of Destiny*, 187–88; compare Spraggett, *Kathryn Kuhlman*, 12–13.

34. Buckingham, *Daughter of Destiny*, 185–87 (quoting the doctor's letter).

35. Buckingham, *Daughter of Destiny*, 188–89; compare Spraggett, *Kathryn Kuhlman*, 58–61.

36. Russ Llewellyn, "Religious and Spiritual Miracle Events in Real-Life Experience," in *Religious and Spiritual Events*, vol. 1 of *Miracles: God, Science, and Psychology in the Paranormal*, ed. J. Harold Ellens (Westport, CT: Praeger, 2008), 241–63 (255), citing his interview with Dr. Burgos.

Chapter 13 Some Medically Attested Twenty-First-Century Cures

1. Clarissa Romez, David Zaritzky, and Joshua W. Brown, "Case Report of Gastroparesis Healing: 16 Years of a Chronic Syndrome Resolved after Proximal Intercessory Prayer," *Complementary Therapies in Medicine* 43 (2019): 289–94. Except where noted otherwise, I am closely following the report in the journal.

2. The exception is what is thought to be postviral gastroparesis, but it normally resolves within two years, in stark contrast to this case, which was the more common form of gastroparesis.

3. Romez, Zaritzky, and Brown, "Case Report," 293.

4. Phone interview, April 27, 2020.

5. Romez, Zaritzky, and Brown, "Case Report."

6. Phone interview, April 27, 2020. Chris's story also appears in Bruce Van Natta, *A Miraculous Life: True Stories of Supernatural Encounters with God* (Lake Mary, FL: Charisma House, 2013), 177–79.

7. Phone interview, May 30, 2010; Chauncey W. Crandall IV, *Raising the Dead: A Doctor Encounters the Miraculous* (New York: FaithWords, 2010), 50–52.

8. Phone interview, May 30, 2010.

9. Crandall, *Raising the Dead*, 39, 152–53.

10. Dr. Crandall provided details in a phone interview, May 30, 2010.

11. Crandall, *Raising the Dead*, 176–78, 181–82.

12. Phone interview, May 28, 2010.

13. Phone interview, May 28, 2010. The account also appears in Crandall, *Raising the Dead*, 171.

14. Phone interview, May 30, 2010. In our May 28 interview, Dr. Crandall pointed out that obvious miracles do not happen every day, but they happen often enough.

15. Phone interview, May 30, 2010. At the time of our interview, media clips of interviews with Dr. Crandall's patients who experienced cures, including Jeff Markin, were still available online; various other video accounts since then may still be accessed by googling Jeff Markin and Chauncey Crandall together.

16. Carl Cocherell, phone interview, May 2, 2009. In this interview Cocherell also noted other healings he has received. Because two locations were involved, it took some time to obtain the medical documentation for his healed ankle, which reached me on June 17, 2009. John Piippo also supports Cocherell's account (personal correspondence, June 15, 2009; June 18, 2009).

17. For ancient analogies for the hyperbole, see Craig S. Keener, *The Gospel of John: A Commentary* (Grand Rapids: Baker Academic, 2003), 2:1241–42.

18. Interviewing Michael O'Neill, Dr. Oz notes cures in religious contexts that lack natural explanations ("Is God behind Miraculous Cures That Have No Earthly Explanation?," Dr. Oz website, accessed July 15, 2020, https://www.doctoroz.com/episode/god-behind-miraculous-cures-have-no-earthly-explanation).

19. Debra Gussman, "The Impossible Pregnancy," in *Miracles We Have Seen: America's Leading Physicians Share Stories They Can't Forget*, ed. Harley A. Rotbart (Deerfield Beach, FL: Health Communications, 2016), 265–67.

20. Russ Llewellyn, "Religious and Spiritual Miracle Events in Real-Life Experience," in *Religious and Spiritual Events*, vol. 1 of *Miracles: God, Science, and Psychology in the Paranormal*, ed. J. Harold Ellens (Westport, CT: Praeger, 2008), 255, citing his interview with her.

21. Again, Llewellyn, "Religious and Spiritual Miracle Events," 255, citing his interviews with her. Llewellyn also notes a "miraculous" outcome reported by Dr. John T. Dearborn (259), and his own healing (260).

22. Interview, Irving, TX, Oct. 29, 2009.

23. Mirtha Venero Boza, interview, Santiago de Cuba, Aug. 6, 2010.

24. Tonye Briggs, phone interviews, Dec. 14, 16, 2009.

25. Documentation from June 2005 through Feb. 2009, in my possession, courtesy of Dr. David Zaritzky (sent in May 2009). Other cases of salivary restoration appear in Keener, *Miracles* (2011), 1:282, 2:716, though it should be observed that salivary glands can recover gradually after radiation treatment.

26. William P. Wilson, "How Religious or Spiritual Miracle Events Happen Today," in Ellens, *Religious and Spiritual Events*, 264–79 (269–70) (reporting that X-ray evidence confirmed the healing at this stage). His friend reported that the non-Christian attending physician admitted that it was a miracle.

27. Wilson, "How Religious or Spiritual Miracle Events Happen Today," 270–73.

28. William Standish Reed, *Surgery of the Soul* (Old Tappan, NJ: Revell, 1969; Spire, 1973), 35, 43–48, 52–53.

29. Christopher Woodard, *A Doctor's Faith Holds Fast* (London: Max Parrish, 1955), esp. some cases in 63–99 passim.

30. Ronda Wells, personal correspondence, May 28–29, 2019. Persistent fetal circulation can resolve quickly, but this child "had not reverted after days on the ventilator and the prognosis was grim"; now she "turned pink and opened her eyes" and the nurses rapidly reduced the oxygen (Wells, personal correspondence, Jan. 30, 2020).

31. Dave Walker, *God in the ICU: The Inspirational Biography of a Praying Doctor* (Sun Valley, South Africa: Tricycle, 2011), 63–66.

32. David Kimberlin, "Whatever the Outcome, It Will Be Okay," in Rotbart, *Miracles We Have Seen*, 80–81.

33. Ginney MacPherson, FaceTime interview, Aug. 26, 2020. MacPherson's husband, Peter, an Anglican minister in Melbourne, also contributed to the interview. Ginney MacPherson notes the broader context of infertility healings after Ken Fish prays.

34. Kathleen Farrell, "The Man All Dressed in White," in Rotbart, *Miracles We Have Seen*, 169–70.

35. Richard Westcott, "A Vacation Like No Other," in Rotbart, *Miracles We Have Seen*, 57–60, revisiting his earlier report in "Can Miracles Happen?," *British Medical Journal* 325 (7363, Sept. 7, 2002): 553, https://doi.org/10.1136/bmj.325.7363.553. For one well-informed, current Eastern Orthodox approach to Jesus's miracles, see Metropolitan Hilarion Alfeyev, *The Miracles of Jesus*, vol. 3 of *Jesus Christ: His Life and Teaching* (Yonkers, NY: St. Vladimir's Seminary Press, 2020).

36. Westcott, "Vacation Like No Other," 59.

Chapter 14 Cancer Cures

1. ELCA pastor Mark Mathews, who notes cancer remissions—including stage 4 remissions—after he has prayed, also observes how often this explanation is offered after a healing by those who do not feel free to mention potentially divine sources (personal correspondence, Jan. 1, 2021).

2. For the healing of untreatable metastatic cancer, sometimes directly following a revelatory word, see, e.g., Robert Canton, *Miracles Never Ending* (Stockton, CA: Aimazing Publishing & Marcom, 2015), 85–88, 115–17; compare 120–21, 125.

3. The complete medical documentation in my possession makes it clear that the existing, serious, so-far-untreated cancer disappeared after being initially biopsied, but because a biopsy often removes the entirety of a localized tumor, I did not consider the account sufficiently naturally "inexplicable" to elaborate it here.

4. See Mirko D. Grmek, *Diseases in the Ancient Greek World*, trans. Mireille Muellner and Leonard Muellner (Baltimore: Johns Hopkins University Press, 1989), 6.

5. Although not all would agree, Grmek (*Diseases in the Ancient Greek World*, 71–72) even goes so far as to suggest that in the ancient world cancer accounted for far "less than 1 case for every 1,000" deaths, as opposed to more than 20 percent of deaths in the modern West (compare pp. 151, 350). Whether the varied incidence has more to do with less chemical pollution in the ancient world, generally shorter life spans, or other factors remains debated. Vivian Nutton (*Ancient Medicine*, 2nd ed. [New York: Routledge, 2013], 23) also considers it rare, except for breast cancer.

6. Letters to Edith Myerscough, Aug. 17, 1944; one mentioned in Cyril Yesson's letter to Edith Myerscough, Sept. 4, 1944. David Emmett provided me with all the information cited here, including access to W. F. P. Burton, *Signs Following* (Luton, UK: Assemblies of God Publishing House, 1949), from which I have extracted quotations. For Burton generally, see now David Emmett, *W. F. P. Burton (1886–1971): A Pentecostal Pioneer's Missional Vision for Congo* (Leiden: Brill, 2021).

7. *Redemption Tidings* 21 (4, Feb. 16, 1945): 5.

8. *Redemption Tidings* 21 (13, June 22, 1945): 7.

9. *Congo Evangelistic Mission Report* 112 (May 1945): 896.

10. *Redemption Tidings* 21 (20, Sept. 28, 1945): 6; *Congo Evangelistic Mission Report* 114 (Sept. 1945): 912.

11. Before knowing Burton's own story, I reported some accounts that Burton shared about others in my *Miracles* (2011), 1:329, 418, 551.

12. H. Richard Casdorph, *The Miracles: A Medical Doctor Says Yes to Miracles!* (Plainfield, NJ: Logos, 1976), 25–33; Casdorph, *Real Miracles: Indisputable Evidence That God Heals* (Gainesville, FL: Bridge-Logos, 2003), 21–32. For the video testimony, see "Lisa Larios's Testimony," originally from *I Believe in Miracles*, vol. 13, *Testimonies*, Kathryn Kuhlman Foundation (2002), available as a

YouTube video, March 1, 2015, 22:37, https://www.youtube.com/watch?v=KofEHt_xy_U (accessed Jan. 29, 2020). For the testimony of Dr. Casdorph himself, see "July 16th Miracle via Kathryn Kuhlman: 'Run Lisa, Run!!,'" YouTube video, posted by Ian Francis, July 17, 2017, 6:56, https://www.youtube.com/watch?v=s-BnQza6ONQ (accessed Aug. 7, 2020).

13. Casdorph, *Real Miracles*, 17.

14. Casdorph, *Real Miracles*, 18–20.

15. Compare also a reported case of X-rays attesting bone restoration, along with healing of osteosarcoma, in C. Bernard Ruffin, *Padre Pio: The True Story*, 3rd rev. ed. (Huntington, IN: Our Sunday Visitor, 2018), 454–55.

16. James L. Garlow and Keith Wall, *Real Life, Real Miracles: True Stories That Will Help You Believe* (Minneapolis: Bethany House, 2012), 206–8; compare dramatically rapid bone healing on 238.

17. Garlow and Wall, *Real Life, Real Miracles*, 243–45.

18. Micael Grenholm, whom I follow very closely here but in translated form, copies relevant medical documentation in figures 7.2a, 7.2b, and 7.2c in *Dokumenterade Mirakler: Vetenskap, Helande och Guds Existens* (Örebro, Sweden: Sjöbergs, 2019). Further explanation came from personal correspondence with Grenholm, Jan. 29, 2020. For another report of terminal pancreatic cancer being healed, see Randy Clark, *Eyewitness to Miracles: Watching the Gospel Come to Life* (Nashville: Nelson, 2018), 30–32; the man healed, Tony Ellis, eventually began praying for the sick himself.

19. Harold J. Sala, *What You Need to Know about Healing: A Physical and Spiritual Guide* (Nashville: B&H, 2013), 106–8, which includes personal correspondence with Dr. Cope, Feb. 14, 2011, as well as correspondence with John Margosian's family. Sala notes other dramatic cancer healings, e.g., on pp. 149–50 (and various dramatic healings on 35–38, 50, 129–33, 147–48), noting also one reported in Charles Swindoll, *Flying Closer to the Flame* (Dallas: Word, 1993), 198–200. From a then-forthcoming book with Maxie Dunnam (*Healing Prayer Is God's Idea* [Amazon, 2021]), David Chotka also shared with me from his pastoral experience a healing from terminal, metastasized pancreatic cancer.

20. Brian Wills, *10 Hours to Live: A True Story of Healing and Supernatural Living* (New Kensington, PA: Whitaker House, 2010), 19. A program for *The 700 Club* shows some medical documentation and interviews some of the medical doctors familiar with Wills's case: "Brian Wills' Testimony of Healing on *The 700 Club*," YouTube video, posted by Healing4Nations, Nov. 16, 2012, 6:46, https://www.youtube.com/watch?v=hIsndQ_aglk (accessed May 12, 2020).

21. Wills, *10 Hours to Live*, 22.

22. Wills, *10 Hours to Live*, 27.

23. Daniel Fazzina, *Divine Intervention: 50 True Stories of God's Miracles Today* (Lake Mary, FL: Charisma House, 2014), 150–53. A 2007 medical report (provided on p. 221 of Fazzina), partly based on the doctor's interview of John, also reports John's left frontal craniotomy to remove the pituitary tumor and its absence in the more recent MRI.

24. Garlow and Wall, *Real Life, Real Miracles*, 176–82.

25. Personal conversation, May 22, 2010; follow-up personal correspondence, May 22, 26, 2010; June 7, 9, 2010; June 26, 2020. I have withheld Carol's surname at her request. Although Carol's recovery was not instantaneous and the biopsy was inconclusive about whether the tumor was malignant, even benign brain tumors "typically do not disappear" (Dr. Nicole Matthews, personal correspondence, May 25, 2010).

26. Candy Gunther Brown, *Testing Prayer: Science and Healing* (Cambridge, MA: Harvard University Press, 2012), 254–55, shares his story (albeit under a pseudonym, out of concern for discrimination at the time).

27. Fred Ankai-Taylor, WhatsApp interview, Aug. 31, 2020. Pastor Ankai-Taylor was referred to me by a valued mutual friend, Victor Agbeibor, also a medical doctor.

28. Mark J. Mathews, personal correspondence, Jan. 1, 2, 5, 6, 2021; Carol Halme, personal correspondence, March 3, 5, 2021. This ELCA pastor has been involved in "about three dozen healing events," along with some other anomalies too unusual for me to share (Mark Mathews, personal correspondence, March 8, 2021).

29. Patrick Marnham, *Lourdes: A Modern Pilgrimage* (New York: Coward, McCann & Geoghegan, 1981), 191; see also Ruth Cranston, *The Miracle of Lourdes: Updated and Expanded Edition by the Medical Bureau of Lourdes* (New York: Image Books, 1988), 289–90.

30. Barbara A. Neilan, "The Miraculous Cure of a Sarcoma of the Pelvis: Cure of Vittorio Micheli at Lourdes," *Linacre Quarterly* 80 (3, 2003): 277–81 (277–78). I owe this reference to Dr. Joseph Bergeron. Neilan notes also a report of the case in *Journal of Orthopedic Surgery*.

31. Marnham, *Lourdes*, 195–96 (Micheli's full dossier appears on 198–216).

32. Neilan, "Miraculous Cure," 279.

33. Jim Garner, "Spontaneous Regressions: Scientific Documentation as a Basis for the Declaration of Miracles," *Canadian Medical Association Journal* 111 (Dec. 7, 1974): 1259. See also Neilan, "Miraculous Cure," 280; compare Cranston, *Miracle of Lourdes*, 306.

34. S. J. Dowling, "Lourdes Cures and Their Medical Assessment," *Journal of the Royal Society of Medicine* 77 (8, 1984): 634–38, https://doi.org/10.1177/014107688407700803; Cranston, *Miracle of Lourdes*, 311.

35. Cranston, *Miracle of Lourdes*, 127–29.

36. Allen Spraggett, *Kathryn Kuhlman: The Woman Who Believes in Miracles* (Cleveland: World, 1970), 29–30. For a reported healing of terminal throat cancer, see Ruffin, *Padre Pio*, 377.

37. J. Harold Ellens, "Biblical Miracles and Psychological Process: Jesus as Psychotherapist," in *Religious and Spiritual Events*, vol. 1 of *Miracles: God, Science, and Psychology in the Paranormal*, ed. J. Harold Ellens (Westport, CT: Praeger, 2008), 1–14 (11); for higher rates, compare Patrick McNamara and Reka Szent-Imrey, "What We Can Learn from Miraculous Healings and Cures," in Ellens, *Religious and Spiritual Events*, 208–20 (209); for lower ones, compare Jeanne Lenzer, "Citizen, Heal Thyself," *Discover: Science, Technology, and the Future* 28 (9, Sept. 2007): 54–59, 73.

38. Ken Fish shared with me that in particular periods of his ministry, he saw the vast majority (he estimated more than 99 percent) healed of the hundreds of stage 4 (on the 0–4 scale) cancer patients for whom he and colleagues prayed (phone interview, Jan. 22, 2020).

Chapter 15 Doctors Cured of Cancer

1. C. Bernard Ruffin, *Padre Pio: The True Story*, 3rd rev. ed. (Huntington, IN: Our Sunday Visitor, 2018), 434–36.

2. See Ruth Lindberg, "The Story of My Healing," *Ruth Lindberg* (blog), accessed March 2, 2021, http://ruthlindberg.com/the-story-of-my-healing/.

3. As noted earlier, they can be found in Lindberg, "Story of My Healing."

Chapter 16 Do Blind People Still Receive Sight? Witnesses

1. E.g., Mark 8:22–26; 10:46–52; Matt. 11:5//Luke 7:22; Matt. 12:22; 15:30–31; 21:14; Luke 7:21; John 9:7.

2. Augustine, *Confessions* 9.7.16. See also Nathan M. Herum, "Augustine's Theology of the Miraculous" (MDiv thesis, Beeson Divinity School, 2009), 43–45.

3. Quoted in James Moore Hickson, *Heal the Sick*, 2nd ed. (London: Methuen, 1924), 65–66; the informant notes that he has heard of other cases that he has not yet investigated.

4. Hickson, *Heal the Sick*, 76.

5. C. Bernard Ruffin, *Padre Pio: The True Story*, 3rd rev. ed. (Huntington, IN: Our Sunday Visitor, 2018), 372–75, citing significant evidence. See also another visual improvement on pp. 376–77.

6. Allen Spraggett, *Kathryn Kuhlman: The Woman Who Believes in Miracles* (Cleveland: World, 1970), 26.

7. See Keener, *Miracles* (2011), 1:510–23. For subsequently published accounts of healed blindness, see, e.g., Colin Dye, *The God Who Heals: Hope for a Hurting World* (Weybridge, UK: New Wine, 2013), 27; Randy Clark, *Eyewitness to Miracles: Watching the Gospel Come to Life* (Nashville: Nelson, 2018), 3–9.

8. Bungishabaku Katho, interview, Wynnewood, PA, March 12, 2009.

9. Yolanda, who had become a close friend of my family, reported this account orally in 2006 and confirmed it for me in writing on Oct. 3, 2008; Paul Mokake reconfirmed the story for me on May 13, 2009.

10. Ethan Lintemuth, personal correspondence, Feb. 24, 2019; March 11, 2019; May 5, 2019. A student when I lectured in Nigeria also shared a healing of blindness of a person for whom he had prayed, with photos of the person before and after (May 29, 2013).

11. Shelley Hollis, phone interview, Jan. 10, 2009.

12. Bruce Collins, phone interview, April 11, 2009.

13. Julie C. Ma, *Mission Possible: The Biblical Strategy for Reaching the Lost*, 2nd ed. (Oxford: Regnum, 2016), 80–81.

14. Clark, *Eyewitness to Miracles*, 7–9. Clark reports restoration of sight in Fortaleza, Brazil, to a man born with a disconnected optic nerve (Randy Clark and Mary Healy, *The Spiritual Gifts Handbook: Using Your Gifts to Build the Kingdom* [Bloomington, MN: Chosen Books, 2018], 163).

15. Phone interview, March 27, 2021; for greater detail, see Lee Strobel, *The Case for Miracles: A Journalist Investigates Evidence for the Supernatural* (Grand Rapids: Zondervan, 2018), 18–19, 26.

16. Robert Canton, *Miracles Never Ending* (Stockton, CA: Aimazing Publishing & Marcom, 2015), 147–48; for other claims of blindness from birth healed, see 168, 195.

17. Canton, *Miracles Never Ending*, 143. For other testimonies regarding vision, see Canton, 135–48, 196, 248; Daniel Kolenda, *Impact Africa: Demonstrations of the Real Power of Jesus Christ Today* (Orlando: Christ for All Nations, 2015), 61, 86, 94, 106, 116, 120, 124–25, 145, 157, 222, 226, 262, 285–89, 298, 322–23; Damian Stayne, *Lord, Renew Your Wonders: Spiritual Gifts for Today* (Frederick, MD: The Word Among Us Press, 2017), 105, 123.

18. Alice Kirsch, personal correspondence, April 12, 14, 2012.

19. Tom Parrish, interview, Birmingham, AL, Feb. 5, 2014; personal correspondence, Feb. 8, 2014.

20. Chester Allan Tesoro, interview, Baguio, Philippines, Jan. 30, 2009.

21. Flint McGlaughlin, personal correspondence, Feb. 6–7, 2009.

22. Robin Shields, personal correspondence (with photographs), Feb. 7–8, 2009.

23. Rolland Baker and Heidi Baker, *Always Enough: God's Miraculous Provision among the Poorest Children on Earth* (Bloomington, MN: Chosen Books, 2003), 76 (noting other such incidents on 171–73). Most research indicates that surgery is the only option for cataracts (Dr. Nicole Matthews, personal correspondence, April 1, 2009).

24. Personal correspondence, May 28, 2016. The dissertation is Donald R. Kantel, "The 'Toronto Blessing' Revival and Its Continuing Impact on Mission in Mozambique" (DMin diss., Regent University, 2007).

25. Don Kantel, "Development Aid as Power Evangelism: The Mieze Model," in *Supernatural Missions: The Impact of the Supernatural on World Missions*, ed. Randy Clark (Mechanicsburg, PA: Global Awakening, 2012), 375.

Chapter 17 Do Blind People Still Receive Sight? Doctors

1. Clarissa Romez et al., "Case Report of Instantaneous Resolution of Juvenile Macular Degeneration Blindness after Proximal Intercessory Prayer," *Explore: The Journal of Science and Healing* 17 (1, Jan.–Feb. 2021): 79–83, https://doi.org/10.1016/j.explore.2020.02.011.

2. Following privacy protocols, the journal does not name the patient.

3. Romez et al., "Case Report of Instantaneous Resolution," 2.

4. In this case, it was an extreme form of Stargardt disease (Romez et al., "Case Report of Instantaneous Resolution," 3).

5. Romez et al., "Case Report of Instantaneous Resolution," 3.

6. Note also the healing after twelve years of paralysis recounted in Mary Healy, *The Gospel of Mark*, Catholic Commentary on Sacred Scripture (Grand Rapids: Baker Academic, 2008), 108.

7. Andrea Anderson, phone interviews, June 24, 2020; July 17, 2020; Aug. 5, 2020; I learned the story first from Dean Merrill, *Miracle Invasion: Amazing True Stories of the Holy Spirit's Gifts at Work Today* (Savage, MN: BroadStreet, 2018), 27–29. A video may be viewed online: "Andrea's Testimony 'Healed of Blindness,'" Vimeo video, posted by Bethel Sarnia, accessed May 13, 2020, 5:53, https://vimeo.com/196310250. Dean Merrill reports another case of blindness due to diabetes, also healed, in his account of Elvira Higgins (Merrill, *Miracle Invasion*, 100–102).

8. Andrea Anderson, phone interview, Aug. 5, 2020; Tim Gibb, personal correspondence, Aug. 5, 2020; Cayden Gibb, personal correspondence, Nov. 24, 2020.

9. Tim Gibb, personal correspondence, June 22, 2020.

10. Henri Nissen, *The God of Miracles: A Danish Journalist Examines Healings in the Ministry of Charles Ndifon* (Copenhagen: Scandinavia Publishing House, 2003), 7–9, 23–30. The book recounts many other healings, including that of Mariam Ghias, a fugitive from Iran who was utterly astonished at her own healing when Charles Ndifon prayed (89–92, noting the television interview); other cases of blindness (106, 121–22, 204); an epileptic atheist healed and converted (115); and deafness (140, 151). Dr. Dragos Bratasanu brought this source to my attention.

11. Lee Schnabel, personal correspondence, Jan. 29, 2020, with copies of eye exams and a link to Kent Gross's testimony: Lee Schnabel, "Men Legally Blind Has Vision Restored to 95% in Albany, OR," YouTube video, July 7, 2019, 1:00, https://www.youtube.com/watch?v=wKDKzf9h5kA (accessed Jan. 29, 2020; May 20, 2021). See also Gross's larger testimony at Lee Schnabel, "Video Healing Testimonies," Capaz: Capacitación interactive de discípulos, accessed March 2, 2021, https://capaz .info/healing-testimonies/; Kent Gross, personal correspondence, Dec. 19, 2020.

12. Carolyn Moore, Zoom interview, Dec. 15, 2020; personal correspondence, Dec. 15, 2020; Cheryl Scroggins testimony video, sent to me by Carolyn Moore on Dec. 15; Cheryl Scroggins, personal correspondence, Jan. 4, 2021.

13. Medical records include an ophthalmology electroretinography report and Goldmann perimetry visual fields ophthalmic diagram (May 20, 1999); a case description from Richard G. Weleber, MD, to Bradley Seely, MD (May 31, 1999); the report of John Boyer, OD, to Linda Mock of the Oregon Commission for the Blind (June 23, 1999); a case description from Patrick McDonnell of the Oregon Commission for the Blind (Nov. 3, 1999). Greg Spencer's testimony (with the documentation) appears online at https://youtu.be/i7WJeyEomhs (accessed March 23, 2021).

14. "Cleansing the Mind," Men's Retreat, April 19–21, 2002.

15. Medical records include a report from Jon Burpee, MD (May 3, 2002); see also a notice from the Social Security Administration (June 12, 2003). For the story, see also Terrell Clemmons, "Jesus of Testimony," *Right Angles* (blog), Feb. 27, 2014, https://terrellclemmons.com/2014/02/27/jesus-of-testimony/. I first learned of this case when Elliott and Ethan Nesch interviewed me for their *Jesus of Testimony* video.

16. Joel Lantz, personal correspondence, Nov. 1–2, 4, 2014; Jan. 16, 2015; Lantz, *Bridges for Honest Skeptics*, 3rd ed. (n.p.: Joel Lantz, 2016), 616–67, available at no cost at https://www.obooko.com /free-philosophy-books/bridges-for-honest-skeptics-lantz.

17. Nonyem E. Numbere, *A Man and a Vision: A Biography of Apostle Geoffrey D. Numbere* (Diobu, Nigeria: Greater Evangelism Publications, 2008), 121 (compare 186, 189–90, 210); Nonyem E. Numbere, personal correspondence, Jan. 6, 13, 2010. Our mutual friend Danny McCain introduced us (personal correspondence, July 11, 2009).

18. Wayne E. Warner, *Kathryn Kuhlman: The Woman behind the Miracles* (Ann Arbor, MI: Servant, 1993), 132–34; Allen Spraggett, *Kathryn Kuhlman: The Woman Who Believes in Miracles* (Cleveland: World, 1970), 71–75, 137.

19. Rex Gardner, *Healing Miracles: A Doctor Investigates* (London: Darton, Longman & Todd, 1986), 20–21; Gardner, "Miracles of Healing in Anglo-Celtic Northumbria as Recorded by the Venerable Bede and His Contemporaries: A Reappraisal in the Light of Twentieth-Century Experience," *British Medical Journal* 287 (Dec. 24–31, 1983): 1929.

20. Renay Poirier with Jane A. G. Kise, *I Once Was Blind: The Miracle of How Renay Poirier Regained His Sight* (Allen, TX: SunCreek Books, 2003). Sadly, several years after his healing, a news report indicates that Poirier was charged with an occasion of lewd behavior, but as Poirier noted before this, healing was not something that he (or anyone else) merited; it was a gift from God.

21. Poirier, *I Once Was Blind*, 19; for the injury, see 13–20.

22. Poirier, *I Once Was Blind*, 196; for the miracle, see 192–200.

23. Paul P. Parker, "Suffering, Prayer, and Miracles," *Journal of Religion and Health* 36 (3, 1997): 205–19 (216). For the healing of another pierced eye, see Jacalyn Duffin, *Medical Miracles: Doctors, Saints, and Healing in the Modern World* (Oxford: Oxford University Press, 2009), 64.

Chapter 18 Do Disabled People Still Walk? Reflex Sympathetic Dystrophy

1. I draw this account from a combination of "God's Voice" (a Christmas *It's a Miracle* episode aired in 1998) and an episode in the series *Unsolved Mysteries*, aired Sept. 20, 1996.

2. Ema McKinley with Cheryl Ricker, *Rush of Heaven: One Woman's Miraculous Encounter with Jesus* (Grand Rapids: Zondervan, 2014). I first learned of this account from Daniel Fazzina, *Divine Intervention: 50 True Stories of God's Miracles Today* (Lake Mary, FL: Charisma House, 2014), 211–14. For video testimony from McKinley and those who knew her, as well as photographs, see Christian Broadcasting Network, "A Christmas Eve Miracle Restores a Crippled Life," *The 700 Club*, YouTube video, Dec. 25, 2012, 6:40, https://www.youtube.com/watch?v=htMhEUv9aGQ (accessed July 14, 2020).

3. McKinley, *Rush of Heaven*, 198.

4. McKinley, *Rush of Heaven*, 206.

5. McKinley, *Rush of Heaven*, 217–18.

6. McKinley, *Rush of Heaven*, 219–20.

7. McKinley, *Rush of Heaven*, 221.

8. McKinley, *Rush of Heaven*, photo gallery (following p. 96).

9. The medical report, from the Mayo Clinic, appears in Fazzina, *Divine Intervention*, 223. Full reports appear (albeit in retypeset form) in McKinley, *Rush of Heaven*, 243–65.

Chapter 19 Do Disabled People Still Walk? Marlene's Cerebral Palsy

1. Dean Merrill, *Miracle Invasion: Amazing True Stories of the Holy Spirit's Gifts at Work Today* (Savage, MN: BroadStreet, 2018), 67–73; Marlene Klepees, phone interview, June 16, 2020. Marlene's testimony can also be viewed online at Christian Broadcasting Network, "Woman Healed of Cerebral Palsy through Vision," *The 700 Club*, YouTube video, March 25, 2010, 5:24, https://www.youtube.com/watch?v=z4TN2uxS7DA (accessed May 13, 2020). This video also displays some of the medical documentation; other details appear in Marlene's interview with Sid Roth on *It's Supernatural!* (https://www.youtube.com/watch?v=4bsKnpOYMUs, accessed March 23, 2021). I also consulted Randall Bach, who previously interviewed Marlene and read her physician's statement (personal correspondence, May 22, 2020). This interview can be viewed (after her testimony) at "Healing—Full Klepees Interview," Vimeo video, posted by Open Bible Churches, accessed March 2, 2021, 29:16, https://vimeo.com/208727554. For a slightly abridged written form, see "Miraculously Healed of Cerebral Palsy: An Interview with Marlene Klepees and Scott Emerson," *Message of the Open Bible*, March 2017, 4–7.

2. Merrill, *Miracle Invasion*, 71.

3. See Christian Broadcasting Network, "Healed from 'Suicide Disease' with a Touch and a Prayer," *The 700 Club*, accessed July 23, 2020, https://www1.cbn.com/healed-suicide-disease-touch-and-prayer.

Chapter 20 Do Disabled People Still Walk? Bryan's Spinal Injury

1. Matthew Suh, FaceTime interview, Aug. 26, 2020; Bryan and Meg LaPooh, FaceTime interview, Aug. 29, 2020; Ken Fish, text message, Aug. 26, 2020; video of Bryan's healing and also his emotional video testimony (the latter is available at "Miraculous Healing from God," YouTube video, posted by Memorable Moments, Sept. 11, 2019, 27:34, https://www.youtube.com/watch?v=vYMMYbkKz0U&feature=youtu.be, accessed Aug. 27, 2020), sent by Bryan and Meg LaPooh, Aug. 27, 2020; interview by Eric Metaxas, "Ken Fish and Bryan La Pooh, Kingdom Fire Ministries," *The Eric Metaxas Radio Show*, YouTube video, Nov. 7, 2019, 1:06:35, https://www.youtube.com/watch?v=Z9UX2oGzdJc&feature=emb_logo&ab_channel=TheEricMetaxasRadioShow (accessed Aug. 30, 2020); Julia Voytovich Ososkalo, personal correspondence, Oct. 1, 2020, including attached iPhone videos of Bryan walking for the first time.

2. Julia Ososkalo, personal correspondence, Oct. 1, 2020.

3. Julia Ososkalo, personal correspondence, Oct. 1, 2020.

4. Julia Ososkalo, personal correspondence, Oct. 3, 2020.

5. June 18, 2020, medical report, sent to me Sept. 1, 2020, along with pre-healing reports from May 10, 2018, and Feb. 14, 2019.

Chapter 21 Do Disabled People Still Walk? Vignettes

1. See Keener, *Miracles* (2011), esp. 1:523–36.

2. E.g., Robert Fort, chairman of the United Evangelical Churches, reports an event in which a man paralyzed on his left side for sixteen years was healed and ran around the church (Dean Merrill,

Miracle Invasion: Amazing True Stories of the Holy Spirit's Gifts at Work Today [Savage, MN: BroadStreet, 2018], 139–41); Bruce Van Natta, *A Miraculous Life: True Stories of Supernatural Encounters with God* (Lake Mary, FL: Charisma House, 2013), 117–19, recounts the complete healing of a paralyzed woman for whom he prayed in Honduras in August 2009 (compare also foot healings on 144–45). For many eyewitness accounts, see Daniel Kolenda, *Impact Africa: Demonstrations of the Real Power of Jesus Christ Today* (Orlando, FL: Christ for All Nations, 2015), 78, 82, 101, 110, 132, 168, 170, 186, 190, 331, 336, 342 (paralysis in 41, 45, 172, 196, 237, 248, 290); Randy Clark, *Eyewitness to Miracles: Watching the Gospel Come to Life* (Nashville: Nelson, 2018), 10–23; Robert Canton, *Miracles Never Ending* (Stockton, CA: Aimazing Publishing & Marcom, 2015), 174–97; Damian Stayne, *Lord, Renew Your Wonders: Spiritual Gifts for Today* (Frederick, MD: The Word Among Us Press, 2017), 105, 123.

3. Vince Nguyen's letter in Canton, *Miracles Never Ending*, 194–95.

4. For an eyewitness account of a leg growing six inches over the course of several days, so that the adult could, for the first time, walk unaided, see Francis MacNutt, *The Power to Heal* (Notre Dame, IN: Ave Maria, 1977), 51–54.

5. Brandon Hammonds, shared in our doctoral seminar on Nov. 2, 2020; follow-up personal correspondence, Nov. 13, 2020.

6. Marianne Sommer, interview, Bouaké, Côte d'Ivoire, July 23–24, 2012; personal correspondence, Oct. 19, 2012. See also Dwight Haymon, *When Lambs Become Lions* (Atlanta: Lifegate, 2013), 11–12.

7. Marianne Sommer, interview, Bouaké, Côte d'Ivoire, July 24, 2012; personal correspondence, Oct. 19, 2012, with some medical documentation.

8. See C. Douglas Weaver, *The Healer-Prophet: William Marrion Branham; A Study of the Prophetic in American Pentecostalism* (Macon, GA: Mercer University Press, 2000), 57. Compare David Edwin Harrell Jr., *All Things Are Possible: The Healing and Charismatic Revivals in Modern America* (Bloomington: Indiana University Press, 1975), 35. For the preacher's (Branham's) exaggerations, see "Congressman Upshaw," Believe the Sign, last modified March 24, 2020, http://en.believethesign.com /index.php/Congressman_Upshaw.

9. David Chang, FaceTime interview, Aug. 30, 2020.

10. Matthew Suh, FaceTime interview, Aug. 26, 2020 (video with explanation sent Aug. 29, 2020); Suh's healing was also noted by Ken Fish, personal correspondence, Aug. 23, 2020.

11. Tim Stafford, *Miracles: A Journalist Looks at Modern-Day Experiences of God's Power* (Minneapolis: Bethany House, 2012), 11–19, 24–27, 30–32, 214–15.

12. Clark, *Eyewitness to Miracles*, 10–12. Randy recounts a similar experience of averted amputation on 12–14; for another dramatic healing situation, see Randy Clark and Mary Healy, *The Spiritual Gifts Handbook: Using Your Gifts to Build the Kingdom* (Bloomington, MN: Chosen Books, 2018), 162. For the healing of a freshly cut thumb tendon within a day after prayer, canceling expected surgery, see Stayne, *Lord, Renew Your Wonders*, 130.

13. Available at "Eyewitness to Miracles," Global Awakening, accessed June 10, 2020, https:// globalawakening.com/eyewitnesstomiracles.

14. Clark, *Eyewitness to Miracles*, 19–21; some additional details surface in the video "Eyewitness to Miracles," mentioned in the previous note.

15. Mary Healy, *The Gospel of Mark*, Catholic Commentary on Sacred Scripture (Grand Rapids: Baker Academic, 2008), 108; supplemented with details from personal correspondence, June 11, 2020; July 1, 2020.

16. Green's story, including reports from close witnesses, appears in Christian Broadcasting Network, "Jermaine Green Walks after Being Paralyzed (2 Years in Wheelchair)," YouTube video, posted by Michelle Wilson Media, April 25, 2019, 5:35, https://www.youtube.com/watch?v=wvf-xWedRSc (accessed July 15, 2020).

17. James L. Garlow and Keith Wall, *Miracles Are for Real: What Happens When Heaven Touches Earth* (Minneapolis: Bethany House, 2011), 190–96.

18. Garlow and Wall, *Miracles Are for Real*, 191.

19. For example, although her recovery was not instantaneous or (as of the time of my interview) complete, full medical records attest the traumatic (and usually deadly) spinal column injury and unusually positive recovery of Diane M. Young of Spokane, Washington (phone interview, Dec. 21,

2014, with sixteen corroborating medical documents). Young had been a medical massage therapist for two decades and so knew how to obtain the documentation.

20. For some other cases of fully functional cures despite continuing organic conditions, see, e.g., Ruth Cranston, *The Miracle of Lourdes: Updated and Expanded Edition by the Medical Bureau of Lourdes* (New York: Image Books, 1988), 136; Caryle Hirschberg and Marc Ian Barasch, *Remarkable Recovery: What Extraordinary Healings Tell Us about Getting Well and Staying Well* (New York: Riverhead, 1995), 113–15; Stayne, *Lord, Renew Your Wonders*, 130. Note also the account of Sarah Norwood's broken neck: Douglass Norwood, interview, Philadelphia, June 6, 2006 (in Keener, *Miracles* [2011], 1:438). In another case, Ronald Coyne appeared to see from an empty eye socket. After Martin Ward convincingly showed me how magicians can plausibly fake such sight (Feb. 20, 2019), I concluded that Coyne was seeing through the other, patched eye, through a slight opening beneath the patch. Dr. Joseph Bergeron, however, challenged me to consider the firmly positive conclusion of ophthalmologist Elizabeth Vaughan, who personally examined Coyne and knows how to tape eyes (personal correspondence, Aug. 20, 2020). See Gypsy Hogan, "'The Man with the Miracle Eye' Uses His Power to Spread Word of God," *Oklahoman*, May 16, 1982, https://oklahoman.com/article/1983808/the-man-with-the-miracle-eye-uses-his-power-to-spread-word-of-god.

21. Linnette Pilar, FaceTime interview, Aug. 27, 2020; eyewitness confirmation of the healing also by Ken Fish, phone interview, Aug. 23, 2020; Matt Bennett, personal correspondence, Aug. 26, 2020.

22. Ken Fish, personal correspondence and videos, March 31, 2021; YouTube Live discussion by Fish and two coworkers, April 21, 2021.

23. Robert A. Larmer, *The Legitimacy of Miracle* (Lanham, MD: Lexington Books, 2013), 200–202; Larmer, personal correspondence, Aug. 4, 2009.

24. Other healings from MS are also reported; see, e.g., Dustin Hedrick, *A Warrior's Battle* (Olin, NC: DHM Publishing, 2016), chaps. 7–8, esp. pp. 85–86, 107–12 (including the photograph on 110).

25. *Healing Prayer Is God's Idea: Embracing God's Invitation to Intercede* (Amazon, 2021). I am grateful for personal correspondence with David Chotka (Feb. 27, 2021), which included some further healing accounts, and with Maxie Dunnam (Feb. 24, 26, 2021).

26. David sent me (March 4, 2021) the doctor's note from Jan. 16, 2013, attesting that Elizabeth had been "symptom free from her FSH muscular dystrophy for the last 3 years."

27. Maura Poston Zagrans, *Miracles Every Day: The Story of One Physician's Inspiring Faith and the Healing Power of Prayer* (New York: Doubleday, 2010), 144–45.

28. Chauncey W. Crandall IV, *Raising the Dead: A Doctor Encounters the Miraculous* (New York: FaithWords, 2010), 152.

29. Crandall, *Raising the Dead*, 155.

30. Mirtha Venero Boza, interview, Santiago de Cuba, Aug. 6, 2010. Before the healing, doctors had immobilized the leg because it was so bent.

31. Teri Speed, *The Incurables: Unlock Healing for Spirit, Mind, and Body* (Lake Mary, FL: Creation House, 2007), 17–23 (Speed is the doctor and an eyewitness).

32. Michael McClymond, personal correspondence, unpublished manuscript and phone conversation, Jan. 3, 2011; extensive before-and-after medical documentation (including detailed Mayo Clinic test results) sent to me Jan. 5, 2011.

33. Nonyem E. Numbere, *A Man and a Vision: A Biography of Apostle Geoffrey D. Numbere* (Diobu, Nigeria: Greater Evangelism Publications, 2008), 415; Numbere, personal correspondence (including photographs), Jan. 6, 13, 2010.

Chapter 22 Are Lepers Still Cleansed? Visible Healings

1. The leprosy addressed by, for example, Father Damien of Molokai, Dr. Paul Brand, Dr. Ruth Pfau, and many others today is Hansen's disease. For discussion regarding skin diseases and leprosy in antiquity, see, e.g., Mirko D. Grmek, *Diseases in the Ancient Greek World*, trans. Mireille Muellner and Leonard Muellner (Baltimore: Johns Hopkins University Press, 1989), 157–71; esp. more recent work by Vivian Nutton, *Ancient Medicine*, 2nd ed. (New York: Routledge, 2013), 29–30; Laura M. Zucconi, *Ancient Medicine: From Mesopotamia to Rome* (Grand Rapids: Eerdmans, 2019), 48,

137–38; Matthew Thiessen, *Jesus and the Forces of Death: The Gospels' Portrayal of Ritual Impurity within First-Century Judaism* (Grand Rapids: Baker Academic, 2020), 44–50.

2. Ebenezer Peter Perinbaraj, interviews, Wilmore, KY, Dec. 25, 2012; May 10, 2014; personal correspondence, May 11, 14, 2014.

3. Interview, Wilmore, KY, April 22, 2016; personal correspondence, April 24, 2016.

4. Yost shared this account (which I have greatly condensed) on Steve Addison's podcast (https://content.blubrry.com/movements/230-Jims_Story.mp3?fbclid=IwAR2oyVCHJOtySf-rxlwGyaePT5NqKRb-8pj-FQMwK6Teq3Xt_0asf5Btmx4), to which I listened on Sept. 6, 2020. With Addison's help, I followed up with Yost on Sept. 7, 2020; I also confirmed his reliability from a mutual colleague.

5. Medical documentation received Sept. 26, 2014, from Joel Lantz and Bruce Van Natta; Bruce Van Natta, personal correspondence, Sept. 29, 2014. See also the accounts published earlier (though I discovered them later) in James L. Garlow and Keith Wall, *Real Life, Real Miracles: True Stories That Will Help You Believe* (Minneapolis: Bethany House, 2012), 48–56; Bruce Van Natta, *A Miraculous Life: True Stories of Supernatural Encounters with God* (Lake Mary, FL: Charisma House, 2013), 47–56.

6. Garlow and Wall, *Real Life, Real Miracles*, 53. Garlow and Wall themselves do include an account of a six-year-old boy run over by a school bus (estimated at 25,000 pounds) who, "after eight days in the hospital . . . was released with not so much as a cast or a bandage," with bones healing "so quickly that the breaks were hard to detect at his next doctor appointment" (238).

7. Joel Lantz, *Bridges for Honest Skeptics*, 3rd ed. (n.p.: Joel Lantz, 2016), 55–68, available at no cost at https://www.obooko.com/free-philosophy-books/bridges-for-honest-skeptics-lantz and other sites.

8. Karsten Harns (personal correspondence, May 3, 2021) shared with me both the written and the recorded audio testimony of Bob Reid (now deceased), one of his mentors who was then assisting minister Joe Jordan. Bob also recounts the experience around minutes 48–53 in "History of Faith Tech Ministries," https://www.youtube.com/watch?app=desktop&v=tCt94OcmcSI&noapp=1 (accessed May 6, 2021). The authenticity of the account was confirmed by Bob's widow, Karen Reid (personal correspondence, May 5, 2021). Bob's son, Ted Reid, who watched from roughly ten to twelve feet away, also witnessed and confirmed the incident (personal correspondence, May 6, 2021). In each case the formation of fingernails followed more gradually over the course of weeks, although the indentation for them had already formed. Bob noted afterward how the incident had challenged his own faith.

9. Several eyewitness goiter-disappearance accounts appear in my 2011 book, *Miracles*, 1:269–72, 319, 2:745–46 (compare also 1:296n216, 307n301, 401, 406n403, 406n413, 407n414, 416–17, 423, 531, 2:650). For more recent accounts, see, e.g., Don Schulze, *A Life of Miracles* (Carol Stream, IL: Tyndale, 2014), 172–74. For reports of various growths visibly disappearing, see, e.g., Robert Canton, *Miracles Never Ending* (Stockton, CA: Aimazing Publishing & Marcom, 2015), 103, 195, 251; Damian Stayne, *Lord, Renew Your Wonders: Spiritual Gifts for Today* (Frederick, MD: The Word Among Us Press, 2017), 105, 117.

10. David Neil Emmett, personal correspondence, May 16, 2020; May 18, 2020; May 21, 2021.

11. Jacques Vernaud's daughter Liliane shared the testimony with me probably around 1980; Jacques Vernaud confirmed it in personal correspondence, Aug. 29, 2005, and I met with them together in Kinshasa on July 23, 2008.

12. See Dean Merrill, *50 Pentecostal and Charismatic Leaders Every Christian Should Know* (Bloomington, MN: Chosen Books, 2020), chap. 46; a minority of those with ruptured brain aneurysms recover fully, but this one was unusual. It is my favorite, however, because I am friends with Wonsuk and Julie. For a report of another serious brain aneurysm healed, in Costa Rica on May 1, 2011, see Michael O'Neill, *Exploring the Miraculous* (Huntington, IN: Our Sunday Visitor, 2015), 81.

13. Julie C. Ma, *Mission Possible: The Biblical Strategy for Reaching the Lost*, 2nd ed. (Oxford: Regnum, 2016), 81–82. Insofar as I can tell from the description, the toxic goiter was probably linked with thyroid cancer.

14. This conversation took place on July 15, 2014.

15. Maura Poston Zagrans, *Miracles Every Day: The Story of One Physician's Inspiring Faith and the Healing Power of Prayer* (New York: Doubleday, 2010), 100, 217. For more recent reports, see, e.g., Tracy Wujak, "5 Guys and a Faith Healer: After Dismal Diagnoses, They Believe in Miracles,"

ABC Detroit, May 17, 2019, https://www.wxyz.com/news/5-guys-and-a-faith-healer-after-dismal
-diagnoses-they-believe-in-miracles (accessed March 5, 2020).

16. Mirtha Venero Boza, interview, Santiago de Cuba, Aug. 6, 2010.

17. Personal correspondence, June 1, 2009; July 11, 2009; Sept. 21–22, 27, 2010; interview, Wilmore,
KY, July 17, 2011; Nov. 24, 30, 2014.

18. Tonye Briggs, phone interviews, Dec. 14, 16, 2009, providing eyewitness confirmation for the
account in Nonyem E. Numbere, *A Man and a Vision: A Biography of Apostle Geoffrey D. Numbere*
(Diobu, Nigeria: Greater Evangelism Publications, 2008), 246–47.

19. James Moore Hickson, *Heal the Sick*, 2nd ed. (London: Methuen, 1924), 85.

20. Hickson, *Heal the Sick*, 218.

21. Personal correspondence, May 26, 2016.

Chapter 23 Do Deaf People Still Hear?

1. Joseph Hambrick, shared in class March 1, 2021; confirmed for me in writing, March 10, 2021.

2. Micael Grenholm, *Dokumenterade Mirakler: Vetenskap, Helande och Guds Existens* (Örebro,
Sweden: Sjöbergs, 2019), 122–24. I follow Grenholm's account directly for all this content, except
using English rather than Swedish.

3. Grenholm's figure 7.1 shows the evidence: in May, Johansson's right ear was reduced by 50
decibels (dB) and the left by 60 in the low frequencies. In September, by contrast, the audiologist
reports "normal values in the base to 1 kHz, with curves dropping to 80–90 dB in the treble." The
average hearing loss in May was 61 /> 89 and in September was 21/41.

4. Rex Gardner, *Healing Miracles: A Doctor Investigates* (London: Darton, Longman & Todd,
1986), 202 (the full account is 202–5). For some other reports of healed deafness not included in my
earlier book, see, e.g., Colin Dye, *The God Who Heals: Hope for a Hurting World* (Weybridge, UK:
New Wine, 2013), 22–23; Bruce Van Natta, *A Miraculous Life: True Stories of Supernatural Encounters
with God* (Lake Mary, FL: Charisma House, 2013), 141–42; Don Schulze, *A Life of Miracles* (Carol
Stream, IL: Tyndale, 2014), 173–74.

5. Gardner, *Healing Miracles*, 204. Describing some of the medical report, Gardner claims that
he checked it and found it meticulously accurate.

6. Gardner, *Healing Miracles*, 205 (emphasis in the original).

7. James L. Garlow and Keith Wall, *Real Life, Real Miracles: True Stories That Will Help You
Believe* (Minneapolis: Bethany House, 2012), 79–84.

8. Candy Gunther Brown, "Testing Prayer: Can Science Prove the Healing Power of Prayer?,"
Huffington Post, March 2, 2012, https://www.huffpost.com/entry/testing-prayer-science-of-healing
_b_1299915.

9. Wayne Brodland wrote this account at the request of Robert Larmer, Oct. 13, 2007; I have
greatly condensed the account (found in Robert A. Larmer, unpublished manuscript forwarded to
Craig Keener with personal correspondence, Aug. 4, 2009) here (from eleven paragraphs to one).

10. Randy Clark, *Eyewitness to Miracles: Watching the Gospel Come to Life* (Nashville: Nelson,
2018), 53–54. Clark also recounts other cases of healing (52–57), including the healing of a person
who lacked an auditory nerve (52–53).

11. Randy Clark and Mary Healy, *The Spiritual Gifts Handbook: Using Your Gifts to Build the
Kingdom* (Bloomington, MN: Chosen Books, 2018), 163–64.

12. Clark and Healy, *Spiritual Gifts Handbook*, 161.

13. Robert Canton, *Miracles Never Ending* (Stockton, CA: Aimazing Publishing & Marcom,
2015), 152–53.

14. Canton, *Miracles Never Ending*, 164–65 (for further reports of auditory healings, see 151–69,
196, 248); Damian Stayne, *Lord, Renew Your Wonders: Spiritual Gifts for Today* (Frederick, MD:
The Word Among Us Press, 2017), 105, 108; Daniel Kolenda, *Impact Africa: Demonstrations of the
Real Power of Jesus Christ Today* (Orlando: Christ for All Nations, 2015), 32, 47, 54, 93, 126, 137,
181, 185, 192, 210, 220, 228, 236, 259, 270, 272, 312–13, 320, 328, 332.

15. For deafness, see, e.g., Rolland Baker and Heidi Baker, *Always Enough: God's Miraculous Provision among the Poorest Children on Earth* (Bloomington, MN: Chosen Books, 2003), 157, 169, 173;

Baker and Baker, *Expecting Miracles: True Stories of God's Supernatural Power and How You Can Experience It* (Bloomington, MN: Chosen Books, 2007), 7–8, 39, 43, 78, 108, 114, 163, 172, 180, 183, 192–93; Guy Chevreau, *Turnings: The Kingdom of God and the Western World* (Tonbridge, Kent, UK: Sovereign World, 2004), 142. For blindness, see, e.g., Baker and Baker, *Always Enough*, 145, 169, 174, 182 (and for further accounts of eyes white with blindness changing color as they were being healed: 76, 171–73; Baker and Baker, *Expecting Miracles*, 189); Baker and Baker, *Expecting Miracles*, 8, 39–40, 68, 78 (often), 108, 113, 159, 160, 192, 193 (partial healing); Chevreau, *Turnings*, 19, 166–67 (partial damage). For the healings of persons both deaf and blind, see Chevreau, *Turnings*, 145, 174, 182.

16. Shelley Hollis, phone interview, Jan. 10, 2009. I was interviewing her concerning a different healing when I learned that she had also spent time in Mozambique.

17. Candy Gunther Brown, Stephen C. Mory, Rebecca Williams, and Michael J. McClymond, "Study of the Therapeutic Effects of Proximal Intercessory Prayer (STEPP) on Auditory and Visual Impairments in Rural Mozambique," *Southern Medical Journal* 103 (9, Sept. 2010): 864–69.

18. Brown, "Testing Prayer." See also Brown, *Testing Prayer: Science and Healing* (Cambridge, MA: Harvard University Press, 2012), 207, 219.

19. See Brown, *Testing Prayer*, 207–9, 214–20, 223–30.

Part 5 "The Dead Are Raised" (Matt. 11:5//Luke 7:22)

1. Jordan Howard Sobel, "On the Evidence of Testimony for Miracles: A Bayesian Interpretation of David Hume's Analysis," *Philosophical Quarterly* 37 (1987): 166–86 (186).

2. See Hume's language in *Of Miracles* (La Salle, IL: Open Court, 1985), 27, 29, 32, 34, 36–39, 43, 52–55.

3. Keener, *Miracles* (2011), esp. 1:536–79; with further detail and sources, Keener, "'The Dead Are Raised' (Matthew 11:5//Luke 7:22): Resuscitation Accounts in the Gospels and Eyewitness Testimony," *Bulletin for Biblical Research* 25 (1, 2015): 55–79.

Chapter 24 Are the Dead Still Raised? History

1. Although I use the phrase facetiously, serious questions about defining death exist; see, e.g., M. Pabst Battin, Leslie Francis, and Bruce M. Landesman, *Death, Dying and the Ending of Life* (Burlington, VT: Ashgate, 2007); Robert D. Truog et al., eds., *Defining Death: Organ Transplantation and the Fifty-Year Legacy of the Harvard Report on Brain Death*, Hastings Center Special Report (Hoboken, NJ: Wiley, 2018).

2. For a particularly extensive collection of testimonies through history (though more recent ones are generally more strongly attested), see Albert J. Hebert, *Raised from the Dead: True Stories of 400 Resurrection Miracles* (Rockford, IL: TAN Books, 1986).

3. In Eusebius, *Ecclesiastical History* 4.3.1–2, also cited by Craig A. Evans, *Jesus and His World: The Archaeological Evidence* (Louisville: Westminster John Knox, 2012), 7–8, who suggests the dates of around AD 70–130.

4. William Young, "Miracles in Church History," *Churchman* 102 (2, 1988): 102–21 (110).

5. Irenaeus, *Against Heresies* 2.31.2.

6. Translation from *Ante-Nicene Fathers: Translations of the Writings of the Fathers down to A.D. 325*, ed. A. Roberts and J. Donaldson, rev. A. Cleveland Coxe, 10 vols. (Grand Rapids: Eerdmans, 1975), 1:407.

7. Augustine, *City of God* 22.8.

8. See Keener, *Miracles* (2011), 1:543–50.

9. Bilinda Straight, *Miracles and Extraordinary Experience in Northern Kenya* (Philadelphia: University of Pennsylvania Press, 2007), 136–37.

10. Straight, *Miracles*, 137.

11. Compare Thomas S. Kidd, "The Healing of Mercy Wheeler: Illness and Miracles among Early American Evangelicals," *William and Mary Quarterly* 63 (1, Jan. 2006): 159; Stephen Tomkins, *John Wesley: A Biography* (Grand Rapids: Eerdmans, 2003), 106.

12. See Dieter Ising, *Johann Christoph Blumhardt, Life and Work: A New Biography*, trans. Monty Ledford (Eugene, OR: Cascade Books, 2009), 207, 219.

13. Mike Finley, personal correspondence, Oct. 10, 22, 2010. Note twelve articles in the *Wichita Eagle* between June 11 and July 7, 1907. Christian sources include Frank McCluney, "Correspondence," *Nazarene Messenger* 12 (2, July 11, 1907): 3–4; "Raised from the Dead," *The Apostolic Faith* 1 (9, June 1907): 4.

14. Alpha E. Anderson, *Pelendo: God's Prophet in the Congo* (Chicago: Moody, 1964), 69–70. Compare various reports of healing in Congo dating from roughly that period also in David Neil Emmett, *W. F. P. Burton (1886–1971): A Pentecostal Pioneer's Missional Vision for Congo* (Leiden: Brill, 2021).

15. Eric Greaux, personal correspondence, Aug. 27–28, 2009; Barachias Irons, personal correspondence, Aug. 27, 2009; Sept. 13, 2009; Jan. 19, 2010; Jan. 21, 2010.

16. Iris Lilia Fonseca Valdés, interview, Havana, Cuba, Aug. 11, 2010. For more accounts from Cuba, see Carlos Alamino, *In the Footsteps of God's Call: A Cuban Pastor's Journey*, trans. Osmany Espinosa Hernández, ed. David Peck and Brian Stewart (Mountlake Terrace, WA: Original Media Publishers, 2008), 63–65. I gathered accounts from elsewhere in Latin America from Arlene M. Sánchez Walsh, *Latino Pentecostal Identity: Evangelical Faith, Self, and Society* (New York: Columbia University Press, 2003), 43–44; R. Andrew Chesnut, *Born Again in Brazil: The Pentecostal Boom and the Pathogens of Poverty* (New Brunswick, NJ: Rutgers University Press, 1997), 86; Sheila Heneise, interview, Ardmore, PA, April 5, 2009; Rebecca Pierce Bomann, "The Salve of Divine Healing: Essential Rituals for Survival among Working-Class Pentecostals in Bogotá, Colombia," in *Global Pentecostal and Charismatic Healing*, ed. Candy Gunther Brown (Oxford: Oxford University Press, 2011), 187–205 (195–96); David Pytches, *Come Holy Spirit: Learning How to Minister in Power* (London: Hodder & Stoughton, 1985), 245; Rex Gardner, *Healing Miracles: A Doctor Investigates* (London: Darton, Longman & Todd, 1986), 139–40.

Chapter 25 Are the Dead Still Raised? Africa

1. E.g., Daniel Kolenda, *Impact Africa: Demonstrations of the Real Power of Jesus Christ Today* (Orlando: Christ for All Nations, 2015), 36, 150–51. Kolenda also shared one of these accounts with me directly in personal correspondence.

2. Luis Bush and Beverly Pegues, *The Move of the Holy Spirit in the 10/40 Window*, ed. Jane Rumph (Seattle: YWAM, 1999), 52. This presumably means not that they occur always but that they are widely known (Tadesse Woldetsadik, personal correspondence, Nov. 1, 2009).

3. André Mamadzi, interview, Yaoundé, Cameroon, Jan. 17, 2013.

4. Sadly, one of the ministers in this story is later reported to have experienced a personal moral failure; unfortunately, many African pastoral and academic settings lack the safeguards against such failure sometimes put in place in the West. Nevertheless, Aimé remains adamant that the many healings were authentic (personal correspondence, May 18, 2020). By contrast, Aimé steered me away from a different person whom he suspected might exaggerate while giving testimony.

5. Ifeanyichukwu Chinedozi, interview, Lynnfield, MA, Nov. 22, 2017; personal correspondence, Feb. 24, 2018. Ifeanyi had other eyewitness accounts of raisings. Other accounts from Nigeria are not uncommon: e.g., E. G. Ojo, "The Healing Miracles of Jesus Christ and Its Relevance to the Contemporary Situation in Nigerian Churches," in *Religion, Medicine, and Healing*, ed. Gbola Aderibigbe and Deji Ayegboyin (Lagos: Nigerian Association for the Study of Religions and Education, 1995), 48; William Young, "Miracles in Church History," *Churchman* 102 (2, 1988): 102–21 (117); Nonyem E. Numbere, *A Man and a Vision: A Biography of Apostle Geoffrey D. Numbere* (Diobu, Nigeria: Greater Evangelism Publications, 2008), 136–37, 140–42.

6. David Neil Emmett, personal correspondence, May 18, 2020; May 19, 2020 (citing the confirmation of Claude Kapenga and Ngoy Kilumba).

7. Cedric Kanana with Benjamin Fischer, *Dying in Islam, Rising with Christ: Encountering Jesus beyond the Grave* (Nampa, ID: Pembroke Street, 2018), esp. 93–100. I received some further explanation from Cedric Kanana, personal correspondence, Feb. 18, 2020.

8. Benjamin Fischer, personal correspondence, Feb. 16, 2020.

Chapter 26 Are the Dead Still Raised? Asia

1. Numerous cases have come to my attention since I finished my earlier book *Miracles* (2011). These include Jerry Trousdale, *Miraculous Movements* (Nashville: Nelson, 2012), 136–39; Paul

Hattaway, *Henan: Inside the Greatest Christian Revival in History* (Manchester, UK: Piquant, 2021), 243–44. I mention "highly respected" because of Hume's insistence that miracles lack respectable witnesses with something to lose. I prefer accounts from persons whose integrity I can generally attest or that can be attested by others who know them, since not all claims merit being taken at face value; see, e.g., Craig S. Keener, "Do the Dead Still Rise?," *Christianity Today*, June 2019, 46–50.

2. Andrew White, *Faith under Fire: What the Middle East Conflict Has Taught Me about God* (Oxford: Monarch, 2011), 44, 84. Canon White has won the William Wilberforce award (Timothy C. Morgan and Kate Tracy, "Andrew White: Being Jesus in the Kill Zone," *Christianity Today*, May 6, 2014, https://www.christianitytoday.com/ct/2014/may-web-only/andrew-white-being-jesus-in-kill-zone.html).

3. He spoke there on March 22, 2014. The account is now reported in Andrew White, *Glory Zone in the War Zone: Miracles, Signs, and Wonders in the Middle East* (Shippensburg, PA: Destiny Image, 2020), 126–27, as one of "eight dramatic resurrections" (124).

4. A similar response appears in some other accounts of raisings: e.g., "I am hungry" in Surprise Sithole with David Wimbish, *Voice in the Night* (Bloomington, MN: Chosen Books, 2012), 73. Compare Mark 5:43.

5. Interview, Makassar, Indonesia, April 1, 2015.

6. Interview, Makassar, Indonesia, April 2, 2015.

7. Shelley Hollis, phone interview, Jan. 10, 2009; personal correspondence, Nov. 6, 8, 2009; April 23, 2010. I received fuller details from Noel's wife, Shanthi Fernando, on Oct. 7, 2019, facilitated through Prof. Chrissokumar Hendry, who knows the family. Shelley also noted that her daughter interviewed Noel at length about his experience of heaven. Additionally, James D. Hernando, "Pneumatological Function in the Narrative of Acts: Drawing Foundational Insight for a Pentecostal Missiology," in *Trajectories in the Book of Acts: Essays in Honor of John Wesley Wyckoff*, ed. Paul Alexander, Jordan Daniel May, and Robert G. Reid (Eugene, OR: Wipf & Stock, 2010), 241–76 (272n81), mentions Mark Hollis's account of this raising.

8. Forceful efforts to revive someone are of course worth the risk of broken ribs, since someone who remains dead will not have much need for the ribs!

9. E.g., Willie Soans, personal correspondence, Nov. 3, 2010; Luis Bush and Beverly Pegues, *The Move of the Holy Spirit in the 10/40 Window*, ed. Jane Rumph (Seattle: YWAM, 1999), 57–58, 59, 60 (three accounts); Jon Thollander, *He Saw a Man Named Mathews: A Brief Testimony of Thomas and Mary Mathews, Pioneer Missionaries to Rajasthan* (Udaipur, Rajasthan, India: Native Missionary Movement, Cross & Crown, 2000), 88.

10. See, at some length, Christiaan Rudolph De Wet, "Signs and Wonders in Church Growth" (MA thesis, Fuller School of World Mission, Dec. 1981), 110–11, following R. R. Cunville, "The Evangelization of Northeast India" (DMiss diss., Fuller Theological Seminary, 1975), 156–57.

11. Donald E. Miller and Tetsunao Yamamori, *Global Pentecostalism: The New Face of Christian Social Engagement* (Berkeley: University of California Press, 2007), 151–52.

12. Willie Soans, personal correspondence, acquired for me and shared with me Nov. 3, 2010, through Ivan Satyavrata and Jacob Mathew, with photos of the boy and family after the event.

13. Interview, April 22, 2016; personal correspondence, April 24, 2016.

14. Keener, *Miracles* (2011), 1:566–67.

15. Hattaway, *Henan*, 235–36, quoting from 236. His colleagues indicated that he had also witnessed two other raisings. A different resuscitation account appears on 265. I thank John Lathrop for bringing this source to my attention.

16. Hattaway, *Henan*, 242–43.

17. Hattaway, *Henan*, 244.

18. Hattaway, *Henan*, 244–45.

19. Hattaway, *Henan*, 245.

Chapter 27 Raised in the West? Cases in the News

1. See, e.g., "Fabrice Muamba Tells of His Miraculous Recovery," *The Telegraph*, April 22, 2012, https://www.telegraph.co.uk/sport/football/teams/bolton-wanderers/9219191/Fabrice-Muamba-tells-of-his-miraculous-recovery.html; Richard Dewsbury, "Fabrice Muamba Says God Saved His Life

after Cardiac Arrest on Pitch," *New Life Publishing*, May 29, 2016, https://www.newlifepublish ing.co.uk/latest-articles/tbg/fabrice-muamba-cardiac-arrest-god-saved-my-life-says-former-bolton -footballer/.

2. "Teen Whose Heart Stopped for 20 Minutes Says He Saw Jesus," Newsmax, May 15, 2015, https://www.newsmax.com/health/people/zack-clements-heart-stopped-jesus/2015/05/15/id/644913 /; "Teen Whose Heart Stopped for 20 Minutes Says He Saw Jesus," Fox 10 Phoenix, May 16, 2015, https://www.fox10phoenix.com/news/teen-whose-heart-stopped-for-20-minutes-says-he-saw-jesus.

3. Christy Wilson Beam, *Miracles from Heaven: A Little Girl, Her Journey to Heaven, and Her Amazing Story of Healing* (New York: Hachette, 2016).

4. See, e.g., Don Piper with Cecil Murphey, *Ninety Minutes in Heaven: A True Story of Death and Life* (Grand Rapids: Revell, 2004), 13–20, 37, 42–45.

5. E.g., Michael Rubincam, "Pennsylvania Toddler Survives Near-Drowning after 101 Minutes of CPR," NBC10 Philadelphia, March 20, 2015, https://www.nbcphiladelphia.com/news/national -international/toddler-survives-cpr-pennsylvania-icy-creek/132703/. See also Tim Pedley, "Miracle Toddler Who Fell in Stream Brought Back to Life after 101 Minutes of CPR," *Mirror*, March 21, 2015, https://www.mirror.co.uk/news/world-news/miracle-toddler-who-fell-stream-5377435; Josie Ensor, "Drowned Toddler Brought Back to Life after 101 Minutes of CPR," *The Telegraph*, March 20, 2015, https://www.telegraph.co.uk/news/worldnews/northamerica/usa/11487010/Drowned-toddler -brought-back-to-life-after-101-minutes-of-CPR.html; "Toddler Survives Near Drowning, 101 Min- utes of CPR," *CBS News*, March 20, 2015, https://www.cbsnews.com/news/toddler-survives-near -drowning-101-minutes-of-cpr/ (also found in "Pennsylvania Toddler Survives Near-Drowning after 101 Minutes of CPR," *Chicago Tribune*, March 19, 2015, https://www.chicagotribune.com/nation -world/chi-toddler-revived-after-near-drowning-20150319-story.html); Derek Burnett, "Dead for an Hour and 41 Minutes: The Incredible Rescue of Baby Gardell," *Healthy*, July 30, 2020, https://www .rd.com/true-stories/survival/rescue-baby-stream/ (all accessed Feb. 17, 2020).

6. Frank Maffei and Richard L. Lambert, "A Spirit of Calm, an Aura of Awe," in *Miracles We Have Seen: America's Leading Physicians Share Stories They Can't Forget*, ed. Harley A. Rotbart (Deerfield Beach, FL: Health Communications, 2016), 93–100, esp. 98–99.

7. See "Toddler Revived after 101 Minutes of CPR," CNN video, accessed Feb. 17, 2020, 2:09, https://www.cnn.com/videos/tv/2015/03/20/lead-pkg-darlington-toddler-revived-after-near-drowning .cnn.

8. E.g., "Teen Who Fell in Icy Pond Makes 'Miraculous' Recovery," *5 on Your Side* (KSDK), Feb. 4, 2015, https://www.ksdk.com/article/news/teen-who-fell-in-icy-pond-makes-miraculous-re covery/211167177; Kay Quinn, "Mom Prays, Dead Son Comes Back to Life," *USA Today*, Feb. 4, 2015, https://www.usatoday.com/story/news/2015/02/04/inspiration-nation-mom-prays-son-back-to -life/22883985/. See also "SSM Health Cardinal Glennon Children's Hospital—John Smith," SSM Health Cardinal Glennon Children's Foundation, YouTube video, Nov. 16, 2015, 5:12, https://www .youtube.com/watch?v=pAnloqg4W4c.

9. Joyce Smith with Ginger Kolbaba, *The Impossible: The Miraculous Story of a Mother's Faith and Her Child's Resurrection* (New York: FaithWords, 2017). See also the concise account in Dean Merrill, *Miracle Invasion: Amazing True Stories of the Holy Spirit's Gifts at Work Today* (Savage, MN: BroadStreet, 2018), 13–18. Other accounts of restoration after drowning flourish: e.g., that of Annie Powell, who recovered after not breathing for ten minutes; see Dan Van Veen, "From Tragic Death to Miraculous Life," Assemblies of God, May 5, 2020, https://news.ag.org/en/Features/From -Tragic-Death-to-Miraculous-Life.

10. Ryan Moore, "An Analytical Look at Survivable Submersion Times," *Site Zed*, March 19, 2013.

11. As for cases of full recovery at the temperature at which John drowned, only two cases appear in M. J. Tipton and F. S. Golden, "A Proposed Decision-Making Guide for the Search, Rescue and Resuscitation of Submersion (Head Under) Victims Based on Expert Opinion," *Resuscitation* 82 (2011): 819–24, as cited in Moore, "Analytical Look."

12. Dr. Sutterer's letter is reproduced in Smith, *The Impossible*, appendix B (pp. 241–43), and it includes the words "I was privileged to witness a miracle." Dr. Sutterer has also repeated his obser- vations in media reports and at the public thanksgiving service for John's recovery. See also, clearly, Jeremy Garrett, "A Bona Fide Miracle," in *Miracles We Have Seen: America's Leading Physicians*

Share Stories They Can't Forget, ed. Harley A. Rotbart (Deerfield Beach, FL: Health Communications, 2016), 114–17 (116–17).

13. Smith, *The Impossible*, 44.

14. Garrett, "Bona Fide Miracle," 116.

15. Garrett, "Bona Fide Miracle," 116.

16. Jason Noble, personal correspondence, April 15, 21, 2019. Note also, concisely, Jason Noble with Vince Antonucci, *Breakthrough to Your Miracle: Believing God for the Impossible* (Bloomington, MN: Chosen Books, 2019), 24–25.

17. Garrett, "Bona Fide Miracle," 116.

18. John Smith, phone interview, Jan. 30, 2020.

19. See Smith, *The Impossible*, 225–26.

20. Noble, *Breakthrough to Your Miracle*, 84–85, 112–13, 124–27.

21. Noble, *Breakthrough to Your Miracle*, 95–96 (through his wife, Paula), 140–46.

22. Dan Van Veen, "Doctors Say John Smith Is 'Bona Fide Miracle,'" *Assemblies of God News*, Feb. 13, 2015; Merrill, *Miracle Invasion*, 16.

23. Personal correspondence, June 6, 2020.

Chapter 28 Raised in the West? Cases That Don't Make the News

1. Interview, Lexington, KY, July 22, 2016; personal correspondence, July 25, 2016; July 29, 2016.

2. James L. Garlow and Keith Wall, *Real Life, Real Miracles: True Stories That Will Help You Believe* (Minneapolis: Bethany House, 2012), 168–75.

3. Józef Bałuczyński with Rob Starner, *Be Not Afraid, Only Believe* (n.p.: Xulon, 2015), 53–58; Rob Starner, personal correspondence, Aug. 27, 2014; Sept. 1, 2014.

4. Margaret J. Cotton, as told by Charlie Mada and Florentina Mada, *Raised! An Inspirational True Story of Two Courageous Young Parents in the Midst of a Tragic Accident, and the Love, Grace, and Miracles That Saved Three Lives* (Meadville, PA: Christian Faith, 2018); interview with the Madas, Phoenix, AZ, Jan. 15, 2019; personal correspondence with the Madas, Jan. 14, 27, 29, 2019; Feb. 11, 16, 2019; March 9, 2019; personal correspondence with Margaret Cotton, June 18, 2018; Aug. 23, 2018; Dec. 5–7, 26, 2018; Jan. 14, 2019; Feb. 16, 2019; meeting, Wilmore, KY, June 26, 2021.

5. A Romanian scholar friend verified the translation for me. The available documentation appears in the back pages of Cotton, Mada, and Mada, *Raised!*

6. E.g., among accounts not already in my book *Miracles* (2011), James Garlow notes the restoration to life of someone he knew (Garlow and Keith Wall, *Miracles Are for Real: What Happens When Heaven Touches Earth* [Minneapolis: Bethany House, 2011], 155–59) and also recounts the return to life of Ron Earl (35–40).

Chapter 29 Doctors Who Witness Raisings

1. See also, e.g., Christopher Woodard, *A Doctor's Faith Holds Fast* (London: Max Parrish, 1955), 97; John Stegeman, "A Woman's Faith," in *Faith Healing: Finger of God? Or, Scientific Curiosity?*, ed. Claude A. Frazier (New York: Nelson, 1973), 35–37.

2. Harley A. Rotbart, ed., *Miracles We Have Seen: America's Leading Physicians Share Stories They Can't Forget* (Deerfield Beach, FL: Health Communications, 2016), 91–122. For extraordinary awakenings where "brain death and a vegetative state seemed certain," see 123–39.

3. Rotbart, *Miracles We Have Seen*, 91.

4. Dave Walker, *God in the ICU: The Inspirational Biography of a Praying Doctor* (Sun Valley, South Africa: Tricycle, 2011), 99–104.

5. Walker, *God in the ICU*, 100.

6. I borrow some of the following wording from my 2015 *Bulletin for Biblical Research* article, "The Dead Are Raised." I have Dr. Ascabano's general account from Jan. 9, 2009, with personal correspondence from Feb. 6, 2009.

7. Todd Stokes, personal correspondence, Aug. 29–30, 2020.

8. Matthew Suh, phone interview, Aug. 26, 2020.

9. Arthur Williams, personal correspondence, Aug. 27, 31, 2020.

10. Chauncey W. Crandall IV, *Raising the Dead: A Doctor Encounters the Miraculous* (New York: FaithWords, 2010), 4. For further information, see Daniel Fazzina, *Divine Intervention: 50 True Stories of God's Miracles Today* (Lake Mary, FL: Charisma House, 2014), 203–6; James L. Garlow and Keith Wall, *Miracles Are for Real: What Happens When Heaven Touches Earth* (Minneapolis: Bethany House, 2011), 164–67.

11. Although the local and national secular media links are no longer posted at the same web addresses (cited in Keener, *Miracles* [2011], 1:578–79), they were available in 2009, when I reviewed them. An explicitly Christian report remains posted at "Dr. Chauncey Crandall: Raising the Dead," Christian Broadcasting Network, accessed July 24, 2020, http://www.cbn.com/tv/1432634071001.

12. Chauncey Crandall, phone interview, May 30, 2010. This observation responds to Hume's argument that no credible eyewitness with something to lose reports miracles. Compare Howard Clark Kee, *Miracle in the Early Christian World: A Study in Sociohistorical Method* (New Haven: Yale University Press, 1983), 11–12.

13. Personal correspondence, Nov. 8, 2013. See the full account, with medical documentation, at Sean George, *The Miracle Story of Dr Sean George* (website), accessed Jan. 30, 2020, https://seangeorge.com.au/. The account also appears in James L. Garlow and Keith Wall, *Real Life, Real Miracles: True Stories That Will Help You Believe* (Minneapolis: Bethany House, 2012), 22–28.

14. See George, *Miracle Story*, https://seangeorge.com.au/.

Chapter 30 Friends Who Used to Be Dead or Met Those Who Had Been

1. Francis Kashimawo, Lagos, Nigeria, May 2013.

2. Chinyereugo Adeliyi, personal correspondence, May 10, 11, 12, 2014; also Johnson Adelaja Tolowoetan, interview, Lagos, Nigeria, May 29, 2013.

3. Timothy Olonade, personal correspondence, May 12, 13, 16, 22, 2014; interview, Wilmore, KY, Feb. 20, 2015.

4. For another account of a resuscitated person moving (in this case within the body bag), see Surprise Sithole with David Wimbish, *Voice in the Night* (Bloomington, MN: Chosen Books, 2012), 176.

5. For one such event in the Democratic Republic of Congo, see Mahesh Chavda with John Blattner, *Only Love Can Make a Miracle: The Mahesh Chavda Story* (Ann Arbor, MI: Servant, 1990), 9, 13–15, 78–79, 131–41 (see esp. 137–41). The documentation includes the death certificate. This account is also noted in academic studies: e.g., Candy Gunther Brown, *Testing Prayer: Science and Healing* (Cambridge, MA: Harvard University Press, 2012), 111, 113.

6. Sarah Speer, phone interview, Jan. 7, 2009; personal correspondence, Aug. 20, 2009.

7. Patrice Nsouami, phone interview, April 29, 2010.

8. Keener, *Miracles* (2011), 1:558–60; Keener, "'The Dead Are Raised' (Matthew 11:5//Luke 7:22): Resuscitation Accounts in the Gospels and Eyewitness Testimony," *Bulletin for Biblical Research* 25 (1, 2015): 55–79 (62–63).

9. Jeanne Mabiala, interview, Brazzaville, Republic of Congo, July 29, 2008.

10. Another non-African account would be that of, e.g., Dick and Debbie Riffle (Dec. 13, 2007), trusted US friends of my brother Chris; the story is recounted in my *Miracles* (2011), 1:574.

11. Elaine Panelo, interview, Baguio, Philippines, Jan. 30, 2009. For stories from elsewhere in the Philippines, see Chester Allan Tesoro, interview, Baguio, Philippines, Jan. 30, 2009. For other accounts from Asia, see, e.g., William Young, "Miracles in Church History," *Churchman* 102 (2, 1988): 102–21 (117–18); Rex Gardner, *Healing Miracles: A Doctor Investigates* (London: Darton, Longman & Todd, 1986), 138; Gardner, "Miracles of Healing in Anglo-Celtic Northumbria as Recorded by the Venerable Bede and His Contemporaries: A Reappraisal in the Light of Twentieth-Century Experience," *British Medical Journal* 287 (Dec. 24–31, 1983): 1932; David Pytches, *Come Holy Spirit: Learning How to Minister in Power* (London: Hodder & Stoughton, 1985), 242–44; Mark R. Mullins, "The Empire Strikes Back: Korean Pentecostal Mission to Japan," in *Charismatic Christianity as a Global Culture*, ed. Karla Poewe (Columbia: University of South Carolina Press, 1994), 87–102 (91); Tony Lambert, *China's Christian Millions: The Costly Revival* (London: Monarch, 1999), 109, 118–19; Philip Jenkins, *The New Faces of Christianity: Believing the Bible in the Global South* (New York: Oxford University Press, 2006), 114; Chin Khua Khai, "The Assemblies

of God and Pentecostalism in Myanmar," in *Asian and Pentecostal: The Charismatic Face of Christianity in Asia*, ed. Allan Anderson and Edmond Tang (Oxford: Regnum, 2005), 261–80 (270); Deng Zhaoming, "Indigenous Chinese Pentecostal Denominations," in Anderson and Tang, *Asian and Pentecostal*, 437–66 (451); Sung-Gun Kim, "Pentecostalism, Shamanism, and Capitalism within Contemporary Korean Society," in *Spirits of Globalization: The Growth of Pentecostalism and Experiential Spiritualities in a Global Age*, ed. Sturla J. Stålsett (London: SCM, 2006), 23–38 (32); Julie C. Ma, "Pentecostalism and Asian Mission," *Missiology* 35 (1, Jan. 2007): 23–37 (31); Alexander F. Venter, *Doing Healing: How to Minister God's Kingdom in the Power of the Spirit* (Cape Town, South Africa: Vineyard International, 2008), 294–95.

12. Yusuf Herman, interview, Wilmore, KY, July 10, 2011; Dominggus Kenjam, phone interview, Aug. 7, 2011. For other accounts of raisings in Indonesia, see, e.g., Kurt Koch, *The Revival in Indonesia* (Grand Rapids: Kregel, 1970), 129, 138, 141–42; Don Crawford, *Miracles in Indonesia: God's Power Builds His Church!* (Wheaton: Tyndale, 1972), 26–28. For the severity of internal decapitations and one survival and recovery considered miraculous, see Richard Roberts, "Decapitated," in *Miracles We Have Seen: America's Leading Physicians Share Stories They Can't Forget*, ed. Harley A. Rotbart (Deerfield Beach, FL: Health Communications, 2016), 149–51.

13. James Watson, correspondence, Nov. 27, 2009; sent by Deborah to me with correspondence, Nov. 30, 2009; Deborah Watson, personal correspondence, Dec. 9, 2009.

14. E.g., Obadiah Avong, interview, Lagos, Nigeria, May 29, 2013; Sung Wha Park, spiritual formation assignment, May 2015; personal correspondence, Jan. 30, 2020.

15. Davie Ferraro, recorded interview, Dec. 22, 2017.

16. Dimbiniaina Randrianasolo, interview, April 18, 2019.

17. Matthew Maresco, personal correspondence, May 18–19, 2021.

18. Margufta Bellevue, personal correspondence, Jan. 30, 31, 2020.

Chapter 31 Raised in Our Family

1. Albert Bissouessoue, interview, Brazzaville, Republic of Congo, July 29, 2008; fuller interview with him by Dr. Emmanuel Moussounga, provided to me Dec. 17, 2009; Julienne Bissouessoue, interview by Emmanuel Moussounga, Dec. 15, 2009.

2. Interview, Dolisie, Republic of Congo, July 12, 2008.

3. Ngoma Moïse confirmed his recollection of the event in a brief phone interview, May 14, 2009.

4. Ngoma Moïse, phone interview, May 14, 2009.

5. Thanks to physics PhD Christopher Keener and engineering student Keren Keener for consultation on the estimates.

Chapter 32 Do Nature Miracles Still Happen?

1. See Keener, *Miracles* (2011), 1:579–99 (esp. 593, 595); Keener, "The Historicity of the Nature Miracles," in *The Nature Miracles of Jesus: Problems, Perspectives, and Prospects*, ed. Graham H. Twelftree (Eugene, OR: Cascade Books, 2017), 41–65, 195–200. Note more recent reports: e.g., James L. Garlow and Keith Wall, *Real Life, Real Miracles: True Stories That Will Help You Believe* (Minneapolis: Bethany House, 2012), 235; Surprise Sithole with David Wimbish, *Voice in the Night* (Bloomington, MN: Chosen Books, 2012), 178. I have even found reports of invisibility in the face of assailants: e.g., Médine Moussounga, personal journal, June 26, 1999; Józef Bałuczyński with Rob Starner, *Be Not Afraid, Only Believe* (n.p.: Xulon, 2015), 26–27; Rob Starner, personal correspondence, Sept. 1, 2014; July 18, 2015.

2. Hwa Yung, "The Integrity of Mission in the Light of the Gospel: Bearing the Witness of the Spirit," *Mission Studies* 24 (2007): 174; Gary B. McGee, "Miracles," in *Encyclopedia of Mission and Missionaries*, ed. Jonathan J. Bonk (New York: Routledge, 2007), 252–54 (253); McGee, *Miracles, Missions, and American Pentecostalism*, American Society of Missiology Series 45 (Maryknoll, NY: Orbis Books, 2010), 51, 242.

3. Dieter Ising, *Johann Christoph Blumhardt, Life and Work: A New Biography*, trans. Monty Ledford (Eugene, OR: Cascade Books, 2009), 215. For an earlier account, see Francis Asbury in John Wigger, *American Saint: Francis Asbury and the Methodists* (Oxford: Oxford University Press, 2009), 193.

4. Sources cited in Paul L. King, *Moving Mountains: Lessons in Bold Faith from Great Evangelical Leaders* (Bloomington, MN: Chosen Books, 2004), 15–16, 20, 42, 46 (compare 38).

5. King, *Moving Mountains*, 15–16.

6. King, *Moving Mountains*, 20.

7. King, *Moving Mountains*, 38, 42, 46.

8. Watchman Nee, *Sit, Walk, Stand* (Carol Stream, IL: Tyndale, 1977), 60–72; see also Angus Kinnear, *Against the Tide: The Story of Watchman Nee* (Wheaton: Tyndale, 1978), 92–97.

9. Alpha E. Anderson, *Pelendo: God's Prophet in the Congo* (Chicago: Moody, 1964), 43–47.

10. Mangapul Sagala, interview, Jakarta, Indonesia, March 27, 2015; Dr. Sagala also noted two other such incidents. For other reports of nature miracles, see, e.g., Edith L. Blumhofer, *Aimee Semple McPherson: Everybody's Sister* (Grand Rapids: Eerdmans, 1993), 184–85 (noting the public prayer and instant stopping of rain, cited also in the *Wichita Eagle*, May 30, 1921, 1); Jerry Trousdale, *Miraculous Movements* (Nashville: Nelson, 2012), 80–81; Nonyem E. Numbere, *A Man and a Vision: A Biography of Apostle Geoffrey D. Numbere* (Diobu, Nigeria: Greater Evangelism Publications, 2008), 206–7; a sea storm in Kurt Koch, *The Revival in Indonesia* (Grand Rapids: Kregel, 1970), 143; Mel Tari and Nona Tari, *The Gentle Breeze of Jesus* (Harrison, AR: New Leaf, 1974), 154–56; Petrus Octavianus in Don Crawford, *Miracles in Indonesia: God's Power Builds His Church!* (Wheaton: Tyndale, 1972), 75; Kurt Koch, *Charismatic Gifts* (Quebec: Association for Christian Evangelism, 1975), 106–7.

11. Sai Krishna Gomatam, interview, Feb. 3, 2020; follow-up correspondence, Feb. 7, 2020.

12. Personal correspondence, June 1–2, 2016. For other instances of selective rainfall, see, e.g., Trousdale, *Miraculous Movements*, 125–26. For examples from Indonesia, see, e.g., Koch, *Revival in Indonesia*, 144; independently, Mel Tari with Cliff Dudley, *Like a Mighty Wind* (Carol Stream, IL: Creation House, 1971), 44–45; Tari and Tari, *Gentle Breeze of Jesus*, 91.

13. David Chotka, personal correspondence, March 3, 4, 5, 7, 11, 12, 2021; also recounted in his book *Power Praying: Hearing Jesus' Spirit by Praying Jesus' Prayer* (Terre Haute, IN: PrayerShop, 2009), 9–11.

14. Fred Hartley, personal correspondence, March 11, 2021; Michael Plunket, personal correspondence, March 4, 2021. Hartley, a graduate of Wheaton and Gordon-Conwell, is pastor of Lilburn Alliance Church. Plunket is pastor at Risen King Alliance Church and has taught at Alliance Theological Seminary.

15. Michael Plunket, "Assessing the College of Prayer International's Ministry in Uganda 2007–2009 and Its Long-Term Effects" (DMin diss., Alliance Theological Seminary, 2014), 15–17.

16. On a larger scale, some Adventist sources have reported something like manna in the wilderness in a drought-stricken village in Angola at times (e.g., *Signs of the Times* 62 [19, May 12, 1947]: 1, 6; *Believers Today*, Sept. 18, 2018; courtesy of Esteban Hidalgo); reports of water turned to wine (see p. 182) also may reflect a larger scale than the Cana wedding (John 2:1–11).

17. Jacalyn Duffin, *Medical Miracles: Doctors, Saints, and Healing in the Modern World* (Oxford: Oxford University Press, 2009), 28; Terence L. Nichols, "Miracles, the Supernatural, and the Problem of Extrinsicism," *Gregorianum* 71 (1, 1990): 23–41 (32–33); Rex Gardner, *Healing Miracles: A Doctor Investigates* (London: Darton, Longman & Todd, 1986), 13, 71; René Laurentin, *Miracles in El Paso?* (Ann Arbor, MI: Servant, 1982), 100–102.

18. See William Young, "Miracles in Church History," *Churchman* 102 (2, 1988): 102–21 (118–19); Gani Wiyono, "Timor Revival: A Historical Study of the Great Twentieth-Century Revival in Indonesia," *Asian Journal of Pentecostal Studies* 4 (2, 2001): 269–93 (286); Tari and Tari, *Gentle Breeze of Jesus*, 117–18 (for days, as in 1 Kings 17:14–16), 42–43; Tari, *Like a Mighty Wind*, 47–49; Corrie Ten Boom with John and Elizabeth Sherrill, *The Hiding Place* (New York: Bantam, 1974), 202–3; Laurentin, *Miracles in El Paso?*, 4–5, 49, 95–97 (six different occasions, with dates and witnesses, 110–12); William P. Wilson, "How Religious or Spiritual Miracle Events Happen Today," in *Religious and Spiritual Events*, vol. 1 of *Miracles: God, Science, and Psychology in the Paranormal*, ed. J. Harold Ellens (Westport, CT: Praeger, 2008), 276–77; Gardner, *Healing Miracles*, 38, 71; Rolland Baker and Heidi Baker, *Always Enough: God's Miraculous Provision among the Poorest Children on Earth* (Bloomington, MN: Chosen Books, 2003), 52 (also noted in Baker and Baker, *Expecting Miracles: True Stories of God's Supernatural Power and How You Can Experience It* [Bloomington, MN: Chosen Books, 2007], 198; by another witness in Heidi Baker, *Birthing the Miraculous* [Lake Mary, FL: Charisma House, 2014],

166; on other occasions in their ministry to the needy, Guy Chevreau, *Turnings: The Kingdom of God and the Western World* [Tonbridge, Kent, UK: Sovereign World, 2004], 214–15). For multiplied blankets for homeless persons, see Garlow and Wall, *Real Life, Real Miracles*, 229.

19. Larry Eskridge, *God's Forever Family: The Jesus People Movement in America* (Oxford: Oxford University Press, 2013), 81–82. Eskridge recounts five specific reports from the context of his larger interviews; around 1977, in similar circles, I heard a report on a much lesser scale.

20. Dean Merrill, *Miracle Invasion: Amazing True Stories of the Holy Spirit's Gifts at Work Today* (Savage, MN: BroadStreet, 2018), 41–43.

21. Randy Clark and Mary Healy, *The Spiritual Gifts Handbook: Using Your Gifts to Build the Kingdom* (Bloomington, MN: Chosen Books, 2018), 166. For earlier Catholic stories of food multiplying, see Albert E. Graham, *Compendium of the Miraculous* (Charlotte: TAN Books, 2013), 176–78; see also the well-documented case at the Ribera del Fresno parish on Jan. 25, 1949 (Michael O'Neill, *Exploring the Miraculous* [Huntington, IN: Our Sunday Visitor, 2015], 80–81).

22. Grant LeMarquand, interview, Wilmore, KY, Oct. 17, 2020. His wife, Wendy, a medical doctor, also has witnessed healings and authored a report in their newsletter about this incident.

23. Baker and Baker, *Always Enough*, 51–52 (a clear, credible, eyewitness case, also noted in Baker and Baker, *Expecting Miracles*, 198; Sithole, *Voice in the Night*, 145); additional occasions in their ministry to the needy are recounted in Chevreau, *Turnings*, 214–15.

24. Baker and Baker, *Always Enough*, 52.

25. Personal correspondence, May 30, 2016.

26. Don Kantel, "Development Aid as Power Evangelism: The Mieze Model," in *Supernatural Missions: The Impact of the Supernatural on World Missions*, ed. Randy Clark (Mechanicsburg, PA: Global Awakening, 2012), 370–73, 377–81; personal correspondence, May 28, 2016.

27. Personal correspondence, Aug. 14, 2020.

28. *Mully* (Bardis Productions, 2015; see Mullymovie.com); also mentioned in "Adopting Hope [2]: The Mully Children's Family," *Christianity Today* podcast, Dec. 4, 2020 (Sasha Parker interview with Kara Bettis).

29. Personal correspondence, June 6, 2016. For other prayers for rain, see, e.g., Luis Bush and Beverly Pegues, *The Move of the Holy Spirit in the 10/40 Window*, ed. Jane Rumph (Seattle: YWAM, 1999), 64; Sithole, *Voice in the Night*, 169–70; Dennis Balcombe, *China's Opening Door* (Lake Mary, FL: Charisma House, 2014), 118–19; other sources in Keener, *Miracles* (2011), 1:593, 595. For water, see also Donna Arukua, interview, Baguio, Philippines, Jan. 29, 2009 (in Keener, *Miracles* [2011], 1:593).

30. See Koch, *Revival in Indonesia*, 208–17 (esp. his eyewitness testimony, 212–17); Koch, *Charismatic Gifts*, 107 (citing himself for the incident on July 18, 1969, and naming eight witnesses of that incident, including foreign educators and a local governor); Wiyono, "Timor Revival," 285–86 (citing interviews with eyewitnesses); Young, "Miracles in History," 119; Crawford, *Miracles in Indonesia*, 26; Yusuf Herman, interview, July 10, 2011 (naming witnesses he knows); Tari, *Like a Mighty Wind*, 78–84 (multiple occasions; Tari says that he checked carefully on one occasion, 79–84).

31. See, e.g., Julia Theis Dermawan, "A Study of the Nias Revival in Indonesia," *Asian Journal of Pentecostal Studies* 6 (2, 2003): 247–63 (256, regarding 1916–1922); Crawford, *Miracles in Indonesia*, 26; Tari, *Like a Mighty Wind*, 43–47 (citing the witnesses); Tari and Tari, *Gentle Breeze of Jesus*, 41 (the same event).

32. Phone interview, April 15, 2014; follow-up personal correspondence, April 15, 2014. I also draw some details from Dr. Jennifer Miskov's videotaped interview with Tari, July 23, 2020; and especially from Tari, *Like a Mighty Wind*, 43–47.

33. Interview, Makassar, Indonesia, April 1, 2015; personal correspondence, April 10, 2015.

Chapter 33 Do You Know Any Witnesses to Nature Miracles?

1. Emmanuel Itapson, interview, April 29, 2008; reiterated in a phone interview, Dec. 15, 2009. My English pun in the sentence admittedly does not work in the original Hausa.

2. Kevin Burr, account in class, March 15, 2016; personal correspondence, March 17, 2016; April 14, 2016; May 29, 2016; reports from Paul Murphy (March 15, 2016); Bridget A. Lindsay (March 17, 2016); Jonathan Lindsay (March 17, 2016); Branson Bridges (March 21, 2016).

3. I checked online weather records, and they are consistent with F2 and F3 tornadoes in the area on April 2, 2006.

4. A copy of the photograph is also in my possession.

5. Brian Shockey, class and personal discussion, Nov. 2, 2020; follow-up personal correspondence, Nov. 2, 4, 16, 2020.

6. See, e.g., David Crump, *Knocking on Heaven's Door: A New Testament Theology of Petitionary Prayer* (Grand Rapids: Baker Academic, 2006), 13, detailing the witness's trustworthiness. Other naturally impossible car reports appear in, e.g., Larry Eskridge, *God's Forever Family: The Jesus People Movement in America* (Oxford: Oxford University Press, 2013), 82.

7. Personal correspondence, March 19, 2013.

8. I first heard this story from Dr. Joseph Harvey in Congo (interview, July 25, 2008) but confirmed and corrected that account on the basis of a phone interview with Sandy Thomas (Aug. 26, 2008).

9. See Craig Keener and Médine Moussounga Keener, *Impossible Love: The True Story of an African Civil War, Miracles, and Love against All Odds* (Bloomington, MN: Chosen Books, 2016), 103, 106–7.

10. Interview, Wilmore, KY, April 8, 2016; personal correspondence, April 9, 2016; May 28, 2016.

11. I heard Ayo Adewuya tell this story on Nov. 22, 2009; he confirmed it in a phone interview, Dec. 14, 2009. On traditional religion, see, e.g., Tabona Shoko, *Karanga Indigenous Religion in Zimbabwe: Health and Well-Being* (Burlington, VT: Ashgate, 2007), 37, 41.

12. Interviews, June 3, 2006; May 13, 2009.

13. Benjamin Ahanonu, interview, Sept. 29, 2009; confirmed by Simon Hauger, phone interview, Dec. 4, 2009.

14. Interview, Wilmore, KY, March 16, 2012.

15. The seminary, Hood Theological Seminary, is affiliated with the A.M.E. Zion Church.

16. Craig Keener, personal journal, Nov. 6, 1993.

Chapter 34 A Firsthand Witness?

1. This happened on Sept. 13–14, 2017.

2. This consultation was on Sept. 18, 2017. Similarly, when my dentist referred me for a root canal (Oct. 8, 2001) but I was extremely limited financially, I was praying for the Lord's help. When I reached the endodontist, he examined me for the root canal and declared that my tooth must have done its own root canal (Nov. 12, 2001). (I still needed a filling, though!) I noted earlier the disappearance of cancer in a member of my small home group, without treatment, after her malignant tumor was biopsied, but because biopsies sometimes remove the entire malignancy, I do not elaborate further.

3. This story also appears in Craig S. Keener, *Gift and Giver: The Holy Spirit for Today* (Grand Rapids: Baker Academic, 2001), 59.

4. See Acts 2:4; 10:46; 19:6; 1 Cor. 12:10, 28; 14:5–6, 18, 39. For one recent, readable study of the gift, see Sam Storms, *The Language of Heaven* (Lake Mary, FL: Charisma House, 2019).

5. Mesfin Negusse, by phone, Dec. 15, 2008; he later confirmed for me again his lack of knowledge on the first occasion (March 29, 2019, in person, in Addis Ababa, Ethiopia).

Chapter 35 Why Don't We See More Miracles in the West?

1. Dale S. Adler, "Father Karl's Miraculous Timing," in *Miracles We Have Seen: America's Leading Physicians Share Stories They Can't Forget*, ed. Harley A. Rotbart (Deerfield Beach, FL: Health Communications, 2016), 9–12. For other examples of "spectacular serendipity," see Rotbart, *Miracles We Have Seen*, 7–42. See, similarly, Ronald Sider's experience noted on his blog, Feb. 1, 2021.

2. Besides sources cited in chaps. 2–3, see, e.g., the articles in *Christian History* 76 (4, 2002); and again, e.g., John Hedley Brooke, *Science and Religion: Some Historical Perspectives* (New York: Cambridge University Press, 1991); Derrick Peterson, *Flat Earth and Fake Footnotes: The Strange Tale of How the Conflict of Science and Christianity Was Written into History* (Eugene, OR: Cascade Books, 2020); today, e.g., Elaine Howard Ecklund, *Science vs. Religion: What Scientists Really Think* (Oxford: Oxford University Press, 2010). Compare Ps. 115:16; Prov. 6:6; 25:2.

3. Jacalyn Duffin, *Medical Miracles: Doctors, Saints, and Healing in the Modern World* (Oxford: Oxford University Press, 2009), 113.

4. For observations concerning the language of "miracles," see, e.g., Richard A. Horsley, *Jesus and Magic: Freeing the Gospel Stories from Modern Misconceptions* (Eugene, OR: Cascade Books, 2014); Luke Timothy Johnson, *Miracles: God's Presence and Power in Creation* (Louisville: Westminster John Knox, 2018), 21–75 (esp. helpfully 41). For the term "signs," I follow here Lukan and Johannine, rather than Markan, usage.

Chapter 36 Spiritual Factors and Miracles

1. See, e.g., Mel Tari, phone interview, April 15, 2014; Rolland Baker, *Keeping the Fire: Discovering the Heart of True Revival* (Bloomington, MN: Chosen Books, 2016).

2. For a fuller set of comparisons and contrasts, see Craig S. Keener, *The IVP Bible Background Commentary: New Testament*, rev. ed. (Downers Grove, IL: InterVarsity, 2014), 337.

3. For the variations, see esp. Thomas Lyons, "Revisiting the Riddle in Samaria: A Social-Scientific Investigation of Spirit Reception in Luke-Acts in Historical Perspective" (PhD diss., Asbury Theological Seminary, 2020), chap. 4, including healings in the Welsh revival. For other examples of miraculous experiences in revivals, see, e.g., Kurt Koch, *The Revival in Indonesia* (Grand Rapids: Kregel, 1970), 208–17; Julia Theis Dermawan, "A Study of the Nias Revival in Indonesia," *Asian Journal of Pentecostal Studies* 6 (2, 2003): 247–63; Solomon Bulan and Lillian Bulan-Dorai, *The Bario Revival* (Kuala Lumpur, Malaysia: HomeMatters, 2004), 92, 113–16, 141, 149, 166.

4. Michelle Moran, "The Spirituality at the Heart of the Catholic Charismatic Renewal Movement," *Transformation* 30 (4, Oct. 2013): 287–91, esp. 287–88.

5. See, e.g., Gary B. McGee, "The Radical Strategy in Modern Mission: The Linkage of Paranormal Phenomena with Evangelism," in *The Holy Spirit and Mission Dynamics*, ed. C. Douglas McConnell (Pasadena: William Carey Library, 1997), 69–95; McGee, "Shortcut to Language Preparation? Radical Evangelicals, Missions, and the Gift of Tongues," *International Bulletin of Mission Research* 25 (July 2001): 118–23; Allan Heaton Anderson, *To the Ends of the Earth: Pentecostalism and the Transformation of World Christianity* (New York: Oxford University Press, 2013), 12–13.

6. See esp. Mark Shaw, *Global Awakening: How 20th-Century Revivals Triggered a Christian Revolution* (Downers Grove, IL: IVP Academic, 2010); on modern revivals and awakenings in general, see Edith Blumhofer and Randall H. Balmer, eds., *Modern Christian Revivals* (Urbana: University of Illinois Press, 1993); Michael McClymond, ed., *Encyclopedia of Religious Revivals in America*, 2 vols. (Westport, CT: Greenwood, 2007).

7. See, e.g., Emmanuel Hooper, "The Great Awakening of 1905: The Welsh Revival and Its Influence on the American Revival," in *Revival, Renewal, and the Holy Spirit*, ed. Dyfed Wyn Roberts (Eugene, OR: Wipf & Stock, 2009), 222–32.

8. On Ramabai, see Nalini Arles, "Pandita Ramabai and Amy Carmichael: A Study of Their Contributions toward Transforming the Position of Indian Women" (MTh thesis, University of Aberdeen, 1985); Ruth Vassar Burgess, "Pandita Ramabai: A Woman for All Seasons: Pandita Ramabai Saraswati Mary Dongre Medhavi (1858–1922)," *Asia Journal of Pentecostal Studies* 9 (2, July 2006): 183–98; Robert Eric Frykenberg, *Christianity in India: From Beginnings to the Present* (New York: Oxford University Press, 2010), 382–410.

9. See, e.g., Allan Anderson, *An Introduction to Pentecostalism: Global Charismatic Christianity* (Cambridge: Cambridge University Press, 2004), 39–45; Cecil M. Robeck, Jr., *The Azusa Street Mission and Revival: The Birth of the Global Pentecostal Movement* (Nashville: Nelson, 2006).

10. See, e.g., Tony Lambert, *China's Christian Millions: The Costly Revival* (London: Monarch, 1999); Rolland Baker and Heidi Baker, *Always Enough: God's Miraculous Provision among the Poorest Children on Earth* (Bloomington, MN: Chosen Books, 2003).

11. Eyewitness Anna D. Gulick (*Captured: An Atheist's Journey with God* [Lexington: Emeth, 2012]) notes that some students' desperate prayer for revival preceded the second Asbury revival (as well as the Hebrides revival).

12. See Edward Warren Capen, *The Significance of the Haystack Prayer Meeting* (New York: Committee on the Centennial Anniversary of the Haystack Prayer Meeting, 1906).

13. See Richard Burgess, *Nigeria's Christian Revolution: The Civil War Revival and Its Pentecostal Progeny (1967–2006)* (Eugene, OR: Wipf & Stock, 2008).

14. Moses, for example, could not negotiate his way out of his calling (Exod. 3:11–4:17); and sometimes we ask for gifts that we are better off without (compare Mark 10:35–40 with 15:27).

15. David Kimberlin, "Whatever the Outcome, It Will Be Okay," in *Miracles We Have Seen: America's Leading Physicians Share Stories They Can't Forget*, ed. Harley A. Rotbart (Deerfield Beach, FL: Health Communications, 2016), 81.

16. Howard Taylor and Mrs. Howard Taylor, *Hudson Taylor and the China Inland Mission: The Growth of a Work of God*, 4th ed. (London: Morgan & Scott, 1920), 265.

Chapter 37 When Healing Is Temporary

1. Lyle W. Dorsett, citing his own conversation with the doctor, in "Helen Joy Davidman (Mrs. C. S. Lewis) 1915–1960: A Portrait," C. S. Lewis Institute, accessed March 3, 2021, http://www.cslewis institute.org/node/31, based on Dorsett, *A Love Observed: Joy Davidman's Life and Marriage to C. S. Lewis* (Wheaton: Harold Shaw, 1998). Compare other remissions in C. Bernard Ruffin, *Padre Pio: The True Story*, 3rd rev. ed. (Huntington, IN: Our Sunday Visitor, 2018), 384–86.

2. See C. S. Lewis, *A Grief Observed* (New York: Seabury, 1961).

3. Candy Gunther Brown, *Testing Prayer: Science and Healing* (Cambridge, MA: Harvard University Press, 2012), 254–55; Brown, "Empirical Perspectives on Prayer for Healing: Viewing Prayer through Multiple Cameras Produces a More Complete Picture," *Psychology Today*, April 10, 2012, https://www .psychologytoday.com/us/blog/testing-prayer/201204/empirical-perspectives-prayer-healing. For a list of some other perceived cures, both temporary and longer-term, see Henri Nissen, *The God of Miracles: A Danish Journalist Examines Healings in the Ministry of Charles Ndifon* (Copenhagen: Scandinavia Publishing House, 2003), 169–78, noting results from Majbrit Bruun Anderson, "Physiological and Psychological Experiences with Religious Treatment in Relation to the Patients' Comprehension of Their Illness and Their Experiences with the Public Health Service" (Pregraduate study, Syddansk Universitet, 2002).

4. Wayne E. Warner, "Still Healed of TB—after Fifty-Two Years," *Pentecostal Evangel*, July 8, 2001, 28; Warner, "'Living by Faith': A Story of Paul and Betty Wells," *Assemblies of God Heritage* 16 (4, Winter 1996–1997): 3–4, 24 (noting that someone remained healed after sixty-five to seventy-five years).

5. Wayne E. Warner, *The Woman Evangelist: The Life and Times of Charismatic Evangelist Maria B. Woodworth-Etter*, Studies in Evangelicalism 8 (Metuchen, NJ: Scarecrow, 1986), 180–81; Romer wrote his testimony to Warner on July 20, 1981.

6. Warner, *Woman Evangelist*, 181; the testimony is from his family and a letter to Warner in 1978.

7. Dirk J. Kruijthoff et al., "'My Body Does Not Fit in Your Medical Textbooks': A Physically Turbulent Life with an Unexpected Recovery from Advanced Parkinson Disease after Prayer," *Advances in Mind-Body Medicine* 35 (2, Winter 2021): 4–13 (compare also the abstract online at https://pubmed.ncbi.nlm.nih .gov/33620331/). In 2021, Rose Marie Straeter shared with me her own healing from Parkinson's in 2010.

8. Bob Neff, *Spiritual End-Time Warfare* (n.p.: Robert Neff, 2009), 13–14.

Chapter 38 When Miracles Don't Happen

1. See here the very relevant account in Mary Healy, *Healing: Bringing the Gift of God's Mercy to the World* (Huntington, IN: Our Sunday Visitor, 2015), 109–12.

2. Books about miracles, whatever their varied approaches, often conclude with such observations: see, e.g., Keener, *Miracles* (2011), 2:766–68; Lee Strobel, *The Case for Miracles: A Journalist Investigates Evidence for the Supernatural* (Grand Rapids: Zondervan, 2018), 235–53 (esp. sharing the story of our mutual friends Doug Groothuis and the now deceased Rebecca Merrill Groothuis); Tony Cooke, *Miracles and the Supernatural throughout Church History* (Shippensburg, PA: Harrison, 2020), 311–19. Compare also Damian Stayne, *Lord, Renew Your Wonders: Spiritual Gifts for Today* (Frederick, MD: The Word Among Us Press, 2017), 109–10.

3. See his testimony in Nabeel Qureshi, *Seeking Allah, Finding Jesus* (Grand Rapids: Zondervan, 2016).

4. Clarissa Romez et al., "Case Report of Instantaneous Resolution of Juvenile Macular Degeneration Blindness after Proximal Intercessory Prayer," *Explore: The Journal of Science and Healing* 17 (1, Jan.–Feb. 2021): 79–83, https://doi.org/10.1016/j.explore.2020.02.011.

5. Discussed briefly in Craig S. Keener, *1–2 Corinthians* (New York: Cambridge University Press, 2005), 240.

6. Chauncey W. Crandall IV, *Raising the Dead: A Doctor Encounters the Miraculous* (New York: FaithWords, 2010), 7–131 passim.

7. Danny McCain, personal correspondence, Nov. 30, 2014.

Chapter 39 What Does the Bible Say about Non-healing?

1. Cyprian, *Treatise 7 (On Mortality)*, 8 (trans. *Ante-Nicene Fathers*, ed. Roberts and Donaldson).

2. Cyprian, *Treatise 7 (On Mortality)*, 16.

3. Cyprian, *Treatise 7 (On Mortality)*, 15.

4. See Gary B. Ferngren, "Demonstrating the Love of Christ: At the Very Beginning of the Church, Christians Were Known for Their Compassion in Times of Illness," *Christian History* 135 (2020): 12–15, esp. 14–15. Cyprian is quoted in the inset.

5. On Dowie, see Ralph H. Major, *Faiths That Healed* (New York: D. Appleton-Century, 1940), 208–22; Grant Wacker, "Marching to Zion: Religion in a Modern Utopian Community," *Church History* 54 (1985): 496–511; Robert Bruce Mullin, *Miracles and the Modern Religious Imagination* (New Haven: Yale University Press, 1996), 203–8; Jonathan R. Baer, "Perfectly Empowered Bodies: Divine Healing in Modernizing America" (PhD diss., Yale University, 2002), 212–19; James Opp, *The Lord for the Body: Religion, Medicine, and Protestant Faith Healing in Canada, 1880–1930* (Montreal: McGill-Queen's University Press, 2005), 91–120; Kimberly Ervin Alexander, *Pentecostal Healing: Models in Theology and Practice* (Blandford Forum, UK: Deo, 2006), 58–63.

6. For the view, see David Edwin Harrell Jr., "Divine Healing in Modern American Protestantism," in *Other Healers: Unorthodox Medicine in America*, ed. Norman Gevitz (Baltimore: Johns Hopkins University Press, 1988), 215–27 (217–18); Mullin, *Miracles and the Modern Religious Imagination*, 204; John Wilkinson, *The Bible and Healing: A Medical and Theological Commentary* (Grand Rapids: Eerdmans, 1998), 280; Neil Hudson, "Early British Pentecostals and Their Relationship to Health, Healing, and Medicine," *Asian Journal of Pentecostal Studies* 6 (2, July 2003): 283–301 (290); Opp, *Lord for the Body*, 52–53; Hudson, "British Pentecostals," 290.

7. Opp, *Lord for the Body*, 103–11, 115 (despite the flimsiness of most of the court cases by today's standards; the individuals could have died even with treatment). Dowie was inflexibly consistent, blaming even his daughter's burning to death on sin (Baer, "Perfectly Empowered Bodies," 249).

8. Heather D. Curtis, *Faith in the Great Physician: Suffering and Divine Healing in American Culture, 1860–1900* (Baltimore: Johns Hopkins University Press, 2007), 194; Gary B. McGee, *Miracles, Missions, and American Pentecostalism* (Maryknoll, NY: Orbis Books, 2010), 148–49; Allan Anderson, "Signs and Blunders: Pentecostal Mission Issues at 'Home and Abroad' in the Twentieth Century," *Journal of Asian Mission* 2 (2, Sept. 2000): 193–210 (207).

9. One cannot fault a mother's love for trying or her church for standing with her, but the outcome is not always what people hope. *Christianity Today* asked me to address this issue in "Every Grieving Parent Can Hope for Resurrection," *Christianity Today*, Dec. 19, 2019, http://christianitytoday .com/ct/2019/december-web-only/pray-to-raise-dead-bethel-resurrection-jesus-talitha-koum.html (accessed July 26, 2020).

10. Indeed, many studies do suggest health benefits of religious practice (see sources cited in my *Miracles* [2011], 2:620–30), benefits that believers may view as divinely built into nature. Such studies are valuable but do not by themselves speak to the issue of theism.

11. See esp. 1 Cor. 15:3–8; Michael R. Licona, *The Resurrection of Jesus: A New Historiographical Approach* (Downers Grove, IL: IVP Academic, 2010); N. T. Wright, *The Resurrection of the Son of God* (Minneapolis: Fortress, 2003).

12. The meaning of the passage is understandably debated; for my interpretation, see Craig S. Keener, *Matthew* (Downers Grove, IL: InterVarsity, 1997), 360–62; Keener, *The Gospel of Matthew: A Socio-Rhetorical Commentary* (Grand Rapids: Eerdmans, 2009), 604–6. Elsewhere in Matthew,

disciples are Jesus's siblings (12:50; 28:10) who could be received with food and drink (10:8–13, 42); whoever received them would receive Jesus (10:40–42).

13. Andrew White, *Faith under Fire: What the Middle East Conflict Has Taught Me about God* (Oxford: Monarch, 2011), 64.

14. The tree borrows imagery for a mighty empire; compare Nebuchadnezzar's kingdom in Dan. 4:11–12, a pale shadow of the final kingdom of God (2:44; 4:3, 34). Compare 1 Cor. 15:35–44.

15. Enid Mojica-McGinnis, phone interview, Aug. 5, 2020.

Chapter 40 Closing Personal Thoughts

1. Lee Strobel, *The Case for Miracles: A Journalist Investigates Evidence for the Supernatural* (Grand Rapids: Zondervan, 2018).

Appendix A Did Prayer Make Things Worse?

1. See "About Us," Unity Worldwide Ministries, https://www.unity.org/about-us/what-we-do (accessed April 15, 2020).

2. Candy Gunther Brown, *Testing Prayer: Science and Healing* (Cambridge, MA: Harvard University Press, 2012), 88. On page 92, Brown notes a metastudy that incorporated Buddhist and other prayer results with those from Unity. Leanne Roberts, Irshad Ahmed, and Andrew Davison ("Intercessory Prayer for the Alleviation of Ill Health," *Cochrane Database of Systematic Reviews* 2 [April 15, 2009]: CD000368, https://doi.org/10.1002/14651858.CD000368.pub3) are more ambivalent, although their study is excoriated from an explicitly atheistic standpoint, one that dismisses religion altogether, in Karsten Juhl Jørgensen, Asbjørn Hrøbjartsson, and Peter C. Gøtzsche, "Divine Intervention? A Cochrane Review on Intercessory Prayer Gone beyond Science and Reason," *Journal of Negative Results in Biomedicine* 8 (7, June 10, 2009), https://doi.org/10.1186/1477-5751-8-7.

3. Note that critics argued this with regard to external, not internal, effects. Some studies suggest that contemplative prayer may healthily stimulate the meditator's own brain's anterior cingulate, although this does not seem limited to theistic or spiritual beliefs. See Britta K. Holzel et al., "Differential Engagement of Anterior Cingulate and Adjacent Medial Frontal Cortex in Adept Meditators and Non-meditators," *Neuroscience Letters* 421 (2007): 16–21; Yi-Yuan Tang et al., "Short-Term Meditation Induces White Matter Changes in the Anterior Cingulate," *Proceedings of the National Academy of Sciences of the United States of America* 107 (35, 2010): 15649–52, https://doi.org/10.1073/pnas.1011043107; Shaowei Xue, Yi-Yuan Tang, and Michael I. Posner, "Short-Term Meditation Increases Network Efficiency of the Anterior Cingulate Cortex," *NeuroReport* 22 (12, 2011): 570–74; Andrew B. Newberg, "The Neuroscientific Study of Spiritual Practices," *Frontiers in Psychology* 5 (215, March 18, 2014), https://doi.org/10.3389/fpsyg.2014.00215. On a popular, Christian level, compare Mike McHargue, "How Your Brain Is Wired for God: Research Shows That Belief May Well Be Part of Our Design," *Relevant*, July 1, 2014, https://relevantmagazine.com/god/how-your-brain-wired-god/ (accessed March 5, 2020).

4. From a nonreligious perspective, note essentially the same objection, articulated more fully, in Richard P. Sloan and Rajasekhar Ramakrishnan, "Science, Medicine and Intercessory Prayer," *Perspectives in Biology and Medicine* 49 (4, Autumn 2006): 504–14 (506–8).

5. C. E. B. Cranfield, *The Gospel according to Saint Mark*, rev. ed., Cambridge Greek Testament Commentary (Cambridge: Cambridge University Press, 1966), 258, on Mark 8:11–12, comments regarding Jesus's critics' "spiritual blindness: unable to recognize the signs which God gives them, they demand signs of their own choosing." In the Gospels, Jesus does not perform miracles for his own benefit or to draw public attention to himself apart from his Father (see, e.g., Matt. 4:1–11// Luke 4:1–12).

Appendix B Some of Hume's Other Arguments

1. See Charles Taliaferro and Anders Hendrickson, "Hume's Racism and His Case against the Miraculous," *Philosophia Christi* 4 (2, 2002): 427–41; C. L. Ten, "Hume's Racism and Miracles,"

Journal of Value Inquiry 36 (2002): 101–7; Craig S. Keener, "A Reassessment of Hume's Case against Miracles in Light of Testimony from the Majority World Today," *Perspectives in Religious Studies* 38 (3, Fall 2011): 289–310.

2. E.g., Kenneth L. Woodward, *The Book of Miracles: The Meaning of the Miracle Stories in Christianity, Judaism, Buddhism, Hinduism, and Islam* (New York: Simon & Schuster, 2000), 21; Robert Wuthnow, *After Heaven: Spirituality in America since the 1950s* (Berkeley: University of California Press, 1998), 122; Baylor surveys cited in David Briggs, "Belief in Miracles on the Rise," *Huffington Post*, Oct. 30, 2012.

3. Keener, *Miracles* (2011), 1:242–49.

4. Sources are legion; see, e.g., Ari Kiev, ed., *Magic, Faith, and Healing: Studies in Primitive Psychiatry Today* (New York: Free Press, 1964); Larry Peters, *Ecstasy and Healing in Nepal: An Ethnopsychiatric Study of Tamang Shamanism* (Malibu, CA: Undena, 1981); Richard Katz, *Boiling Energy: Community Healing among the Kalahari Kung* (Cambridge, MA: Harvard University Press, 1982); Edith Turner et al., *Experiencing Ritual: A New Interpretation of African Healing* (Philadelphia: University of Pennsylvania Press, 1992); Edith Turner, *The Hands Feel It: Healing and Spirit Presence among a Northern Alaskan People* (DeKalb: Northern Illinois University Press, 1996); Turner, *Among the Healers: Stories of Spiritual and Ritual Healing around the World* (Westport, CT: Praeger, 2006); James McClenon, *Wondrous Healing: Shamanism, Human Evolution, and the Origin of Religion* (DeKalb: Northern Illinois University Press, 2002); Linda L. Barnes and Susan S. Sered, eds., *Religion and Healing in America* (New York: Oxford University Press, 2005); Linda L. Barnes and Inés Talamantez, eds., *Teaching Religion and Healing* (Oxford: Oxford University Press, 2006); Sidney M. Greenfield, *Spirits with Scalpels: The Culturalbiology of Religious Healing in Brazil* (Walnut Creek, CA: Left Coast, 2008).

5. E.g., John Dawson, "Urbanization and Mental Health in a West African Community," in Kiev, *Magic, Faith, and Healing*, 305–42 (328–29); Raymond Prince, "Indigenous Yoruba Psychiatry," in Kiev, *Magic, Faith, and Healing*, 84–120 (91); John S. Mbiti, *African Religions and Philosophies* (Garden City, NY: Doubleday, 1970), 204, 258; Gananath Obeyesekere, "Sorcery, Premeditated Murder, and the Canalization of Aggression in Sri Lanka," *Ethnology* 14 (1975): 1–24; Jeanne Favret-Saada, *Deadly Words: Witchcraft in the Bocage*, trans. Catherine Cullen (Cambridge: Cambridge University Press, 1980), 123–27; Frank Hoare, "A Pastoral Approach to Spirit Possession and Witchcraft Manifestations among the Fijian People," *Mission Studies* 21 (1, 2004): 113–37 (127–28); Godwin Ehi Azenabor, "The Idea of Witchcraft and the Challenge of Modern Science," in *Studies in Witchcraft, Magic, War, and Peace in Africa*, ed. Beatrice Nicolini (Lewiston, NY: Mellen, 2006), 21–35 (27); Tabona Shoko, *Karanga Indigenous Religion in Zimbabwe: Health and Well-Being* (Burlington, VT: Ashgate, 2007), 123.

6. Negatively, see, e.g., Num. 22:6; Deut. 23:4–5.

7. Keener, *Miracles* (2011), 2:843–56.

8. Fasil Woldemariam, interview, Wilmore, KY, March 8, 2016. Accounts of healings from Ethiopia could be multiplied; I (with examples supplementing those in my earlier book), David Black of Southeastern Seminary (at http://daveblackonline.com/), and others even from the West have collected numerous accounts. Compare also the psychic healers converted in Henri Nissen, *The God of Miracles: A Danish Journalist Examines Healings in the Ministry of Charles Ndifon* (Copenhagen: Scandinavia Publishing House, 2003), 93.

Appendix C False Signs

1. On such forces, see Keener, *Miracles* (2011), 2:769–856, and the scores of sources there. For more recent accounts, see, e.g., Keener, "Crooked Spirits and Spiritual Identity Theft: A Keener Response to Crooks?," *Journal of Mind and Behavior* 39 (4, Autumn 2018): 345–72; Robert Gallagher, *Demonic Foes: My Twenty-Five Years as a Psychiatrist Investigating Possessions, Diabolic Attacks, and the Paranormal* (New York: HarperOne, 2020).

2. Keener, *Miracles* (2011), 2:613–44.

3. For power encounters, see Keener, *Miracles* (2011), 2:843–56.

4. For studies of spirit possession and related issues, see, e.g., material in Keener, *Miracles* (2011), 2:769–856; Joy Ames Vaughan, "Spirit Possession in Luke-Acts and Modern Eyewitnesses: An Analysis

of Anthropological Accounts as Evidence for the Plausibility of the Lukan Accounts" (PhD diss., Asbury Theological Seminary, 2020).

5. *Didache* 11.6.

6. For calls for discernment from the charismatic sector of Christianity, see, e.g., Michael L. Brown, *Playing with Holy Fire: A Wake-Up Call to the Pentecostal-Charismatic Church* (Lake Mary, FL: Charisma House, 2018); Eddie L. Hyatt, *Angels of Light* (n.p.: Hyatt Press, 2018); Paul L. King, *Is It of God? A Biblical Guidebook for Spiritual Discernment* (Newberry, FL: Bridge Logos, 2019).